Continuity and Change in Ancient Umbrian Cult Places

Mnemosyne Supplements

HISTORY AND ARCHAEOLOGY
OF CLASSICAL ANTIQUITY

Series Editor

Jonathan M. Hall (*University of Chicago*)

Associate Editors

Jan Paul Crielaard (*Vrije Universiteit Amsterdam*)
Benet Salway (*University College London*)

VOLUME 485

The titles published in this series are listed at *brill.com/mns-haca*

Continuity and Change in Ancient Umbrian Cult Places

By

Arianna Zapelloni Pavia

BRILL

LEIDEN | BOSTON

This is an open access title distributed under the terms of the CC BY-NC-ND 4.0 license, which permits any non-commercial use, distribution, and reproduction in any medium, provided no alterations are made and the original author(s) and source are credited. Further information and the complete license text can be found at https://creativecommons.org/licenses/by-nc-nd/4.0/

The terms of the CC license apply only to the original material. The use of material from other sources (indicated by a reference) such as diagrams, illustrations, photos and text samples may require further permission from the respective copyright holder.

This publication was supported by the Cooperatio Program provided by the Charles University, research area Archaeology, implemented at the Faculty of Arts of Charles University.

Cover illustration:
Terracotta foot (inv. N. 124019; by permission of the Soprintendenza ABAP dell'Umbria).
Highly schematic warrior figure (inv. N. 721867; by permission of the Polo Museale dell'Umbria).
Schematic head (MTM_63: inv. N. 721806; by permission of the Polo Museale dell'Umbria)
Fragment of male head (inv. N. 232366; by permission of the Polo Museale dell'Umbria)
Terracotta head (inv. N. 361899; by permission of the Soprintendenza ABAP dell'Umbria).

The Library of Congress Cataloging-in-Publication Data is available online at https://catalog.loc.gov
LC record available at https://lccn.loc.gov/2024052440

Typeface for the Latin, Greek, and Cyrillic scripts: "Brill". See and download: brill.com/brill-typeface.

ISSN 2352-8656
ISBN 978-90-04-54516-8 (hardback)
ISBN 978-90-04-71217-1 (e-book)
DOI 10.1163/9789004712171

Copyright 2025 by Charles University, Faculty of Arts, Prague. Published by Koninklijke Brill BV, Leiden, The Netherlands.
Koninklijke Brill BV incorporates the imprints Brill, Brill Nijhoff, Brill Schöningh, Brill Fink, Brill mentis, Brill Wageningen Academic, Vandenhoeck & Ruprecht, Böhlau and V&R unipress.
Koninklijke Brill BV reserves the right to protect this publication against unauthorized use.

This book is printed on acid-free paper and produced in a sustainable manner.

Contents

Acknowledgments IX
List of Figures and Tables X

1 Introduction 1
   1 Chronology and Geographic Scope 3
   2 Outline of the Study 4

2 Cultural Change in the Sanctuaries of Central Italy 8
   1 Cultural Change and the Roman Conquest 8
      1.1 *Cultural Change in Ancient Umbria* 14
   2 Cultural Change in the Religious Sphere of Central Italy 16
   3 Cultural Change in the Religious Sphere of Ancient Umbria 25
   4 Conclusions 28

3 For an Archaeology of Religion and Ritual 30
   1 Introduction 30
   2 Archaeology of Religion 31
   3 Archaeology of Ritual 33
   4 Votive Religion 38
      4.1 *Votive Offerings in Central Italy* 42
      4.2 *Votive Offerings in Ancient Umbria* 43
   5 Conclusions 46

4 History of the Umbrian Territory 48
   1 Introduction 48
   2 The Boundaries of Ancient Umbria 50
      2.1 *The Existence of an Umbrian Identity: An Ongoing Debate* 57
      2.2 *Umbria's Geography* 63
   3 The History of Pre-Roman Umbria 64
      3.1 *Sixth–Fourth Century BCE* 65
      3.2 *Sacred Spaces* 69
   4 Late Fourth–Early First Century BCE: The Roman Conquest of Umbria 70
      4.1 *Fourth and Third Centuries BCE* 71
      4.2 *Second and First Centuries BCE* 75
   5 Conclusions 77

5 A Micro-Scale Approach to the Archaeology of Umbrian Cult Places 84

1 Introduction 84
  1.1 *Methodology Notes* 86
2 Southern Umbria 87
  2.1 *Grotta Bella* 87
  2.2 *Pantanelli Sanctuary* 96
  2.3 *Monte San Pancrazio Sanctuary* 100
  2.4 *Monte Torre Maggiore Sanctuary* 102
  2.5 *Monte Moro Sanctuary* 109
  2.6 *Monte Santo Sanctuary* 113
3 Umbrian Valley 117
  3.1 *La Rocca Sanctuary* 117
  3.2 *Monte Subasio Sanctuary* 122
4 Northern Umbria 125
  4.1 *Monte Ansciano Sanctuary* 125
  4.2 *Monte Acuto Sanctuary* 129
5 Apennine Umbria 133
  5.1 *Colle Mori Sanctuary* 133
  5.2 *Cancelli Sanctuary* 138
  5.3 *Campo La Piana Sanctuary* 143
  5.4 *Monte Pennino Sanctuary* 147
  5.5 *Sanctuary of Cupra at Colfiorito* 149
6 Conclusions 156

6 Conclusions: A Macro-Scale Approach to the Archaeology of Umbrian Cult Places 159

1 Introduction 159
2 Umbrian Pre-Roman Sanctuaries in Context 161
  2.1 *Topographical Aspects* 161
  2.2 *Architectural Aspects* 162
  2.3 *Function of Pre-Roman Sanctuaries* 164
  2.4 *Towards an Understanding of the Ritual Function of Umbrian Votive Offerings* 168
  2.5 *Display of Votive Offerings* 172
3 Umbrian Sanctuaries between the Late Fourth and the Early First Century BCE 175
  3.1 *Votive Offerings in the Hellenistic Period* 175
  3.2 *Anatomical Votives Revisited* 176
  3.3 *Continuity and Abandonment of Pre-Roman Cult Places* 181

CONTENTS VII

3.4 *Monumentalization of Umbrian Sanctuaries: Architectural Features* 184
3.5 *Monumentalization of Umbrian Sanctuaries: Possible Agents* 187
4 Conclusion and Looking Forward 189

Appendix 1: Types of Umbrian Figurative Votive Offerings 193
Appendix 2: Tabulated Catalog of Umbrian Figurative Votive Offerings 205
Appendix 3: Catalog of Umbrian Figurative Votive Offerings 208
Bibliography 299
Index 324

Acknowledgments

The genesis of this book traces back to my dissertation research defended in 2020 at the University of Michigan. Several people and institutions have enabled and assisted me in bringing this project to life. The work would not have been possible without the steadfast support of the Soprintendenza Archeologia Belle Arti e Paesaggio dell'Umbria and the Polo Museale dell'Umbria.

I am deeply thankful to the archaeologists Giorgio Postrioti, Elena Roscini, Gabriella Sabatini, Giovanni Altamore, Luca Pulcinelli, and Luana Cenciaoli. Also, to the technical staff, in particular Enrico Bizzarri and Luca Bartolini, not only for facilitating the obtainment of the study permits but also for assisting me in my research and study trips across Umbria.

This research is the result of a long journey that encompassed the evolution from full confidence to loss of confidence and eventually to a restoration of confidence. Many people contributed to making this lonely yet thrilling adventure unforgettable. Their mentorship, counsel, friendship, and firm support immensely contributed to this endeavor: Nicola Terrenato, Celia Schultz, Elaine Gazda, Chris Rattè, Monika Trümper, Tesse Stek, Greg Woolf, David Potter, Andrea Gaucci, Vishal Kanhdelwahl, Paolo Maranzana, Gregory Tucker, Alexander Hoer, Emily Hurt, Antonios Vonofakos, and the Italian community I found in Ann Arbor.

The manuscript was written during my post-doc appointment at Charles University in Prague and published thanks to the kind support of the Faculty of Arts. I extend my gratitude to my colleagues at the Institute of Classical Archaeology for their consistent encouragement during the completion of this project. I dedicate this book to my parents, who gave me the freedom to chase my dreams.

Figures and Tables

Figures

1 Modern Umbria (in red) and the location of the Umbrian sanctuaries analyzed in this book   4

2 Planimetry and cross sections of the cave derived from the most recent topographic survey (after Zapelloni and Larocca 2023, 40 fig. 1)   90

3 Graph showing the type distribution of the Grotta Bella votive figurines between the sixth and the fourth century BCE   91

4 Graph showing the type distribution of the Grotta Bella figurative votive offerings between the late fourth and the early first century BCE   96

5 Graph showing the type distribution of the Pantanelli votive figurines between the late sixth and the fourth century BCE   98

6 Revetment slab from Pantanelli (after Monacchi 1997, 179)   99

7 Graph showing the type distribution of the Pantanelli figurative votive offerings between the late fourth and the early first century BCE   99

8 Graph showing the type distribution of the San Pancrazio sanctuary's votive figurines between the sixth and the fourth century BCE   101

9 On the right: foundations of the third-century and the first-century temples (temples A and B). Notice the channel and the pit inside the *pronaos* of temple B (after Bonomi Ponzi 1988, 23, tav. V). On the left: section of the *pronaos* of temple A and of the funnel-shaped pit (after Bonomi Ponzi 2006, 116, fig. 6)   104

10 Graph showing the type distribution of the Monte di Torre Maggiore sanctuary's votive figurines between the late sixth and the fourth century BCE   105

11 Well identified in 2006 in the sacred area of Monte di Torre Maggiore (courtesy of the Soprintendenza Archeologia Belle Arti e Paesaggio dell'Umbria)   107

12 Plan of the Monte di Torre Maggiore sanctuary with the two temples (after Bonomi Ponzi 2006, 113, fig. 5)   107

13 Graph showing the type distribution of the Monte di Torre Maggiore figurative votive offerings between the late fourth and the early first century BCE   108

14 Graph showing the type distribution of the Monte Moro votive figurines between the fifth and the fourth century BCE   111

15 The Monte Moro sanctuary's structures (after Sisani 2013, 18 fig. 2)   112

16 Graph showing the type distribution of the Monte Moro figurative votive offerings between the late fourth and the early first century BCE   113

FIGURES AND TABLES

XI

17 Graph showing the type distribution of the Monte Santo votive figurines between the fifth and the fourth century BCE 115

18 Graph showing the type distribution of the La Rocca sanctuary's votive figurines between the late sixth and the fourth century BCE 119

19 Architectural terracottas from La Rocca (after Pani 2011, fig. 20–23) 120

20 Graph showing the type distribution of the La Rocca figurative votive offerings between the end of the third and the early first century BCE 120

21 Graph showing the type distribution of the Monte Subasio votive figurines between the fifth and the fourth century BCE (the unspecified figurines are those mentioned by Helbig) 124

22 Plan of the sanctuary on Monte Ansciano (after Malone and Stoddart 1994, 146, fig. 5.2) 127

23 Graph showing the type distribution of the Monte Ansciano votive figurines between the fifth and the fourth century BCE 128

24 Excavation plan of the Monte Acuto sanctuary. A: entrance; B: precinct; C: *sacellum*; D: votive pit (after Cenciaioli 1998, 46) 130

25 Graph showing the type distribution of the Monte Acuto sanctuary's votive figurines between the sixth and the fourth century BCE 132

26 Plan of the Colle Mori Umbrian settlement. On the right: the sacred area (after Bonomi Ponzi 2010, 184 fig. 25) 134

27 Plan of the *sacellum*: letters A, B, and C indicate the walls of the *cella*; E is the pit; F is the cistern inside the *pronaos* (modified after Stefani 1935, 156, fig. 2) 135

28 Graph showing the type distribution of the Colle Mori votive figurines between the sixth and the fourth century BCE 136

29 Colle Mori cistern clad in bricks (after Bonomi Ponzi 2010, 189, fig. 35) 137

30 Graph showing the type distribution of the Colle Mori figurative votive offerings between the late fourth and the early first century BCE 137

31 Graph showing the type distribution of the Cancelli votive figurines between the sixth and the fourth century BCE 140

32 Plan of the excavation. The features in green belong to the first phase of the structure, while the ones in brown belong to the second-century BCE phase (after Manca et al. 2014, 31, fig. 10) 141

33 Graph showing the type distribution of Cancelli figurative votive offerings between the end of the fourth and the first century BCE 142

34 Drawing of the walls identified by Ticchioni in loc. Campo La Piana. Letter D indicates the space where materials were found (after Brizio 1891, 309) 144

35 Graph showing the type distribution of the Campo La Piana votive figurines between the sixth and the fourth century BCE 146

36 Graph showing the type distribution of Campo La Piana figurative votive offerings between the late fourth and the early first century BCE 147

37	Graph showing the type distribution of the Monte Pennino votive figurines between the sixth and the fourth century BCE 148
38	Graph showing the type distribution of the Sanctuary of Cupra votive figurines between the sixth and the fourth century BCE 151
39	Plan of the Sanctuary of Cupra (after Bonomi Ponzi 2010, 180 fig. 21) 154
40	Revetment slab from the Sanctuary of Cupra (after Manca and Menichelli 2014, 27) 154
41	Graph showing the type distribution of the Sanctuary of Cupra figurative votive offerings between the late fourth and the early first century BCE 155
42	Graph showing the types of figurines dedicated in each Umbrian sanctuary 167
43	Graph showing the percentage of votive figurines dedicated in each Umbrian sanctuary 168
44	Graph showing the groups of votive figurines dedicated in each Umbrian sanctuary 169
45	Graph showing the groups of figurative votive objects dedicated in each Umbrian sanctuary 177
A1	Schematic representation of a man (inv. N. 41; by permission of the Soprintendenza ABAP dell'Umbria) 208
A2	Schematic representation of a man (inv. N. 50306; by permission of the Soprintendenza ABAP dell'Umbria) 209
A3	Schematic representation of a man (inv. N. 50709; by permission of the Soprintendenza ABAP dell'Umbria) 209
A4	Schematic representation of a man (inv. N. 50351; by permission of the Soprintendenza ABAP dell'Umbria) 209
A5	Schematic representation of a female figure (inv. N. 50709; by permission of the Soprintendenza ABAP dell'Umbria) 210
A6	Schematic representation of a warrior (inv. N. 50227; by permission of the Soprintendenza ABAP dell'Umbria) 210
A7	Schematic representation of a warrior (inv. N. 50744; by permission of the Soprintendenza ABAP dell'Umbria) 210
A8	Schematic representation of a female figure (inv. N. 50311; by permission of the Soprintendenza ABAP dell'Umbria) 211
A9	Schematic representation of a female figure (inv. N. 50309; by permission of the Soprintendenza ABAP dell'Umbria) 211
A10	Schematic representation of a female figure (inv. N. 50707; by permission of the Soprintendenza ABAP dell'Umbria) 211
A11	Schematic representation of a bovine (inv. N. 50770; by permission of the Soprintendenza ABAP dell'Umbria) 212
A12	Schematic representation of an ox (inv. N. 50417; by permission of the Soprintendenza ABAP dell'Umbria) 212

FIGURES AND TABLES

A13 Schematic representation of a sheep (inv. N. 50419; by permission of the Soprintendenza ABAP dell'Umbria) 212

A14 Schematic representation of an unidentifiable animal, likely a ferret (inv. N. 50724; by permission of the Soprintendenza ABAP dell'Umbria) 213

A15 Schematic representation of a warrior (inv. N. N/A; by permission of the Soprintendenza ABAP dell'Umbria) 213

A16 Schematic representation of a warrior (inv. N. 50785; by permission of the Soprintendenza ABAP dell'Umbria) 213

A17 Bronze leg (inv. N. NA; by permission of the Soprintendenza ABAP dell'Umbria) 214

A18 Bronze arm (inv. N. NA; by permission of the Soprintendenza ABAP dell'Umbria) 214

A19 Bronze leg (inv. N. NA; by permission of the Soprintendenza ABAP dell'Umbria) 214

A20 Bronze foot (inv. N. 114336; by permission of the Soprintendenza ABAP dell'Umbria) 215

A21 Schematic head (inv. N. 50425; by permission of the Soprintendenza ABAP dell'Umbria) 215

A22 Schematic head (inv. N. 50423; by permission of the Soprintendenza ABAP dell'Umbria) 215

A23 Schematic head (inv. N. 50424; by permission of the Soprintendenza ABAP dell'Umbria) 216

A24 Lead schematic representation of a warrior (inv. N. 50436; by permission of the Soprintendenza ABAP dell'Umbria) 216

A25 Lead schematic representation of a warrior (inv. N. 50430; by permission of the Soprintendenza ABAP dell'Umbria) 216

A26 Lead schematic representation of a female (inv. N. 50704; by permission of the Soprintendenza ABAP dell'Umbria) 217

A27 Lead schematic representation of a female (inv. N. 50431; by permission of the Soprintendenza ABAP dell'Umbria) 217

A28 Lead schematic representation of a female (inv. N. 50433; by permission of the Soprintendenza ABAP dell'Umbria) 217

A29 Lead *episema*. One side represents an arm fastened to the shield; the other depicts three men under a tree (inv. N. 50435; by permission of the Soprintendenza ABAP dell'Umbria) 218

A30 Lead *episema*. One side represents an arm fastened to the shield; the other depicts three men under a tree (inv. N. 50437; by permission of the Soprintendenza ABAP dell'Umbria). Below: drawing of the side of the shield with the three men 218

A31 Lead *episema*. One side represents an arm fastened to the shield; the other

XIV FIGURES AND TABLES

depicts three men under a tree (inv. N. 50440; by permission of the Soprintendenza ABAP dell'Umbria) 218

A32 Lead *episema* with gorgoneion (after Monacchi 1988, tav. 36) 219

A33 Lead *episema*. One side represents an arm fastened to the shield; the other depicts a radiating sun (inv. N. 50440; by permission of the Soprintendenza ABAP dell'Umbria) 219

A34 Terracotta breast (inv. N. NA; by permission of the Soprintendenza ABAP dell'Umbria) 219

A35 Terracotta breast (after Monacchi 1988, tav. 36) 220

A36 Worshiper holding a patera and standing on a base (inv. N. 3038; by permission of the Soprintendenza ABAP dell'Umbria) 220

A37 Worshiper holding a patera (inv. N. 50225; by permission of the Soprintendenza ABAP dell'Umbria) 220

A38 Worshiper with outstretched arms (inv. N. 50304; by permission of the Soprintendenza ABAP dell'Umbria) 221

A39 Lead schematic representation of a warrior (inv. N. NA; by permission of the Soprintendenza ABAP dell'Umbria) 221

A40 Fragment of a lead figurine representing a human figure (inv. N. NA; by permission of the Soprintendenza ABAP dell'Umbria) 221

A41 Lead *episema* with *gorgoneion* (inv. N. NA; by permission of the Soprintendenza ABAP dell'Umbria) 222

A42 Lead *episema* with zigzag and knobs motif (inv. N. NA; by permission of the Soprintendenza ABAP dell'Umbria) 222

A43 Terracotta foot (inv. N. 124019; by permission of the Soprintendenza ABAP dell'Umbria) 222

A44 Highly schematic male figures (from left to right: inv. N. 721816, 721817, 721818; by permission of the Polo Museale dell'Umbria) 223

A45 Highly schematic male figure (inv. N. 721836; by permission of the Polo Museale dell'Umbria) 223

A46 Highly schematic female figure (inv. N. 721862; by permission of the Polo Museale dell'Umbria) 223

A47 Highly schematic female figure (inv. N. 721863; by permission of the Polo Museale dell'Umbria) 224

A48 Highly schematic female figure (inv. N. 721861; by permission of the Polo Museale dell'Umbria) 224

A49 Highly schematic female figure (inv. N. 721860; by permission of the Polo Museale dell'Umbria) 224

A50 Schematic representation of a leg (from left to right: inv. N. 721864 and 721865; by permission of the Polo Museale dell'Umbria) 225

A51 Schematic representation of an arm (inv. N. 721820; by permission of the Polo Museale dell'Umbria) 225

FIGURES AND TABLES

A52   Schematic representation of an arm (inv. N. 721821; by permission of the Polo Museale dell'Umbria)   225

A53   Schematic heads (from left to right: inv. N. 721875–79; by permission of the Polo Museale dell'Umbria)   226

A54   Schematic crests with eyes (from left to right: inv. N. 721872–74; by permission of the Polo Museale dell'Umbria)   226

A55   Highly schematic warrior figure (inv. N. 721867; by permission of the Polo Museale dell'Umbria)   227

A56   Schematic warrior figure (after Colonna 1970, tav. LII–LIII)   227

A57   Schematic figure turned sideways (inv. N. 721871; by permission of the Polo Museale dell'Umbria)   228

A58   Schematic figure of an ox (inv. N. 721819; by permission of the Polo Museale dell'Umbria)   228

A59   Terracotta half-head (inv. N. 721815; by permission of the Polo Museale dell'Umbria)   229

A60   Highly schematic male figure (inv. N. NA; by permission of the Soprintendenza ABAP dell'Umbria)   229

A61   Extremely schematic male figure (inv. N. NA; by permission of the Soprintendenza ABAP dell'Umbria)   230

A62   Extremely schematic male figure (from left to right: inv. N. 209173, 209133; by permission of the Soprintendenza ABAP dell'Umbria)   230

A63   Extremely schematic warrior figures (from left to right: inv. N. 209173, 209133; by permission of the Soprintendenza ABAP dell'Umbria)   230

A64   Highly schematic female figure (inv. N. 721809; by permission of the Polo Museale dell'Umbria)   231

A65   Highly schematic female figure (inv. N. 721809; by permission of the Polo Museale dell'Umbria)   231

A66   Schematic figure of a striding male (inv. N. 721805; by permission of the Polo Museale dell'Umbria)   231

A67   Schematic figure of a striding male (inv. N. 721808; by permission of the Polo Museale dell'Umbria)   232

A68   Highly schematic figure of a warrior (inv. N. 721807; by permission of the Polo Museale dell'Umbria)   232

A69   Schematic head (MTM_63: inv. N. 721806; by permission of the Polo Museale dell'Umbria. MTM_64: inv. N. NA; by permission of the Soprintendenza ABAP dell'Umbria).   232

A70   Schematic head (MTM_63: inv. N. 721806; by permission of the Polo Museale dell'Umbria. MTM_64: inv. N. NA; by permission of the Soprintendenza ABAP dell'Umbria).   233

A71   Bronze hand (inv. N. 273867; by permission of the Soprintendenza ABAP dell'Umbria)   233

A72	Schematic representation of a foot (inv. N. 313; by permission of the Soprintendenza ABAP dell'Umbria) 233
A73	Schematic representation of a warrior (inv. N. 94422; by permission of the Soprintendenza ABAP dell'Umbria) 234
A74	Schematic representation of a warrior (inv. N. 209104; by permission of the Soprintendenza ABAP dell'Umbria) 234
A75	Schematic representation of a warrior (inv. N. 113484; by permission of the Soprintendenza ABAP dell'Umbria) 235
A75b	Schematic representation of a warrior (inv. N. 94420; by permission of the Soprintendenza ABAP dell'Umbria). 235
A76	Schematic crest with eyes (inv. N. 113414; by permission of the Soprintendenza ABAP dell'Umbria) 236
A77	Schematic head of a bull (inv. N. 338233; by permission of the Soprintendenza ABAP dell'Umbria) 236
A78	Schematic head of a bull (inv. N. 94429; by permission of the Soprintendenza ABAP dell'Umbria) 236
A79	Male worshiper holding a patera (inv. N. 721804; by permission of the Polo Museale dell'Umbria) 237
A80	Male worshiper holding a patera. Still visible underneath the figurine's feet are the traces of the cubic travertine small base that supported the figurine (inv. N. 209160; by permission of the Soprintendenza ABAP dell'Umbria) 237
A81	Female worshiper holding an acerra (inv. N. 212196; by permission of the Soprintendenza ABAP dell'Umbria) 237
A82	Hand wearing a ring (inv. N. NA; by permission of the Soprintendenza ABAP dell'Umbria) 238
A83	Fragments of a foot (modified after Bononi Ponzi 1989, 26 fig. 21) 238
A84	Fragments of a male head (inv. N. 341470; by permission of the Soprintendenza ABAP dell'Umbria) 238
A85	Fragments of a female head (inv. N. 209163; by permission of the Soprintendenza ABAP dell'Umbria) 239
A86	Highly schematic male figure (inv. N. 183026; by permission of the Polo Museale dell'Umbria) 239
A87	Highly schematic male figure (inv. N. 230054; by permission of the Polo Museale dell'Umbria) 240
A88	Highly schematic male figure (inv. N. 230054; by permission of the Polo Museale dell'Umbria) 240
A89	Schematic crest with two eyes (from left to right: inv. N. 183031 and 183034; by permission of the Polo Museale dell'Umbria). 241
A90	Schematic crest with two eyes (from left to right: inv. N. 183031 and 183034; by permission of the Polo Museale dell'Umbria). 241

FIGURES AND TABLES

A91   Highly schematic warrior figure (inv. N. 230034; by permission of the Polo Museale dell'Umbria)   241

A92   Schematic figure of a horse (inv. N. 230045; by permission of the Polo Museale dell'Umbria)   242

A93   Schematic figure of an ox (inv. N. 230023; by permission of the Polo Museale dell'Umbria)   242

A94   Schematic head (inv. N. 230026; by permission of the Polo Museale dell'Umbria)   242

A95   Fragment of a uterus (inv. N. 232367; by permission of the Polo Museale dell'Umbria)   243

A96   Schematic head (inv. N. 232368; by permission of the Polo Museale dell'Umbria)   243

A97   Fragment of a right hand (inv. N. 232345; by permission of the Polo Museale dell'Umbria)   243

A98   Fragment of a left hand (inv. N. 183019; by permission of the Polo Museale dell'Umbria)   244

A99   Fragment of a nose (inv. N. 232369; by permission of the Polo Museale dell'Umbria)   244

A100   Fragment of a foot (inv. N. 232376; by permission of the Polo Museale dell'Umbria)   244

A101   Fragment of male genitalia (inv. N. 232374; by permission of the Polo Museale dell'Umbria)   245

A102   Fragment of male head (inv. N. 232366; by permission of the Polo Museale dell'Umbria)   245

A103   Fragment of male head (inv. N. 232375; by permission of the Polo Museale dell'Umbria)   245

A104   Fragment of hairdo of a veiled head (inv. N. 232373; by permission of the Polo Museale dell'Umbria)   246

A105   Base of terracotta head (inv. N. 232370; by permission of the Polo Museale dell'Umbria)   246

A106   Highly schematic warrior figure (inv. N. 342; by permission of the Soprintendenza ABAP dell'Umbria)   247

A107   Schematic figure of a striding male (inv. N. 358; by permission of the Soprintendenza ABAP dell'Umbria)   247

A108   Schematic figure of a striding male (inv. N. 348; by permission of the Soprintendenza ABAP dell'Umbria)   248

A109   Schematic figure of a striding male (inv. N. 325; by permission of the Soprintendenza ABAP dell'Umbria)   248

A110   Highly schematic male figure (inv. N. 349; by permission of the Polo Museale dell'Umbria)   249

FIGURES AND TABLES

A111 Highly schematic male figure (inv. N. 356; by permission of the Polo Museale dell'Umbria) 249

A112 Highly schematic female figure (inv. N. 382; by permission of the Polo Museale dell'Umbria) 249

A113 Highly schematic female figure (inv. N. 382; by permission of the Polo Museale dell'Umbria) 250

A114 Schematic warrior figure (inv. N. 332; by permission of the Soprintendenza ABAP dell'Umbria) 250

A115 Schematic warrior figure (Inv. N. 334; by permission of the Soprintendenza ABAP dell'Umbria) 251

A116 Schematic warrior figure (inv. N. 333; by permission of the Soprintendenza ABAP dell'Umbria) 251

A117 Schematic warrior figure (inv. N. 330; by permission of the Soprintendenza ABAP dell'Umbria) 252

A118 Schematic figure of a warrior (inv. N. 322; by permission of the Soprintendenza ABAP dell'Umbria) 252

A119 Schematic female figure (inv. N. 380; by permission of the Soprintendenza ABAP dell'Umbria) 253

A120 Schematic female figure (inv. N. 337; by permission of the Soprintendenza ABAP dell'Umbria) 253

A121 Schematic female figure (inv. N. 302; by permission of the Soprintendenza ABAP dell'Umbria) 254

A122 Schematic figure of a bull (inv. N. 392; by permission of the Soprintendenza ABAP dell'Umbria) 254

A123 Schematic figure of a horse (inv. N. 396; by permission of the Soprintendenza ABAP dell'Umbria) 255

A124 Schematic head (inv. N. 385; by permission of the Soprintendenza ABAP dell'Umbria) 255

A125 Schematic head (inv. N. 310; by permission of the Soprintendenza ABAP dell'Umbria) 255

A126 Schematic head (inv. N. 319; by permission of the Soprintendenza ABAP dell'Umbria) 256

A127 Schematic warrior figure (inv. N. 303; by permission of the Soprintendenza ABAP dell'Umbria) 256

A128 Schematic warrior figure (inv. N. 308; by permission of the Soprintendenza ABAP dell'Umbria) 257

A129 Schematic warrior figure (inv. N. 307; by permission of the Soprintendenza ABAP dell'Umbria) 257

A130 Schematic Heracles (inv. N. 304; by permission of the Soprintendenza ABAP dell'Umbria) 257

FIGURES AND TABLES

XIX

A131 Highly schematic male figure (inv. N. 109558; by permission of the Polo Museale dell'Umbria) 258

A132 Highly schematic male figure (inv. N. CS1729; by permission of the Polo Museale dell'Umbria) 258

A133 Highly schematic male figure (inv. N. CS1728; by permission of the Polo Museale dell'Umbria) 258

A134 Highly schematic warrior figure (inv. N. 109578; by permission of the Polo Museale dell'Umbria) 259

A135 Highly schematic warrior figure (inv. N. 109559; by permission of the Polo Museale dell'Umbria) 259

A136 Highly schematic warrior figure (inv. N. 337381; by permission of the Polo Museale dell'Umbria) 260

A137 Schematic figure of a striding male (inv. N. 305069; by permission of the Polo Museale dell'Umbria) 260

A138 Schematic figure of a striding male (inv. N. CS172; by permission of the Polo Museale dell'Umbria) 261

A139 Bronze arm (inv. N. 305671; by permission of the Polo Museale dell'Umbria) 261

A140 Fragments of feet, toes, and fingers (inv. NN. 305628, 305631—feet; 305626, 305627—toes; 305629, 305630—fingers; after Pani 2011, fig. 23) 262

A141 Fragments of two uteri (inv. NN. 305645 and 305645) 262

A142 Fragment of male genitalia (inv. N. 275102) 263

A143 Fragment of a head (left) and veiled head (right) (inv. NN. 305632 and 305652) 263

A144 Fragment of a terracotta bovine (inv. N. 305623) 264

A145 Highly schematic male figure (inv. N. 10; after Monacchi 1986, tav. 38b) 264

A146 Schematic figure of a striding male (inv. N. NA; after Monacchi 1986, tav. 38b) 265

A147 Schematic figure of a warrior with situla (inv. N. 1; after Monacchi 1986, tav. 38a) 265

A148 Dancing figure (inv. N. 18; after Monacchi 1986, tav. 39c) 266

A149 Pendant in the shape of a quadruped (inv. N. 12; after Monacchi 1986, tav. 38d) 266

A150 Schematic figure of female worshiper (left and center) and arm of worshiper with patera (right) (inv. NN. 10, 13, and 18; Monacchi 1986, tav. 39a–c) 266

A151 Highly schematic male figures (from left to right: inv. NN. 625958, 625959, 625960; by permission of the Soprintendenza ABAP dell'Umbria) 267

A152 Highly schematic male figure (inv. N. 41; by permission of the Soprintendenza ABAP dell'Umbria) 267

A153 Highly schematic male figure (inv. N. 93; by permission of the Soprintendenza ABAP dell'Umbria) 268

A154	Highly schematic male figure (inv. N. 146; by permission of the Soprintendenza ABAP dell'Umbria) 268
A155	Extremely schematic warrior figure (inv. N. 80; by permission of the Soprintendenza ABAP dell'Umbria) 268
A156	Highly schematic female figure (inv. N. 625955; by permission of the Soprintendenza ABAP dell'Umbria) 269
A157	Highly schematic female figure (inv. N. 625954; by permission of the Soprintendenza ABAP dell'Umbria) 269
A158	Highly schematic female figure (inv. N. 65; by permission of the Soprintendenza ABAP dell'Umbria) 269
A159	Highly schematic warrior figure (inv. N. 44; by permission of the Soprintendenza ABAP dell'Umbria) 270
A160	Extremely schematic warrior figure (inv. N. 46; by permission of the Soprintendenza ABAP dell'Umbria) 270
A161	Fragment of terracotta head (inv. N. 625969; by permission of the Soprintendenza ABAP dell'Umbria) 270
A162	Hand holding a patera (inv. N. 73; by permission of the Soprintendenza ABAP dell'Umbria) 271
A163	Highly schematic male figure (inv. N. 122218; by permission of the Soprintendenza ABAP dell'Umbria) 271
A164	Highly schematic male figure (inv. N. 122218; by permission of the Soprintendenza ABAP dell'Umbria) 271
A165	Highly schematic female figure (inv. N. 114347; by permission of the Soprintendenza ABAP dell'Umbria) 272
A166	Highly schematic female figure (inv. N. 11686; by permission of the Soprintendenza ABAP dell'Umbria) 272
A167	Highly schematic warrior figures (inv. NN. 116864 and 116847; by permission of the Soprintendenza ABAP dell'Umbria) 272
A168	Highly schematic figure of a pig (inv. N. 1222412; by permission of the Soprintendenza ABAP dell'Umbria) 273
A169	Highly schematic figure of a sheep (inv. N. 114341; by permission of the Soprintendenza ABAP dell'Umbria) 273
A170	Highly schematic figure of an ox (inv. N. 116848; by permission of the Polo Museale dell'Umbria) 273
A171	Highly schematic figure of a goat (inv. N. 116845; by permission of the Polo Museale dell'Umbria) 274
A172	Highly schematic figure of a quadruped (inv. N. 116845; by permission of the Soprintendenza ABAP dell'Umbria) 274
A173	Schematic male figure (inv. N. 113498; by permission of the Polo Museale dell'Umbria) 274

FIGURES AND TABLES

XXI

A174 Schematic male figure (inv. N. 113498; by permission of the Soprintendenza ABAP dell'Umbria) 275

A175 Highly schematic warrior figure (inv. N. 113499; by permission of the Soprintendenza ABAP dell'Umbria). 275

A176 Highly schematic warrior figure (inv. N. 116871; by permission of the Soprintendenza ABAP dell'Umbria) 275

A177 Highly schematic figure of a male striding forward (inv. N. 114344; by permission of the Soprintendenza ABAP dell'Umbria) 276

A178 Highly schematic figure of a male striding forward (inv. N. 116846; by permission of the Polo Museale dell'Umbria) 276

A179 Bronze heads (inv. NN. NA; by permission of the Soprintendenza ABAP dell'Umbria) 276

A180 Bronze leg (inv. N. NA; by permission of the Soprintendenza ABAP dell'Umbria) 277

A181 Bronze arm (inv. N. 116872; by permission of the Soprintendenza ABAP dell'Umbria) 277

A182 Bronze hand (inv. N. 116844; by permission of the Soprintendenza ABAP dell'Umbria) 277

A183 Highly schematic male figure (inv. N. 361784; by permission of the Soprintendenza ABAP dell'Umbria) 278

A184 Highly schematic male figure (inv. N. 361875; by permission of the Soprintendenza ABAP dell'Umbria) 278

A185 Highly schematic male figure (inv. N. 88988; by permission of the Soprintendenza ABAP dell'Umbria) 278

A186 Highly schematic warrior figure (inv. N. 174766; by permission of the Soprintendenza ABAP dell'Umbria) 279

A187 Lower half of terracotta head (inv. N. 361878; by permission of the Soprintendenza ABAP dell'Umbria) 279

A188 Female worshiper holding a patera (inv. N. 211373; by permission of the Soprintendenza ABAP dell'Umbria) 280

A189 Terracotta head (inv. N. 361899; by permission of the Soprintendenza ABAP dell'Umbria) 280

A190 Terracotta head (inv. N. 364985; by permission of the Soprintendenza ABAP dell'Umbria) 281

A191 Highly schematic warrior figure (inv. N. 637473; modified after Manca et al 2014, 56 n. 31). 281

A192 Highly schematic warrior figures (inv. NN. NA; modified after Picuti 1999, 25 n. 11) 282

A193 Highly schematic male figure (inv. N. 646185; after Manca et al. 2014, 56 n. 36) 282

A194	Highly schematic female figure (inv. N. 637518; after Manca et al. 2014, 56 n. 35) 283
A195	Highly schematic warrior figure (inv. N. 643123; after Manca et al. 2014, 56 n. 34) 283
A196	Schematic figure of a bull (inv. N. 679455; after Manca et al. 2014, 56 n. 34) 283
A197	Highly schematic warrior figure (inv. N. 637436, after Manca et al. 2014, 56 n. 32) 284
A198	Highly schematic male figure (inv. N. 737440; after Manca et al. 2014, 56 n. 37) 284
A199	Schematic crest with eyes (inv. N. 637443; after Manca et al. 2014, 56 n. 38) 284
A200	Schematic head (inv. N. 637459; after Manca et al. 2014, 56 n. 39) 285
A201	Bronze arm (inv. N. 637466; after Manca et al. 2014, 56 n. 39) 285
A202	Drawing of Hellenistic worshiper figure (Picuti 2009, 9) 285
A203	Fragment of a foot (inv. N. 695199; after Manca et al. 2014, 51 n. 5) 286
A204	Fragment of the upper half portion of a male head (inv. N. 643009; after Manca et al. 2014, 51 n. 4) 286
A205	Highly schematic male figure (inv. N. NA; by permission of the Soprintendenza ABAP dell'Umbria) 286
A206	Highly schematic figure of a male striding forward (inv. N. NA; by permission of the Soprintendenza ABAP dell'Umbria) 287
A207	Terracotta head of a male wearing a tall hat (inv. N. NA; by permission of the Soprintendenza ABAP dell'Umbria) 287
A208	Highly schematic human figures (inv. NN. NA; by permission of the Soprintendenza ABAP dell'Umbria) 288
A209	Highly schematic male figures (inv. N. 764031; by permission of the Soprintendenza ABAP dell'Umbria) 288
A210	Highly schematic male figure (inv. N. 721905; by permission of the Polo Museale dell'Umbria) 289
A211	Highly schematic female figure (inv. N. 721900; by permission of the Polo Museale dell'Umbria) 289
A212	Highly schematic female figure (inv. N. 763932; by permission of the Polo Museale dell'Umbria) 289
A213	Extremely schematic male figures (inv. N. 764033; by permission of the Soprintendenza ABAP dell'Umbria) 290
A214	Extremely schematic male figure (inv. N. 721902; by permission of the Polo Museale dell'Umbria) 290
A215	Highly schematic female figure (inv. N. 601919; by permission of the Soprintendenza ABAP dell'Umbria) 291

FIGURES AND TABLES

A216 Highly schematic female figure (inv. N. 341593; by permission of the Soprintendenza ABAP dell'Umbria) 291

A217 Highly schematic warrior figure (inv. N. A1748; by permission of the Polo Museale dell'Umbria) 292

A218 Highly schematic warrior figure (inv. N. 76318; by permission of the Soprintendenza ABAP dell'Umbria) 292

A219 Schematic figure of a striding male (inv. N. 601918; by permission of the Soprintendenza ABAP dell'Umbria) 292

A220 Schematic figure of a striding male (inv. N. 721906; by permission of the Polo Museale dell'Umbria) 293

A221 Highly schematic figure of a horse (inv. N. 764006; by permission of the Soprintendenza ABAP dell'Umbria) 293

A222 Highly schematic figure of an ox (inv. N. 721896; by permission of the Polo Museale dell'Umbria) 293

A223 Highly schematic warrior figure (inv. N. 341637; by permission of the Soprintendenza ABAP dell'Umbria) 294

A224 Schematic warrior figure (inv. N. 354776; by permission of the Soprintendenza ABAP dell'Umbria) 294

A225 Schematic warrior figure (inv. N. 351595; by permission of the Soprintendenza ABAP dell'Umbria) 295

A226 Schematic representation of a foot (inv. N. 601896; by permission of the Soprintendenza ABAP dell'Umbria) 295

A227 Schematic figure with bird-like features (inv. N. A1732; by permission of the Soprintendenza ABAP dell'Umbria) 296

A228 Schematic figure with bird-like features (inv. N. 76350; by permission of the Soprintendenza ABAP dell'Umbria) 296

A229 Schematic figure with bird-like features (inv. N. 764035; by permission of the Polo Museale dell'Umbria) 296

A230 Schematic figure with monkey-like features (inv. N. 601926; by permission of the Soprintendenza ABAP dell'Umbria) 297

A231 Terracotta foot (inv. N. 601922; by permission of the Soprintendenza ABAP dell'Umbria) 297

A232 Tanagra figurines (inv. NN. 602018 and 602016; by permission of the Soprintendenza ABAP dell'Umbria) 298

A233 Schematic figure of Heracles (inv. N. 341601; by permission of the Soprintendenza ABAP dell'Umbria) 298

A234 Right hand (inv. N. 316; by permission of the Soprintendenza ABAP dell'Umbria). 256

Tables

1.1 Chronology of Italic religion 3

CHAPTER 1

Introduction

What difference did the Roman expansion make in the transformation of ancient Italy? With its conservative nature and abundant material evidence, the religious sphere represents a unique lens through which we can study this process over time and across different sites. Tracking the transformation of Italy as a result of Rome's expansion, this book explores the issue of Romanization and sheds light on the different processes of adaptation that occurred during the Roman conquest.

During the Middle and Late Republican periods, cult places dotted the Italian landscape, with many concentrated in the ancient region of Umbria. From the layout and location of these sanctuaries to the paraphernalia associated with their cult practices, the archaeological record suggests that a shift in the location, architecture, and ritual practices occurred after Rome's progressive expansion in the region at the end of the fourth century BCE. However, this transformation doesn't adhere to a singular, uniform pattern. Certain sanctuaries witnessed a decline in ritual practices, while others underwent substantial reconstruction, often acquiring their initial permanent architectural elements. Meanwhile, a few sites persisted in their pre-Roman setup without any evident alterations.

Although sanctuaries do not follow a single pattern with regard to their architecture and location, they seem to do so with votive assemblages. During the Roman period, the range of objects associated with cult practices at these sanctuaries expanded. Between the fourth and third centuries BCE, as the Roman presence in Umbria spread and became a permanent fixture in the area, the bronze figurines that characterize votive deposits of the archaic period noticeably decreased. In their stead, we find a wider array of offerings including black-slip pottery, coins, and, in particular, anatomical terracottas, which remain the most popular type of offering into the first century BCE.

While much has been written on the religious landscape of Central and Southern Italy (Lucania, Etruria, Samnium, and Latium), a comprehensive overview of the religious sphere of ancient Umbria before and after the Roman conquest is still missing. The limited scholarship on the topic has focused on individual sanctuaries and, in line with traditional approaches to Central Italian cult places, has largely considered Roman expansion as the cause of apparent changes in the use of Umbrian sanctuaries and in the composition of votive material.

© CHARLES UNIVERSITY, FACULTY OF ARTS, PRAGUE, 2025 | DOI:10.1163/9789004712171_002

This is an open access chapter distributed under the terms of the CC BY-NC-ND 4.0 license.

In attempting to point out the limitations of this argument, this research investigates how the Roman conquest affected religious behavior in the region of Umbria and the role played by cult places and religious phenomena in the integration of the region into the broader Roman state in the last few centuries BCE; did the socio-economic and political role of cult places influence their pattern of change? In order to address these questions, my exploration of Umbrian sanctuaries begins in the archaic period (sixth–fourth centuries BCE) and ends in the early first century BCE, before all the inhabitants of the peninsula gained Roman citizenship and all Italy was enfranchised (with the exception of Transpadane Gaul, the area beyond the Po River).

A multi-scalar approach to Umbrian sanctuaries and their votive material is used here to evaluate the various contexts—historical, religious, political, and socio-cultural—in which the sanctuaries functioned. Theories on cultural interactions and ritual are employed to provide an interpretation of the repercussions of Roman expansion in the religious sphere of the region and to seek out the meaning behind the practice of dedicating figurative votive objects during the pre-Roman period. Both goals are essential for moving the discussion about cultural change and ritual tradition forward: in this region in particular, a prevalent trend in scholarship considers the period after the fourth century BCE as a moment of radical change in the religious life of local peoples due to the Rome's occupation of the region and downplays the ritual practices of the Umbrian worshipers before this century. As a result, the use of sanctuaries during the fourth–first centuries BCE and the appearance of terracotta heads and anatomical votives are believed to be closely linked to the Roman cultural imposition on the religious sphere. My work explicitly tackles these assumptions, testing them against the hard evidence from Umbrian sanctuaries and their figurative votive offerings: I examine both those finds that have been published and displayed in local museums and those that have been, quite literally, left to molder in dusty boxes in the depots of museums and the Soprintendenza Archeologia Belle Arti e Paesaggio dell'Umbria or have simply been lost and are only mentioned in archival and excavation reports.

This ample material has not been gathered together before, nor has it been brought to bear on questions of continuity and change. No work has been done to evaluate the change in the location, architecture, and ritual behaviors of the Italic sanctuaries during the Republican period, or their significance for Italic communities at a crucial historical moment: the aftermath of Roman expansion at the end of the fourth century BCE. Integration among topographical, architectural, and votive data from Umbrian sanctuaries and a focus on the region's archaic and Roman social and political developments are the tools that enable my project to cast a new light and bring an altogether new approach

INTRODUCTION

TABLE 1.1   Chronology of Italic religion

Archaic/classical period. I also refer to this period as pre-Roman.	Sixth–fourth centuries BCE	Appearance of the first significant evidence of Italic religion
Hellenistic period. I also refer to this period as the Roman period or the Middle Republican period.	Late fourth– early first century BCE	Roman conquest and its aftermath: most Italic peoples were conquered by Rome and entered into alliances with the *urbs*.
Late Republic	91 BCE to 14 CE.	Italy became largely homogenized with the Social War and the concession of full Roman citizenship.

to the study of the ancient religious landscape. As the following chapters will demonstrate, the change that happened in the religious sphere of the region has little to do with Roman influence and more with extant local customs, long-lived ritual practices, and contemporary socio-political events.

1   Chronology and Geographic Scope

In this study, I use the chronology of Italic religions outlined by Guy Bradley and Fay Glinister.[1] Since Italic peoples were profoundly affected by Roman expansion and its aftermath, the historical period of Italic religion can be classified in connection to the three main stages of this process, which can be summarized in Table 1.1.

With respect to the geographic scope of this work, it is important to note that ancient Umbria embraced a larger territory than the modern region designated by the same name. The latter excludes the northern part of the Adriatic side of the Apennines (the modern regions of Le Marche and Emilia Romagna) and includes areas that were originally Etruscan, such as Perusia and Volsinii. As my study of Umbrian sanctuaries is closely dependent upon the permission of the Soprintendenza Archeologia Belle Arti e Paesaggio dell'Umbria to analyze the material, I limit my investigation to the Umbrian sacred places that fall

---

1   Bradley and Glinister 2013, 176.

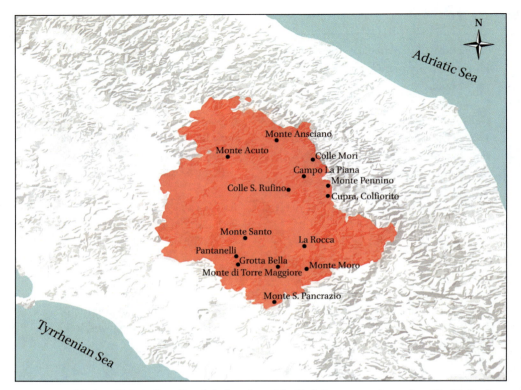

FIGURE 1   Modern Umbria (in red) and the location of the Umbrian sanctuaries analyzed in this book.

into the area of responsibility of this Soprintendenza (fig. 1.1).[2] Excluded from my investigations are therefore the cult places that belong to the authority of the Soprintendenza Archeologia Belle Arti e Paesaggio delle Marche and the Soprintendenza Archeologia dell'Emilia Romagna.

2   **Outline of the Study**

If we exclude the Introduction, this study consists of five chapters and three appendices.

---

2   Excluded from this map are the sanctuaries that have not yielded pre-Roman votive offerings, such as the important sanctuary of Villa Fidelia and the sanctuary at Iguvium Hortensis, for which the Soprintendenza did not grant me a study permit. Furthermore, I have not included isolated votive offerings whose provenance is lacking. These are published by Colonna 1987.

INTRODUCTION 5

Chapter 2 outlines the theoretical methods that provide a framework for my investigation. They include the most dominant and influential approaches that scholars have applied to the study of cultural change on the Italian peninsula following the Roman expansion, with particular attention to religious contexts. Moving from the general to the specific, I offer a detailed analysis of the way these topics have been dealt with in the geographical context of Umbria and highlight how the discussion falls behind the stimulating debate on cultural change in other areas of the peninsula.

After laying out these theoretical principles, Chapter 3 delves into the ways anthropologists and sociologists have approached the study of ritual and how archaeologists have looked at the physical evidence for ritual practices. There is a tendency in the scholarship to concentrate on the study of anatomical terracottas—and their alleged significance as a marker of the spread of Roman religious beliefs—and Etruscan religion, perhaps due to its importance for later Roman tradition, such as divination techniques. As a result of this overly narrow focus, little attention has been given to understanding the meaning of other types of votive depositions. Umbria is no exception to this trend. Here, the abundance of bronze votive figurines of the pre-Roman period has been used to assign socio-political meanings to Umbrian society, while the appearance of anatomical terracottas in the Roman period is seen as an indication that local religious customs had changed following the Roman conquest. Ultimately, approaching the study of this material from a different angle, namely the ritual meanings of their deposition, can allow us to engage with broader questions on how and why anatomical terracottas made their appearance towards the end of the fourth century BCE.

Chapter 4 places Umbrian sanctuaries in the broad geographical and historical context of the region, from the pre-Roman period to the Social War in the early first century BCE. Special attention is paid to the question of ethnicity and the dynamics of Roman expansionism. Following a close reading of the literary sources, traditional interpretations of the historical trajectories of the region have regarded the Umbrians as a cohesive *ethnos* and the middle centuries of Roman expansion (the third and second centuries BCE) as crucial to the political, social, and cultural changes that happened in the region. Recent studies on ethnicity and identity in the Mediterranean and the intricate dynamics of the interactions between Roman and local elites complicate these traditional interpretations of the process of Roman expansion. In this chapter, I highlight the archaeological and epigraphical evidence from Umbria that corroborates these new approaches and sheds light on the existence of both diverse local identities (rather than a single monolithic one) and of factionalism and personal agendas that members of the Umbrian elite could pursue in order to manipulate the

Roman imperialistic machinery into working in their favor. This analysis provides a fundamental framework through which we can interpret the change that happened in the cult places of the region.

Chapter 5 introduces the archaeological record available for Umbrian sanctuary sites and traces their development between the sixth and the first centuries BCE. For each of them, I provide an overview of the topographical location, the architectural and spatial organization, and the votive material—published, unpublished, and archival objects—with particular attention paid to figurative votive offerings (anthropomorphic, zoomorphic, and anatomical offerings). These are further described at length and cataloged in the Appendices (1–3). The results of this analysis allow us to address crucial questions regarding central Italian sacred places: was the abandonment of cult places related to the *laissez-faire* policy of Rome? Is the presence of anatomical terracottas an indication of a change in the cult sphere that followed the spread of more homogenized religious beliefs? The artifactual evidence from Umbrian sanctuaries answers these questions and tells us a different story from the one generally discussed by scholars. It demonstrates, first, that sanctuaries continued to thrive into the Roman period regardless of their proximity to significant Roman religious centers, and second, that anatomical terracottas are hardly related to the Roman presence in the region, since the practice of dedicating anatomical votive offerings and terracotta heads was already widespread from the sixth to the fourth centuries BCE. Once it is shown that one-way influence from Rome into Umbria is untenable, I focus on what the contextual analysis of sanctuaries and their votive objects can, in fact, reveal with respect to the broader patterns in cultural practices that spread through the region following the Roman expansion into the peninsula.

Drawing from the data analyzed and discussed in the previous section, in Chapter 6 I advance several hypotheses that account for the continuation of Umbrian sanctuaries during the Roman period and the apparent longevity of the ritual practice of dedicating anatomical objects. In doing so, I trace a macro-scale picture of the socio-economic and cultural trends visible in the region's cult places from the archaic to the Hellenistic periods. In the first section of the chapter, I focus on the function of sacred places from the sixth to the fourth centuries BCE and use topographical data and information provided by the figurative votive offerings to argue that sanctuaries function in close connection with individual communities. Furthermore, I explore the possible meanings for the deposition of bronze figurines during this period and propose that it constituted a ritual of well-being for the individual as well as for the community. The second section considers the development of cult places after the Roman expansion. First, I analyze the change in ritual depositions

INTRODUCTION

and suggest that the adoption of terracottas needs to be considered as a new medium—advantageous both in technique and in fashion—used to express an already long-established practice. Second, I provide an interpretation of the decrease in ritual activities at certain sanctuaries and the monumentalization of other sanctuaries with Italic and Hellenistic architectural features. While the former appears to be connected to regional economic trends, the latter ties into the dynamics of interconnection and negotiation among Umbrian and Roman elites, who, for different reasons, had a shared interest in showing public munificence to pursue their civic and political goals. On the basis of this interpretation of the evidence, the model I propose to use to approach the topic of cultural change in the religious sphere does not leave much room for the imposition of one culture onto the local people; rather, I advocate for a theoretical framework of analysis which finds similarities with the Middle Ground theory first proposed by Richard White. This "space in between," however, was not solely the one shared by Romans and the Umbrians but rather one that reflected and was informed by a complex network of dynamic relationships and associations that involved the broader Italic peninsula and the Mediterranean as a whole.

Three appendices conclude the book. In Appendix 1, the types of offerings that make up Umbrian votive deposits are described in detail, with a focus on their stylistic elements and, if available, the scholarly discussion of their interpretation. Appendix 2 is a tabulated catalog in the form of an Excel database. It collects all the votive figurines of Umbria, mostly unpublished, that I studied first-hand in the museums and depots of the region. Information regarding find spot, date, measurements, and chronological range is provided, followed by a bibliography (if present) and appropriate comparanda. Appendix 3 is a photo catalog of the figurative votive offerings discussed in Chapter 5.

On a final note, I hope that this work will also provide a useful method of investigation in other areas of research on Italic cult places, especially those that either have not yet been examined, such as the ones in Picenum, or are still discussed within the conventional framework of "Religious Romanization." As the example of Umbria abundantly demonstrates, a careful analysis of the material evidence from sanctuaries has the potential to rewrite some of the basic assumptions of Roman cultural influence and to shed new light on local traditions, their persistence through time, and their adaptation to new sociopolitical events.

CHAPTER 2

Cultural Change in the Sanctuaries of Central Italy

The investigation of cult places represents a unique opportunity for understanding broader issues of cultural continuity and change. As has been widely demonstrated by scholars working in central and southern Italy, people living in the fortified centers and the surrounding areas used sacred spaces not only to express their religious sentiments but also to gather as a community. Moreover, as leading scholars have argued, religion represented an extension of social life, with its functions in and implications for daily life. As such, sanctuaries provide essential social, political, and economic information about past societies.

Approaches to sacred spaces and their material culture have changed over time as a result of new data and changing perspectives in anthropological and archaeological methods. In this chapter, I review the most dominant and influential ways that scholars have thought about and discussed sacred spaces within the timeframe of this book, from the sixth to the early first centuries BCE. The discussion is organized into two sections: the first part of the chapter discusses the scholarly approaches to cultural change within the frame of the Roman conquest. At the end of this section, significant contributions to the cultural change that happened in Umbria following the Roman expansion are identified. The second part of the chapter deals with the topic of cultural change in religious contexts, and the ways scholars used rural sanctuaries, colonies, and *municipia* to formulate and support their theories. Although ongoing and stimulating debates on cultural change in the Italian peninsula have challenged some traditional interpretations of this topic, the discussion about the changes that happened in Umbria and its sacred spaces following the Roman expansion seems, unfortunately, to remain anchored to old assumptions and outdated historical analysis.

1 Cultural Change and the Roman Conquest

The process of cultural, socio-political, and economic change in Italy and the provinces during the Roman conquest, often called Romanization, has been the object of extensive debate for over two hundred years. One of the theoretical methodologies employed in examining cultural change and processes of conquest, especially in the past, is the colonialist approach.[1] Its first theorist,

---

1   Haverfield 1912; Freeman 2007, 27–50; Hingely 2000.

© CHARLES UNIVERSITY, FACULTY OF ARTS, PRAGUE, 2025 | DOI:10.1163/9789004712171_003

This is an open access chapter distributed under the terms of the CC BY-NC-ND 4.0 license.

Francis Haverfield, saw the process of Romanization as beginning primarily in a post-conquest society (e.g., Gaul and Britain), where direct Roman policy from the top prompted an increase in the Roman population of the province through the establishment of veteran colonies. According to this view, Romanization was a deliberate policy on the part of the government of Rome that imparted a systematic and standardized process of acculturation. The moral mission attributed to Rome is evident in Haverfield's claim that "Rome acted for the betterment and happiness of the world" and his suggestion that the use of "Roman things" indicated that conquered territories "realized their value and ceased any national hatred towards them."[2]

This unilinear view of cultural change—where the Romans change the provincials, but the provincials have no impact on Rome in return—has been maintained by other scholars, especially citizens of modern colonial empires. Scholars living in Britain, France, and Germany seem to have felt a sort of kinship towards the ancient Romans and were particularly interested in topics related to the Roman conquests, the process of acculturation, and the conceptualization of the identity of the "other."[3] Archaeological studies were interested mainly in the perspective of the colonizers (whether Greek or Roman), while the native population was either largely overlooked or treated as the "passive recipient of new habits."[4] The acculturation process was seen as a one-way street, with the indigenous elites (and, after a spell, the rest of the population) emulating the customs and the crafts of the invaders. This approach to Romanization has been much criticized, since it implies an idea of "a triumph of a superior and more advanced culture over primitive communities," resulting in "the creation of a very uniform political and cultural entity."[5]

In the later twentieth century, after the collapse of the great colonizing empires, scholars began to open a new debate about the concepts of Romanization and to stress adaptation over acculturation, negotiation over emulation, and hybridity over monoculturalism. Most importantly, scholars such as Martin Millett, Greg Woolf, Chris Gosden, Andrew Wallace-Hadrill, Nicola Terrenato, and David Mattingly have attempted to reconstitute the voice of the local people, whom they now view as a fundamental agent in the acceptance or rejection of Roman culture. These approaches, many of which draw on postcolonial studies in history and anthropology, address the complex effects of colonization,

---

2 Haverfield 1923, 9.
3 Hingley 2000.
4 Lyons and Papadopoulos 2002, 5.
5 Terrenato 2001, 3.

colonialism, and decolonization on cultural formation by placing emphasis on the perspectives of the colonized and striving to develop a new understanding of colonialist experiences, often emphasizing the agency of indigenous people.[6]

Millet's *The Romanization of Britain* is an influential contribution to the post-colonial reaction to Rome's role in the lives of provincial and native societies.[7] He focuses on the native and local developments of Roman culture in Britain and argues that the provincial elite had a direct self-interest in adopting elements of Roman culture and identifying themselves with the imperial power. Provincial elites would have, therefore, "self-romanized" through the adoption of material culture, language, and beliefs that they used to reinforce their position within local society. These Roman customs then spread to other levels of society through a sort of trickle-down effect based upon the material benefits of Roman identity to everyone. In studies of Italy, the paradigm of self-Romanization takes an even more extreme turn. In the view of scholars such as Emilio Gabba and Mario Torelli, Italic elites imitated Roman cultural and political norms.[8]

The concept of self-Romanization has been widely criticized. First, the model focuses narrowly on elites, assuming that the rest of the population passively emulated them. Scholars such as Woolf and Mattingly have argued that, although Millett's model frees the process of conquest from a strictly Romano-centric perspective, it does not allow for a diversity of responses to Roman dominion by different groups within a local population.[9] Indeed, it does not allow the possibility that some groups could have opposed the new order.

A second point of critique is the simplistic use of "Roman material culture." Millett assumed that Roman goods adopted by the local elites had an intrinsic Roman identity, and he did not consider the possibility that these could have been perceived differently in different areas of the Roman empire. In his review of Millett's book, P.W.M. Freeman successfully demonstrated that new "Roman" goods and traits did not necessarily carry a Roman identity but could incorporate alternative meanings depending, for example, on different geographical contexts.[10] For example, the appearance of villas and of Samian pottery may "reflect regional pre-Roman social practices" rather than "a desire to

---

6   Liebmann-Riez 2008; Given 2004.
7   Millett 1990.
8   Gabba 1994; Torelli 1995.
9   Hingley 1996; Woolf 1992, 1998; Mattingly 2011.
10   Freeman 1993.

be 'Roman.' "[11] Most importantly, the adoption of goods may have represented an efficient and technologically new practice, an improvement over what was used before, regardless of their origin. Freeman and others have shown that labeling goods as "Roman" is a simplification and that their adoption by local people does not automatically imply the simple acceptance of the material elements of Roman civilization.[12] Terrenato reflects critically on the label "Roman" applied to architectural forms and techniques of the Middle and Late Republican period and its inappropriate use in scholarship. He provocatively uses the term "Romanization of Rome" to highlight, on the basis of recent discoveries in the field of Roman architecture, that many of the alleged Roman elements, such as concrete-enabled complexes, did not originate in Rome, nor could Rome boast of being a mediator of Greek culture during the Hellenistic period.[13]

In more recent years, the dynamics of interaction between locals and Romans have been further problematized. Scholars have moved away from the binary opposition Romans/locals and have developed more complex models of the interrelation between settlers and the indigenous population. One such model is the Middle Ground theory,[14] initially used by Richard White to describe the encounters between early European settlers and Native Americans. According to White, people in a new or unfamiliar social context adapt to diverse cultural practices and values while continuing to use their own social conventions. This interaction between people of different cultural backgrounds creates new cultural structures, a middle ground in which peoples live—sometimes for some centuries.[15] White's theory has been applied to the Roman world by Gosden, who emphasized the local hybrid forms created by the contacts between Rome and indigenous people during the imperial period.[16]

Creolization, code-switching, bricolage, and discrepant identities are other notions used by scholars who have tried to explain the process of cultural change that occurred with the incorporation of indigenous societies into the Roman state and to account for the inclusion of non-elite groups in such pro-

---

11 Freeman 1993, 444.
12 Barrett 1997; Fincham 2002; Mattingly 1997, 2004; Webster 2001; Woolf 1992.
13 Terrenato 2021. Marble columns, marble wall paintings, baths, and masonry theaters are attested elsewhere in central Italy earlier than they are in Rome. Interestingly, even less urbanized regions such as Samnium experimented with stone theaters before Rome did.
14 Lyons and Papadopoulos 2002.
15 White 1991.
16 Gosden 2004, 104–113.

cesses. Jane Webster borrowed the word "creolization" from linguistics, where it was used to indicate the emergence of a mixed speech that derives from two different languages and applied it to the study of the Roman provinces. Focusing on creolization as a mixture of cultural traits recognizable in material culture, Webster stressed that the interaction between Romans and the provinces resulted in a cultural negotiation and mediation involving defined cultural change.[17] In Webster's view, the result of colonial interaction is "not a single, normative colonial culture, but mixed cultures" that are evidenced by the various uses of material culture.[18] Similarly, Herring refers to differential acculturation in his analysis of the interactions between the native peoples of Southern Italy and the Greeks in the religious sphere during the fifth and fourth centuries BCE. With this term, he refers to the specific choices of indigenous peoples concerning the assimilation of Greek elements. In his view, they selected what best suited their changing native society and was the closest to their traditional native practices while at the same time maintaining some traditional elements of their own belief system.[19]

Rather than looking for instances of the creation of something entirely new, Andrew Wallace-Hadrill has emphasized code-switching, another term taken from linguistics and used to describe how individuals move between diverse but coexisting culture-systems. Wallace-Hadrill rejects the traditional belief in cultural superiority and hierarchy and focuses on the set of choices and practices by which a group constructs, interprets, and reproduces its own identity in diverse culture-systems. Switching between different languages to best communicate a message depending on the situation, he argues, may not only be confined to bilingualism/multilingualism but may also map onto expressions of material culture. Therefore, Wallace-Hadrill looks at the archaeological record of the Italian peninsula from the Mid-Republican period onward as a manifestation of diverse culture-systems, "in full awareness of their diversity and code-switching between them."[20] He argues that cultural modes of expression are added to an individual's repertoire, rather than the local being replaced by the Roman, as maintained by colonial and postcolonial theories—Ennius, for example, could maintain his *tria corda* without having to choose one of them. In short, Wallace-Hadrill's code-switching theory does not require a third space of interaction like the Middle Ground theory, where two different cultures merge to form a new single entity. Instead, he proposes that cultural cues

---

17   Webster 2001.
18   Webster 2001, 2018.
19   Herring 1996.
20   Webster 2001, 30.

survive alongside each other in particular social contexts and that people are able to "switch" from one code to the other strategically according to the context.

In the context of his exploration of change and continuity at Volterra, Nicola Terrenato offers another theoretical model for cultural encounters. He sees cultural processes within the Roman conquest as processes of bricolage through which old objects acquire "new meaning to serve new purposes within new contexts."[21] That is, an object that already carried a sedimented message can take over new functions according to specific needs. With the adoption of new meanings attributed to pre-existing cultural items, new cultural patchworks come into existence and could be made of different elements: old, new, local, and imported. Each community reacted to the process of Roman expansion in a different way, thereby creating a different bricolage. In the process of Roman expansion, Terrenato highlights the role played by Roman and Italian elites' agendas and encourages consideration of the political scene of the Italians, the existence of factions, and even political parties that manipulate the new cultural choices available to them for their own purposes.[22]

David Mattingly similarly focuses on local populations' strategic use of cultural elements. He stresses the diversity of assimilation to Roman control among different groups according to class, occupation, and gender. He proposes the model of discrepant identities,[23] closely akin to code-switching, according to which individuals and groups in the Roman period possessed a range of overlapping identities and expressed themselves differently in different contexts. In the case of burial practices, for example, he notices that the Libyan-Phoenician elite in Lepcis Magna sometimes built tombs in the Roman architectural style but also used Neo-Punic characters inside the tombs, even on the interior or exterior of burial urns. Mattingly interprets this as showing that the local elite of Lepcis selected elements of Roman culture to show their connection to the power structure of the empire, while at the same time they maintained local traditions to differentiate themselves from outsiders and visitors.

Despite their differences, the various models are united in their rejection of a binary opposition between native and Roman cultures as too simplistic for so multifaceted a phenomenon as Roman expansion in the Italian peninsula and the provinces. These newer approaches rightly emphasize the specificities

---

21   Terrenato 1998, 23.
22   Terrenato 2014, 45–60; Terrenato 2019, 155–191.
23   Mattingly 2011.

of cultures, the role of the inhabitants of different regions, and their negotiation and cultural exchange with the Roman peoples. Furthermore, they make it clear that cultures can take on foreign ways of doing or being while still remaining conscious of their own identity. As such, they open a new perspective for analyzing the dynamic interplay of different groups and currents during the period of Roman expansion. Ultimately, I will demonstrate that the effects of Roman expansion in the religious sphere of Umbria can be explained with the help of the Middle Ground approach. The encounter between Romans and Umbrians creates a middle ground space where no side is clearly the master. Rather, what seems to emerge from this interaction in the sanctuaries of the region is a new set of cultural forms where the preexisting practices and traditions are both preserved and integrated with new ones.

1.1 Cultural Change in Ancient Umbria

The cultural change brought about in Umbria during the Roman conquest of this area has only very recently been the object of sustained scholarly attention. Debate on cultural change in central Italy has revolved mainly around the better-investigated regions of Etruria, Latium, and Samnium.[24] However, the last two decades of archaeological discoveries and historical rethinking have begun to increase our knowledge of ancient Umbria, making this region a promising field of study.

Scholars investigating Romanization in this region have long been influenced by William Harris' monograph *Etruria and Umbria*.[25] In this work, not only does Harris overestimate the cultural influence of Rome in the process of the conquest of the region, but he also treats Umbria as a distant second behind Etruria, with its much better documented history and archaeology. In the conclusion of his book, Harris holds that after the Social War, the inhabitants of the towns of Etruria and Umbria "were Romans, not Etruscans and Umbrians."[26] According to Harris, the spread of Latin and the adoption of Roman magisterial institutions were clear signs of the replacement of one identity and culture (Etruscan, Umbrian) by another (Roman).

Simone Sisani's *Fenomenologia della conquista* extends Harris' arguments and adds an extensive discussion of the archaeological evidence to what was previously limited to literary sources.[27] Sisani praises Harris' take on Roman

---

24   Manconi 2017 for a detailed explanation of the reasons why ancient Umbria has only been recently investigated.
25   Harris 1981.
26   Harris 1981, 318.
27   Sisani 2009.

cultural influence and downplays local Umbrian cultural traits that he considers evanescent. He focuses on Romanization as a voluntary choice by local populations, and he maintains that the latter underwent a process of self-Romanization and acculturation. According to him, starting from the fourth century BCE, Etruscan and Umbrian centers shared a similar acculturation process that would be completed by the Romans in the first century BCE. Sisani argues that, in the decades following the Social War, Italy became a "geographical and political unity, if not a nation ... unified by the Roman politics and inseparable from the notion of *romanitas*."[28]

Recently, Guy Bradley reacted against the idea that Umbrians were the passive recipients of Roman culture.[29] His consideration of social change and urbanism during the conquest shows the complexity of the transformations that occurred in the region. He argues that many of these developments are caused not only by external factors (i.e., Rome) but also by internal ones, such as the local environment (proximity to cities as opposed to rural areas) and Umbrian participation in the Roman army. In addition, he uses archaeological evidence to show the presence of locals in the newly established colonies of the region and advocates for more intricate patterns of cohabitation both in and outside settlements. Most importantly, he concludes that we should not take cultural change as a sign of a culture replacing another but of the coexistence of different identities. He points out the danger of over-emphasizing the influence of Rome and reassesses the role played by the Umbrian communities in the period of the Roman conquest. In doing so, Bradley responds to Caroline Malone and Simon Stoddart's *Territory, Time and State* and Pierre Fontaine's *Cités et encientes de l'Ombrie antique*, both of which envision an ancient Umbria that was mostly undeveloped, had little if any state structural systems prior to the Social War, and owed its governmental institutions primarily to Roman intervention in the region.[30]

Bradley raises new and exciting questions and challenges for those who study cultural change in Umbria. His problematization of the dynamics of cultural interaction represents a starting point for my investigation of Umbrian sacred spaces and how they developed following the conquest.

---

28 Sisani 2009, 24. Translation by the author.
29 Bradley 2000.
30 Stoddart 1994, 177; Bradley 2000, 10–18.

2   Cultural Change in the Religious Sphere of Central Italy

Recent anthropological and archaeological research has demonstrated that sanctuaries are a suitable avenue for investigating processes of cultural change.[31] In moments of cultural interaction, communities seem to evoke or reinvent their traditions by reshaping religious and ritual institutions. Yet Italic sanctuaries have only been the object of a few comprehensive studies attempting to explain and problematize the change in these places after the Roman conquest. As pointed out by Tesse Stek,[32] one of the obstacles to the study of inland Italic sanctuaries is that many of them have been excavated only recently, and their interpretation lacks a firm archaeological framework. In addition, a lack of written sources and a dearth of epigraphic material has limited historical interpretation. For this reason, until a decade ago, scholars had long advanced a Romanocentric view that emphasized both Rome's policy of non-intervention in rural sanctuaries and Roman colonization as key factors in the spread of Roman religious ideas.[33]

Scholarship on the topic has traditionally assumed that Roman expansion had no repercussions in the religious sphere of conquered people who had not been enfranchised. The received wisdom is that Roman policymakers and representatives did not intervene in the religious matters of unenfranchised areas, which could keep their gods and religious institutions. Conversely, Rome would have had an active role in the religious traditions and material culture of the areas whose inhabitants had gained Roman citizenship, namely colonies and *municipia*.

The notion of a hands-off Roman policy applies in particular to rural sanctuaries. The prevailing view has maintained that the Roman expansion led to a decline in rural cult sites, which did not experience the rapid development of cities in the Roman world. Yet the archaeological data does not support this hypothesis. Many rural sanctuaries continued to be used during the Roman period and some were embellished and even monumentalized. Scholars such as Adriano La Regina, Cesare Letta, and Giovanni Colonna have wondered about the reasons for such investment in rural sanctuaries during the Middle and Late Republican period and have asked whether it relates to Rome's cultural and political role in the peninsula. Specifically, they have tried to tie the motivations behind the temples' visible embellishment to the possible functions of the sanctuaries themselves in the pre-Roman period.

---

31   Cohen 1985; Stek 2009; Battiloro 2019; Zapelloni Pavia and Larocca 2022.
32   Stek 2009, 54.
33   See in particular de Cazanove 2000 and Stek 2009, 17–34.

Among the Apennine and Adriatic regions of central Italy, Samnium is by far the area that has received the most scholarly attention. In recent years, the research and fieldwork carried out in Samnium by teams from several Dutch universities led by Stek have tackled the traditional interpretation of rural sanctuaries and shed new light on the Roman impact on religious structures in non-Roman Republican Italy.

The function and role of rural sanctuaries have often been related to the presence of *tratturi*, ancient paths along which shepherds drove their flocks between cooler mountains pastures and warmer lowlands for grazing. Scholars who have linked rural sanctuaries to the pastoral context of the Italic economy argued that cult places were located along *tratturi* to provide shelter to herdsmen and to offer a place to trade safely.[34] The wealth associated with these activities would have been used to monumentalize and decorate the sanctuaries, often dedicated to the patron deity of herdsmen, Heracles. As Stek has demonstrated, this interpretation is flawed for two reasons. First, evidence for large-scale pastoralism before the Roman period is scant, and second, research in Samnium shows that the link between sacred spaces and *tratturi* is based more on assumptions of a putative topographical correspondence than on hard evidence.[35]

Others have considered Italic sanctuaries as markers of civic, political, and ethnic boundaries.[36] This view, which originated in studies by Francois de Polignac and Pier Giovanni Guzzo on sanctuaries in Greece and Magna Graecia, holds that Italic sanctuaries functioned as markers of the territory belonging to a specific community.[37] The focus of this line of investigation has been

---

34   La Regina 1999; Llyod 1991, 185–185; Dench 1995, 21.

35   Stek (2009, 56–58) shows that, given its position and altitude, the sanctuary of Campochiaro was not accessible from the nearest *tratturi*, which makes it unlikely that it housed a cattle market, as was once believed.

36   D'Ercole 2000.

37   De Polignac's 1991 study of the role of religious practice in the rise of Greek *poleis* argued that sanctuaries located outside city centers functioned as markers of the power of the *poleis* as they formed political boundaries. His main case study is the Argive Heraion. De Polignac notes that during the earlier geometric and archaic periods, when Argos was conducting a non-aggressive policy towards its neighbors, the role of the sanctuary was as a meeting place open to all. However, in the classical period, as Argos established its hegemony in the region, the monumental extra-urban sanctuary publicized the new political reality. Guzzo (1987) created a framework for the identification of the so-called "frontier sanctuaries." According to this model, urban cults were centered in the *agora*, suburban rural cults within the agricultural belt, and frontier sanctuaries in zones of contacts between diverse political entities.

Etruscan sanctuaries, especially those located in the southern part of the region, and Campanian sanctuaries.

Using the concepts of political and frontier sanctuaries as they have been applied to Greek and southern Italian contexts, Corinna Riva and Stoddart suggest that sanctuaries worked to define boundaries on three levels, according to their spatial relationship to the city center.[38] Within this model, sanctuaries outside urban areas were placed in liminal spaces between urban and suburban zones in order to delimit and negotiate territorial control. Similarly to Riva and Stoddart, Andrea Zifferero holds that sanctuaries were positioned in very strategic areas delimiting urban and non-urban areas and between territories belonging to different cities. Thus, he believes that the role of these sanctuaries was to act as a location for the conflicts over territorial control, and their resolution. A similar role has been identified for the sanctuaries of Campania by Paolo Carafa, who emphasizes their role as markers of the edge of a city's influence.[39]

Studies of ethnicity in central Italy have highlighted the difficulty of defining stable ethnic boundaries during both the Archaic and the Republican periods.[40] The presence of ethnic groups is difficult to trace archaeologically, and the concept of ethnicity itself depends on socio-historical moments and is "therefore very sensitive to historical changes."[41] This view is supported by the recent work of Rafael Scopacasa, who shows that users of Italic sanctuaries defined themselves fluidly, regardless of their ethnicity.[42] Scopacasa focuses on Samnium, demonstrating that the architecture and architectural decoration of Samnite sanctuaries reveal the fluidity (what he calls nested identities) with which social groups defined themselves rather than a monolithic ethnic identity. For example, the architectural terracottas from temples at Gildone and Petacciato show that the iconographical traditions current in Tyrrhenian and southern Italy were not only reproduced but also transformed according to particular cultic and aesthetic preferences. On the other hand, the lavish euergetism of temple B at Pietrabbondante and the fact that the place was overtly named "the cult site of the *safinim*," as attested by an inscription found on site,[43] possibly signals that the worshipers at this site wanted to bolster a sense

---

38 Riva and Stoddart 1996.

39 Carafa 2008.

40 See in particular Dench 1995 and Jones 1997. For a more detailed discussion on this topic see *infra*, Chapter 4.

41 Stek 2009, 63.

42 Scopacasa 2015.

43 The inscription in Oscan reads: **safinim sakaraklum**. See Vetter 1953, no. 149.

CULTURAL CHANGE IN THE SANCTUARIES OF CENTRAL ITALY   19

of ethnic unity among the community. Scopacasa interprets this to mean that communities used cult places to articulate their identity differently, according to context, personal interests, and purpose.

Another view popular among scholars is that, in the context of scarce urbanization, rural sanctuaries worked within the so-called *pagus-vicus* system.[44] In Latin, *pagus* refers to the local, territorial districts of the people of the central Apennines, while *vicus* refers to the villages within the larger *pagus*. According to Adriano La Regina, Cesare Letta, and others, in a landscape that lacked secure urban centers, sanctuaries would have functioned as the pole of aggregation on different levels depending on their association to a *touto* (tribe), a *pagus*, or a *vicus*.[45] The presence of rural sanctuaries in the Roman period in central Italy has been, therefore, considered a persistence of the indigenous *pagus-vicus* system.

Undoubtedly, one of the merits of recent scholarship on Italic sanctuaries has been the deconstruction of their association to the *pagus-vicus* system. In 2004, the "Sacred Landscape" survey project, under the supervision of Jeremia Pelgrom and Tesse Stek,[46] demonstrated that the isolation of rural sanctuaries is merely an illusion caused by a lack of research. Fieldwork around the sanctuaries of Colle Rimontato, Cupa, and Castel di Galdo in central Samnium has demonstrated that clusters consisting of settlements and cult sites seem to be the rule in all three case studies. The organization of *pagus-vicus* settlements based on pre-urban centers is therefore debatable. Stek has also questioned the pre-Roman origin of the *pagus-vicus* system in this region.[47] Drawing from the work of Michel Tarpin and Luigi Capogrossi Colognesi, Stek demonstrates that *pagus* and *vicus* were administrative units created by the expanding Roman power: they were not relics of an earlier Italic system of territorial organization. He shows that inscriptions that relate to the involvement of a *pagus* or *vicus* in a cult or sanctuary come from Roman areas. When the epigraphical evidence can be connected to archaeological material, the Roman influence in the religious sphere becomes more manifest. The recently excavated temple at Castel di Ieri is a case in point. The structure is built *ex pagi decreto*, as inscribed on a mosaic at the temple's entrance,[48] and presents strictly Romanizing aspects

---

44   La Regina 1970–1971; 1980, esp. 35–42; 1981; Colonna 1985; Gualtieri 1987; Letta 1992.

45   This dispersed *pagus-vicus* model was conceived as an Italic antithesis to the Greek *polis*, Roman *urbs*, and Etruscan city-state in which the aforementioned functions were supposedly centralized in a single urban agglomeration.

46   Stek and Pelgrom 2008.

47   Stek 2009, 65–75.

48   *AE* 2004, 489.

that suggest the involvement of the *pagus* in Roman religious ideology. Similarly, evidence from the *vici* on the shores of the Fucine Lake points to the adoption of new deities such as Valetudo and Victoria. Cult places associated with *pagi* and *vici* seem, therefore, to function within the Roman reorganization of the land and its people.

As for the fate of religious places after the concession of Roman citizenship at the beginning of the first century BCE, the received wisdom states that all cult places were re-shaped to conform to Rome's model, and Italic rural sanctuaries were closed as they did not serve the new political order. This is most often seen as a consequence of the urbanization process in newly founded *municipia*, a phenomenon amply discussed by Gabba and, more recently, d'Alessio.[49] The responsibilities and privileges that accompanied Roman citizenship and autonomous local administration required the creation of urban areas and public buildings to house the political and economic functions imposed by this new social and administrative organization. Architecture and urbanism served as tangible evidence of the insertion of new citizens into the system of Roman political values. Non-urban centers would have been left out as they did not fall within Rome's sphere of interest. However, new fieldwork carried out at Samnite sanctuaries (especially at Capochiaro, Vastogirardi, Schiavi d'Abruzzo, and S. Giovanni in Galdo) has demonstrated that the archaeological evidence is inconsistent with the traditional view of the abandonment of countryside sacred areas after the Social War. The data show that activities in rural sanctuaries did not cease after the Social War but continued well into the first century BCE.

Contrary to the situation in territories outside direct Roman control, newly established Roman and Latin colonies and *municipia* would have been chosen for the spread of Roman religious ideas in and outside colonial settlements. In this process of "religious Romanization,"[50] on the one hand, Rome imposed its will on local people, and, on the other hand, colonies showed their loyalty to Rome through the emulation of its religious material culture: i.e., the Etrusco-Italic temple model and anatomical votives. This view owes its popularity to the work of scholars such as Frank Brown, Edward Salmon, Daniel Gargola, and Olivier de Cazanove, who believed that Roman colonies followed a purely Roman imprint and were composed primarily of mono-ethnic settlers from Rome and Latium who moved to the colony with a prescribed cult-package.[51]

---

49   Gabba 1972; D'Alessio 2008.

50   This term was first used by de Cazanove (2000).

51   Salmon 1969; Brown 1980; Gargola 1995. The idea that Capitolia are a standard feature of

CULTURAL CHANGE IN THE SANCTUARIES OF CENTRAL ITALY   21

The presence of Etrusco-Italic temples and their terracotta decoration has been considered the main proof that colonial establishments replicated the image of Rome. The Capitolium temple, with three *cellae*, a high podium, a high axial staircase, and a *pronaos*, would have represented an unequivocal symbol of the Roman ideals of urbanity and sophistication and an appeal to the neighboring Italic people who adopted these models from the colonies.[52] Mario Torelli, in particular, concludes that the selection of figures and scenes further contributed to forging a stable relationship between the colony and Rome.

The dedication of anatomical ex-votos and votive heads represents another phenomenon believed to be typical of Roman colonies. During the Middle and Late Republican period, mold-made terracotta offerings became a far-reaching phenomenon in central Italian sanctuaries.[53] They included representations of hands and feet, genitals, internal organs, and parts of the face, such as tongues, eyes, and ears. Their appearance in the Etruscan cities of the Tyrrhenian coast of central Italy as early as the end of the fifth century BCE has been connected to the external influences of either Greece or Magna Graecia. Some scholars associate this tradition with the contacts between southern Etruscan cities and classical Greece, where the custom of dedicating anatomical votives made of clay and other materials became popular in the same century;[54] others trace it to the production of statues of worshipers and heads in the Veian and Faliscan area in which they recognize the influence of the masks from Sicily and Magna Graecia associated with chthonic cults.[55]

Although there is no agreement on the origin of the Italic custom of dedicating anatomical fictile votive offerings, most scholars agree that there is a connection between the growing presence of these objects in the Italian peninsula in the fourth and third centuries BCE and Rome's colonizing ventures. Simply put, since Etruscan cities were among the first ones to be conquered by the Romans, the spread of anatomical votives outside Etruria and Latium has been read as the direct consequence of the exposure to, and the influence of, Roman hegemony.[56] According to this view, the arrival of Roman and Latin colonists

---

Roman colonies goes back at least to Du Cange's *Glossarium Mediae et Inmae Latinitatis*, published in 1737. For a review of the studies on Capitolia see Quinn and Wilson 2013.

52 Torelli 1993; 1999, 127. For a recent discussion on the characteristic features of Etrusco-Italic temples see Edlund-Berry 2008 and Warden 2012.

53 Glinister 2006a.

54 Lesk 2002, 200; Haynes 2000, 172–173; Huges 2017.

55 Comella 1981, 771–775, Fabbri 2010, 30.

56 Torelli 1973, Torelli 1999; Fenelli 1975; Comella 1981; Coarelli 2000; Sisani 2007; de Cazanove 2000; 2015; 2017, 75; Fabbri 2019, 16.

caused local Italian communities to adopt religious practices from Rome and Latium. These votives have consequently become a convenient instrument to measure the religious Romanization of Italy. Some scholars go as far as to suggest that Rome deliberately used terracotta votives to integrate Roman ideology into non-Roman communities on a cultural level.[57] In this frame of reference, it is argued that colonies facilitated the spread of Roman ideology and function, as Olivier de Cazanove puts it, as "religious staging posts of Roman expansion."[58]

Within this traditional Romano-centric view, an often-posited assumption is that anatomical offerings had a healing meaning. Scholars traditionally maintain that they were dedicated as a request for, or in the hope of, a cure for some disease and therefore associate them with healing and fertility cults such as that of Asclepius.[59] According to this conventional view, votive representations of feet, hands, etc. symbolized the body parts that needed healing by the god or those that had already been healed.[60]

In the past two decades, this prevailing view of Roman colonial policy that resulted in the phenomenon of the "religious Romanization" of Italy has been contested and problematized. First, recent scholarship has shown that the model that assumes a deliberate likeness between Rome and the mid-Republican colonies, derived mainly from Rome-centered literary sources, is untenable in light of the archaeological evidence.[61] Michael Crawford, Elizabeth Fentress, and Edward Bispham, among others, have demonstrated that the evidence at our disposal does not show any clear and consistent link between

---

57   Coarelli 2000; de Cazanove 2001, 191.

58   De Cazanove 2000, 75.

59   See, for example, Turfa 1994; Potter and Wells 1985; Comella 1981; Dicus 2012; Hughes 2017; Draycott and Graham 2017 with previous bibliography. In addition to the healing function of the anatomical votives, the last two authors also explore the possibility that they may indicate concerns about the fragmentation of the body and the relation between the whole and single parts. For a revisionist approach to this view see Chapter 6.

60   According to the account written in Ovid's *Metamorphoses*, Asclepius was introduced to Rome because of an epidemic in 293 BCE: Ov. *Met.* 14.940.

61   Ancient historical accounts portray the Roman conquest of Italy as the first stage in the city's inevitable rise to world domination. Whilst such narratives offer an invaluable basis for our understanding of how Rome extended its territory and power, they also pose serious challenges. Except for Polybius, most of the surviving texts were written from the mid-first century BCE onwards, at least two hundred years after the events that they describe. These authors wrote about the mid-Republican past in view of their own political agendas and anxieties as upper-class Romans of the late Republic and Principate. See Dench, 2005; Kraus and Woodman 1997; Bispham 2006; Bradley 2006; and Patterson 2006.

the construction of *capitolia* and the award of colonial or municipal status.[62] A growing body of epigraphic, numismatic, and archaeological sources shows, in fact, that the trend of building *capitolia* only really develops after 200 BCE. The public buildings at Cosa, which include a *capitolium*, for example, emerge only in the second century BCE, one century after the establishment of the colony.[63] These reviewed chronologies reveal that Cosa and other classic Latin colonies, such as Fregellae and Alba Fucens, were more lacking in monumental buildings during the Mid-Republican period than previously thought.

Scholars have also questioned Rome's supposed role as the sole influence on colonial town building. Fay Glinister emphasizes the efforts and motivations of individuals and small groups not only among the commissioners and the colonists but also among the locals and settlers from various parts of Italy, who, in many cases, appear to have been included in the colony.[64] Jamie Sewell has pointed to the Greek influence on Roman and Latin colonies, such as the length of *insulae* and the fortification system, and has thus underlined the differences between colonies and Rome rather than similarities.[65] Amanda Coles focuses on the role of cult in the makeup of each colony and how it facilitated the integration of diverse social and ethnic groups. At Fregellae, for example, the placement of urban sanctuaries next to the Via Latina may point to an effort to reinforce community cohesion and boundaries.[66] Given this evidence, Cole invites us to consider "the uniqueness of each colony's set of gods, temples, and rituals" rather than their alleged similarity to Rome.[67]

The claim that anatomical votives map the extension of Roman expansion and function as an instrument of Roman domination on a cultural level has been similarly contested. Glinister and Gentili have recently pointed out that there is no good reason to argue that the diffusion of anatomical models coincides geographically with the spread of Roman political influence. First, the tradition of dedicating anatomical votives predates the major phase of Roman colonization in the fourth and third centuries BCE. Excavations at the Italic sanctuaries of Lagole, San Pietro Montagnon, Marzabotto, Lake of the Idols, among others, have brought to light anatomical votives in bronze dated as early as the sixth century BCE.[68] Additionally, it seems that in the Latin colonies of

---

62   Fentress 2000, Crawford 2006, Bispham 2000 and 2006. The discussion is here limited to the religious aspects that are associated to Roman colonization.

63   Fentress 2000, Cooley 2016, 378–400.

64   Glinister 2015; see also Tarpin 2014.

65   Sewell 2014.

66   Coles, 2009, 167–168.

67   Coles 2009.

68   Glinister (2006a, 13) does not give a precise location where these anatomical bronzes

Paestum, Salerno, and Carseoli anatomical terracotta votives date to at least fifty years before the colonial foundations.[69] Secondly, the archaeological focus on Campania, Latium, and Etruria has led to a biased picture of the distribution pattern of anatomical votives, which does not consider other regions of the peninsula. Glinister pays particular attention to the evidence from Abruzzo and notes that the "the map will suffice to show that few of these sanctuaries lie anywhere near significant foci of Romanization such as colonies or roads."[70] If to this evidence we add the fact that "on all interpretations, the findspots of the earliest anatomical terracottas lie outside Rome,"[71] it becomes apparent that the distribution pattern of these votives does not back up the claim that Rome was the epicenter of their distribution.

The findings of Glinister and Gentili have far-reaching implications. By questioning the Romanness of anatomical terracottas, they laid the groundwork for a revisionist approach to the idea of the influence of Rome on the religious traditions of Italic peoples. Over the past few years, other scholars have contributed to this debate and emphasized the influence of local traditions on the appearance of anatomicals during the Roman period. Marlene Turneer's work, for example, focuses on the anatomical votives from three colonies in central Italy and concludes that the pattern of political influence and artistic expression was much more complicated than suggesting a "Roman connection" as the primary source for anything created outside Rome. Similarly, Scopacasa focuses on the use of anatomical votives in the Apennines to argue that local cultural practice had an impact on the political change in these areas during the fourth century BCE.[72]

In sum, recent archaeological breakthroughs challenge traditional interpretations of central Italian sanctuaries. Previous studies have emphasized the role of isolated rural sanctuaries as a persistent feature of Italic life, thus emphasizing the hands-off policy of Rome. The embellishment of some sacred spaces during the Roman period has been explained in connection with their function as marketplaces, boundary markers, or vestiges of *pagus-vicus* settlements. Research and fieldwork in Italy show that these explanations are hardly feasi-

---

are located. Zapelloni Pavia's study on pre-Roman sanctuaries in Central and Northern Italy demonstrates that from as early as the fifth century BCE, the use of small bronze votive offerings emerged as a widespread practice across various cult sites (Zapelloni Pavia 2024).

69   Gentili 2005, 372.

70   Glinister 2006a, 18.

71   Glinister 2006a, 17. Gentili notices that terracotta heads appear in Rome two centuries after their occurrence in Etruria, Latium, and Campania (Gentili 2005, 370).

72   Turmeer 2016, Scopacasa 2015.

ble. In particular, the *pagus-vicus* model relied on anachronistic terminology and a rigid polarization between *polis* and dispersed settlement which does not correspond to the variety of community forms and structures throughout the peninsula. Steks's and Scopacasa's research demonstrates that cult places defy any simplistic ethnic characterization. Instead, Samnite sanctuaries provide evidence that Samnite identity was itself shifting and unstable. It varied in its geographical scope according to the needs and interests of the groups "who defined themselves through the shared use of sanctuaries."[73]

In addition to questioning the function of Italic rural cult places, there are several counterarguments to the proposition that Rome influenced colonial cult places and the presence of anatomical terracottas. Even if it is true that many colonies emulated certain aspects of Roman architecture, such as temples, this trend only spread in the Late Republican period. Similarly, anatomical votives do not geographically or chronologically overlap with Roman expansion.

Ultimately, the archaeological record shows that while colonies may have had some Roman political framework by which they set up their community, there was no blanket imposition of Roman culture on the non-Roman or local populations. Rather, each colony took a different religious trajectory shaped by different traditions observed by Roman governmental representatives and settlers, the local environment, and interaction with the local population. These new archaeological studies not only expand and complicate our understanding of the Romanization process but also encourage expanding the research's focus to other areas of central Italy.

3 Cultural Change in the Religious Sphere of Ancient Umbria

In Umbria proper, detailed studies of Umbrian cult places and their topographical and cultural developments are limited. They fall in line with some of the abovementioned traditional approaches and, with the exclusion of Bradley's remarkable contribution, have not been revised according to new scholarship on the topic.

Scholars such as La Regina, Colonna, and Bonomi Ponzi have explored the function of Umbrian sacred spaces.[74] Drawing on the type of votives and the rural location of the sanctuaries, they interpret Umbrian sacred spaces within

---

73   Scopacasa 2015a, 236; Stek 2009.
74   Bonomi Ponzi 1989, 1990, 1997; Monacchi 1986, 1988; Giontella 1995, 43–49; La Regina 1970, 1975.

a *pagus-vicus* system. In other words, they include Umbrian sanctuaries in the broader category of Apennine sacred places that were assumed to have functioned as political and economic centers in the absence of "real" urban units, subject to the demands of the ruling class. They also agree that the elite group, whose power is visible in the funerary sphere, controlled these cult places and used them to display their status through the dedication of bronze offerings.

Similarly, theories linking the continuation of Umbrian sanctuaries into the Roman period and the presence of anatomical votives in the region have their roots in traditional thinking. Manconi, Tomei, and Vezar connect the endurance of Umbrian sanctuaries after the fourth century BCE to the new Roman presence in, and control over, the region. They argue that if, on the one hand, sanctuaries near a Roman area were more likely to be abandoned, those located in the central Apennine zone had more chances "di una piú prolungata continuità."[75] The presence of anatomical votives in some of these sanctuaries is explained by Monacchi, Sisani, and others as an unequivocal sign of a Roman presence. Assuming that terracotta ex-votos represented a distinctive Roman cultural practice exported during the conquest, they consider them the indicator of Roman expansion and, in some cases, the proof of "the physical presence of Roman colonists in the region" or of the arrival of new cults.[76]

This line of thought on the function and continuity of Umbrian sanctuaries has been revised by Bradley, who in 1987 authored an article titled "Archaic Sanctuaries in Umbria," and a few years later, in 2000, published the first monograph on the region.[77] Concerning the function of sacred spaces within the *pagus-vicus* model, Bradley rightly points out that the model imposes ideal and institutional systems of a socio-political level onto physical remains. He emphasizes the region's geographical diversity and the fact that sanctuaries lie in areas hardly classifiable according to the dichotomy of urban/non-urban. According to his analysis, Umbrian communities may well have functioned as self-sufficient centers, even in the absence of cities such as those in the more "urbanized" lowlands of Latium and Campania. Using recent scholarship on related problems concerning Greece, he notes that not all states were *poleis* and that the absence of a centralized settlement system is not automatically "an example of an earlier tribal form of society that had yet to evolve into a

---

75   Manconi et al. 1981, 373.

76   Monacchi 1986; Sisani 2013, 134. See also Bonomi Ponzi 1991; Manca and Menichelli 2014, 33.

77   Bradley 1997 and 2000a. Cf. Bradley 2000b on the emergence of state identity in the region.

CULTURAL CHANGE IN THE SANCTUARIES OF CENTRAL ITALY   27

polis."[78] At Plestia, for example, evidence from burials, hillforts, and the Cupra Sanctuary point to social complexity, craft specialization, and, ultimately, to a communal organization that had a solid collective identity, despite the absence of a "proper" town.

Furthermore, he notes that no archaeological evidence validates the hypothesis that the aristocracy assumed socio-political authority and, even more so, that cult places were under the control of specific kinship associations. I corroborate this argument in the next chapter, where I examine the material evidence used by scholars to track the elite active presence in the sanctuaries, namely the votive figurines. Although we cannot exclude the fact that the elite may have had control of sacred spaces, the iconographic and stylistic analysis of these objects does not allow us to link them to any specific social class.

Although Bradley refutes the existence of the *pagus-vicus* settlement type, he accepts the hypothesis that sacred places could have had functions that were not purely religious. By comparison with other central Italian sanctuaries, he puts forth the possibility that they could also function as marketplaces or have some political function. Bradley sees a strong link between archaic Umbrian sanctuaries and their territory, following the land-community model studied by de Polignac and applied to Greece. In addition, he notes the high number of sanctuaries in Umbria and the ample presence of locally produced votive offerings. Although he does not elaborate on this topic much further, he suggests that this may hint at the importance played by religious spaces "in the creation of community identities."[79]

As for the issue of the continuity of Umbrian sanctuaries, it is again Bradley who rebuts the consensus view based on his analysis of archaeological data. Cases supporting his argument are the Monte Ansciano sanctuary, which is not located in a Romanized territory but is a place where ritual activity decreases noticeably starting in the fourth century BCE, and the Grotta Bella cave, which is located in southern Umbria and continued to be used until at least the fourth century CE. The continuation of sanctuaries into the Roman period, he concludes, is not due to the Roman presence in the region but to some other reason, such as the location of sanctuaries far from growing urban centers where new sanctuaries "took over the function of the old mountain top sanctuaries."[80] Although he does not directly engage with the issue of votive offerings, Bradley suggests caution in considering anatomical votives simply as a sign of Roman-

---

78 Bradley 2000, 121.
79 I will return to the function of Umbrian sacred places in Chapter 6.
80 Bradley 1997, 128.

ization and considers the variety of votive deposits in the Roman period within the broader frame of central Italian cultural koine, one influenced mainly by Roman expansion.

Bradley taps into the ongoing discussion on cultural change and demonstrates that the changing landscape of the region represents an exciting avenue for the investigation of how sacred spaces and ritual behaviors changed following Roman expansion—not only in non-urban but also in urban contexts. New excavation data has accumulated since his initial publication on Umbria, but it has not yet been gathered together, nor has it been brought to bear on questions of continuity and cultural change.[81] The latest monograph on ancient Umbria by Amann provides a detailed overview of Umbrian culture, but it only addresses religion and ritual in one chapter and mostly summarizes earlier scattered research. She laments the absence of a comprehensive study on this topic, which may be the reason why she does not attempt to draw any conclusion regarding the development of sacred spaces in the region.[82] No work has been done to evaluate the change in location, architecture, and ritual behaviors of the Italic sanctuaries during the Middle and Late Republican period or their significance for Italic communities in a crucial historical moment: the aftermath of the Roman expansion in the fourth century BCE. In addition, no attempt has been made to assess the relationship between the Roman conquest and the social and political context within which Umbrian sanctuaries were constructed and functioned.

4 Conclusions

Traditional approaches to assessing the impact of Rome on its neighbors in central Italy have focused on new Roman and Latin territories with an emphasis on the supposedly Roman character of the region's sanctuaries and their votive deposits. The spread of the Etrusco-Italic temple type and the presence of anatomical votives have been largely interpreted as an immediate by-product of the increasing Roman presence in the area. Conversely, non-urban cult sites would have been scarcely involved in the historical developments of the Middle and Late Republican periods. According to this view, the demise of some sanctuaries was caused by their loss of importance after the Roman conquest, mainly due to their distance from major city centers. Other rural sanctuaries

---

81   Publications on individual sites are listed in Chapter 3.
82   Amann 2011.

that continued into the Roman period have been considered a vestige of old rural traditions, a sign of the "immutable character of rustic life."[83]

Recent studies have begun to dispel these axioms and to problematize the Romano-centric image of Roman expansion in central Italy, with significant consequences for many aspects of Italic sanctuaries, from their architecture and votive deposits to the ability of the local populations to adapt to new modes of worship while continuing their own. Umbria, located just east of Latium, has not yet been a prominent part of this re-evaluation. Although Bradley has questioned traditional views on the function and development of local sanctuaries during the Roman period, and Glinister has remarked that anatomical votives existed in central Italy well before the conquest, the assumption that the Roman conquest brought cultural assimilation is still widespread. Before turning to the archaeological record to gauge an understanding of the evolution of Umbrian cult practices before and after the Roman conquest, we need to situate this research in the context of the relatively new fields of the archaeology of religion and ritual in general and of votive religion in particular.

---

83   Stek and Burgers 2015, 4.

CHAPTER 3

For an Archaeology of Religion and Ritual

1 Introduction

In recent years, archaeologists have successfully applied new approaches to the investigation of rituals and their material remains and have made significant and novel contributions to the contextualization of ritual theory. There is a growing consensus among archaeologists that religion and religious practices are significant components of human culture and social life and should not be ignored in archaeological investigation. These developments in archaeology have led to new interpretations that have helped articulate the relationship between religious belief and practice and, further, to explore the materiality of religion in ancient life.

The discussion is organized into three parts. In the first and second parts, I review different approaches used by archaeologists to study religion and religious rituals and to understand the role that both play in shaping a community's cultural identities. Within the discipline of archaeology, religion has often been treated as particularly impenetrable. As a consequence of deep-rooted aversions towards archaeological studies of religion, ritual has been used as a catch-all term for anything that archaeologists find to be odd and without immediate functional value. In the past thirty years, however, religion and religious rituals have become an essential topic within archaeological investigation. Building on anthropological and sociological understandings of religion, archaeologists have begun to address the material remains of religion. The archaeology of ancient ritual is now a dynamic and growing field that continues to generate numerous ongoing debates and areas of new research.

The third part considers how these material remains have been used to reconstruct ancient ritual through considerations of their continuity across time and their connection to social identity. This discussion highlights the limitations of the existing studies of central Italian votive offerings, which largely focus on anatomical terracottas as a proxy for the spread of Roman conquest. Scholars have given scant attention, however, to the ritual function of archaic votives and how it developed during the Roman period. The study of Umbrian votive figurines in particular has suffered from this narrowly focused interest and no attempts have been made to consider the ritual meaning of their deposition and how it may have varied over time. It is time for a new study of votive material.

© CHARLES UNIVERSITY, FACULTY OF ARTS, PRAGUE, 2025 | DOI:10.1163/9789004712171_004
This is an open access chapter distributed under the terms of the CC BY-NC-ND 4.0 license.

2   Archaeology of Religion

In an influential article from 1954, Christopher Hawkes[1] argued that "religious institution and spiritual life" represent the least appropriate venue for archaeological inquiry. In the years since, archeologists have been daunted by using religion as a lens of interpretive analysis. The reason why archaeologists have considered religion to be such an impenetrable realm for analysis lies in the alleged divide between religious belief and religious practice. These two domains have traditionally been carefully separated in archaeological investigations because archeologists viewed religion as primarily metaphysical and abstract, and, therefore, in clear contrast with the object of their study, the material world. The "New Archaeology" of the 1960s–1970s further strengthened this view, as it portrayed religion as epiphenomenal and downplayed its practical dimension, considering it "materially unidentifiable."[2]

This tendency to view religion as abstract has also manifested in more recent discussions of the archaeology of religion. In his 2004 monograph, Timothy Insoll holds that religion is all-pervasive, informing and influencing even aspects of life that archaeologists have typically considered secular. Although Insoll emphasizes the all-encompassing nature of religion, he also stresses the difficulty of delving into its essence. In his view, the numinous character of religion "defies rationality" and thus represents an obstacle for archaeologists.

Despite this history of strict separation, in the last thirty years, cultural anthropologists, sociologists, and scholars of religion have developed theories for understanding ancient religion and have paid progressively closer attention to the ways in which religious beliefs and practices are embodied and performed in social contexts and how broader cultural and political factors shape them. Their theoretical understandings of religion have formed the cornerstone of new archaeological approaches to both religion and ritual.[3]

Practice theorists such as Pierre Bourdieu, Ernst Bloch, and Catherine Bell advocate for the embeddedness of religion within human actions and emphasize the different ways that religion is present in people's daily lives.[4] Applying the ideas of Bourdieu's *Theory of Practice*, where ritual is considered a specific form of social practice that reproduces social relationships, Bell identifies ritual as a form of human action and as an active component of religious practice

---

1   Hawkes 1954, 155–168.
2   Droogan 2012, 79.
3   For an extensive review of the most common anthropological approaches to religion see Cunningham 1999, Morris 2006, Verhoeven 2002.
4   Bourdieu 1977; Bloch 1989; Bell 1992, 1997.

that creates and alters religious beliefs.[5] Others emphasize ritual's potential to foster social change and the effect that ritual has on the power relationships between participants.[6]

These approaches explicitly reject the structural approach that has traditionally dominated the discussions of religion.[7] The structuralist perspective emphasizes the stability of religion as a long-lasting cultural phenomenon. According to this view, ritual is a form of human action that enacts religious principles and must be stable over time. This theory has been contested by, among others, practice theorists as being "ill-suited to the consideration of diachronic change."[8] Rather than focusing on the stability of ritual actions, practice theorists follow Bourdieu's *Theory of Practice* and highlight the experiential aspects of ritual and how it is continuously reconstructed and modified.[9]

So too, the cognitive approach also relates religious beliefs to practice and material culture. Cognitive theories analyze the relationship between the human mind/brain system and external reality. Anthropologists such as Merlin Donald, Robert McCauley, and Thomas Lawson emphasize the dialectic between surroundings and the mind, and they recognize external elements as crucial in cognitive development.[10] In their foundational book, *Rethinking Religion*, McCauley and Lawson posit a unified theory that exemplifies the cognitive approach to religious ritual.[11] According to these two authors, religious rituals are actions guided by the same cognitive system that guides everyday practice.

Despite minor divergences, both of these interpretative frameworks offer a significant contribution to archaeological studies by emphasizing that religion is not merely a spiritual phenomenon but is made manifest in the material world. Therefore, the construction of religious architecture, the offerings of objects to gods, and the performance of sacrifice all have the potential to leave material remains that archaeologists can study. As will become apparent in the next part of this chapter, these theories can be particularly applicable to archaeology.

---

5   Bell 1997, 138–170.

6   Kelly and Kaplan 1990, Kertzer 1988, DeMarrais et al. 1996, Demarest and Conrad 1992, Fox 2012.

7   Levi-Strauss 1969, 1966; Leach 1976.

8   Koutrafouri and Sanders 2017, 111.

9   See also the work of other practice theorists such as Connerton 1989, Hobsbawm and Ranger 1983, Comaroff 1985, Humphrey and Laidlaw 1994, Ortner 1989.

10   Donald 2001, Lawson and McCauley 1990.

11   Lawson and McCauley1990.

Following the lead of anthropological and sociological studies, in the past ten years, archaeology has increasingly incorporated religion into its interpretative repertoire. Rather than focusing on religion's unknowable and transcendental aspects, scholars have begun to shift their attention to materiality, agency, practice, memory, movement, and performance; in short, they have started to consider religion as centrally embedded in human actions. This recent emphasis on practice is critical for the archaeological study of religion. As Lars Fogelin has emphasized,[12] religion is something that people do, and therefore it leaves material traces. Archaeologists, in turn, can examine these traces and, through careful research and investigation, reconstruct what people did and the religious ideology underlying those actions.

3 Archaeology of Ritual

The study of ritual is another field of inquiry that has been largely overlooked in archaeology. For a long time, archaeologists have grappled with the challenges of recognizing and understanding ancient rituals based on archaeological evidence. Explicit methodologies for reconstructing ancient rituals and religion have been mostly absent, with the belief that this was an unsuitable area for archaeological inquiry. The main reason for this neglect is the longstanding divide between human beliefs and social practices. Alongside religion, ritual has been considered immaterial (or intangible?), related to beliefs, transcendence, or the supernatural. As a result, archaeological data were regarded as insufficient to interpret ritual practices. As Ian Hodder points out,[13] anything that archaeologists have found odd and without immediate functional value has been associated with ritual, leading to various definitions and interpretations of ritual practices.[14]

In recent years, however, the shift from belief to practice in anthropological and sociological studies on religion has positively affected archaeology. Archaeologists have made increased efforts to bridge the apparent divide between ancient rituals and archaeological data.[15] As Bell observes, in the current schol-

---

12   Fogelin 2008.
13   Hodder 1982.
14   The problem of finding a shared definition for ritual has led Bell (2007, 277–289) to state that there is never going to be agreement on such a definition because ritual has too many functions and meanings and, according to her, no scientific field moves forward because of a good definition.
15   Particularly illustrative of these attempts is Joyce Marcus' paper on the necessity of mak-

arship on ancient rituals there seems to be a shared agreement to define ritual as a "set of crystallized" forms of human action, or set activities, that leave material traces in the archaeological record.[16] Since archaeologists attempt reconstructions based on observed patterns, ritual is more likely to be tracked than many other activities.

Colin Renfrew first noted that the presence of repetitions and patterns in the archaeological record was characteristic of ritual. In his seminal work on the Bronze Age Cycladic shrine of Phylakopi, Renfrew attempts to systematize the archaeological identification of religious sites by providing a list of indicators of ritual that includes attention focusing (with place, equipment, and symbols), boundary zones, the presence of the deity, participation, and offerings.[17] Although this checklist has attracted some criticism,[18] it has substantially impacted subsequent work.

The attention given by anthropologists in recent years to a more practice-oriented understanding of religion has resulted in an increased focus on material evidence. More recent archaeological research places the primacy of ritual practice at the forefront, emphasizing the agency of humans and objects as well as ritual practices' experiential and behavioral aspects.[19] These studies are influenced by various theories, including Alfred Gell's "object agency," Bruno Latour's Actor-Network Theory, and Hodder's concept of "entanglement" between humans and things[20] Material-based studies of ancient religion explore the embeddedness of religion in the material world in different ways.

---

    ing the study of ritual a scientific endeavor; see Kyriakidis 2007, 43–77. A list of the most recent archaeological publication on ancient ritual includes Fogelin 2007, Insoll 2001, 2004; Kyriakidis 2007, Plunket 2002, Whitley and Hays-Gilpin 2008, McAnany and Wells 2008, Pauketat 2013, Renfrew and Morley 2009, Brumfiel 2001, Gonlin and Lohse 2007, Hayden 2003, Leone 2005, Swenson 2015, Droogan 2012, Raja 2015, Pakkanen and Bocher 2015.

16   Kyriakidis 2007, 297.

17   Renfrew 1985.

18   Insoll 2004, 96–97.

19   For an overview on the topic, see Hicks 2010. A very recent trend in "object agency" stems from the "posthumanism" of Bruno Latour's Actor-Network Theory. Posthumanist theory is still a very new theoretical direction within Classics. Broadly speaking, archaeologists who apply this theory to their research emphasize nonhuman entities and downplay the differences between human and nonhuman agency. For a recent discussion about posthumanism in archaeology, see Kipnis 2015 and Selsvold and Webb 2020. Braidotti (2013) offers a good introduction and major contribution to contemporary debates on the posthuman.

20   Gell 1998, Hodder 2012.

Gell challenges the traditional dichotomy between people and objects by arguing that objects are not just mere reflections of human agency. Instead, he asserts that they are active devices that play a role in "securing the acquiescence of individuals in the network of functionalities in which they are enmeshed." In short, artifacts are social agents in themselves. Similarly, Latour's Actor-Network Theory (ANT) considers the interactions that occur between humans and nonhuman actors. He maintains that people and things cannot be separated as they have a symmetrical relationship in which each affects the other. This proposition is not dissimilar to Karl Knappett's argument that suggests that humans and objects have a relationship in which they "bring each other into being."[21]

Unlike Latour, Hodder considers the relationship between things and humans to be asymmetrical because the dependencies that one can have on the other lead "to entrapments in particular pathways from which it is difficult to escape."[22] He holds that the materiality of things creates a set of dependencies between objects and people (entanglements), which he breaks down into four types: human-thing, thing-human, thing-thing, and human-human.

This "material turn" is part of a broad range of new approaches to archaeology that have been defined as relational or posthuman. These approaches challenge traditional notions of human exceptionalism and individual subjectivity and instead consider the agency and intentionality of objects. The aim is to move away from anthropocentric views of the world and towards a more holistic understanding of the relationships between people and things.[23]

Among recent practice-based approaches to archaeology, the work of Lynn Meskell, John Barrett, and Bill Sillar,[24] who work on Egypt, Greece, and the Andes respectively, has been particularly influential. They emphasize that different objects—from human-made items to natural features of the landscape—have agency and intentionality that shape religious traditions. Likewise, Chris Gosden focuses on the replacement of Iron Age objects from southern Britain with Roman objects and analyzes how the objects' form and style influenced people. He draws on Gell's idea that objects have their own logic and that human behavior and thoughts may "take the shape suggested by the object, rather than objects simply manifesting pre-existing forms of thought."[25]

---

21 Knappett 2005, 170.
22 Hodder 2012, 19.
23 For a definition of posthuman approaches as applied to archaeological investigation see Harris and Cipolla 2017, 17.
24 Meskel 2004, Barrett, 1994 and 2000, Sillar 2009.
25 Gosden 2005: 196.

These scholars observe the inseparability of beliefs and other internal cognitive or emotional experiences from material culture: objects express and shape symbolic meanings, identities, relationships, and perceptions. For these reasons, they argue that agency lies in the social relationship that people have with the material world and that material objects can have social identities. These approaches emphasize the posthuman tendency of decentering of the human: they enable us to understand the archaeological record as the visible materialization of the interdependence between objects and humans and challenge the limitations of modernist, western perspectives on the world.

The discussion of the centrality of change within ritual is a significant development in recent research. Scholars have emphasized the importance of understanding how rituals are subject to change through human agency and may change for reasons beyond human control. Additionally, research has shown that rituals change those who perform or observe them. The "Ritual Dynamics" project at Heidelberg University has contributed to this discourse by investigating the dynamics of ritual practices in various historical and contemporary cultures.[26] The project's focus on the performative character of ritual emphasizes the creativity and meaning-creating character of ritual, and its case studies, ranging from modern and ancient Asia to the Near East, illustrate the centrality of change in ritual practice. The project's findings challenge the notion that rituals are stereotyped and invariant events and highlight the significance of change within and through rituals.

The recent collection of papers, *Ritual Dynamics in the Ancient Mediterranean: Agency, Emotion, Gender, Representation*, edited by Angelos Chaniotis, clearly illustrates the application of practice theory in archaeology as emphasized by the "Ritual Dynamics" project and exemplifies the latest trends in the study of ritual performances in the Ancient Mediterranean.[27] The contributors to the volume utilize diverse source material to identify and explain evidence of changes in the Mediterranean (Egypt, Greece, Northern Italy, North Africa, and the Roman East) through the lens of agency, emotion, gender, and representation. For example, Ioanna Patera's account of modifications over time in

---

26 Heidelberg University's collaborative research center SFB 619 "Ritual Dynamics" is the world's largest research association exclusively investigating rituals as well as their change and dynamics and, at the same time, one of the largest humanities collaboration research centers in Germany. The scholars and scientists involved in the project come from the fields of ancient and medieval history, anthropology of South Asia, Assyriology, classical and modern Indology, East Asian art history, Egyptology, history of South Asia, Islamic studies, Jewish studies, medical psychology, musicology, religious studies, and theology. Their contributions are published in Brosius et al. 2013.

27 Chaniotis 2011.

Eleusinian rites and Eftychia Stavrianopoulou's study of how Greek written text codified practice both focus on tradition invoked as a rationale for change.[28] In the case of Eleusis, Chianotis notes that many innovations in Greek rituals affected the staging and aesthetics of the ritual actions rather than of the essential form of the ritual that, instead, remains unchanged. Similarly, scholars such as Barbara Mills and William Walker, and Ruth Van Dyke and Susan Alcock, have emphasized the dynamic aspects of ritual.[29] Although specific rituals may remain the same over long periods, their meaning for society is constantly recontextualized.

Practice theory elucidates how the ritual experience has the potential to reaffirm, create, or challenge the dominant social order.[30] Research often focuses on ritual symbolism and the materialization of ritual symbols. Once materialized, symbolic objects can be controlled and manipulated by people in order to achieve specific aims. Elizabeth DeMarrais and John Robb productively apply these insights in their examination of how the elite could limit access to material symbols such as icons, rituals, monuments, and written text or change their underlying meaning.[31] Jerry Moore and Lars Fogelin, among others, employ a practice approach more focused on how people experienced ritual in the past.[32] They emphasize the ways in which different religious architectural layouts promoted different experiences that either served the interests of authority or resistance to authority.

These practice-based perspectives in the archaeology of ritual emphasize the effects of ritual on the social relations between ritual participants and focus on how ritual change over time informs and reflects the development of those relationships. As such, practice approaches downplay the importance of symbolism in the study of ancient rituals and favor the analysis of the use of symbols and the goals of the people who deployed them.

Against these formulations that consider ritual to be a "transformative performance,"[33] scholars who support a structuralist perspective emphasize the stability of religion.[34] They view it as a long-lasting, static cultural phenomenon and stress its anachronistic and invariant elements. Cultural materialists such as Roy Rappaport and Elizabeth Sobel also hold onto the stability of religion

---

28 Chaniotis, 2012, 85–103 and 119–137.
29 Mills and Walker 2008, Van Dyke and Alcock 2003.
30 Bradley 1998, DeMarrais et al. 1996, Fogelin 2006, Lucero 2003, Moore 1996.
31 DeMarrais, 1996, Robb 1998.
32 Moore 1996, Fogelin 2006.
33 Turner 1992, 75.
34 Cf. *supra*, 41.

and argue that ritual actions have the function of retaining and passing down social information over time[35]

As noted by Lars Fogelin,[36] few archaeologists follow either the practice-oriented or the structural approach to the archaeology of ritual. More typically, they employ insights from both perspectives in their research without overcoming the contradictions that the two perspectives pose. Similarly, Insoll points out that the current problem that archaeologists face is to find a balance between understanding ritual as subject to change and the existence of an underlying core of stability in practice and belief concerning ritual.[37]

As this discussion has shown, religion and ritual are now far from being tangential to archaeological research. In the past few years, scholars have questioned the impenetrability of religion, and new research questions and approaches have opened new perspectives for the development of the field of the archaeology of religion. Following the lead of sociological and anthropological studies, archaeologists are paying increasing attention to material culture as a source to reconstruct ritual and cult practices. A proliferation of new studies on the archaeology of ancient religion examine the complex interactions between humans and objects, their agency, and the role of religion in society. As scholars focus on the agency of objects and participants in a ritual in their specific social, local, and historical context, they are aware that the meaning of ritual is far from static, but rather can change over time. As archeologists begin to engage with this material, they also use new approaches to understand it, such as the entanglement between human and object agencies, religion as a causal force for social change, and change and re-contextualization of religious rituals. These ongoing investigations contribute to making the archaeology of religion and ritual a fundamental component in debates over the interactions and interrelationships between individuals, communities, and structures of power.

4 Votive Religion

In societies accustomed to giving gifts to transcendent beings for supernatural returns, such as Italic and Roman societies, votive offerings represent the

---

35 Rappaport 1979, Sobel and Bettles 2000. On the structuralist perspective on ancient ritual see also Geertz 1973.
36 Fogelin 2007, 66.
37 Insoll 2011, 3.

most ubiquitous evidence of ritual activity.[38] Any object could be vowed, but generally, votives consisted of perishable items (grains and plants, milk, wine, honey, cakes); personal items (toys, amulets, jewelry); practical items (fish hooks, loom weights, tools, utensils, incense burners); statuettes/statues (gods, men, women, swaddled babies, animals); body parts (miniaturized models of every description); altars, *cippi*, and bases; ceramic items (miniaturized pottery, lamps, temple models); and coins. These offerings are both abundant and ubiquitous. As indicated by Ingrid Edlund-Berry's research on votive depositions at Etruscan sanctuaries, people seeking or receiving the god's attention would leave votive offerings on display in a wide range of settings, including urban, rural, extramural, extra-urban, spring, lake, mountain, cave, state, and private cults.[39]

The quantity and variety of votive types have inspired the term "votive religion," since votives are concrete and provide long-lasting evidence for the principle of reciprocity.[40] As Walter Burkert has emphasized, votive offerings embody the principle of exchangeability—*do ut des* (I give so that you will give)—that granted divine aid in exchange for the donor's vow.[41] As such, they are considered visible expressions of the interaction and communication between the donors and the deities. Thus, the beliefs and motives of the worshiper must have played an essential role in the selection of the dedication. The function of votive offerings as gifts that bind together an individual and the gods makes this class of material a vital tool for exploring cultural and ritual dynamics in ancient societies. First, votive offerings illuminate the complex relationship between people and things and between people and gods.[42] Second, recent publications demonstrate that votive offerings can provide valuable information for reconstructing aspects of ancient economies,[43] social and political structures,[44] and ritual practices.[45]

Although the relevance of votive religion in Greek and Roman contexts has been recognized,[46] the study of votive offerings has long been neglected by archaeologists. Robin Osborne points out a number of reasons for this over-

---

38   Griffith 2013, 325.
39   Edlund-Berry 1987.
40   On vows and votive religion, see Rudhardt 1992, 187–202; Burkert 1985, 68–70.
41   Burkert 1987, 43–44.
42   Osborne 2004.
43   Nijboer 2001.
44   Schultz 2006.
45   Gleba and Becker 2008, de Grummond 2011.
46   Glinister 2006a and 2006b, Karyakidis 2007, Pakkanen and Bocher 2015.

sight.[47] Firstly, archaeologists have devoted their attention primarily to the classification of objects rather than assemblages. The consequence of this predilection for object types, which are believed to provide chronological information, is that we have overlooked the potential of artifacts' assemblages to understand ritual practices. Secondly, it can be difficult to differentiate between objects that have been dedicated and those that have been simply discarded, one of the primary complications in the interpretation of ritual in the archaeological record.[48] Similarly challenging is the question of how much votive material is needed to classify a site as a ritual space and whether a few objects are sufficient to classify a site within the corpus of sacred spaces. Finally, Osborne rightly points out the hesitance among scholars in agreeing on one term to refer to dedicated objects. These objects are variously called dedications, offerings, votives, hoards, or simply deposits, depending on what feature of the object the writer wants to emphasize the most (permanence of the gift/action of giving/connection with prior vow/quantity/circumstances of the act of depositing).[49]

Minoan and archaic Greek votive practices are particularly prominent in studying Mediterranean religion and its connection with culture, politics, and society. Since the beginning of archaeological work on Crete in the nineteenth century, archaeologists have nurtured a fascination for the origin of ritual practices and belief systems in the Aegean, and their connections to contemporaneous socio-political phenomena. In the past thirty years, works such as Renfrew's *The Archaeology of Cult* and Warren's *Minoan Religion as Ritual Action* have pioneered new approaches to performance and ritual action, with a specific focus on material culture.[50] Both authors underscore the importance of performance in ritual actions and of votive (as well as iconographic) material to reconstruct religious practices.

Experiential and cognitive approaches have been applied to Minoan archaeology with the result that votive material is used to reconstruct how people experienced rituals. In her dissertation on mountain peak sanctuaries, Elissa Faro explores the material culture in the ritual spaces of the island and their meaning within the network of the Minoan ritual landscape. She analyzes assemblages from extra-urban and urban ritual spaces and clarifies that their

---

47 Osborne 2004, 5–6.
48 For a summary, see Kyriakidis 2007, 20–23.
49 For this research, I will use these terms interchangeably. In addition, I have resolved that the basic evidence for the identification of a site as ritual is the secure presence of material culture that indicates participation in the Umbrian wide ritual complex. As will be made clear later in this section, this polythetic set consists mainly of small bronze figurines.
50 Renfrew 1985, Warren 1988.

differences provide evidence for distinct ritual practices. Moreover, she demonstrates that votive assemblages changed over time according to the specific needs of the elite who sought to redefine their status in the new power structure of the Neopalatial period.[51] Similarly, Camilla Briault studies votive deposits from Minoan sacred places. She concludes that the interpretation of data patterning is a productive way to approach ritual in the Bronze Age Aegean.[52]

The recent publication *Cult Material: From Archaeological Deposits to Interpretation of Early Greek Religion* further elaborates on the theory and practice of interpreting cult and religion, with particular attention paid to votive deposits in their archaeological context.[53] The contributors to this volume emphasize the role of votive deposits in monitoring processes of change and transformation. Indeed, one of their central arguments is that the analysis of cult places using archaeological methods enables us to observe shifts in structural patterns that reflect on ritual behavior and social agency.

Emma-Jayne Graham's study of the anatomical votives from Fregellae and Punta della Vipera in Latium emphasizes the multivalent nature of anatomical votives and focuses on how these objects impacted the lives of their worshipers.[54] She argues that anatomical votives not only created permanent relationships between humans and the gods but also made manifest the power of the gods in the real world. These material remains thus shed light on "how people conceptualized, performed, and constructed their knowledge of the gods."[55] Pursuing this line of research even further, in her recent monograph, she uses a method called new materialism to explore how the process of reassembling the material remains of religious practices and beliefs can help us to better understand the lived experience of ancient religion.[56]

While Graham's study explores the impact of anatomical votives on worshipers in Latium, Battiloro's work on Lucanian sanctuaries sheds light on the ritual performances associated with votive offerings in southern Italy.[57] Battiloro's focus on the rituals associated with votives sets her research apart from most of the work on Italic religion, which treats votive deposits mainly in terms of their socio-political meaning and relationship to the Roman con-

---

51   Faro 2008.

52   Briault 2007.

53   Pakkanen and Bocher 2015.

54   Graham and Draycott 2017, 45–63.

55   Graham and Draycott 2017, 49.

56   Graham's perspective is that religion is primarily practiced as a lived experience, highlighting how individuals' experiences are formed through tangible, situational, and physical acts of rituals: Graham 2020.

57   Battiloro 2018.

quest. Together, Graham's and Battiloro's studies contribute to a growing body of research that emphasizes the importance of analyzing votive deposits in their archaeological and ritual contexts to appreciate the diverse ways in which ancient people interacted with their gods.

4.1 Votive Offerings in Central Italy

For decades, the study of votives in central Italy has suffered from a narrow scholarly focus on anatomical terracottas and the rituals and beliefs of the Etruscans. The current discourse on votive offerings in this area centers around the vast number of votive terracotta deposits in Etruscan and Italic societies dedicated between the late fourth and first centuries BCE. Scholars have primarily focused on this material to track "Romanization," following Torelli's 1973 argument that the distribution of these objects was linked to Rome and the foundation of Latin colonies. Notwithstanding the attempts to deconstruct the ideological aspect of anatomical terracottas, the paradigm of Romanization is still widespread in the studies of ancient votives, as demonstrated by de Cazanove's paper in Tesse Stek and Gert-Jan Burgers' recent publication.[58] This scholarly insistence that anatomical votives are a sign of Roman cultural influence overly simplifies the interactions between Romans and locals and overlooks other categories of ancient Italic votive offerings.

As for the use of votives as a means to reconstruct ancient ritual practices in central Italy, research has been sporadic and focused almost entirely on the region of Etruria. Much ink has been spilled over the "most religious of men,"[59] and recent work considers the potential of votive offerings to shed light on Etruscan religious beliefs and practices. The collection of papers in the volume edited by Nancy de Grummond and Ingrid Edlund-Berry, *The Archaeology of Sanctuaries and Ritual in Etruria*, illustrates the recent trends in the study of Etruscan votive religion.[60] De Grummond's contribution, for example, encourages archaeologists to look carefully for variation in votive contexts and to consider the ritual implications of broken or misshapen objects in sanc-

---

58   Stek and Burgers 2015; esp. De Cazanove, pp. 29–67.
59   Liv. 5.1.; for Etruscan religion, see de Grummond and Simon 2006 and Turfa 2013 with extensive bibliography.
60   De Grummond and Edlund-Berry 2011. Etruscan ritual is also approached in the volume edited by Gleba and Becker (2009), where the authors consider mortuary customs, votive rituals and other religious and daily life practices. It is worth mentioning also the framework developed by Bonghi Jovino (2005) and Bagnasco (2005) for Pian di Civita, Tarquinia. They distinguish four main ritual categories (propitiation, foundation, celebration, obliteration) and their physical "containers" (natural or artificial, open or closed, etc.).

FOR AN ARCHAEOLOGY OF RELIGION AND RITUAL

tuary contexts.[61] Helen Nagy has also found that comparative approaches shed new light on Etruscan rituals. By comparing votive terracottas from Veii and Cerveteri, she prompts further questions about male and female participation in ritual and raises the possibility that not only certain rituals but also specific ritual spaces were gendered in the ancient landscape.[62]

4.2   *Votive Offerings in Ancient Umbria*

More than two thousand figurative votive offerings representing bronze worshipers, warriors, animals, and anatomical parts and heads have been retrieved from the sanctuaries of ancient Umbria. While Guy Bradley acknowledges the importance of this material in providing insight into Umbrian religion, scholars have largely overlooked it. With only a few site-specific catalogs available, the topic is mostly confined to rare appearances in broad discussions on Italic religions. One issue with the limited research that has been done is that it tends to focus on the socio-political meaning of the votives and on anatomical terracottas as markers of the "Romanization" process brought about by Rome's expansion. As a consequence, the ritual significance of dedicating votive objects in the region and how it changed from the third to the first century BCE has received little attention.

Studies of the figurative votive offerings from the region have been influenced by the seminal work of Giovanni Colonna, entitled *Bronzi votivi Umbro-Sabellici a figura umana*. Colonna categorizes pre-Roman bronze votive figurines into groups according to their stylistic affinities and labels the groups with one of their main find sites, even if this is not always their likely place of manufacture.[63] Although individual workshops are difficult to identify, the fact that some types recur in higher proportion in specific sanctuaries of the region has led him to hypothesize that the bronze figurines were produced by local workshops that could travel and sell their products across Umbria and in the neighboring regions. The votive types classified by Colonna go from a low level of sophistication, with figurines of the so-called "Esquiline Group," "Amelia Group," and "Nocera Umbra Group," to the stylistically more sophisticated figures of the "Foligno Group."[64] Colonna identifies the figures of warriors as the most common type and calls them "Mars in Assault."[65] Moreover, he rec-

---

61   De Grummond and Edlund-Berry 2011, 68–89.
62   De Grummond and Edlund-Berry 2011, 127–139.
63   Colonna 1970.
64   For a full overview of pre-Roman (and Roman) types of votive offerings, see Appendix 1.
65   Colonna's classifications are included in Appendix 1, where I describe the types of Umbrian figurative votives.

ognizes some figures as *oranti*, or worshipers, and others as Hercules, walking figures, and dancers; besides these, but not discussed by Colonna, figurative votive offerings of the pre-Roman period include simple representations of parts of the body, small warrior crests, and animals, including pigs, oxen, goats, and sheep.

Since Colonna's study, little research has been done on Umbrian votive bronzes that goes beyond his classification. Even if we include published catalogs of Umbrian bronzes,[66] which are purely lists of objects, scholars studying votive bronzes in the region have made no attempts to interpret the nature of the ritual associated with the votives that go beyond the traditional association between the presence of votive body parts and salutary cults.[67] The trend among scholars in the past years has been to confer socio-cultural meaning upon bronze figurines or note their presence in the Roman period alongside other types of votives and assess the presence of traditions "salvaguardate dalla romanizzazione."[68]

The likelihood that bronze figurines were publicly displayed in Umbrian sanctuaries has led scholars to understand these votives as an ostentatious means by which the donors competed within the context of sanctuaries. Laura Bonomi-Ponzi, for example, interprets the subject matter of the figurines of domestic animals and warriors as a representation of the basis of the aristocratic power, while Bradley understands the more sophisticated types of bronzes as a sign of the active presence of Umbrian elites in the sanctuaries.[69] By the same token, Luana Cenciaioli interprets the presence of schematic and straightforward figurines as markers that people from outside the social elite frequented the sanctuaries.[70]

Scholars focusing primarily on the representation of animals and warriors favor an interpretation that sees the sanctuaries as the *foci* of the pastoral population interested in warfare. Monacchi, for example, has suggested that the more schematic bronzes of animals are offerings of thanks for the protection of the donor's herd and that they show Umbrian society's interest in stock-raising.[71] Along similar lines, Bradley argues that the "Mars in assault" types ought to be interpreted as a manifestation of an agricultural and pastoral

---

66 Roncalli 1989, 1990; Roncalli and Bonfante 1991.
67 Bruschetti 1989, 114 and 124. For a revisionist approach to this view, see Chapter 6.
68 Sisani 2007.
69 Bonomi Ponzi 1990, 64; Bonomi Ponzi 1991, 59.
70 Cenciaioli 1991, 212.
71 Monacchi 1984, 80–81; cf. Cenciaioli 1998.

FOR AN ARCHAEOLOGY OF RELIGION AND RITUAL

community while the worshiper types were representations of the donors.[72] According to these authors, the pastoral lifestyle of the pilgrims reflected in the type of bronzes is further indicated by the high altitude of several Umbrian sanctuaries.

These socio-economic interpretations are open to debate as most archaeological records from Umbrian cult places show no indication of the social classes involved in the cult.[73] This holds true in particular for votive figurines. While the refinement of the figurines, their size, and their manufacture may indicate the level of investment put into the dedication,[74] in the absence of any inscription there is no direct or concrete indication of the wealth of the person who bought and donated a given votive. A refined object is not necessarily the dedication of an elite member of a high social class. It may instead represent a significant investment of money by a lower-class person who cared particularly for their dedication to the god or desired to be self-represented in the religious sphere through the offering, for example, of a well-refined warrior figurine. If we look at the more schematic figurines, it is also possible, as Bradley wisely suggests,[75] that they were the dedications of elite members who left many votives each. Unlike grave goods, which point to the presence of elite members,[76] individual offerings dedicated in sacred spaces could result from the noticeable economic effort of less affluent and elite individuals. It seems, therefore, unsound to make inferences about the social status of the worshipers of Umbrian sanctuaries and to identify them based strictly on iconography. This type of analysis may indicate the investment made in the practice of dedicating offerings, but any interpretation of the donor's social class remains pure speculation.

By attempting to shed some light on the socio-economical composition of Umbrian communities, previous works on Umbrian bronze votive figurines

---

72   Bradley, 2000, 68.

73   Glinister (1997, 73) rightly points out that among Italic people, elite involvement in sanctuaries becomes visible from the second century BCE, when members of the elite begin to leave inscriptions at rural sanctuaries.

74   Colonna's close examination of the stylistic details of votive groups can hint at the type of monetary investment spent for the pre-Roman dedications. The presence of a significant number of simple figurines without much refinement may indicate a meager monetary investment in the purchase while the offer of an elaborated object, carefully modeled and of significant size, can be interpreted as a sign of a more substantial investment in the religious activity.

75   Bradley 1997, 118.

76   See Chapter 4 for a list of wealthy pre-Roman necropoleis in Umbria. For a discussion of how the expenditure on votive offerings in the region can inform us about larger social trends related to the function of Umbrian sanctuaries, see Chapter 6.

have overlooked what ritual practice was associated with them. The only effort to address the ritual aspect of Umbrian cult places is made by Stoddart, when he discusses the results of the Gubbio Project.[77] He addresses the peak sanctuary of Monte Ansciano and its votive deposits in order to hypothesize the ritual landscape present at Gubbio in the archaic period. Stoddart points to the simplicity of the ritual enclosure as suggesting a small scale of investment and low-key participation. However, he does not evaluate the ritual meaning of the deposition of the objects dedicated in the enclosure.

Between the fourth and third centuries, as the Roman presence in Umbria spread and became a permanent fixture, the bronze figurines that characterize votive deposits of the archaic period noticeably decreased. We find a more extensive array of votives in their stead, including coins, miniature pottery, *balsamaria*, and figurative votive offerings. The latter consists primarily of bronze figurines of worshipers of the so-called Hellenistic worshiper type—female and male with the head wrapped by a wreath of vine leaves or diadem, a patera in the right hand and acerra in the left—and anatomical terracottas, an offering which began to fade in popularity in the first century BCE.

Although, as noted in the previous chapter, Glinister and Gentili highlight that the exponential increase in the available material does not validate the widespread view that connects anatomical votives to the Roman conquest, the social perspective has also left its mark on the studies on these votives. Scholars have used anatomical terracottas in Umbria to draw simple conclusions about the Romanization of the area or the influence of Roman ritual customs on local ones.[78] Conversely, their absence or paucity has been connected to concepts such as "resistance" and "safeguarding of local traditions." As for the Hellenistic worshiper type, given their popularity, they are simply defined as typical of the Etrusco-Italic koine of the Hellenistic period.[79]

5   Conclusions

In recent times, there has been a renewed interest in the archaeological study of religion due to a recognition of a gap in our understanding of symbolic

---

77   Stoddart and Malone 1994, 149–152. The Gubbio Project, led by Simon Stoddart and Caroline Malone from the University of Cambridge, has ended fieldwork and excavation at Monte Ansciano and Monte Ingino, in the ancient Umbrian town of Iuguvium. The project culminated in a publication in 1994 (Stoddart and Malone 1994).

78   Cf. n. 78.

79   Bonomi Ponzi 1994; Calvani et al. 2000, 331; Bonfante and Nagy 2015, 179.

behavior. Object-oriented approaches that focus on physical evidence for ritual practices have been identified as important developments in this area. While some publications have discussed the potential of this approach, there is still a lack of work on votive religion in central Italy. In particular, the ritual significance of the deposition of offerings in Umbria has been overlooked in favor of anatomical terracottas and Etruscan rituals and beliefs.

Little attention has been given to the ritual meaning of dedicating votive objects in Umbria and how it changed from the third to the first century BCE. This lack of interest has prevented archaeologists from examining the role of these material objects in the associated ritual. Recognizing this connection is critical to understanding the enactment and transformation of the rituals performed in ancient Umbrian sanctuaries.

To address broader research questions, it is necessary to abandon the traditional socio-economic approach to studying Umbrian votive offerings and find evidence to refute the conventional view of anatomical terracottas as proof of "religious Romanization" throughout the peninsula. Only then can we use these and other Umbrian figurines to analyze the transformation of ritual practices from the third to the first century BCE. This, in turn, can help us understand the role of material objects in religious practices and the broader societal changes that occurred in ancient Italy. While the analysis of sanctuaries and their votive deposits will be discussed in Chapter 5, the next chapter provides a historical background to the study of Umbrian sacred spaces and their material manifestation.

CHAPTER 4

History of the Umbrian Territory

1   Introduction

In order to explore Umbrian sanctuaries and their material culture in the pre-Roman and Roman periods, it is paramount to situate the sacred spaces of ancient Umbria within their geographical and historical context. Both factors, in fact, contributed to the role that sanctuaries had during the archaic period and how they developed during the Roman period.

This chapter aims first to introduce the region's geographical boundaries and then to provide a historical context for understanding how the region's social, political, and economic organization changed throughout time. This account offers a historical foundation for the rest of the chapters that follow. By the end of the chapter, the reader will see the Umbrians as a much less well-defined ethnic group and the region's conquest by the Romans as a much more complicated process than has been traditionally assumed.

Research carried out in the region over the last two decades has shed light on the material culture of the ancient Umbrians and their historical trajectory from the pre-Roman period to the incorporation of Umbria in the Augustan *regio sexta*. Despite this scholarly progress, a debate is still ongoing regarding the applicability of the concept of Umbrian identity as a cohesive *ethnos*. The question of whether a solid Umbrian identity existed is partially related to the fuzzy nature of Umbria's boundaries as described in ancient sources, which often provide contrasting information about the area occupied by these ancient people. For this reason, this chapter examines ethnic identity, which is an essential factor in drawing exact regional boundaries and in seeing ethnic Umbrian identity reflected in the archaeological record.

In the first section of this chapter, I present ancient authors' accounts of the Umbrians and their territories to outline the boundaries of the ancient region. I do not introduce the authors chronologically or divide them into Roman or Greek, but rather, I put together authors who offer similar accounts of the region. Although doubts about the exact boundaries of the area remain, it is possible to extrapolate information from ancient sources and draw a general picture of the region. In the pre-Roman period, it reached northward to the Po valley, extended to the south and west, covering the whole of the modern region of Umbria as far as the left bank of the Tiber, and spread eastward to the Adriatic Sea, running from Ravenna to Ancona.

© CHARLES UNIVERSITY, FACULTY OF ARTS, PRAGUE, 2025 | DOI:10.1163/9789004712171_005
This is an open access chapter distributed under the terms of the CC BY-NC-ND 4.0 license.

HISTORY OF THE UMBRIAN TERRITORY

After this geographical overview, I focus on the history of the Umbrian territory during the pre-Roman and Roman periods. Interest in the archaeology of the ancient region of Umbria was sporadic for most of the twentieth century, and no research was carried out on the protohistory of the Umbrians. The fact that ancient Umbria includes three modern regions (Umbria, Marche, and Emilia-Romagna) and that the modern region of Umbria corresponds to three Augustan regions contributed to making the study of this Italic people more complicated, generating overlaps, ambiguity among scholars, and a lack of clarity.

However, in the past three decades, new excavations and studies have rekindled interest in this *gens antiquissima*, to use a renowned attribution given by Pliny the Elder to the Umbrians.[1] Scholars have begun to investigate different aspects of these peoples, from their settlements to their funerary and religious practices. The efforts of scholars such as Bonomi Ponzi, Cenciaioli, and Sisani, together with the field projects carried out by the University of Cambridge, the British School of Rome, and the University of Perugia, have given detail to the continuous occupation of the historic settlements of the Umbrians from the Iron Age to the Roman period or beyond.[2]

While individual sites and their topographical location will be discussed in the next chapter, in this section of the book I focus on providing an outline of the region's historical trajectory. After a short overview of earlier periods, I begin with the rise of a what might be called an Umbrian culture at the end of the seventh century BCE and trace it down to the concession of Roman citizenship to all Italic communities at the beginning of the first century BCE. In brief, over this span of seven centuries, Umbria saw proto-urban settlements develop into territorial polities that controlled the hinterlands and that, ultimately, were highly involved in the Roman conquest and colonization.

Although religious places will be treated in greater detail in the following two chapters, this section also includes a short overview of cult places, starting from their first archaeological traces in the sixth century BCE. Sacred spaces represent the "nodal points in the cultic, political, and socio-economic networks of the manifold communities that populated the Italian peninsula" and cannot be

---

1 Plin. *Nat.* 3.14.112.
2 Particularly active in this respect are the Faculty of Classical Archaeology of Perugia and the Department of Classical Studies at Cambridge. Two excavations, at ancient Tuder and at Urvinum Hortense, are being carried out by a team led by Professor Gianluca Grassigli from the University of Perugia. As mentioned above, the Gubbio Project has conducted excavations at Monte Ansciano and Monte Ingino, in the ancient Umbrian town of Iuguvium.

excluded from an overview of the history of the Umbrian territory.[3] As will be shown, the appearance of cult places in the region is the outcome of the socio-economic transformation that occurred during the archaic period. The second section of this chapter deals with Roman expansion in the region, which we can piece together with the aid of ancient literary authors, epigraphy, and archaeology. Most of the information for this period comes from ancient authors such as Livy. Consequently, it is essential to remember that they couch the details of colonization in terms of their understanding of the late Republican ideology of colonization, also offered by Cicero and Dionysius of Halicarnassus, "in which colonization was seen as an ordered, state-controlled process which played a vital part in the success of the Roman Empire."[4]

The end of the fourth century BCE marks the beginning of a long process of Roman interaction in the region. After the foundation of the Roman colony of Narnia, the Roman conquest of Umbria is evident with the establishments of the colonies of Sena Gallica (293 BCE), Ariminum (268 BCE), and Spoletium (241 BCE); in the same year, the Via Amerina was built, connecting northern Lazio with Umbrian centers and with the Etruscan cities of Perugia and Chiusi.

2   The Boundaries of Ancient Umbria

The modern region of Umbria is not identical to the ancient region. Modern Umbria occupies a central location within the Italian peninsula and was created with the unification of Italy in 1861. It includes most of the southern part of ancient Umbria but excludes the strip of land east of the Apennines, which is now included in the region of Marche. Moreover, modern Umbria incorporates the Etruscan cities of Orvieto and Perugia and the Sabine center of Norcia.

Ancient Umbria occupied a much vaster territory. In the words of ancient authors, the Umbrians appear as one of the oldest people on the peninsula, who occupied an extended area of central Italy. In the first century CE, both Pliny the Elder and Dionysius of Halicarnassus show an awareness that pre-Roman Umbria had occupied a vaster area than the *sexta regio* of Augustan Italy, between the left bank of the Tiber and the Apennines.[5] However, as

---

3   Stek and Burgers 2015, 1.
4   Bradley 2006, 69.
5   Plin. *Nat.* 3.50: *Umbrorum gens antiquissima Italia existimatur, ut quos Ombrios a Graecis putent dictos quod in inundatione terrarum imbribus superfuissent.* ("The Umbrians are believed to be the most ancient people of Italy; According to belief, the Greeks dubbed them "Ombrii" due to their endurance through the tempest after the land was engulfed by floods.")

ancient authors make clear, the boundaries of ancient Umbria in the period that preceded the Augustan reorganization of the Italian territory are not easily traceable.[6]

The Greek authors Herodotus and Dionysius of Halicarnassus report the great extent of the Umbrian territory and its origins.[7] According to both authors, the Umbrian territory covered the southeast Po valley and the central Adriatic coast,[8] with Herodotus extending it as far north as the Alps.[9] Both report that Etruscans expanded into former Umbrian areas, conquering, among others, the cities of Perugia and Cortona.[10] This account dovetails with

---

    Dion. Hal. *Ant. Rom.* 1.19.1: πολλὰ δὲ καὶ ἄλλα χωρία τῆς Ἰταλίας ᾤκουν Ὀμβρικοί, καὶ ἦν τοῦτο τὸ ἔθνος ἐν τοῖς πάνυ μέγα τε καὶ ἀρχαῖον. ("The Umbrians extended their presence across various regions of Italy, establishing themselves as a profoundly significant and ancient population.")

6   The uncertainty of ancient sources about ethnic boundaries is not limited to Umbrians and Etruscans but encompasses the whole Italian peninsula. Ancient authors often apply the same ethnicity to different communities at different points in their narratives. For specific examples, see Farney and Bradley 2017, 109.

7   For an extensive review of the Umbrians in the ancient Greek literature, see Maddoli 2009.

8   Dion. Hal. *Ant. Rom.* 1.19.1: οἱ δὲ διὰ τῆς μεσογείου τραπόμενοι, τὴν ὀρεινὴν τῆς Ἰταλίας ὑπερβαλόντες, εἰς τὴν Ὀμβρικῶν ἀφικνοῦνται χώραν τῶν ὁμορούντων Ἀβοριγῖσι. ("However, those who ventured inland traversed the mountainous terrain of Italy, eventually reaching the domain of the Umbrians, who were adjacent to the Aborigines.")

9   Hdt. 4.49.2: Ἰλλυριῶν δὲ ῥέων πρὸς βορέην ἄνεμον Ἄγγρος ποταμὸς ἐσβάλλει ἐς πεδίον τὸ Τριβαλλικὸν καὶ ἐς ποταμὸν Βρόγγον, ὁ δὲ Βρόγγος ἐς τὸν Ἴστρον· οὕτω ἀμφοτέρους ἐόντας μεγάλους ὁ Ἴστρος δέκεται. ἐκ δὲ τῆς κατύπερθε χώρης Ὀμβρικῶν Κάρπις ποταμὸς καὶ ἄλλος Ἄλπις ποταμὸς πρὸς βορέην ἄνεμον καὶ οὗτοι ῥέοντες ἐκδιδοῦσι ἐς αὐτόν. ("The Angrus River courses northward from Illyria into the Triballic plain, where it meets the Brongus River. Subsequently, the Brongus flows into the Ister (Danube), which assimilates the contributions of these two significant waterways. Originating from the northern reaches of the Umbrian territory, the rivers Karpis and Alpis also flow northward and join the Ister.") Herodotus extends the Umbrian territory to reach even the Alps.

10   Dion. Hal. *Ant. Rom.* 1.20.4 ἔπειτα μοῖρά τις αὐτῶν οὐκ ἐλαχίστη, ὡς ἡ γῆ πᾶσιν οὐκ ἀπέχρη, πείσαντες τοὺς Ἀβοριγῖνας συνάρασθαί σφισι τῆς ἐξόδου στρατεύουσιν ἐπὶ τοὺς Ὀμβρικοὺς καὶ πόλιν αὐτῶν εὐδαίμονα καὶ μεγάλην ἄφνω προσπεσόντες αἱροῦσι Κρότωνα· ταύτῃ φρουρίῳ καὶ ἐπιτειχίσματι κατὰ τῶν Ὀμβρικῶν χρώμενοι, κατεσκευασμένῃ τε ὡς ἔρυμα εἶναι πολέμου ἀποχρώντως καὶ χώραν ἐχούσῃ τὴν πέριξ εὔβοτον, πολλῶν καὶ ἄλλων ἐκράτησαν χωρίων τοῖς τε Ἀβοριγῖσι τὸν πρὸς τοὺς Σικελοὺς πόλεμον ἔτι συνεστῶτα πολλῇ προθυμίᾳ συνδιέφερον, ἕως ἐξήλασαν αὐτοὺς ἐκ τῆς σφετέρας. ("Afterwards, a considerable part of the Pelasgians, as the land was not sufficient to support them all, prevailed on the Aborigines to join them in an expedition against the Umbrians, and marching forth, they suddenly fell upon and captured Croton, a rich and large city of theirs. And using this place as a stronghold and fortress against the Umbrians, since it was sufficiently fortified as a place of defense in time of war and had fertile pastures lying round it, they made themselves masters also of a great many other places and with great zeal assisted the Aborigines in the war they were still engaged in against the Sicels, till they drove them out of their country."); Hdt.

52   CHAPTER 4

Pliny's mention of three hundred Umbrian *oppida*, probably located along the Tiber, fully occupied by Etruscans.[11]

Additional information on the geographical rivalry between Etruscans and Umbrians is gained from Strabo, who lived in the first century BCE. In book five of his *Geography*, he maintains that Umbria bordered on the land of the Etruscans and extended from the Apennines to the Adriatic: to the north, it reached Ravenna and Ariminum, whereas its southern border was the river Aesis, the modern Esino.[12] He continues his description of the Umbrians by recounting their expansion north of the Apennines, where, together with the Etruscans, they founded colonies in the area of the Po.[13] In this area, in addi-

---

1.94.6: ἀποπλέειν κατὰ βίου τε καὶ γῆς ζήτησιν, ἐς ὃ ἔθνεα πολλὰ παραμειψαμένους ἀπικέσθαι ἐς Ὀμβρικούς, ἔνθα σφέας ἐνιδρύσασθαι πόλιας καὶ οἰκέειν τὸ μέχρι τοῦδε. ("They [scil. the Tyerrenians] sailed away to seek a livelihood and a country; until at last, after sojourning with one people after another, they came to the Ombrici, where they founded cities and have lived ever since.") The mention of these two cities as previously Umbrian is in Dion. Hal. *Ant. Rom.* 1.26 (Cortona) and Serv. *Aen.* 10. 201 (Perugia).

11   Plin. *Nat.* 3.113: *trecenta eorum oppida Tusci debellasse reperiuntur.* ("We find that 300 of their towns [Umbrian] were conquered by the Etruscans.")

12   Strab. 5.2.1: οἱ δ᾽ Ὀμβρικοὶ μέσοι μὲν κεῖνται τῆς τε Σαβίνης καὶ τῆς Τυρρηνίας, μέχρι δ᾽ Ἀριμίνου καὶ Ῥαουέννης προΐασιν, ὑπερβάλλοντες τὰ ὄρη. ("The Ombrici lie between the eastern boundaries of the land of the Tyrrheni and the Sabini, but extend beyond the mountains as far as Ariminum, and Ravenna."); 5.2.10: πρότερον μέν γε τὸν Αἶσιν ἐποιοῦντο ὅριον, πάλιν δὲ τὸν Ῥουβίκωνα ποταμόν. ἔστι δ᾽ ὁ μὲν Αἶσις μεταξὺ Ἀγκῶνος καὶ Σήνας, ὁ δὲ Ῥουβίκων μεταξὺ Ἀριμίνου καὶ Ῥαουέννης, ἄμφω δ᾽ ἐκπίπτουσιν εἰς τὸν Ἀδρίαν. ("they made the Esino the boundary; afterwards the river Rubicon: the Esino being between Ancona and Sena, and the Rubicon between Ariminum and Ravenna, both of them falling into the Adriatic.") Cf. Strab. 5.1.11: τὸ δὲ Ἀρίμινον Ὄμβρων ἐστὶ κατοικία, καθάπερ καὶ ἡ Ῥάουεννα ("Ariminum is a colony of the Umbrians, as it is Ravenna.")

13   Strab. 5.1.10: τοῖς δὲ Ῥωμαίοις ἀναμέμικται καὶ τὸ τῶν Ὀμβρικῶν φῦλον, ἔστι δ᾽ ὅπου καὶ Τυρρηνῶν. ταῦτα γὰρ ἄμφω τὰ ἔθνη πρὸ τῆς τῶν Ῥωμαίων ἐπὶ πλέον αὐξήσεως εἶχέ τινα πρὸς ἄλληλα περὶ πρωτείων ἄμιλλαν, καὶ μέσον ἔχοντα τὸν Τίβεριν ποταμὸν ῥαδίως ἐπιδιέβαινεν ἀλλήλοις. καὶ εἴ πού τινας ἐκστρατείας ἐποιοῦντο ἐπ᾽ ἄλλους οἱ ἕτεροι, καὶ τοῖς ἑτέροις ἔρις ἦν μὴ ἀπολείπεσθαι τῆς εἰς τοὺς αὐτοὺς τόπους ἐξόδου· καὶ δὴ καὶ τῶν Τυρρηνῶν στειλάντων στρατιὰν εἰς τοὺς περὶ τὸν Πάδον βαρβάρους καὶ πραξάντων εὖ, ταχὺ δὲ πάλιν ἐκπεσόντων διὰ τὴν τρυφήν, ἐπεστράτευσαν οἱ ἕτεροι τοῖς ἐκβαλοῦσιν· εἶτ᾽ ἐκ διαδοχῆς τῶν τόπων ἀμφισβητοῦντες πολλὰς τῶν κατοικιῶν τὰς μὲν Τυρρηνικὰς ἐποίησαν τὰς δ᾽ Ὀμβρικάς· πλείους δὲ τῶν Ὀμβρικῶν, οἱ ἐγγυτέρω ἦσαν. οἱ δὲ Ῥωμαῖοι παραλαβόντες καὶ πέμψαντες ἐποίκους πολλαχοῦ συνεφύλαξαν καὶ τὰ τῶν προεποικησάντων γένη. ("The Ombrici nation and some of the Tyrrheni are also intermixed with the Romans. Before the Romans' rise, these two nations had disputes over precedence. With only the river Tiber between them, they easily waged war on each other. If one launched an expedition against a nation, the other sought to do the same with equal force. The Tyrrheni, after a successful campaign against the barbarians around the Po, lost their gains due to their own indulgence, prompting the Ombrici to retaliate against those who had expelled them. Disputes erupted between the Tyrrheni and Ombrici over

HISTORY OF THE UMBRIAN TERRITORY

tion to Ravenna,[14] ancient authors identify the cities of Butrium[15] and Mantua[16] as Umbrian, while Spina is considered an Umbrian city conquered by the Etruscans.[17]

Ancient assertions are supported by the archaeological evidence, which offers a substantial chronological anchor for the expansion of the Etruscans into previously Umbrian areas and for Umbrian colonization in the Po valley. Starting from the end of the seventh century BCE, the territories of Arezzo, Cortona, and Perugia show a significant range of Etruscan materials, with influences mainly from the Etruscan cities of Chiusi and Orvieto.[18] This data should be considered in the broader context of Etruscan expansion towards the left side of the Tiber up to the offshoot of the Apennines, which led to the shrinking of the western Umbrian boundary.[19] It is possible to situate Umbrian and Etruscan expansion into the Po valley during the same century (sixth) since the archaeological data includes a sixth–fifth century BCE *facies* with clear signs of Italic and Umbrian influence.[20]

The limits of the region to the east and to the south are much more extensive in the *periplos* of Pseudo-Skylax (perhaps an Athenian who wrote around 338–335 BCE) and in the *periplos* of Pseudo-Skymnos (second century BCE).[21] The first "circumnavigation" describes the coasts of the Mediterranean and the Black Sea, naming hundreds of towns along with geographical features such as rivers, harbors, and mountains. It begins at Gibraltar, moves along the north shore of the Mediterranean, circles the Black Sea, and returns to its starting point through Asia Minor, the Levant, and the coast of Egypt and North Africa. The unknown author maintains that the Umbrians occupied a long stretch of the Adriatic coast between the Etruscans and the Greek inhabitants of Spina to the north and the Picentes to the south; and Ancona is described as an

---

ownership rights to these territories, leading both nations to establish numerous colonies. However, the Ombrici's colonies were more abundant as they were closer to the region. When the Romans rose to power, they established colonies in various places but retained those founded by their predecessors.")

14   Nonetheless considered Sabine by Pliny: Plin. *Nat.* 3.15.115: *Ravenna Sabinorum oppidum.*
15   Plin. *Nat.* 3.15.115: *nec procul a mari Umbrorum Butrium.*
16   Serv. *Aen.* 10.201.
17   Iust. 20.1.11.
18   Aigner Foresti 1991, 14.
19   For an ample discussion of the middle valley of the Tiber and the Etruscan boundaries, see Patterson and Coarelli 2008, 15–45.
20   Colonna, 1974. The presence of the Umbrians in the Po valley has been recently examined by Sassatelli and Macellari 2002; Sisani 2014, 86.
21   Marcotte 1986.

54   CHAPTER 4

Umbrian city.[22] Pseudo-Skymnos' *periegesis*, dedicated to a King Nicomedes of Bithynia, gives a similar report of the extent of the Umbrian area. In this periegetic account of the world written in the second century BCE, Umbria extended almost to Apulia.[23]

The reason for the uncertainty in ancient descriptions of Umbrian boundaries probably lies in the blurry ethnic boundaries between Umbria and Etruria, which prevented ancient authors from differentiating between their corresponding territories.[24] As modern scholarship has demonstrated, the mutability of ethnic boundaries was indeed a characteristic of ancient Italy. In contrast to the view that ethnic boundaries were a social fact to which ethnic groups *a priori* belonged,[25] most archaeologists now embrace the social anthropological model first proposed by the cultural anthropologist Fredrik Barth.[26] According to this model, ethnicity is just one of the many social identities— alongside family, social, sexual, political, and other identities—that individuals decided to perform. Understood in this way, it becomes clear that ethnic boundaries need to be considered permeable and not simply defined in relation to allegedly monolithic ethnic groups.[27] Movement between communities of different ethnic backgrounds and the absorption of communities into local citizen bodies was frequent for groups and individuals.[28]

Indeed, cross-cultural contacts and social movement are apparent in the region from the ninth century BCE. In the Iron Age, the links that local elites developed with neighboring regions of Italy demonstrate the fluid nature of ancient Umbria's topographical and cultural boundaries. The presence of a rich chariot in an Umbrian burial at Todi, in the necropolis "La Loggia," provides

---

22   Scyl. 16M: μετὰ δὲ Σαυνίτας ἔθνος ἐστὶν Ὀμβρικοί, καὶ πόλιδ ἐν αὐθῇ Αγχών ἐστι. τοῦτο δὲ τὸ ἔθνος τιμᾷ Διομήδην, εὐεργετηθὲν υπ' αὐτοῦ· καὶ ἱερόν ἐστιν αὐτοῦ. ("After the Samnites, there are the Umbrians, and in this region there is the city of Ancona. This people worship Diomede, for the benefits received from him, and there is a sanctuary dedicated to him.")

23   Skymn. 366: Μεσσαπίων δ' οἰκοῦσιν ⟨πρός δύσι⟩ Ὀμβρικοί (...) ("West of the Messapians live the Umbrians").

24   A list of all the primary sources mentioning the territory of the Umbrians and their translation (into Italian) can be found in Sisani 2009, 19–41; Sisani 2014. For a recent discussion on the western boundaries of Umbria with Etruria see Patterson and Coarelli 2008, 15–87.

25   For a discussion of this topic, see Bradley 2000b and Scopacasa 2017. For a review of some of the most recent archaeological to the ethnicity, see Knappett 2014.

26   Barth 1989; cf. Eriksen 1992 and Jones 1996, 76–79.

27   See below for further discussion of this topic.

28   For some examples of crossing ethnic barriers and state boundaries in central and southern Italy, see Fulminante 2012, 89–108. An excellent excursus on mobility in pre-Roman Italy is in Bourdin 2012, 515–785.

HISTORY OF THE UMBRIAN TERRITORY

an example. At Todi, strategically located between the inland Apennine area and Etruscan territory, the importance of the community's *princeps* is highlighted by the remains (in a possible chamber tomb) of a chariot decorated with embossed sheet bronze. This symbol of social class is typical of the Etruscan world and confirms the close ties between this region and Umbria and the permeability of ethnic boundaries and common customs. In the archaic period, there is additional evidence of the mobility of the aristocracy, as indicated by the presence of Umbrian groups in the Etruscan cities of Perugia and Orvieto. Here, sixth-century BCE tombs contain aristocratic Umbrian names and point to the peaceful coexistence between the two groups, most likely through intermarriage.[29]

Also, as Mario Torelli has suggested, it is possible that the intertwined deeds and fates of Etruscans and Umbrians were another reason for the vagueness of Umbrian boundaries. According to Torelli, the Etruscan expansion in Umbrian territories beyond the Tiber and into the Po valley caused vagueness, malleability in regional boundaries, and confusion in the accounts of ancient authors.[30]

A quick scrutiny of the linguistic evidence supports the impression of an overall blurring of edges, rather than a sharply divided region. The Umbrian language, a subfamily of the Osco-Umbrian,[31] is known almost entirely from the sacred text of the Iguvine Tablets, the seven bronze tablets found in the town of Iguvium (modern Gubbio) in 1444.[32] These tablets, which date to about the second century BCE, have a twofold importance. First, their content is fundamental for our knowledge of Italic religion and cult practice. As will be discussed in further detail in the next chapter, the Iguvine Tablets describe a communal purification ritual at Iguvium and instruct the community to shun their neighbors. Second, the tablets represent the longest text in any non-Latin language of ancient Italy (4000 words).

Otherwise, our knowledge of Umbrian comes from thirty-two shorter inscriptions, which include public inscriptions, sacred dedications, boundary terms, funerary inscriptions, artist signatures, and coin legends. Most are dated from the third to the first century BCE (in the Umbrian alphabet and in the

---

29   See Benelli 2017 for a discussion on the archaeological evidence shared among central Italic cultural groups.

30   Torelli 2010, 219–230.

31   The most complete editions of the Sabellic texts are Rix 2002 and Crawford 2011. The standard grammar of the Sabellic languages remains Buck (1928), supplemented by works on aspects of the grammar such as Meiser 1986 and Dupraz 2012.

32   For the most recent examination of this text, see Weiss 2010.

56   CHAPTER 4

Latin alphabet), with only a handful of inscriptions dated from between the fifth and the fourth century BCE. The distribution of these inscriptions clearly defies any scholarly attempts to map the Umbrian language onto distinct regional variations.[33] First, Umbrian inscriptions appear in limited areas of the region described by the ancient sources, as they are concentrated only in the northeastern sector of the modern region of Umbria. Second, Umbrian inscriptions are often found together with Etruscan ones; and, in towns such as Tuder there are more Etruscan inscriptions than Umbrian. Thus, as Enrico Benelli has recently argued,[34] it is impossible to define neat linguistic borders between cultures.[35] Besides indicating the presence of mixed language use, this evidence further emphasizes the permeability of regional boundaries and the difficulty of drawing clear regional boundaries.

Ultimately, if we piece together these different accounts from ancient authors, it seems likely that, at least until the end of the archaic period, the region of Umbria would have covered central and northern Italy, almost as far as the Alpine region. In the north, this broad area extended up to the Po valley and included the cities of Ravenna, Rimini, Butrium, and Mantua, which were conquered by the Boii and Lingones in the fifth century.[36] In the west, it may have included the Etruscan centers of Perugia, Cortona and Chiusi/Camars at least until the end of the seventh century BCE or the beginning of the sixth century BCE.[37] Following the course of the Tiber, the southern border would have reached Ocriculum, and then followed the Adriatic coast bordering Picene territory between Camerino and Sentinum. However, in the fourth century BCE, Umbria lost the swath of Adriatic territory north of the river Esinus (the northern area of modern Marche) to the Senones, the last Gallic tribe to arrive in the Italian peninsula.[38] Most likely, the mountainous area on the eastern side

---

33   Pallottino 1940; Sisani 2009, 180–184.

34   Benelli 2017, 89–103.

35   On the use of archaeological data to map ancient Italic peoples, see Bradley 2000, 111–113.

36   For the Gallic invasion of the Italian peninsula, see Zecchini 2009. Cf. Liv. 5.35.2: "Then, over the Poenine Pass, came the Boii and Lingones, who finding everything taken up between the Po and the Alps, crossed the Po on rafts, and drove out not only the Etruscans, but also the Umbrians from their lands; nevertheless, they kept on the further side of the Apennines."

37   A skeptical position regarding the "umbricità" of these northern Etruscan cities is held by Sisani (2008, esp. 69). According to him, the literary traditions that mention these centers of northern internal Etruria as Umbrian reflect the presence of foreign elements within the social structure of the Etruscan archaic communities.

38   Liv. 5.35.2. "Then the Senones, the latest to come, had their holdings from the river Utens all the way to the Aesi."

HISTORY OF THE UMBRIAN TERRITORY 57

of the river Nera would have belonged to the Sabines, though it is difficult to pinpoint an exact border between ethnic groups.[39]

Ancient Umbria becomes a clear geographical unit during the Augustan age as a consequence of the division of the peninsula into fourteen administrative regions: Umbria Ager Gallicus became the sixth region.[40] Pliny the Elder (*Nat.* 3.112–114) records the extent of Umbria and states that its southern border consisted of the Nar and Tiber rivers and that it encompassed the Apennine slopes bordering the Adriatic from Camerinum to Mevaniola and from Aesis to Pisaurum on the coast. In this geographical reorganization of ancient Italy, the Tiber came to define the limit between Etruria (Regio VII) and Umbria (Regio VI).[41]

2.1 The Existence of an Umbrian Identity: An Ongoing Debate

Considering the contrasting views of the Umbrian boundaries provided by ancient sources, it is not entirely surprising that scholars cannot agree on the ethnic identity of the Umbrians. Indeed, the question remains as to whether it is possible to identify an Umbrian distinctiveness that could have supported the formation of Umbrian ethnicity as described by the literary sources. As noted above in the discussion of the boundaries of the ancient region, the question of ethnicity is a much-debated topic among scholars of ancient Umbria, and of the ancient Mediterranean more broadly. Despite modern research that emphasizes the fluidity of ethnic identity and problematizes the existence of pre-Roman monolithic ethnic groups, archaeologists working in Umbria still resist the impossibility of tracing one Umbrian ethnic group. Although a discussion on scholarly work on ethnicity is beyond the scope of the present work, it is worth noting some of the most dominant approaches to the topic here.

Looming large over this debate is Jonathan Hall's book *Ethnic Identity in Greek Antiquity*. Hall examines the construction, meaning, and function of ethnic identity among Greek communities.[42] He argues that ethnicity is a contingent phenomenon and considers territoriality and genealogy as essential

---

39 The most recent discussion on the borders of the ancient region of Sabina is in the article by Gary D. Farney and Giulia Masci in Bradley 2017, 543–558.

40 A full account of the literary sources for the Roman period (from the expansion of Rome in Umbrian territory to the formation of the *regio sexta*) is in Sisani 2007, 299–367.

41 This limit was just an administrative one since the awareness of earlier group identities did not cease to exist. The previously Etruscan center of Vettona, satellite of Perusia and now in the Regio VI, retained the title of *praetor Etruriae*. See Koch 1954.

42 Hall 1997.

factors in the definition of ethnic identities. Consequently, he argues that ethnicity is fungible and in continuous flux. Similarly, Sian Jones argues that ethnic identity is situational and subjective yet connected to people's experiences and social practices.[43]

These ideas have been expanded in the past decade to include contexts other than mainland Greece. Denise Demetriou, for example, focuses on Greek *emporia* and trade ports such as Emporion, Gravisca, Naukratis, Pisitiros, and Pireus in order to explain how different ethnic, social, linguistic, and religious groups encountered each other and how each group shaped its identity while interacting with others.[44] She concludes that the various populations in these emporia created their identities in relation to themselves and others by utilizing cultural aspects such as law, political institutions, and religion.

Several other approaches to this topic are described in the recent *Companion to Ethnicity in the Ancient Mediterranean* and in the edited volume *Creating Ethnicities and Identities in the Roman World*.[45] These works cover different time periods and regions and highlight the flexible and functional aspects of ethnic identity, while recognizing the limitations of providing a comprehensive analysis and the need to rely on specific case studies.

Theories on the flexibility and contingency of ethnicity are also extremely popular among scholars who closely investigate identities in ancient Italy. Emma Blake is aware of the difficulties of studying group ethnic identity in archaeology. To shed some light on identity formation in the murky period of the Bronze Age, she applies network analysis and path dependence to the distributions of imports and other distinctive objects.[46] She argues that members of an ethnic group interact and communicate through networks that thus can be identified by examining the material traces of communication between sites. In Bronze Age Etruria and in Latium, she identifies the "proto-Etruscan" and the "proto-Latin" groups, whose close interaction determined, according to the author, the rise of their ethnic identities of the later first millennium.

The extensive work by Stephan Bourdin on the peoples of pre-Roman Italy emphasizes the flexibility of pre-Roman ethnic groups, the so-called *nomina*.[47] His arguments, largely based on scrutiny of the mentions of ancient peoples

---

43   Jones 1997.

44   Demetriou 2012.

45   McInerney 2015, Gardner et al. 2013.

46   Blake 2014.

47   Bourdin (2012) examines minutely the ancient application of terms such as *populus* and *nomen* and whether it had any political content and how the reality of settlement and organization of the territory related to questions of identity.

in ancient literary sources, are centered on the opposition between independent political groups, *populi*, and larger ethnic groups, *nomina*, which group together the *populi* (e.g., Rome is a *populus* of the *nomen* Latinum). Bourdin holds that if the *populus* represents a relatively stable group, the ethnic representations, the *nomina*, are highly mobile. He contends that these manipulations were deliberate and voluntary, and could be attributed to political motives.

This view is only partially shared by Rafael Scopacasa, who also acknowledges the importance of local identities as well as shared ethnic identities but argues for a situational use of both ethnic and local identities by ancient peoples.[48] He uses epigraphical evidence to demonstrate that people could use different levels of identities (e.g., ethnic identity and local identity) depending on the context.[49] The *lustratio* described in the Iguvine Tablets, written between the third and the first century BCE but reflecting an earlier period, aims to protect the people of Iguvium and curse their nearest neighbors, who also may have defined themselves as Umbrian. This example clearly illustrates the importance of considering ethnic identity as situational: communities belonging to the same *ethnos* could "pursue very different foreign policies when it suited them."[50]

Tesse Stek further reiterates the importance of local identity in his discussion of Italic identities and the Romanization of Italy.[51] First, he reiterates the fleetingness of the concept of ethnic identity, which is closely tied to historical circumstances. For example, the ethnic *safinim* (Samnite), attested by the sixth century in Abruzzo, is used in the second century in Molise, likely as part of the antagonizing strategy against Roman dominion in this period. Thus, Stek suggests setting aside the "search" for ethnic groups in favor of a focus on more local identities and the varieties among them. Drawing from recent archaeological research that shows local variegation in material culture and practice, he shows that in cases such as Samnium and Latium, ethnic identity is characterized by local varieties that stray from a unified political organization. The importance of local civic identities is particularly noticeable in the case of Latium. Here, evidence of shared rituals such as at the sanctuary of Jupiter Latiaris or at the

---

48   Scopacasa 2017.

49   Scopacasa 2017, 117.

50   Scopacasa 2017, 118. An interesting development of this concept is in Farney 2007. The results of Farney's research on Roman political culture suggest that aristocratic families manipulated their identity for political or social goals. For this reason, according to the author, the *praenomina* of aristocrats are more important than *nomina* because they reflect their choice to self-identify themselves with an ethnic membership or descent.

51   Stek 2013.

thirteen altars at Lanuvium seems to establish power relationships among different communities rather than a higher level of political organization. Thus, Stek emphasizes the importance of local civic identity and communal organization over ethnicity as a geographical concept.[52]

The preceding survey offers just a handful of examples of current approaches to ethnicity that are representative of a broader intellectual understanding of ethnic identity as multi-layered, negotiable, and variable. In the case of Umbria, the discussion is not nearly close to an end. As for other peoples of ancient Italy, the narrative of the Umbrian *ethnos* and its distinctiveness is biased by the perspective of authors writing centuries after the period they describe and of Greeks and Romans who perceived the Italians as divided into ethnic groups.[53] Although a few inscriptions dated to the fifth century BCE do mention ethnic groups, much of the controversy related to the identification of an Umbrian ethnic identity is rooted in the fundamentally different views on the extent to which Italian people considered themselves as ethnically distinct.[54]

Archaeologists who study ancient Umbria have differing opinions about the region's cultural and ethnic identity before the Roman period. The Italian school, led by scholars such as Simone Sisani, Laura Bomoni Ponzi, Mario Torelli, and Dorica Manconi, use archaeological and linguistic evidence to argue for the coherence of Umbria as a distinct cultural and ethnic identity.[55] For example, Sisani prioritizes Greek and Late Republican written sources, as

---

52   This concept has been recently emphasized by Benelli (2017). He notes the discrepancy between cultural boundaries and ethnic boundaries in central Italy during the pre-Roman period and suggests that the ethnic identity as people of one region was weaker than local identities, which he sees reflected in distinctive material culture.

53   Dench 1995.

54   Excellent discussions about this evidence and related bibliography are in Suano and Scopacasa 2013 and Scopacasa 2017. For a good review of recent research on ethnogenesis in central Italy (mainly Etruria and Latium Vetus) see Fulminante 2012. Her analysis is particularly innovative as it brings different types of evidence in a relational model to the study of ethnicity both horizontally and vertically. She suggests the use of a combination of material culture, ancient authors, and faunal or vegetal remains in order to explore how ethnic identity is defined. In agreement with previous scholarship, she argues that, for Latium Vetus, the definition and characterization of identity happens in proto-history (tenth–seventh century BCE) and identifies several indicators in the material culture that illustrate how ethnic identity can be investigated.

55   In her synthesis of the historical processes of the region during the seventh century, Bonomi Ponzi (1991, 70) argues that "the presence of the Umbrians in historical sources is clearly attested." Torelli pinpoints the existence of an Umbrian ethnic distinction already in the sixth century and even postulates the existence of a maritime *emporium* at Rimini: Torelli 2010, 29.

HISTORY OF THE UMBRIAN TERRITORY

well as the only inscription of the fifth century BCE that mentions "the plain of Umbria,"[56] to claim that the Umbrians represented a well-defined ethnic group, unified by the existence of an Umbrian league.[57] It is worth noting that this ethnonym is attested from the Sabellic languages only in the South Picene *ombriíen* and there are no known references to the Umbrians using this term to describe themselves. Manconi supports the idea of an independent Umbrian cultural *ethnos*, which, she argues, appeared in the late seventh/sixth century BCE. However, she also admits to recognizing "a common culture, almost a central Italic koinè, in which there are common forms and affinities in pottery, tomb typologies, and funerary rituals,"[58] almost undermining her previous statement about the existence of a clear Umbrian specificity.

British archaeologists have taken a different approach, emphasizing recent theoretical approaches to the archaeology of ethnic groups and highlighting the situational construction of most cultures. Bradley, for example, does not view Umbria as a unified culture, but rather as a region made up of local communities.[59] According to him, the use of the Umbrian collective name was rare until the first century BCE, and local inhabitants of the region preferred to describe themselves in relation to their city. This suggests that in archaic Umbria there was little sentiment of belonging to an Umbrian ethnic group.

In the case of Plestia, located on the eastern side of Umbria, four bronze inscriptions from the fourth century BCE dedicated at the Sanctuary of Cupra read *cupras, matres pletinas, sacru esu*.[60] The Plestini are among the groups mentioned by Pliny in the first century as residing in Umbria.[61] The reference to this group in the inscriptions to the sanctuary's goddess suggests that the local community already had its own identity in the pre-Roman period. The importance of local identity in the region is reinforced in the Iguvine Tablets with the list of the enemies of the city of Iguvium. Bradley rightly points out that the presence, among other *nomina*, of the *naharcer* (the inhabitants of Nahars in lowland Umbria) is a strong indicator of the lack of an overarching Umbrian identity group. The feeling of individual group cohesion, which emerges from these two examples of Umbrian epigraphy, seems to have been more important than, and quite separate from, that of belonging to an Umbrian *ethnos*.

---

56   This inscription is carved on a bronze bracelet dedicated in a shrine in the Pescara valley that mentions "in the territory of the Umbri" or "in the plain of the Umbri": *ombriíen akren*.

57   Sisani 2009; Sisani 2012.

58   Manconi 2017, 606.

59   Bradley 1997; 2000.

60   "I am sacred to Cupra, mother of the Plestini." On this inscription, see Ciotti 1964; Bradley 2000a, 288; Crawford 2011, 115–118.

61   Plin. *Nat.* 3.14.114.

Drawing on studies of identity formation in Greece, Bradley argues that local communities, with their distinctive state identity, grew into a shared ethnic identity through interactions for political and military reasons.[62] In particular, progressive Roman expansion was the decisive threat that increased the cohesive forces of Umbrian communities, which were strengthened after the conquest. Bradley notes that the Umbrians are likely to have fought together more frequently in military units of the Roman army after the conquest than before it and that such service may have played an important role in the definition of Umbrian ethnic identity.[63] As also noted by Benelli, the army provided by local communities (colonies, *civitae sine suffragio* and allied communities) to the Roman military was precisely organized into units, and this may have exercised considerable influence in forging a more fixed definition of perceived ethnic groups.[64]

Simon Stoddart and David Redhouse carry the argument even further.[65] In their most recent article, they examine the role of landscape in the construction of ethnicity and attribute a shadowy identity to the Umbrians, in contrast to other central Italian groups whose identities they consider more developed. They, too, support the existence of local identities in the pre-Roman period and argue that these coalesced into a regional identity in response to the advance of Rome. The landscape development of Iguvium, Tuder, Interamna, Ameria, and Spoletium, to different extents, exhibits traits of community bonds and local political power. The overall picture illustrates the absence of a broader sense of ethnicity and the presence of community identity in several of the major pre-Roman settlements of the region. For this reason, the authors have concluded that "local community was the primary focus of identity."[66]

Considering these contrasting voices on the nature of Umbrian identity, it seems reasonable to use caution when we examine ancient Umbria as a whole. As scholars have shown, the evidence for a strong Umbrian identity is

---

62 Petra Amann (2011, 296) shares Bradley's conclusions about the blurry nature of pre-Roman Umbrian identity: "... existieren derzeit keine echten Indizien dafür, dass neben einem eher lockeren Gefühl der ethnischen Gemeinsamkeit eine Art von dauerhaftem Staatenbund zwischen den einzelnen umbrischen Gemeinden existiert hätte. ... Zweifellos bestand spätestens ab dem 4. Jh.v.Chr. die Notwendigkeit eines gemeinsamen militärischen Vorgehens, die einzelnen umbrischen Gemeinden schlossen sich temporär zu Verteidigungszwechen zusammen, blieben aber politisch autonom und verfügen über keine gemeinsame politische Organisation mit Zentralorganen."

63 Similarly, Stek (2013, 349) argues that, in Latium, Latin speakers could "identify with each other in the face of external threat."

64 Benelli 2017, 100.

65 Stoddart and Redhouse 2014.

66 Stoddart and Redhouse 2014, 117.

HISTORY OF THE UMBRIAN TERRITORY 63

slender and the sense of Umbrian ethnicity was weaker than the identification with specific states such as Tuder, Plestia, and Iguvium.[67] In addition, the absence of a clear concept of Umbrian ethnic identity may likely be responsible for the ambiguity of the boundaries of the region. In the next chapter, I will demonstrate that the study of votive offerings from the region's sanctuaries can provide further evidence of the presence of local ethnic groups rather than overarching Umbrian *ethnos*.

2.2 Umbria's Geography

The region's inland landscape is characterized by a diverse terrain that includes mountains, valleys, and rivers. The Apennine Mountains form a natural boundary to the north and east, but low passes provided access across them, connecting the western and eastern areas of Umbria. Apart from the Apennines, notable peaks include Monte Subasio and Monte Maggiore, which dominate the hills south of Gubbio; the Martani Mountains, which run along the Umbrian valley; and the Amerini Mountains, which dominate the southwest of the region.

Rivers and valleys have historically played an important role in facilitating communication and transportation throughout the region. The Tiber River runs along the western part, while numerous smaller rivers and streams are found in the modern areas of Romagna and Marche. The largest valley is the Valle Umbra, located in the center of the ancient Augustan region. The northern part Umbria is divided between the Gubbio basin and the lower Chiascio basin, while the southern part is occupied by the Terni valley and the northern Tiber valley covers the west.

The geographic and hydrographic features of the Umbrian region, together with its key position on the north–south and east-west routes of ancient Italy, facilitated the early human occupation of this area and favored contact with the other pre-Roman groups of the peninsula. Additional elements that favored human occupation were the presence of clays (from the limestone uplands and Plio-Pleistocene terraces), ore bodies in areas such as Gualdo Tadino and Monteleone di Spoleto, and the presence of forests that guaranteed wood supply. This diverse territory is suitable for different types of productive activities ranging from agriculture to livestock and pastoralism, depending on the ground's elevation.[68]

---

67   If anything, the South Picene inscription, *ombríien akren*, "on Umbrian land," shows that at least one tribe in this region considered themselves members of an Umbrian *ethnos*.

68   For a more extensive description of the region's geography, see Bonomi-Ponzi 1991, Colivicchi and Zaccagnino 2008, and Ammann 2011.

64   CHAPTER 4

3   The History of Pre-Roman Umbria

Human occupation of ancient Umbria began in the northern part of the region
during the Lower Paleolithic, one million to 300,000 years ago. Human habita-
tion has been detected on the terraces above the Tiber, Chiasco, and Topino
rivers, and on Monte Peglia, between Todi and Orvieto. From the late sixth millennium, during the Neolithic period, human occupation is evidenced by more
permanent settlements established in the foothills, with a preference for the
alluvial fans of the Gubbio valley. In the latter phase of the Neolithic period,
evidence is concentrated in the area of Norcia and Terni, in the south.[69]

The Bronze Age represents the first well-known phase in ancient Umbria.
From the seventeenth century BCE to the twelfth century BCE (Middle Bronze
Age), the region came to be dominated by the so-called Apennine culture,
which was widespread throughout the central-southern peninsula in this
period and may have originated in Umbria.[70] This phase is characterized by
seasonal settlements connected to transhumance, especially in the mountains,
where people depended on an economy of pastoralism and large-scale stock-
raising. In the lowlands, we find more stable settlements that appear to have
supported a more mixed economy.[71] The hallmarks of this culture are a distinctive pottery type with incised geometric designs and the deposition of bronze
tools and weapons in inhumation burials.

With the sub-Apennine phase (second half of the eleventh century BCE–
tenth century BCE), corresponding to the Late Bronze Age, important changes
happened in the region partly due to contacts with the Terramare, the Proto-
Villanovan cultures, and the intensification of trade with the Aegean-
Mycenean world and that of central Europe.[72] Although cremation funerary
rites (at Gubbio, Spoleto, and Terni) suggest an egalitarian society, the intensification and specialization of agriculture, the increased demographic scale,
including polyfocal settlements in areas such as Gubbio, and the presence of

---

69   Grifoni Cremonesi 1987.
70   Bonomi Ponzi 1991, 52.
71   The fullest examination of the so-called Apennine culture was done by Salvatore Puglisi,
      who, in 1959, published his work on the Apennine Bronze Agestill, the principal statement
      of the "pastoralist" hypothesis. However, data from the excavation at Luni sul Mignone in
      northern Latium, which led to the discovery of imposing house foundations cut into the
      soft volcanic tufo, suggested that "the Apennine culture had a mixed economy with agri-
      culture and stock-breeding as basic components ... pastoral nomadism cannot therefore
      be looked upon as the primary characteristic feature of the Apennine culture": Östenberg,
      1967, 260.
72   On the sub-Apennine phase, see Peroni 1959.

HISTORY OF THE UMBRIAN TERRITORY 65

metal hoards (e.g., at Gualdo Tadino and Terni) indicate wealth accumulation (or at least conspicuous disposal) and, therefore, suggest social stratification.[73]

The region underwent further political, economic, and cultural changes at the beginning of the Iron Age (tenth to eighth century BCE). Previous settlements were abandoned, and metal hoards ceased to be deposited. Settlements concentrated along the Apennine areas or around large basins and valleys, forming more consistent nucleation of populations in places that endured, such as Todi, Terni, Gubbio, Ameria, the massif of Monte Torre Maggiore and the Colfiorito plateau.[74] The latter, which has been investigated in depth, provides important information on settlement organization and burial practices during this phase.[75] Here, communities appear to be organized in villages consisting of huts located at a regular distance (500 meters) from one another, with a ditch on the eastern side. The necropolis, similar to the one excavated in Terni,[76] is characterized by inhumation, with rectangular graves covered with limestone slabs and marked on the ground by a circle of stones. Grave goods found in the tombs are very simple, local products: an impasto vase and clothing-related objects such as *fibulae*, and razors, none of which suggest social stratification.[77] Overall, during this first phase of the Iron Age, the Umbrian territory shows a general uniformity, closely related to the contemporary Villanovan and Latial cultures.[78]

3.1 Sixth–Fourth Century BCE

The sixth century BCE was marked by an expanded trade in imported luxury objects. Umbria saw the emergence both of nucleated communities and of more diffuse groups occupying fortified upland settlements. Both types of settlements show a division between social classes and the establishment of an aristocratic caste. Some scholars have taken such organization as concrete evidence of an independent cultural identity among the Umbrians.[79] If, during the

---

73   Fulminante 2013, 5.
74   For an overview of settlements in these mountainous areas, see Bonomi Ponzi 1982.
75   Bonomi Ponzi 1988.
76   See the most recently detailed publication on this necropolis, Leonelli 2003.
77   The pottery from the funerary ensembles was made from coarse clay and took simple forms. It was wheel-made in local workshops throughout the region and fired in kilns. The typologies show similarities with the Etruscan-Latin areas and with southern Italy. With regard to the metal objects, the presence of fibulae from the area of Bologna points at the contacts, through the Tiber valley, with the Po valley.
78   Bonomi Ponzi 1991, 61.
79   The traditional interpretation is that during this period a few major cultural groups appeared and their boundaries, even though blurred, roughly corresponded to the geo-

previous phase, communities had begun to settle in more permanent locations, it is starting in this next phase that Umbrian people established settlements at sites that would later be occupied by the cities of archaic times, both in the sub-mountain areas and in the mountains. In the mountainous territories, the occupation of the territories is based on a series of fortified hill settlements, the so-called castella, which in some cases take the place of the previous Iron Age villages.[80] Among these fortified settlements on higher ground we can mention Colle Mori at Gualdo Tadino,[81] Monte Orve in the middle of the Colfiorito plateau, Monte Torre Maggiore at Terni, Colle San Rufino at Assisi, Monteleone at Spoleto, Bevagna, Gubbio, Matelica, Fabriano, and Pitino.[82]

These settlements are located at heights ranging from 500 to 1000 meters and usually overlook communication routes.[83] They comprise areas measuring about 120–150 square kilometers defended by a ditch (4–5 meters wide) and a bank of earth or dry-laid stone walls up to 4 meters high around the highest point in the landscape.[84] The area occupied by the hillforts is divided into several hut villages, each organized to distinguish the living areas from production areas. The presence of streets between villages and common areas such as pastures, sacred areas,[85] and fortifications has led scholars to hypothesize that villages, although divided into separate units, would have been able to cooperate for their maintenance and protection.[86]

Although a detailed study on Umbrian hillforts is lacking,[87] surveys and excavations conducted in the '80s and '90s on some of the Umbrian hillforts,

---

graphical location of pre-Roman people known in historical times and from literary sources. For example, in central Italy, archaeologists have identified distinctive material cultures such as the Villanovan culture, which is characterized by cremation funerary rites in pits and is found primarily in areas west of the Tiber, including modern-day northern Latium and Tuscany. Meanwhile, the rest of the region, along with northern Abruzzo, is thought to have been part of a central Italian "koine" or common cultural group, which practiced inhumation burial in large rectangular pits with stone circles; see Manconi 2017.

80   The previous settlements on the plains were abandoned due to the insecurity of their position. Plestia is a well-studied example of an Iron Age village that, in the sixth century, relocated to a hillfort: Bonomi Ponzi 1985, 214–216.

81   This is the only settlement that has been the object of a systematic excavation.

82   Bonomi Ponzi 1991, 62; Manconi 2017, 609.

83   For a discussion of the function of hillfort settlements in this region, see Bradley 2000, 53–55.

84   These structures have only been dated through association with surface pottery and related cemeteries.

85   See Chapter 6 for a discussion of the connection between hilltop centers and sacred spaces.

86   Bonomi Ponzi 1985 and 1991.

87   Unlike, for instance, the Samnium region, where the Venafro Project of the Freie Univer-

HISTORY OF THE UMBRIAN TERRITORY

such as at Colfiorito and Gualdo Tadino, have revealed that they were organized hierarchically, with minor hillforts gravitating around a more complex central site.[88] The position and richness of the cemeteries associated with the hillfort on Monte Orve, at the center of the Colfiorito Plateau, strongly suggest that it was the most important hillfort in the area and that it controlled the smaller peaks of Monte di Franca and Monte Trella, located elsewhere on the plateau. Another important settlement of this type is at Gualdo Tadino, Colle Mori. Here, a nucleated settlement developed on the hillside of a spur overlooking an upland plain and was surrounded by a fortified circuit. As in the case of Monte Orve, the richness of the cemetery of San Facondino (600 m to the west) has led to the hypothesis that this was the central node of the settlement system made up of some other ten hillforts in the area, which controlled the main roads coming from Perusia and Iguvium, and the trans-Apennine routes leading to the Adriatic coast.[89]

The hierarchical organization of Umbrian hillforts finds a parallel in the aristocratic political and social organization of the communities of the sixth and fifth centuries. Within individual communities, archaeological evidence shows the emergence of clear differentiation among social classes, a phenomenon that in Latial and Etruscan areas emerged in the Orientalizing period, if not before.[90] The presence of an aristocratic elite is clear from the necropoleis that, during this phase, appear in or near a broader spectrum of sites. The necropoleis at Otricoli, Amelia, Todi, Spoleto, Bevagna, Foligno, Nocera, and Gubbio add to the earlier necropoleis of Terni and Colfiorito, which continue to be frequented during this period. Aristocratic burials are signaled by tumuli or stone-circle tombs and, most importantly, by grave goods. These are prestige goods produced locally or obtained through importation mainly from South Etruria, Picenum, the Faliscan territory,[91] and Greece.[92] Women were often

---

      sität di Berlino (Excellence Cluster TOPOI) investigated the settlement dynamics of the region. The results of this investigation merged into the book "Die Höhenbefestigungen Samniums: Eine landschafts- und siedlungsarchäologische Analyse" by Alexander Hoer.

88   Bonomi Ponzi 1985.

89   Bonomi Ponzi 1992, Bonomi Ponzi 2010.

90   See Bradley 2015 for a discussion of the emergence of a stable elite class in these areas.

91   Among some examples we can mention are the embossed bronze laminated shields from Veii found in Colfiorito, Sant'Anatolia di Narco, Pitino di San Severino, Fabriano, Verrucchio, and Capena; and the plates and Faliscan pottery, imported and imitated in Todi, Febbrecce, Tavere di Serravalle, and Pitino di San Severino: Bonomi Ponzi 1991, 70.

92   When Orvieto/Volsinii took over the position of fulcrum of trade between Umbria and Etruria, imported Greek pottery begins to appear in funerary contexts: Bradley 2000, 97; Bonomi Ponzi 1991, 58.

buried with spindle whorls, rocchetti (small, spool-shaped terracotta objects thought to have been used in weaving or as stamping devices), and fibulae. Male burials contained iron weapons indicating the ranks of individual warriors. For example, at Terni, a lance or javelin alone signified a soldier of lower rank; a sword, a lance, and two javelins, someone of higher rank.[93] At the necropoleis of Le Logge and San Raffaele at Todi, the typological analysis of the aristocratic burials' grave goods from the sixth/fifth century BCE suggest the presence of hierarchical communities, centered around leading warrior aristocratic figures, who likely benefitted from the favorable position of this center and from controlling commercial routes.[94] The increasing complexity of Umbrian communities is also manifested by the use of coinage, adopted at Tuder and Iguvium, initially employing a Chiusine Etruscan weight standard of about 200 g.[95] At an earlier date, *aes rude* or bronze fragments, widely accepted as representing portable wealth, were employed, suggesting a progressive formalization of wealth into an accepted political symbol of the community.

Towards the end of the fifth century BCE, the archaic socio-institutional organization drastically changed, and a process of urban re-organization put an end to the hegemony of the aristocratic class of the previous centuries. A change in the settlement patterns can be observed at the well-excavated Colle Mori, where buildings had tiled roofs and stone foundations and were articulated in several rooms.[96] In addition, the presence of a *cippus* with an inscription mentioning the name of the civic community/*touta* (*tarina*) suggests that starting from these centuries, settlements began to re-define their limits, perhaps in connection with a new foundation of the cities themselves.

The rise of a new class that replaced the aristocratic society of the previous centuries is further evidence of the transformation of some archaic centers into centralized cities. This shift is clearly illustrated by the necropoleis of S. Stefano and Peschiera at Tuder, closer to their urban centers than the archaic necropoleis of Le Logge and San Raffaele.[97] Here, grave goods related to the curing of the body, such as *unguentaria*, represent the new urban society. In the Apennine area of Umbria, the centers along communication routes present similar evidence of urban development. The necropolis Vittorina at Iguvium shows the presence of a wealthy class represented by a particular

---

93   Bonomi Ponzi, 1988.
94   Tascio 1988, 16–17.
95   Catalli 1989, 140–152.
96   Sisani 2009, 55–70.
97   Torelli 2010, 30; Sisani 2006, 164; Tascio 1989, 13–17.

HISTORY OF THE UMBRIAN TERRITORY

grave good: an Attic crater with red figures laid at the feet of the deceased. This evidence may indicate the existence of a *lex sumptuaria* that eliminated funerary ostentation and aimed to represent the city in a more egalitarian way.

We should not assume that developments were homogeneous throughout the region. In the necropolis of Colfiorito, located some distance from major roads, evidence from the necropolis reveals that the aristocratic class continued to dominate until the end of the third century BCE. The grave goods from this necropolis show inequality among individuals and the presence of a wealthy class that continued to express itself through weapons and sumptuous banquet vessels. A similar situation appears to hold true at Hispellum in the Umbrian valley, where the necropolis' grave goods demonstrate the prominent role of the warrior until the second century BCE. Although this evidence indicates that these centers had a different social trajectory compared to the more urban cities already mentioned, the lack of systematic investigations in most Apennine and southern Umbrian areas represents an obstacle to any precise reconstruction of the socio-institutional and demographic developments.

3.2 Sacred Spaces

Although it is unlikely that religious activity did not exist before the sixth century BCE, it is only toward the end of this century that sacred places become visible in the archaeological record. As Bradley's survey of Umbrian cult places has shown,[98] except for a small number of sacred places, most archaic Umbrian cult places have only been identified during ground explorations through the presence of ex-votos representing armed figures or simple male and female bronze figurines or human body parts, common also among the Venetic people and the Etruscans.[99] This is due not only to a general lack of excavation and the damaged stratigraphy of the few sites that have been excavated,[100] but also to the nature itself of early cult places, which consisted often only of a pit, a temporary wooden structure, an altar, an enclosure wall, and perhaps a natural

---

98   Bradley 1997.
99   As Malone and Stoddart (1994, 142–143) clarify, in the absence of structural remains, religious sites can be distinguished by "the repetitive act of making distinctive offerings of bronze figurines on simply prepared and demarcated surfaces" and by the fact that these figurines "show clear signs of expressive gesture and action." In general, on Etruscan religion, see Grummond and Simon (2006, with previous bibliography); on Venetic religion, see Maioli and Mastrocinque 1992.
100   Due to the presence of *scavi clandestini* (unofficial excavations).

landmark such as a spring, a lake, or a cave.[101] As Turfa specifies with regard to the Etruscans, a single one of these features was enough for people to make a dedication.[102]

As will be shown in the next chapter, Umbrian communities of the archaic period relied on some cult sites located, in a custom typical of Italic religion, in a prominent location of the landscape, either in strategic places or those of natural significance, from mountain peaks to caves and hills, or in the proximity of settlement sites.[103]

Notwithstanding the different locations, a common characteristic of these early shrines was their votive deposits. The most significant part of the votive material is composed of bronze (rarely lead) miniature figures of animals, men, women, and body parts, all usually under 10 cm. As mentioned in the previous chapter, the Umbrian production of votive bronzes has been amply studied by Colonna, who classified the Umbro-Sabellian bronzes into types and established that they were the product of workshops active either in southern or northern Umbria between the sixth and the fifth century BCE.[104] The next two chapters will show that this vast material has the potential to illuminate not only the ritual practices of the archaic inhabitants of the region but also the function of cult places.

4 Late Fourth–Early First Century BCE: The Roman Conquest of Umbria

The information passed down by Republican and imperial authors such as Livy, Polybius, Appian, Diodorus, and Cassius Dio allows us to partially reconstruct the history of Umbria during the Middle Republican period. However, one must take into consideration that these accounts are very selective and therefore problematic for several reasons. First, as these authors write about events well before their own day, they describe the expansionist enterprise of the Romans in terms of their understanding of the late Republican ideology

---

101   Amann 2011, 373. See also Chapter 6 for an overview of the topography and architecture of Umbrian sanctuaries.

102   De Grummond 2006, 92.

103   On the location of Italic cult places, see Bradley and Glinister 2013, 173–191.

104   The presence of these types beyond the Alps and the Po valley, where the Amelia, Foligno, Nocera Umbra, Esquiline, Fiesole, and Marzabotto types and bronze sheet figurines have been found, has led Colonna to hypothesize the presence of Umbrian peoples in these areas, perhaps "spinti a cercarsi una nuova patria a seguito delle invasion galliche, secondo il modello additato da Livio per i Reti," Colonna 1974, 19.

HISTORY OF THE UMBRIAN TERRITORY

of colonization. In this period, in fact, colonization was seen as "an ordered, state-controlled process which played a vital part in the success of the Roman empire," an idea also disseminated by Cicero.[105] Second, as they write under the influence of their own time and agendas they inevitably alter the narrative. In addition to this, even when they seem to draw on official records, their reliability can hardly be proved. As Bradley wisely advises, it is therefore essential to take into account the possible distortion and selective information provided by the ancient sources when we attempt to reconstruct the Roman conquest of the region.[106]

4.1 Fourth and Third Centuries BCE

The beginning of the fourth century BCE represents the first close involvement of Umbria in the expansionist dynamics of Rome. From the onset of this century, the Romans began to expand for the first time in areas adjacent to the region. Aiming at the control of the Tiber valley after the defeat of Falerii, in 391 BCE Rome attacked first Volsinii and then its allies, the Sappinates, a shadowy group mentioned by Livy that Sisani locates in Umbria.[107] Although the interpretation of Livy's passage is open to debate, the information at our disposal regarding the interactions between Romans and Umbrians becomes clearer by the end of the century. In 310 BCE, as a result of a war between Rome and the Etruscans and Umbrians, a brother of the consul Q. Fabius Maximus Rullianus led an expedition to Umbrian Camerinum on the Adriatic side of the Apennines, with the purpose of signing a treaty of *societate amitiaque*.[108] In 308 BCE,[109] the consul P. Decius Mus suppressed an Umbrian rebellion near Mevania. The initial resistance of the Umbrians was quickly sub-

---

105   Bradley 2006, 163. Cic. *Agr.* 2.73.

106   Bradley 2006, 164.

107   Liv. 5.31. 5. The location of this group is uncertain. Livy locates the *tribus Sapinia* on the northern part of Umbria, not far from the Gauls; Liv. 31. 2.6. Pliny mentiones the Sappinates among the Umbrian groups that do not exist anymore in the region during his time; Plin. *Nat.* 3.14.114. This evidence is enough for Sisani to locate them in Umbria "probabilment non lontano dal Tevere e dal confine volsiniese," likely in the Ameria or in the Tuder areas: Sisani 2006, 30. It is still Livy who recounts another encounter between Romans and Umbrians without specifying the date but writing *in Umbria Gallis hostibus adiunctis, ... gerebant bellum* (Liv. 9.19.3). According to Sisani, this information relates to a Gallic invasion, which, from the North, passed through Umbria to confront the Romans. However, this is pure speculation as it is based only on one, unreliable passage by Livy.

108   Liv. 9.36.7.

109   Liv. 9.41. 8–10.

dued by the Romans; Umbrians capitulated within two days, and the Ocriculani were accepted *in amicitiam*.[110]

In the years following the battle of Mevania, Roman military activity in the region confirmed Umbria's role as a crucial node in Rome's progressive expansion toward the inland of Etruria and its northern extremities. In 300 BCE, the Romans besieged the Umbrian *oppidum* of Nequinum, located at a crucial position that allowed them to reach the Adriatic coast through the Apennines.[111] After the treachery of two townsman, in 299 BCE[112] the Romans established the colony of Narnia and achieved the twofold aim of preventing an Umbrian invasion (Livy specifies that the colony was sent as an outpost *contra Umbros*)[113] and securing the route towards the north, threatened by the Gauls.[114]

As a reaction to the inevitability of Roman dominance over central Italy, shortly after their defeat at Nequinum, the Umbrians joined forces with the Etruscans, the Samnites (who were fighting the third Samnite War against the Romans), and the Gauls.[115] In 295 BCE, after alternating victories and defeats, the Roman army subdued the unified enemy force at Sentinum, at the border between Umbria and Picenum (in the modern region of Le Marche) and occupied the Gallic territory between the rivers Esinus and Rubicon.[116]

Roman expansion in Umbria seems to have been completed in the central years of the third century BCE. The Umbrian centers of Fulginiae and Plestia were incorporated into the Roman state and given *civitas sine suffragio*;[117] the

---

110   The friendship with *Ocriculum* represented an important step in the Roman advance towards north. This center, in fact, occupied a strategic location overlooking the Tiber valley and controlled one of its ports.

111   Liv. 10. 9.8–9.

112   Liv. 10.10.1.

113   Liv. 10.10.5.

114   Liv. 10.10.6–12.

115   Liv. 10.18.2.

116   Liv. 10. 24–31. The participation of the Umbrians in this battle remains dubious. Livy notes that Etruscans and Umbrians were absent from the battle; Polybius concurs with this, although at 30.5 he reports that some of his sources included both peoples at Sentinum. The *Fasti Triumphales* list the triumph of Fabius Maximus Rulianus at Sentinum over Gauls, Samnites, and Etruscans, leaving aside the Umbrians. Stephen Oakley is skeptical of the participation of the Umbrians in this battle. He argues that if the Umbrians were involved in it, the Roman sources would not have marginalized their presence, but, conversely, they would have enhanced the danger faced by the Romans. Sisani opts for a more cautious reading of the sources and concludes that Umbrians participated only marginally in the battle. Sisani 2009, 46; Oakley 2005, 289.

117   Communities granted this status shared the private privileges and obligations of Roman citizenship (*commercium, connubium,* and *militia*) but without the possibility of voting in political elections. The exact dynamics of these types of agreement are elusive. The

HISTORY OF THE UMBRIAN TERRITORY

praefectura of Interamna Nahars,[118] the colonies of Sena Gallica, Ariminum, and Spoletium, and the market town Forum Flaminii were founded.[119] The triumph over the Sassinates, who occupied the northern border of the region, is recorded in 266 BCE, and the final capitulation of the Umbrians in 268–265 BCE.[120] Until the first century BCE, when they opposed the Romans during

---

main problem in determining the details of these agreements is that ancient authors apply this category to communities that had different statuses in relation to Rome. Centers such as Capua could retain their magistrates and local administration, which continued to function independently after the change of status. However, in the case of Anagnia, the concession of the status of citizens without the vote at the end of the fourth century BCE was considered a punishment for rebelling against Rome. Consequently, the city was deprived of autonomy, and magistrates could only perform religious tasks. While Mouritsen (2007, 150–155) suggests that the concept of *civitas sine suffragio* was invented in the late second century BCE and is, therefore, a fiction, Torelli (2016, 265) hypothesizes that this status varies over the centuries. If, at the beginning of the fourth century, it had a favorable connotation and was granted as a type of honor to an allied community (e.g., Caere), starting at the end of the century it implied a loss of self-government and the obligation to serve in the Roman army. Both Plestia and Fulginiae seem to have received Roman citizenship *optimo iure* as praefecturae by the end of the third century BCE. For a discussion of the evidence of the Roman status of these two settlements, see Bradley 2000, 140–143 and Sisani 2007, 271–273 with previous bibliography.

118   Bradley (2000, 129–138) argues that Interamna was a Latin colony, but see Fora (2002) and Sisani (2007, 165–168) for arguments against this interpretation. Sisani suggests that Interamna Nahars was born as a *praefectura* in coincidence with viritane deductions in the area, which he believes are dated to the third century BCE (2007, 146–150). The only juridical difference between the two statuses was the right to vote. While the inhabitants of a praefectura were all Roman citizens and thus could vote in Rome, those of Latin colonies could vote for one tribe in Rome if they lived in the city at the time of the election: Carlà-Uhink 2017, 348. In either of these two instances, what seems to be certain is that the foundation of Interamna did not erase all indigenous political and social structures but should instead be seen as an addition to the existing situation. Bradley has convincingly demonstrated the presence of local people after the Roman conquest. As he points out (2000, 133), the presence of an imperial inscription recording the foundation of the city 704 years earlier shows that the memory that the city foundation pre-dated the arrival of settlers survived at least until the imperial period. This awareness could suggest that the pre-existing Umbrian community was incorporated into the city, regardless of its status as a Latin colony or as a Roman praefectura.

119   For the colonies: Liv. *Per.* 20; Vell. Pat. 1.14.8. For Forum Flaminii: Strab. 5.2.10. Fora were typically new foundations created by a Roman magistrate (Flaminius in this case) in connection with the construction of a road along which the forum was situated. Forum Flaminii almost certainly owed its existence to the building of the Via Flaminia. Here, in fact, the two branches of the Flaminia met again to cross the Apennines on their way to the Adriatic.

120   Liv. *Epitom.* 15.

the Social War, the Umbrians remained generally allied with them and provided support and troops.

From the middle of the third century, important roads were built to connect Umbrian centers with other conquered areas.[121] In 241 BCE, the construction of the Via Amerina, which led from Falerii to Ameria, connected Umbrian centers with northern Latium and to the Etruscan cities of Perugia and Clusium.[122] Most importantly, the Via Flaminia, opened in 220 BCE, became a fundamental route across central Italy.[123] This road crossed the Apennines from Rome to Ariminum on the Adriatic coast and granted the Romans access to the Po valley. Furthermore, the new road passed through the colonies that had been founded in Umbria just a few decades before and thus strengthened Roman control over these territories.[124]

Treaties represented another way Rome controlled those communities in the region that were not given Roman citizenship (*civitates sine suffragio*) or colonized.[125] As already mentioned, Camerinum and Ocriculum stipulated treaties with Rome. To these treaties, Cicero adds a *foedus* between Iguvium and Rome, which was likely stipulated sometime after 292 BCE.[126] Although ancient sources mention only these three *foedera*, we can add other Umbrian towns to the list of allies of Rome. It is likely that the inhabitants of Tuder, Ameria, Mevania, and Asisium, who were not Roman citizens until the Social War (Tuder and Ameria)[127] and who had preserved their local magistracies until 90 BCE (Mevania and Asisium), had been of allied status.[128] In addition to these centers, Polybius mentions a contingent of Umbrians among the allied armies that aided Rome against the Gauls in 225 BCE.[129] These brief mentions,

---

121   Dionysius of Halicarnassus is the only source that mentions a third road, the Via Curia. Although its exact path remains unclear, scholars agree it passed through Reate and connected the Sabine territory (conquered in 290 BCE) with Interamna Nahars in Umbria: Sisani 2006, 122.

122   Frederiksen and Ward Perkins 1957 give a detailed description of this Roman road.

123   Potter 1979, 102–104.

124   Not for nothing Ray Laurence argues that this road created a "Rome-centered" geography, which enabled Latin colonies and allied communities to be linked among themselves and to Rome: Laurence 1999, 23.

125   The fact that the Umbrians are recorded as *socii* when they provided troops to Rome in 279 BCE against Pyrrhus of Epirus, and in 225 BCE and 205 BCE against the Gauls, may suggest that the Romans concluded *foedera* with the Umbrian peoples after the victory at Sentinum in 292 BCE: Sisani 2006, 100–115.

126   Cic. *Balb.* 46–47. With regard to the *foedus* with Iguvium, see Sisani 2001, 225–230.

127   Sisenn. 111 P.

128   For a list of these inscriptions, see Sisani 2006, 101, note 10.

129   Polyb. 2.24: οἱ δὲ τὸν Ἀπεννῖνον κατοικοῦντες Ὄμβροι καὶ Σαρσινάτοι συνήχθησαν εἰς δισμυρίους, μετὰ δὲ τούτων Οὐένετοι καὶ Γονομάνοι δισμύριοι.

HISTORY OF THE UMBRIAN TERRITORY

combined with the epigraphic data from administratively independent centers during the late Republican period, leave open the possibility that other Umbrian communities had treaties with Rome.[130]

It is not clear what the status of allied communities entailed. Based on Cicero's discussion of Roman treaties, scholars have suggested that some treaties were *aequii* and some *iniquii*. However, as Ernst Badian points out, the unequal treaty, where the second party was required to acknowledge and respect the greatness of the Roman people, is unlikely to have been official.[131] Notwithstanding the possible distinctions between individual treaties, the epigraphic and literary evidence suggests that these peoples remained independent, with the obligation to raise and pay troops for Rome and to follow Roman foreign policy.[132] The number of men levied by each community was fixed in a list kept in Rome and called the *formula togatorum*.[133]

4.2 Second and First Centuries BCE

The ancient sources at our disposal for the period between the second century BCE and the Social War are not particularly comprehensive, for Umbria is mentioned only in a few sporadic instances. In 199 BCE a commission of *triumviri*, following a demand from Narnia, was established to increase the number of inhabitants in the colony.[134] The latest colonial settlements are Pisaurum in 184 BCE and Forum Sempronii in 133–130 BCE, founded after the implementation of the *lex Sempronia agraria*.[135] Cicero and other authors mention an Umbrian presence among Marius' troops at the end of the second

---

130 Bradley (2000, 121–122) adds fourteen more Umbrian centers to the list of the cities with a well-known treaty with Rome.

131 Badian 1958, 25–28.

132 The fact that Iguvium and Todi could mint their own coinage indicates their local sovereignty. For coinage as a sign of political organization, see Bradley 2000, chapter 4, s. 6. With respect to the clauses of the *foedera* between Roman and the Umbrian peoples, the only exception seems to be the *foedus* with Camerinum, which had greater freedom in choosing whether to send troops to help Rome or not. Liv. 38, 45, 13.

133 The measures contained in this document are not clear as there are no sources that elucidate them. In the *lex agraria* of 111 BCE it is mentioned that "all allies or members of the Latin name, from whom Romans are accustomed to demand soldiers in the land of Italy *ex formula togatorum*"; see Erdkamp 2007, 116–117. As mentioned above in this chapter, communities' ability to conduct the levy is also considered by Bradley as a further sign of the organization of the region into a city-state communal structure by the time of the conquest.

134 Liv. 32, 6–7. ***.

135 This law entailed the redistribution of public land and its *adsegnatio* to new owners. The nature of this measure is explained by Appian (*BCiv.* I.10). For the foundation of the colony of Pisaurum, see Liv. 39, 44, 10.

76   CHAPTER 4

century BCE.[136] In some instances, beneficiaries of Marius, such as the Camertine cohorts, M. Annius Appius of Iguvium, the Latin colonist, and T. Matrinus of Spoletium, received individual grants of Roman citizenship.

In 91 BCE, Umbrian and Etruscan aristocrats opposed Livius Drusus' proposal to give Roman citizenship to the *socii italicii*.[137] This program, which included distribution of land to poorer citizens and Roman citizenship for all the Latins and Italian allies, threatened the local Umbrian aristocrats, who feared losing their lands.[138] Following a request of the consul, a contingent of Umbrians and Etruscans came to Rome, where they may have played a part in Drusus' murder.[139] The failed scheme to offer Roman citizenship to the Italics triggered the outbreak of the Social War.[140] In 91 BCE and the first part of 90 BCE, neither Umbrians nor Etruscans joined the Italic forces against Rome. However, in 90 BCE, some unidentified Umbrian communities participated in the rebellion a few months before the *lex Iulia* was established.[141] This law, which marked the end of the *bellum italicum* for most Italic communities, allowed the inclusion of all Roman allies within the citizen body and the grant of municipal status to their cities.[142] The municipal ruling class could now openly participate in the Roman political process and lead their communities in support of or in opposition to decision-making in Rome.

The concession of Roman citizenship virtually concluded the process of conquest and incorporation of Umbria into the Roman state. The loss of formal autonomy for the Umbrian centers marked the beginning of a new chapter in the history of this region.

---

136   Cic. *Balb.* 46; 48; Val. Max. 5.2.8; Plut. *Mor.* 202C–D. For a discussion on the different ways to acquire Roman citizenship see Harris 1971, 192–201.

137   App. *BCiv.* 1.36.162. See also the critical reading by Crawford 2012, 737 and 2014, 209–211. Umbrians and Etruscans were the only two groups who opposed both the *lex agraria* and the *rogatio de sociis*. On these issues, see Asdrubali Pentiti 1981–1982.

138   App. *BCiv.* 1.35.

139   App. *BCiv.* 1.36.164.

140   For an extensive treatment on the municipalization of Italy see Bisham 2007, 205–404; Dart 2015. The latter also assesses the repercussions of the Social War, investigating the legacy of the insurgency during the civil wars, and considers its role in reshaping Roman and Italian identity on the peninsula in the last decades of the Republic. For the strategy of urban renewal after the Social War, see Gabba 1994.

141   App. *BCiv* 36.162–164. For a discussion on Umbria's participation to the War, see Harris 1971, 212–229.

142   As Harris (1970, 230) suggests, it is reasonable to hypothesize that a *senatus consultum* was passed to enfranchise the towns that remained in arms during the war.

HISTORY OF THE UMBRIAN TERRITORY

5   Conclusions

Thus far, I have delineated the trajectory of ancient Umbrian history up to the Social War of the early first century BCE. Archaic Umbria appears to have been open to a range of cultural influences from Italy and the wider Mediterranean world. As shown above, the attitudes toward death and burial and symbols of power and wealth linked Umbrian cultural practices with other regions of the Italian peninsula, such as Samnium, Etruria, and Latium. Starting in the seventh century BCE, material evidence from the cemeteries of the region (mainly Interamna, Spoletium, Plestia, and Iguvium) shows that the aristocratic class differentiated itself from the rest of society by means of prestigious goods, some of which were imported from the eastern Mediterranean through Greek traders frequenting the Adriatic coast. Other goods reached this social class through the other major routes that crossed the region, such as the routes from Etruria to Picenum, and the route along the Tiber valley from Volsinii and southern Etruria to Perusia and central Umbria.

In addition to this, the presence of upland hillforts and their organization demonstrates ties with the later Italic urbanization processes in regions such as Samnium and (contemporary) settlements outside Italy in Britain and Gaul.[143] Lastly, the presence of cult places within pre-Roman Umbrian communities and their connection to the territory find parallels in contemporary developments in Greece, northern Italy, and Etruria.

Unlike inland areas such as Plestia and southern areas such as Terni, the areas more closely connected to the Etruscan centers that were situated along communication routes underwent important urban and socio-economic transformation from the end of the fifth century BCE and particularly in the fourth century. The evidence from several pre-Roman centers shows that a new social class took the place of the archaic aristocracy, and urban development became more consistent than in the previous centuries. This new oligarchy, whose presence is visible from the region's necropoleis, found in the new urban structure the social base for its power and the means to control wide territories. Characteristic of the end of the society of the *principes* is the absence of grave goods related to war and the adoption of other modes of self-representation such as strigils and imports of pottery from Etruria and the ager Faliscus as well as

---

143   Due to the lack of excavation data, the date and function of Samnite hillforts have been largely overlooked. However, ongoing studies in the modern region of Lucania and Campania are revealing new information not only on the function of hillforts but also on their organization; see Hoer 2020. For hillforts in Britain and Gaul, see Harding 2012; Oswald et al .2013 with previous bibliography.

intense urban and suburban building activity. Recent excavations at Gualdo Tadino have shown how these new settlements were organized: dwellings had dry-laid stone foundations and wooden supports, with flat and curved roof tiles. With respect to cult places, the presence of architectural terracottas and revetment slabs in the fourth century at the suburban sanctuaries of Pantanelli at Amelia and of Monte Santo at Todi is indicative of Etruscan influence. It is perhaps due to the gradual Roman expansion in Central Italy, and to a lesser extent to the Gallic presence in northern Italy, that during this period some Umbrian centers, such as Ocriculum, Ameria, Spoletium, and Bettona, organized themselves with stone-built city walls and gates that surround their main religious sites.

The last four centuries of the first millennium represent a watershed in the history of the region. Following the expansion of Rome, new cities were founded, some centers gained Roman citizenship but without the right to vote, and some others developed *foedera* with the Urbs. Strategic roads were built to strengthen and connect the conquered territories: the Via Amerina, connected northern Lazio with the Umbria and the Etruscan cities of Perugia and Chiusi, and the Via Flaminia crossed the whole Umbria up to the Marche and the Adriatic (Rimini).

Many scholars consider this period (third and second century BCE) crucial to the political and socio-cultural transformation of Umbria. Above all, they have rushed to the conclusion that most of the changes of this period are linked to the imposition of Roman customs. The list of changes imputable to Rome is long, but a few deserve special note.

The construction of the roads Amerina and Flaminia has been regarded as the main factor that facilitated the adoption of Roman ways. These roads are considered a powerful tool for the spread and the assimilation of Roman models and the subsequent deconstruction of the original local cultural substrate. According to this view, the arrival of Latin and Roman people to the newly founded colonies enhanced the process of acculturation.[144]

The army represents another factor that scholars see as contributing to the alleged "acculturation" process. According to some, since the recruiting systems of Republican Rome required the Italic allies to contribute soldiers to Rome,

---

144   As mentioned in the first chapter, in the past two decades the view of Roman colonization as an acculturation process and of colonies as a medium for this process has been strongly criticized by scholars working mainly in Latium, Etruria, and Samnium. For a more general overview of Roman colonization and its impact on Italic territories, see Bradley 2006, Stek and Pelgrom 2014, Scopacasa 2015 with previous bibliography. For a discussion of Roman colonization and its effects on the sacred sphere see Chapter 2.

HISTORY OF THE UMBRIAN TERRITORY 79

the participation of Umbrians in the Roman military facilitated the process of integration in the Roman world.[145]

Assumptions about the other types of material evidence also loom large in the scholarship on Umbria during the Roman period. Black gloss pottery and votive deposits provide examples. In the region, the growth of Roman political influence is paralleled by an increase in imports of black gloss pottery (such as the *petites estampilles*) from Latium and the ager Faliscus, which have been interpreted as a sign of Roman dominance.[146] Finally, as noted in the first chapter, the presence of the anatomical votives has been considered as conclusive evidence of this process. Sisani, who considers the changes that happened during the years of Roman conquest as a wholesale consequence of a planned strategy,[147] interprets the diffusion of anatomical votives in the region as "un indicatore non equivoco di presenze coloniali."[148]

These views are clearly based upon an outdated view of Roman expansion as a unilateral and purely hegemonic phenomenon for the conquest and control of Italy. They have been notoriously put forth by Mommsen, who in his work *Römische Geschichte* wrote that "their [the Romans'] object was the subjugation of Italy, which was enveloped more closely from year to year in a network of Roman fortresses and roads."[149] This consensus has been subject to dispute on a number of levels. It does not consider the complex interchange of cultural ideas between individual Romans and locals that took place during the last centuries of the Republic.[150]

Indeed, when we take a closer look at the archaeological and literary evidence, we get the impression that the process of Roman expansion into this region had a lesser impact on the local population and was a more complicated process than has been traditionally assumed.

One of these pieces of evidence comes from the epigraphical record that mentions Umbrian political institutions. Two identically named members of the Babrius family are mentioned in two inscriptions from Assisium, one written in the Umbrian language and Latin script,[151] and the other in the Latin

---

145   Harris 1971, 170.
146   Bonomi Ponzi 2006, 66.
147   Sisani 2006.
148   Sisani 2006, 151–152; Bonomi Ponzi 2006, 65.
149   Mommsen 1869, 474.
150   Most of these contributions are mentioned in Chapter 2 in the discussion of cultural change. For a more general discussion of the latest developments see Pelgrom and Stek 2014 and the several contributions to the *Companion to Roman Italy* (Cooley 2016).
151   Um 10: Crawford 2011, 101–102: ager. emps .et termnas .oht(retie)c(aie).u.uistinie.ner.t.babr (ie) Maronatei uois(ie). ner. propartiet. u. uoisiener sacre. Stahu. "A-field bought and

80   CHAPTER 4

language and script.[152] Both inscriptions recall two offices held by Nero Babrius, first the *maro* and then the *uthor*. Both offices were probably already used by Umbrian communities by the sixth BCE; the maronate pertained to the construction of buildings and public monuments,[153] while the *uthor* was a public magistrate who was given a special role during the sacrifices in honor of Puemun-Vesuna.[154]

---

bounded in-the-auctorship of-Cauius/Gaius Vistinius (son)-of-Vibius/Vibis (Osc.) (and) Nero Babrius (son)-of-Titus (and) in-the-maronateship of-Voisienus Propartius (son)-of-Nero (and) Titus Voisienius (son)-of-Vibius/Vibis(Osc.). I-stand sacredly." This inscription refers to a field that has been bought and delimited during the period of office of two *uthors*, C. Vastinius and Nero Babrius, and two *marones*, Voisienus Propartius and Titus Voisienus. In this text, all Umbrian inscriptions are mentioned according to Rix's (2002) catalog of inscriptions.

152   *CIL* 11.390: Post(umus) Mimesius C(ai) f(ilius), T(itus) Mimesius Sert(oris) f(ilius), Ner(o) Capidas C(ai) f(ilius) Ruf(- - -), Ner(o) Babrius T(iti) f(ilius), C(aius) Capidas T(iti) f(ilius) C(ai) n(epos), V(ibius) Voisienus T(iti) f(ilius) marones murum ab fornice ad circum et fornicem cisternâmq(ue) d(e) s(enatus) s(ententia) faciundum coiravere. This inscription is carved over an arch that leads to a Roman cistern and is dated to the second BCE. It records the building of a terrace wall that extended from the arch of the cistern to another arch near the circus during the office of six *marones*, among whom we find Nero Babrius.

153   The civic office of the *maro* is a local Umbrian magistracy and is attested as a collegiate office of two. Since the office doubles the Etruscan MarunuX, it has been suggested that it had become part of the political institution of Umbrian communities at least since the fourth century BCE (Bradley 2000, 258). Indeed, it is during this century that the great Etruscan centers, such as Volsinii and Perusia, began to exert influence on Umbrian communities. From the epigraphic evidence, it is clear that the sphere of influence of the *marones* was limited to the construction of buildings and public monuments. The parallel between maroship and the aedileship is further strengthened by the absence of this office from the Iguvine Tablets, whose religious content excludes the public undertakings associated with the *marones*. This office is attested at Asisium, Fulginiae (Um 6), Tadinum (Um 7).

154   Devoto 1947, 370. This office is mentioned also in the Iguvine Tablets (TI va 2, 15) and at Maevania (Um 25). Here, the *uthor* presides over two moments of the acts and rites of the Atiedian Brethren. In order to define the role and status of this magistracy, early scholarship focused primarily on the mention of the *uthor* in the Iguvine Tablets, by far the most studied among the Umbrian inscriptions. Vetter, Buck, and others (Vetter 1953, 211–212; Buck 1904, 301, Coli 1964, 142–143) held that it was an internal office of the Atiedian Brotherhood, perhaps even appointed by its members, while Devoto maintained that it was a public magistrate who was given a special role during the sacrifices in honor of Puemun-Vesuna. This controversy seems to have been resolved in favor of Devoto, when he found the inscription from Maevania, where the *uthor* is mentioned after the dead man's name in the style of a public magistracy. Recently, the presence of the *uthor* in the Umbrian *cursus honorum* has been further proved by Weiss (2010, 77). The author examines inscription no. 5 and rightly argues that this boundary-marking inscription supports Devoto's argument about the political role of the *uthor*.

Nero's retention of local offices and his use of two languages and scripts to record his achievements are significant for two reasons. First, the former shows that members of the Umbrian elite retained strong political functions in the region during the second century BCE. Second, the latter suggests that the use of languages and scripts in inscriptions is the result of a conscience decision made by the elites. Local magistrates had diverse languages and scripts at their disposal that they could deploy in their civic inscriptions. It is reasonable to imagine that this choice was linked to political behaviors that would have a measurable effect on eventual outcomes.

The recent suggestion by Terrenato that the role of elite agendas ought to be considered seems to be particularly suitable for the case just presented. He encourages consideration of the political scene of the Italians, the existence of factions, and even actual political parties that appropriate the Roman imperial machinery to benefit a specific factional group rather than a political abstraction such as "the Roman empire."[155] It is reasonable to suppose that the decision to have their local magistracies represented in the Latin language, Latin script, or Umbrian language underlies the possibility of gaining some sort of public benefit in response to changing local balances of power and evolving political discourse. Such advantages could be, for example, maintenance of social order, dominance over the local community, and control over tribal formation and composition. The existence of a variety of options open to the Umbrian elite during the period of Roman expansion helps to account for the emergence of diverse of identities found in these inscriptions. this phenomenon aligns with Terrenato's concept of "brokerage," which denotes the intermediation between the burgeoning capital and the Italian communities.: "the adoption of Roman political formulas can mask persistence of local power structures and long standing alliances between aristocratic clans" that "managed to survive and thrive after the Roman conquest and are now using Latin political terminology to legitimize further their dominant position."[156]

---

155 Terrenato 2014, 45–60. The new ongoing project "Non-Roman Elites: Tracking persistence and change in central Italy through the Roman conquest," of which I am part, has the potential to shed further light on the role of individual elite members during the period of Roman expansion. By focusing on two bodies of evidence—burial evidence for local elites and onomastic evidence from regional epigraphy relating to elite family groups, some of which can be reconstructed in stemmatic lineages—in central Italy, this project explores new models for understanding the negotiations as Rome expanded and incorporated new elites into her imperial project. Early results of this research group were presented in January 2019 at the AIA conference in San Diego.

156 Terrenato 2008, 240.

The active role of local people and some sort of factionalism between them and the Romans is also evident from Livy's account of the establishment of the colony of Nahars. In passage 10.10.1, Livy narrates that this city was taken by the Romans thanks to the treachery of two townsmen who made a tunnel and came by this secret passage to the Roman outposts. Interestingly, Bradley notes that this action may be an example of the help offered to the Romans by local elites, who may have had an interest in aiding the Romans. As in the case of the political action of Nero, it is possible to interpret the action of the two townsmen within the frame of elite factionalism and bonds with the Romans, as noted by Terrenato. Nero, through his diplomatic choices, and the townsfolk, by aiding the Romans, could have engaged in reciprocal actions to maintain the privileges of their traditional structures, such as Nero's leadership and the townsfolk's autonomy. The presence of individual agendas underscores the complexity of the consequences of Roman expansion in the region.

A close consideration of the military conflicts between the Romans and the Umbrians also prompts caution when assessing the effects of the Roman expansion. As we have seen, ancient sources account for a series of important wars against the Umbrians, starting at the end of the fourth century. Scholars have traditionally assumed that these wars were part of a long-term vision of Roman imperialist policy. However, recent scholarship has questioned the nature of the wars waged by Rome in the fourth and third centuries BCE and argued that they were haphazard conflicts of short duration rather than strategically planned enterprises.[157] In this respect, the Samnite Wars represent a case in point. Tim Cornell has closely and critically analyzed the accounts of these wars written by early imperial authors and has demonstrated that the Samnite Wars consisted of a series of unrelated clashes rather than a long military operation.[158] Bradley's exploration of Cornell's claims about Roman imperialism emphasizes the importance of the unpredictability of Roman behavior and, consequently, the unlikelihood of a master plan behind Roman expansion.[159]

The conflicts between the Umbrians and the Romans seem to follow a pattern similar to the one just described. Livy describes the conflicts against the Umbrian communities of Ocriculum and Nahars as lasting only a couple of days. There is no reason to doubt Livy's information as he, famous for using every opportunity to add rhetorical elaboration and sensational and romantic coloring, would not have missed an opportunity to aggrandize at length

---

157   For a discussion, see Cornell 2004; Stek 2015, 6–8; Terrenato 2014.
158   Cornell 2004, 115–131.
159   Bradley 2014, 60–73.

HISTORY OF THE UMBRIAN TERRITORY

these Roman campaigns in Umbria. In addition to this, the conflict with Nahars ended with the favorable terms of *amicitia*, one of the many *foedera* that Rome negotiated with local communities. These dynamics seem to suggest that the Roman expansion in the region developed through a series of skirmishes where the Romans most likely followed short-term political and perhaps even personal goals. As the cases of Asisium and Nahars illustrate, not only the Romans but also the local population engaged in such political and personal agendas.

Among scholars studying Umbria, Bradley is the only one who argues that many of the social and urban changes of the Roman period are caused not only by external factors (i.e., Rome) but also by internal ones. However, his call for equal attention to local factors alongside Romanization in the region's history has not gained widespread acceptance among scholars.[160]

In the next chapter, I will examine the development of the sanctuaries of the region and their votive objects from the archaic period up to the end of the Roman expansion process (first century BCE). It will become clear that these objects not only problematize the simplistic views of unilateral cultural exchange but also illuminate the dynamics of acquisition and maintenance of local traditions at play during this period.

---

160   He is echoed by Amann 2011.

CHAPTER 5

A Micro-Scale Approach to the Archaeology of Umbrian Cult Places

1 Introduction

To gain a thorough understanding of the role of Umbrian sanctuaries, the rituals performed there, and the changes that occurred after Roman expansion, it is necessary to explore the development of each sacred space separately. Therefore, this chapter takes a micro-scale approach to Umbrian sanctuaries, examining their topography, architecture, and votive offerings from the sixth century BCE to the beginning of the first century BCE. The focus is on the importance of each sanctuary to the community before and after the Romans established their presence in the region. As architectural elements are often absent in both pre-Roman and Roman period sacred spaces, the attention is on the votive offerings, which provide significant insight into the religious practices in ancient Umbrian sanctuaries.

This chapter categorizes cult places into groups based on their topographical location within the Umbrian territorial region, primarily determined by the geomorphology of the territory. These groups include southern Umbria, the Umbrian valley, northern Umbria, and Apennine Umbria. The focus is on three key aspects of each sanctuary. Firstly, the topographic location is outlined to provide a context within the contemporary settlement system of the region. Secondly, where relevant, the architectural aspects and spatial organization are discussed. Lastly, an analysis of the votive material is presented. The discussions are organized chronologically, in line with the chronology of Italic religions presented in Chapter 1. The chapter begins with the archaic and classical period (sixth–fourth century BCE) and proceeds to the Hellenistic period (late fourth–early first century BCE).

The presented data are the result of an integrated analysis of various sources, including published, unpublished, and archival material. To understand the changes that occurred in religious spaces following Roman encroachment, it is necessary to utilize all available information, including objects that survive only in archaeological documentation. The focus of the discussion of the votive material is on figurative votive offerings, the most widespread type of votive offering in Umbria, particularly before the Roman conquest.[1] This

---

1 All votive types are explained in Appendix 1. In this chapter, they are always described after

© CHARLES UNIVERSITY, FACULTY OF ARTS, PRAGUE, 2025 | DOI:10.1163/9789004712171_006
This is an open access chapter distributed under the terms of the CC BY-NC-ND 4.0 license.

class of objects is examined in greater detail, drawing upon published and archival data as well as objects on display in museums and those stored in local depots.

In the conclusion, it is demonstrated how reviewing the architectural and ritual material from Umbrian sanctuaries can help debunk certain common assumptions regarding sacred spaces in central Italy. Should the widespread observance of the anatomical votive tradition be seen as an indication of a change in the cult sphere as a result of the gradual homogenization of Italy under Rome? Were rural cult places either abandoned or the object of the laissez-faire politics of Rome? The available data and new information collected for this study undermine the conventional scholarly interpretation of central Italian sanctuaries and the role of anatomical votives, thus falling in line with the most recent re-evaluation of sacred spaces advocated by scholars like Stek and Scopacasa.[2] In contrast to the prevailing scholarly consensus, the research findings reveal that sacred spaces remained vital during the Roman period, irrespective of their proximity to significant areas of Romanization, such as colonies or roads. Additionally, it is demonstrated that anatomical votives are not significantly related to the Roman presence in the region. This chapter calls for the abandonment of these conventional assumptions and concludes that the persistence of cult spaces and the apparent change in votive offerings should be examined by focusing on internal indigenous factors rather than solely attributing them to the hegemonic influence of Rome.

This chapter works in concert with the three appendices presented at the end of the book. All the votive figurines introduced in this chapter are linked in the footnotes to their database entry (abbreviation of the sanctuary site followed by a number) listed in Appendix 2 and to the photo catalog in Appendix 3.[3]

---

their first mention. The votive offerings whose rendering can noticeably vary, such as terracotta heads and anatomical votives, or those that are unique for certain sites, will be described on a case-to-case basis. The chronology, if not specified, is the one assigned to the objects by the archaeologists who studied or excavated the material. When this is unknown, I use comparanda from other sites in order to establish a plausible chronological framework. Comparanda are also used if they serve to better define the chronology proposed by the excavators.

2　See Chapter 2 on this topic.

3　Although all the heads, the anatomicals, and the offerings belonging to the group "Other" will be accompanied by a photo, in the case of the Umbrian bronze figurines, the repetitiveness of the types does not necessitate a photo for each specimen. Instead, this Appendix includes photos of the best-preserved specimens from each sanctuary.

1.1 *Methodology Notes*

Various factors hinder obtaining a clear understanding of the life of Umbrian sanctuaries and the role and function of their votive offerings. Firstly, a significant proportion of Umbrian cult places were excavated in the 1960s and 1970s, which meant that stratigraphic analysis and techniques were not frequently employed. Consequently, not all the sanctuaries presented in this chapter are equally documented, and only rarely are quantitative data on their materials available. This lack of consistency arises from differences in the level of site exploration and the degree of relevant research and available publications, as well as archival data. Second, Umbrian votives have not been found in their original depositional position. In some cases, votive objects have been found inside votive pits (such as at Pantanelli and Monte Acuto). However, over time, votive objects were removed to make space for other offerings, as seen in other parts of Italy and Greece.[4] Despite this removal, the sacred value of the votive objects was not lost, as they were often accumulated in votive pits, the so-called "votive deposits," in specific sanctuary areas and where rituals appropriate to their placement were conducted. In other cases, votive objects and other construction materials formed obliteration deposits. They filled wells and/or cisterns when sacred areas were abandoned (Monte Moro) or water facilities went out of use (Monte Torre Maggiore, Colle Mori).[5] In both cases, the accumulation of layers from different periods inside the pits means that the find context offers no information for the reconstruction of relative chronology. Each find can, therefore, be dated only by internal stylistic criteria.

Furthermore, the absence of remains from Umbrian sanctuaries, such as architectural terracottas or decorative elements, presents a challenge in establishing a chronological framework. Without these anchoring artifacts, excavators must rely solely on the findings within each deposit. Complicating matters, several Umbrian votives have been discovered accidentally on the surrounding surface (Monte Pennino, Monte Subasio), often due to the disturbance caused by more recent agricultural production (Monte Santo), or distributed across the sanctuary area in disturbed contexts (Monte Torre Maggiore, Monte San Pancrazio, Monte Moro, Monte Ansciano, La Rocca, Cancelli, Grotta Bella,

---

4 On relocating and burying offerings, see Murgan 2015. The author also discusses the terms employed to describe the different contexts containing depositions of dedicated objects.

5 As a few examples from Etruria show, when dismantled the material from sacred areas was still considered divinely imbued and therefore had to be handled with extreme care: see Nagy 2016.

A MICRO-SCALE APPROACH TO ARCHAEOLOGY   87

Campo La Piana, Colfiorito). As a result, the circumstances of the discovery impact not only the dating of the artifacts, which is often based on comparanda and stylistic criteria, but also determinations about the original purpose of the dedications. Additionally, many sites were looted before being fully excavated, making it difficult to determine the proportion of different votive types and the level of activity at each cult place. Even when archaeological investigations have recovered votive material, it is still challenging to draw accurate conclusions about the site's activity level based solely on the votive deposition. It is possible that some activities continued but left no archaeological evidence.

Therefore, generalization and simplifications are unavoidable in interpreting the available material and any graphics presented in this chapter should be viewed with the proviso that they can only include the potentially biased sample of the available material.

2 Southern Umbria

2.1 *Grotta Bella*

2.1.1 Topographic Location

The site is on the northeastern slope of Monte L'Aiola (756 m above sea level). This mountain is the easternmost extension of the Monti Amerini chain, between the Monte Castellari to the south and the Monte Pianicel Grande to the north. It now makes up the territory of Avigliano Umbro, eight kilometers from the town of Amelia (ancient Ameria) and some two kilometers east of the village of Santa Restituta.

The cult place appears to have been connected to a system of settlements whose fortifications have been identified on the summit of the Amerine hills on the Monte Castellari and the Monte Pianicel Grande. The fortified areas defined by these defensive walls controlled the east-west routes that connected the southern Umbrian centers of Tuder and Ameria with central Etruria. The fulcrum of this territorial organization was the Umbrian town of Ameria, where a permanent settlement seems to have existed at least since the sixth century BCE.[6] A mountainous path connected the cult place with both the Tiber valley and the pre-Roman routes that led to Ameria and were retraced by the Via Amerina in the third century BCE.

---

6   For more information on the settlement history of the Ameria territory, see paragraph 2.2. Pantanelli.

The first known historical reference to the cave's existence dates to 1902, when the geologist Bernardino Lotti had the opportunity to visit it. In a note, he briefly described the underground rooms and mentioned the discovery of a small terracotta head from the Roman period that he found in the Entrance Hall.[7] In addition, he recalled some tunnels in the deepest part of the cave that he did not dare to explore alone. The first scientific exploration of the cave and its innermost recesses took place half a century later. At the end of the 1950s, the site attracted the attention of the Gruppo Grotte Pipistrelli CAI of Terni (cavers from Terni, Umbria). In addition to visiting most of the hypogeal environments, the speleologists from Terni carried out the first topographical examination of the space and surveyed the site in the Catasto delle Grotte dell'Umbria (Cadaster of Umbrian caves, identification position: 19 U/TR). As a result of the speleological investigation, the cave was thoroughly described. At the same time, ancient artifacts, revealed by clandestine diggers, spurred professional archaeological interest for the first time.[8]

In 1970, the Soprintendenza alle Antichità dell'Umbria, in collaboration with the Department of Human Paleontology and Palethnology of the University of Milan, began the first archaeological investigation of the cave. During four consecutive campaigns, the research effort was concentrated on one external trench and three internal ones. In one of these internal trenches, the excavation of a deep stratigraphic sequence, explored to a depth of seven meters from the surface, allowed for the identification of three phases of occupation of the space.[9] The site had been inhabited from Neolithic times (5000–3000 BCE) until the late Bronze Age (1200–1000 BCE) and became a cult place from the archaic to the end of the imperial period (sixth century BCE to fourth century CE). However, from the first century CE to the fourth century CE, the votive offerings noticeably decreased compared to the previous centuries, suggesting more episodic use of the sacred space.[10]

---

7   Lotti 1902.

8   Mattioli 1968.

9   Guerreschi et al. 1992. Evidence of human occupation during the pre- and protohistoric period, from the fifth to the second millennium, can be found in both the first rooms (entrance and Entrance Hall) and the deepest rooms (secondary branches) of the cave. However, recent investigations have shown that there was a complete burial site in the cave, specifically in the Sala dello Scheletro. This suggests that in prehistoric times, there was a living area near the entrance of the cave and a burial area located in the deepest part of the cave. For more information on these earlier phases of occupation, see Zapelloni Pavia and Larocca 2023.

10   A preliminary archaeological report of this excavation was published by Arena (1975–1976). A detailed overview of its materials has been presented by Monacchi (1988) and more recently by Zapelloni Pavia (2020) and Zapelloni Pavia and Larocca 2023.

A MICRO-SCALE APPROACH TO ARCHAEOLOGY   89

In the 1990s, after a decade in which the cave appears to have been widely forgotten and its stratigraphy disturbed by looters, it became a regular destination of the Gruppo Speleologico Todi. This group, made up of professionals in all aspects of caves and cave systems, explored the entire underground system and discovered a number of new areas. In particular, in the deepest parts of the cave they revealed the presence of a room with a large scattering of human skeletal remains. Here, they found a skull embedded on the base of a massive stalagmite—hence the name Sala Dello Scheletro (Skeleton Hall). Unfortunately, this discovery was not followed by a thorough survey of the cave, and, once again, several decades passed before archaeological work in the cave resumed.

In 2019–2021, archaeologists and anthropologists from the Regional Center of Speleology "Enzo dei Medici," an organization specializing in speleo-archaeological research, and the aforementioned Gruppo Speleologico Todi investigated anew the Sala Dello Scheletro. They ascertained the archaeological importance of the site and rekindled scientific interest in the historical stratification of the cave.[11]

2.1.2   Sixth–Fourth Century BCE: Architectural and Spatial Distribution
The cave is set within the hard limestone of the slope of the Monte l'Aiola and consists of several underground segments (figure 2).[12] The first room, the so-called Entrance Hall, is massive: the major axis measures 40 m and the minor axis 30 m; its average height is about 10 m. From the most sunken sector of the Entrance Hall, three distinct tunnels continue into the cave. Each of them has been given a conventional name: 1) Via delle Strettoie (Narrow Passages Route); 2) Ramo delle Firme (Signature Branch); and 3) Condotta Preistorica (Prehistoric Passageway).

---

11   For an updated study of the cave see Larocca 2022 and Zapelloni Pavia and Larocca 2023.
12   For a thorough discussion on the spatial distribution of the cave, see Zapelloni Pavia and Larocca 2023.

90   CHAPTER 5

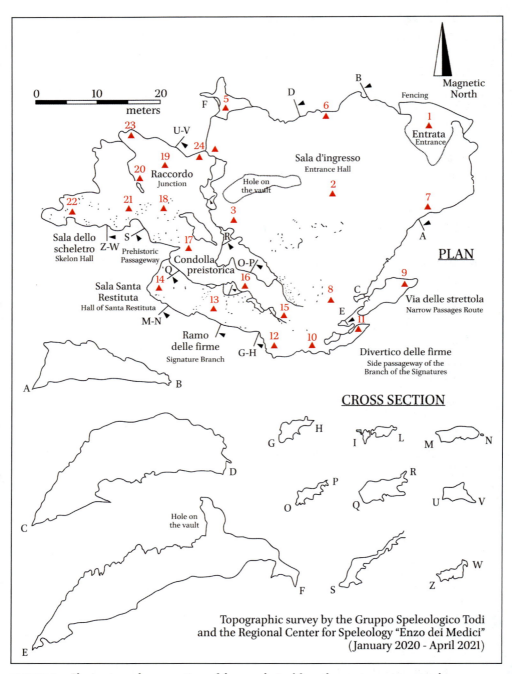

FIGURE 2   Planimetry and cross sections of the cave derived from the most recent topographic survey
(after Zapelloni and Larocca 2023, 40 fig. 1).

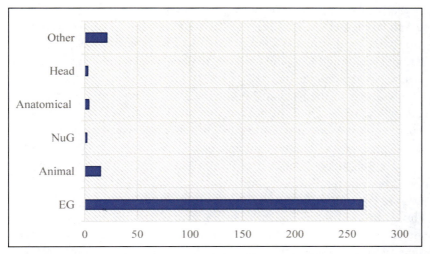

FIGURE 3　Graph showing the type distribution of the Grotta Bella votive figurines between the sixth and the fourth century BCE.

2.1.3　Sixth–Fourth Century BCE: Votive Material

The votive material attributed to this phase consists of twenty-four pieces of *aes rude* and two hundred and eighty-six figurines, mostly made out of bronze and a few of lead (figure 3).[13] Both the fragments of *aes rude* and the figurines were found in disturbed layers of soil during the excavation of the Entrance Hall, mixed with earlier and later objects.

The "Esquiline group" (EG) is, with two hundred and sixty-five specimens, the most attested type of votive figurine (figures A1–10). All figurines of this group have a flat, narrow, and relatively elongated body with stiff arms and legs. The legs are slender and pointed, while the head is elongated with grooves indicating the eyes and an incision representing the mouth. The arms may have transverse grooves to depict the fingers. There are twenty-six females, one hundred and two males, and thirty-five warriors. Females are depicted wearing a long tunic; males are naked with clear genital protuberances; warriors bear a highly schematic crest on their heads and their right arms are pierced to make space for a spear.[14]

13　Lead slugs found in the cave are likely related to the production *in loco* of the lead figurines: Monacchi 1988, 44.

14　Females: GB_41 GB_48 GB_49 GB_50 GB_51 GB_52 GB_53 GB_145 GB_152 GB_163 GB_164 GB_165 GB_166 GB_167 GB_168 GB_169 GB_170 GB_171 GB_205 GB_241 GB_8 GB_9 GB_292 GB_293 GB_294 GB_295. Males: GB_10 GB_47 GB_54 GB_55 GB_56 GB_58 GB_59 GB_60 GB_61 GB_62 GB_63 GB_64 GB_65 GB_66 GB_67 GB_70 GB_71 GB_72 GB_73

Similarly schematic in the rendering of the bodies are fifteen figurines of the type Animal (figure A11–14). These consist of six cows, one goat, two sheep, five pigs, and one unidentifiable animal.[15] Standard features of the type are elongated bodies, pointed feet, and anatomical details rendered by grooves or by small circles carved in the bronze.

Two figurines of the Nocera Umbra type (NuG) represent a warrior, identifiable by the presence of the helmet and a hole for a spear (figure A15,16).[16] The body of the warrior is presented in a flat, filiform style, with only the crest of the helmet rendered in three dimensions. The arms and legs are wide open and lack any significant detail, except for small grooves that suggest anatomical features. The figurine is supported by two spikes situated underneath the feet.[17]

Three votives present schematic heads and four reproduce anatomical parts of the body (figure A17–23). The heads of the former group (figure A21–23) are modeled and rendered like the heads of the schematic EG figures, with the eyes

---

GB_74 GB_75 GB_76 GB_77 GB_78 GB_79 GB_80 GB_81 GB_82 GB_83 GB_84 GB_85 GB_86 GB_87 GB_88 GB_89 GB_90 GB_91 GB_92 GB_93 GB_94 GB_95 GB_96 GB_97 GB_98 GB_99 GB_100 GB_101 GB_102 GB_103 GB_104 GB_105 GB_106 GB_107 GB_108 GB_109 GB_110 GB_111 GB_112 GB_113 GB_114 GB_115 GB_116 GB_117 GB_118 GB_119 GB_120 GB_121 GB_122 GB_123 GB_124 GB_125 GB_126 GB_127 GB_128 GB_129 GB_130 GB_131 GB_132 GB_133 GB_134 GB_135 GB_136 GB_137 GB_138 GB_139 GB_140 GB_141 GB_142 GB_143 GB_146 GB_186 GB_187 GB_188 GB_189 GB_190 GB_191 GB_192 GB_193 GB_194 GB_195 GB_196 GB_197 GB_198 GB_200 GB_201 GB_203 GB_204 GB_206 GB_207 GB_208 GB_209 GB_210 GB_211 GB_212 GB_213 GB_214 GB_215 GB_216 GB_217 GB_218 GB_220 GB_221 GB_222 GB_223 GB_224 GB_225 GB_226 GB_227 GB_228 GB_229 GB_230 GB_231 GB_232 GB_233 GB_234 GB_235 GB_236 GB_237 GB_238 GB_239 GB_240 GB_4 GB_37 GB_38 GB_39 GB_40 GB_57 GB_144 GB_147 GB_148 GB_149 GB_150 GB_151 GB_153 GB_156 GB_161 GB_162 GB_183 GB_184 GB_185 GB_199 GB_202 GB_1 GB_2 GB_3 GB_5 GB_13 GB_14 GB_15 GB_16 GB_19 GB_20 GB_21 GB_22 GB_23 GB_24 GB_25 GB_26 GB_28 GB_29 GB_30 GB_31 GB_32 GB_43 GB_44 GB_296 GB_297 GB_298 GB_299 GB_300 GB_301 GB_302 GB_303 GB_304 GB_305 GB_306 GB_307 GB_308 GB_309 GB_310 GB_311 GB_312 GB_313.

GB_6 GB_7 GB_11 GB_12 GB_17 GB_27 GB_33 GB_34 GB_35 GB_36 GB_42 GB_45 GB_46 GB_68 GB_69 GB_154 GB_155 GB_157 GB_158 GB_159 GB_160 GB_172 GB_173 GB_174 GB_175 GB_176 GB_177 GB_178 GB_179 GB_180 GB_181 GB_182 GB_314 GB_315. Warriors: GB_6 GB_7 GB_11 GB_12 GB_17 GB_27 GB_33 GB_34 GB_35 GB_36 GB_42 GB_45 GB_46 GB_68 GB_69 GB_154 GB_155 GB_157 GB_158 GB_159 GB_160 GB_172 GB_173 GB_174 GB_175 GB_176 GB_177 GB_178 GB_179 GB_180 GB_181 GB_182 GB_314 GB_315.

15   GB_242 GB_243 GB_244 GB_245 GB_246 GB_247 GB_248 GB_249 GB_250 GB_251.

16   GB_252 GB_253.

17   GB_242 GB_243 GB_244 GB_246 GB_248 GB_249 GB_250 GB_247 GB_287 GB_288 GB_289 GB_290 GB_245 GB_291 GB_251. GB_287–290 and GB_291 were recorded by Monacchi (1988, 79), but I could not locate these pieces.

A MICRO-SCALE APPROACH TO ARCHAEOLOGY   93

marked by small grooves and the mouth by a small horizontal incision. The neck is elongated and spiked at the end. The anatomical parts consist of two legs, one foot, and one arm (figure A17–20). The legs are extremely filiform, with little distinction between the upper and lower part. The foot is equally schematic with no rendering of the toes. The arm is represented outstretched and is supported at the elbow's level by a spike; the hand is missing due to a break running above the wrist.[18]

Twenty-one figurines belong to the group "Other." They stand out from the rest of Grotta Bella's figurines for two reasons. First, unlike bronze figurines, which are the result of a process of molding and casting, these are made out of lead sheets, which, still hot, were stamped with a mold and cut with shears or scissors along the edges. Second, they occur exclusively in the Amelia area (Grotta Bella and Pantanelli).[19] The group comprises six female figurines, six warriors, and nine decorated miniature shields (figure A23–32).[20] As suggested by Monacchi, the shields would originally have been molded together with the male figurines, of which there must, therefore, have been at least nine.[21]

Both female and male figures are represented in profile, except for the bust, which is frontal. The former group (figure A26–28) wear long tunics decorated either with a zig-zag motif or with wavy lines, visible also on the back. The hair is held in a sort of ponytail, and the anatomical details are rendered with small, embossed circles. The male figurines (figure A24–25) are shown with wide-open legs and wear short *chitoniskoi* and armor with shoulder straps held by bosses. Their right arms are lifted as in the act of throwing a spear or holding a sword.

The shields are decorated on both sides (figure A29–32). While the back-side of all specimens shows an arm fastened to the shield, the front one, the *episema*, presents three possible motifs. The first one (figure A29–31), attested

---

18   Heads: GB_279 GB_280 GB_281. Foot: GB_278. Legs: GB_275 GB_277. Arm: GB_276.
19   The choice of lead as a material for the figurines in the sanctuaries of Grotta Bella and Pantanelli could be influenced by the characteristics of the cults practiced there. Lead has been associated with various symbolic and mystical properties throughout history, including its connection to oracular and chthonic cults. The choice of locations for the sanctuaries, with Grotta Bella being underground and Pantanelli being connected to a necropolis, further suggests a connection to chthonic cults. These locations may have been considered spiritually significant and appropriate for conducting rituals dedicated to chthonian deities or ancestral spirits.
20   Females: GB_258 GB_259 GB_260 GB_261 GB_263 GB_263. Warriors: GB_262 GB_264 GB_265GB_255 GB_256 GB_257. Shields: GB_266 GB_267 GB_268 GB_269 GB_270 GB_271 GB_272 GB_273 GB_274.
21   Monacchi 1988.

on six specimens, consists of three schematic figures with outstretched arms arranged circularly under a bare tree with several wavy branches. Embossed circles fill the space and are arranged circularly on the outer edge of the *episema*. The second motif (figure A32) is attested on only a single specimen and shows a *gorgoneion* with wide-open eyes, a long nose, and a thin mouth with its tongue extended. The outer edge of the *episema* is decorated with a zig-zag pattern. The last motif (figure A33), also attested on one specimen, depicts a central circle surrounded by either waves or rays.

The closest comparisons to Grotta Bella's lead figurines of warriors, women, and shields are from Laconia. The ancient sanctuary of Artemis Orthia and the Menelaion have yielded a significant number of small figurines of cast lead dated between the eighth and the fourth century BCE, with a peak in the sixth century.[22] These Laconian figurines, carefully classified by Martin Boos, include winged figures, types identified as Olympian deities, warriors, and women. The women are festively dressed and turned either to the left or right, with their arms, in most cases, resting by their sides, with only the head shown in profile. The warrior figures are equipped with a helmet, a spear, a shield, and sometimes greaves. A distinctive feature of the warriors is the shield design which can consist of concentric circles around a central boss, straight lines radiating from a central boss, rosettes, curved lines radiating from a central boss, and, in a few cases, blazons (bucranium, scorpion, and cockerel).

The presence of similar votive offerings in two places in the Mediterranean illustrates how common figurative themes—such as the radiant sun, the male warrior, and the woman—could be adopted by faraway local manufacturers to create standardized votive types that could satisfy the request of the devotees without an expensive investment. Some motifs seem, however, to reflect individual choices and preferences of the worshiping communities. Like the Laconian votives, where artisans used a variety of motifs often inspired by local religious beliefs (demons and gods from the Greek pantheon), the shields depicting men under a tree may have drawn from local myths, local activities of the area (the harvest?),[23] and the ritual context of Grotta Bella. In support of the last interpretation, it is interesting to take note of the leafy motif engraved on the small temple model dedicated in the cave and dated to the third–second

---

22   Cavanagh and Laxton 1984, Muskett 2014, Boos 2000.

23   A similar iconography representing a harvest theme is recognizable in two black-figure Athenian amphoras from Etruria dated to the middle of the sixth century BCE (Beazley 1956, 273.11 and 270.50.). One side of the body of these vases depicts three men harvesting olives.

century BCE.[24] This motif and the tree depicted on the lead shields suggest a connection to the natural surroundings of the sacred cave and possibly evoke the presence of sacred groves, which were commonly found in pre-Roman and Roman Italy as important elements of sacred sites.[25]

2.1.4 Late Fourth–Early First Century BCE: Architectural Aspects and Spatial Organization

No architectural remains belonging to this phase have been unearthed in the cave.

2.1.5 Late Fourth–Early First Century BCE: Votive Material

The material from this phase has been found in disturbed layers inside the cave, mixed with materials from different periods. It consists primarily of ceramics, coins, a small terracotta model of a temple, four anatomical terracottas, and three bronze figurines (fig. 4).

Coins are attested with seventy-nine specimens, mainly asses of the prow series.[26] Besides the coins from the Roman Republic, six belong to the Romano-Campanian series and one appears to have been minted in Tuder. Ceramics include locally produced black gloss, mostly paterae, and miniature vases.

The anatomical terracottas are dated to the fourth–second century and include three feet and one breast (figure A34–45).[27] The terracotta breast (figure A34) is hemispherical and broadens sharply at the bottom. The nipple is rendered in high relief and has a light circular incision around it, indicating the areola. As for the terracotta feet, only the picture of one right foot survives in the archaeological documentation (figure A35). It terminates at the upper ankle, which continues to swell as it rises. The heel is rounded at the back, and the foot tapers at the center and widens toward the toes. These are indicated by small, indented lines that separate them. The bottom of the foot shows evidence of a sole.

The bronze figurines belong to the "Hellenistic worshiper with radiant crown" type and are dated to the third–second century BCE (figure A36–38).[28]

---

24 On this model, with comparisons, see Monacchi 1986, 85–87.
25 Bassani et al. 2019, 141–157.
26 The term "prow series" was used by Crawford (1975, 42) to designate Roman asses that show on the reverse the bow of a ship. Generally, this motif is interpreted as a proclamation of Rome's awareness of her position as a naval power and accordingly these coins are dated from the first Punic war, or soon after it in concomitance with the introduction of the quadrigatus.
27 Feet: GB_283 GB_284 GB_317. Breast: GB_282.
28 GB_285 GB_286 GB_318.

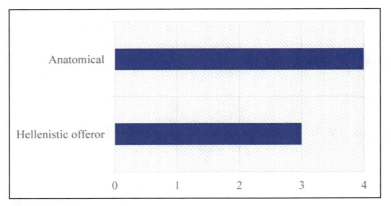

FIGURE 4   Graph showing the type distribution of the Grotta Bella figurative votive offerings between the late fourth and the early first century BCE.

Two are of the male type, which is portrayed holding a patera in the right hand and a round box (*acerra*) in the left (figure A36–37). They wear a long himation draped over the left shoulder; on the head, they wear a wreath of ivy leaves. The third one depicts one of the possible variations of the Hellenistic female worshiper (figure A38). The figurine has cap-like hair and is dressed in a chiton and mantle draped over the left shoulder and arm. The hands are open, the palms directed upwards.

2.2   *Pantanelli Sanctuary*

2.2.1   Topographic Location

The sanctuary site is located in the Pantanelli necropolis, one kilometer southwest of the ancient settlement of Ameria (modern Amelia). The area is distinguished by the presence of mountains that divide the Tiber valley to the west from the Terni basin (Conca Ternana) and the valley to the east and northeast. The morphology of the terrain influenced the placement of the settlement of Ameria, which is located on a limestone spur that overlooks the Tiber river to the east and the Nera river to the west. The Tiber and the roads extending from its valley into Umbrian territory (later replaced by the Via Amerina) made it easier for Ameria to engage in regional commerce and trade with nearby Faliscan and Etruscan areas.

The human occupation of Ameria can be traced back to the Bronze Age, as suggested by the presence of impasto ware fragments. However, the settlement became more substantial starting in the ninth century BCE. During this time, the limestone outcrop served as a temporary shelter for a scattered rural community. The Pantanelli necropolis and sanctuary are the most significant evidence of Ameria's earliest nucleated settlement, which emerged on this site during the seventh/sixth century BCE. These archaeological sites were discovered between 1860 and 1881 when the landowner in the Pantanelli area noticed artifacts emerging from the surface and carried out an excavation. Giovanni Eroli, an archaeology enthusiast from the nearby city of Narni, documented the findings. However, aside from a few votives, the artifacts only survive in his report. About a century later, a number of terracotta slabs were discovered in the Pantanelli area, not far from where Eroli had identified the votive materials and the necropolis.

Based on Eroli's documentation, the Pantanelli necropolis was excavated in the clastic travertine and was used from the sixth to the first century BCE. It consisted of corridors and chamber tombs that yielded fine gold jewelry and Attic vases, likely imported from Etruria. With respect to the sacred area, the excavation produced several votive offerings that date back to the sixth to the second century BCE and fragments of decorated terracotta slabs. Unfortunately, most of these artifacts are now lost, and no further excavation was carried out after the nineteenth-century exploration. As a result, our knowledge of the Pantanelli sacred area is limited and mainly relies on Eroli's brief report and Monacchi's more recent study of the terracotta slabs.[29]

2.2.2 Sixth–Fourth Century BCE: Architectural and Spatial Distribution
No architectural structure of this period was found during the nineteenth-century excavation.

2.2.3 Sixth–Fourth Century BCE: Votive Material
This phase is attested by fragments of *aes rude* and forty-nine votive figurines (figure 5). According to the nineteenth-century excavation report, this material was buried under a thin layer of soil covered by large tufo slabs.

Most of the votive figurines belong to the EG type, but none of them survives. Based on Eroli's succinct account, we know that forty figurines represented women, men, and warriors. Similarly lost are also two cow figurines.

The only bronzes noted by Eroli which survive today are seven figurines that belong to the type "Other." They are made of lead and belong to the same

---

29   Eroli 1860, 118–122; Eroli 1864, 56–59; Eroli 1867, 169–172; Monacchi 1997, 167–194. For an overview on the settlement of Ameria from the Bronze Age to the Roman period, see Matteini Chiari 1996, also with sections on the surviving materials from the Pantanelli necropolis, and Bravi and Monacchi 2017. The latter publication also provides a short summary of the nineteenth-century discovery and suggests a more precise dating for the votive offerings than that of Eroli.

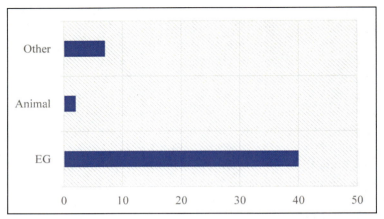

FIGURE 5 Graph showing the type distribution of the Pantanelli votive figurines between the late sixth and the fourth century BCE.

production as the Grotta Bella lead figurines. In particular, the Pantanelli specimens consist of one human figure (figure A40) whose poor state of preservation does not allow further identification, a fragment of a warrior (figure A39), and five decorated warriors' shields (figure A41–42).[30] Like their counterparts from Grotta Bella, the shields' reverse side depicts an arm fastened by three straps, while the motif on the *episema* varies. Three specimens are decorated with a zig-zag motif with the addition of knobs in relief (figure A42), and one with the *gorgoneion* motif (figure A41). The monster's head is schematically rendered with elongated eyes and a waggling tongue.

2.2.4   Late Fourth–Early First Century BCE: Architectural Aspects and Spatial Organization

A rich assemblage of Etrusco-Italic architectural terracotta revetments (*antepagmenta*) spread across the Pantanelli necropolis has been attributed to the monumentalization of the sacred area during the end of the fourth/third century BCE. They are decorated with feathered palmette leaves, lotus flowers, and volutes, sometimes displayed in two rows (figure 6).[31] This decorative motif

---

30 Figurines: PNT_1 PNT_2. Shields: PNT_3 PNT_4 PNT_5 PNT_6 PNT_7.
31 Monacchi (1997) has grouped the Pantanelli revetment plaques into six types. In the first one, a floral-form ornament, or anthemion, consists of one pair of palmettes separated by two volutes. The second is characterized by four palmettes with lanceolate leaves positioned at the four corners of the slab and connected by spirals and smaller palmettes oriented in the opposite direction; buds and berries branch off from the stems. The third type of revetment slab has two rows of palmettes connected by lines of horizontal spirals.

FIGURE 6 Revetment slab from Pantanelli (after Monacchi 1997, 179).

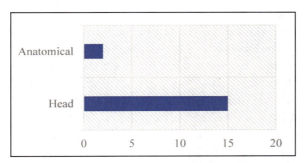

FIGURE 7 Graph showing the type distribution of the Pantanelli figurative votive offerings between the late fourth and the early first century BCE.

belongs to the repertoire of so-called "Etrusco-Italic" architectural decoration. It seems to have been first used in Etruria at the Scasato temple in Falerii in the fourth century and then adopted for the decoration of many sanctuaries of the Italic peninsula during the third and second century BCE.[32]

2.2.5   Late Fourth–Early First Century BCE: Votive Material

The votive material of this phase consists of coins belonging to the Roman series of *aes grave*, fragments of black gloss pottery, fifteen terracotta heads, and two anatomical terracottas (figure 7). Except for one votive foot, this material is entirely lost, and Eroli provides no information about the objects' appearance.

In the fourth type there is an alternation of palmettes and lotus forms, which in the sixth type is organized in three rows. The only decorative motif recognizable in the revetment plaques of the fifth type is a large palmette leaf.

32   Picuti 2006, 205; Strazulla 1981.

100   CHAPTER 5

The single surviving anatomical terracotta, dated to the third–second century BCE, is a fragment of a right foot (figure A43). The poor state of preservation, with the forefoot, toes, and bottom entirely missing, does not allow for secure identification of the object as an isolated foot, leaving open the possibility that it was part of a complete leg. Traces under the heel suggest that the foot rested on a sole.

2.3   *Monte San Pancrazio Sanctuary*

2.3.1   Topographic Location

The sanctuary is situated on Monte San Pancrazio, a southern Umbrian massif located around 9 km east of the ancient settlement of Ocriculum (modern Otricoli). At approximately 1000 meters above sea level, the Monte San Pancrazio massif overlooks the plain known today as the Conca Ternana, providing a strategic vantage point over the Tiber valley and communication routes to the interior. The course of communication in and out of the Conca Ternana was determined by Monte San Pancrazio and Monte Torre Maggiore (2.4. below), making it a crucial crossroads in southern Umbria throughout history.

Our understanding of this site is very limited. In the 1960s, Umberto Ciotti conducted an archaeological investigation of the mountain peak after the accidental discovery of votive material on the slopes. A few travertine blocks were visible on the surface, but the results of the excavation, including the votive objects, were never documented or published. In his brief account of the sanctuary, Ciotti mentions uncovering the remains of a Hellenistic *porticus*. Based on this discovery and the analysis of the votive objects, he suggests that the sanctuary was used until at least the second century BCE.[33]

2.3.2   Sixth–Fourth Century BCE: Architectural and Spatial Distribution

No structure has been attributed to this phase.

2.3.3   Sixth–Fourth Century BCE: Votive Material

Bronze figurines are so far the only evidence of ritual activity on Monte San Pancrazio (figure 8).

The best attested figurine type is the EG, with five male and four female figurines (figure A44–49).[34] Nine votive bronzes represent anatomical parts and heads (figure A50–53).[35] The limbs represented are two legs and two arms (fig-

---

33   Ciotti 1964, 111. See also Bonomi Ponzi 1985, 48.

34   Males: MSP_1 MSP_2 MSP_3 MSP_4 MSP_5. Females: MSP_6 MSP_7 MSP_8 MSP_9. For the description of types already introduced in this chapter, see Appendix 1.

35   Heads: MSP_13; MSP_16 and MSP_17; without the band: MSP_14 and MSP_15. Legs: 18 MSP_19. Arms: MSP_20 MSP_21.

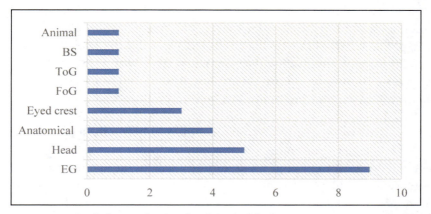

FIGURE 8   Graph showing the type distribution of the San Pancrazio sanctuary's votive figurines between the sixth and the fourth century BCE.

ure A50–51), while the heads depict male individuals (figure A53). Two of them resemble the heads of the EG type, while the remaining three have features of the male heads of the Amelia Group type. They are filed on the front, with the result of two flat surfaces that form an acute angle and end on the upper part with a curved edge. The eyes are indicated by small circles, and the mouth by an incision at the base of the angle that identifies the nose. On the forehead, a linear groove suggests the presence of a band of some sort.

Three specimens belong to the eyed crest type (figure A54).[36] The crests stand on spikes, are filed, and have two grooves made with a punch that resemble eyes. The remaining types are attested only by one specimen.[37] A warrior of the type Foligno Group (FoG) is represented naked and striding towards the left, wearing a crest on his head (figure A55). The eyes, nipples, and navel are rendered with punched roundels and the mouth with a small slit. The figurine is supported by two short spikes situated underneath the feet. A second warrior belongs to the type Todi Group (ToG). This figurine is notable for its size, three times larger than the average size of the other human figurines, and for its high level of detail. The warrior is shown wearing armor with shoulder guards that are hinged, as well as a belt and greaves (figure A56). On his head, he wears an Attic helmet adorned with geometric patterns similar to those seen on the greaves.

36   MSP_23 MSP_24 MSP_25.
37   FoG: MSP_10. ToG: MSP_11.

102   CHAPTER 5

The last two figurines belong to the Bronze Sheet (BS) and Animal types.[38] The former shows a figure cut from a sheet of bronze and turned sideways; an eye in profile is carved into the metal, and a hole above the forehead (figure A57). The state of preservation does not allow the determination of the figure's gender. The Animal type figurine represents an ox and includes additional details, such as the circlets that may symbolize its genitals (figure A58).

2.3.4 Late Fourth–Early First Century BCE: Architectural Aspects and Spatial Organization

There is only limited archaeological information about the appearance of the sanctuary during this phase. Umberto Ciotti opened two trenches on the mountain in 1962 and claimed to have discovered the foundation of a Hellenistic porticus that surrounded the sacred areas and was crossed by a water channel. He also notes that the porticus foundation and the water channel were dug into the rock.

2.3.5 Late Fourth–Early First Century BCE: Votive Material

Among the materials found scattered in the area, only a fragment of a terracotta head and twelve coins can be attributed to the frequentation of the sanctuary during this period. The coins are mostly illegible. The only one with a readable surface depicts a horse's head on the front side, dated to 280–245 BCE.[39]

The terracotta head is of a male figure with wavy hair parted in the center of the crown (figure A59). It is broken under the eyes, but it is clear that they are deeply carved in an almond shape with marked eyelids that develop more laterally than frontally. This particular style can also be found in some of the heads discovered in Vulci and Tessennano, which Martin Söderlind has categorized as belonging to type A1.[40] By comparing this head to others of the same type, we can suggest that it was created during the last fifty years of the second century BCE.

2.4 *Monte Torre Maggiore Sanctuary*

2.4.1 Topographic Location

The sanctuary is situated at the summit of Monte Torre Maggiore, which is 1120 meters above sea level. This mountain is the highest peak of the Monti Martani range and is about 20 kilometers north of the Umbrian settlement of Interamna Nahars (modern Terni). The mountain's elevated position offers

---

38 MSP_12; MSP_26.
39 The material is unpublished. This dating is suggested on the display at the MANU.
40 Söderlind 2002, 62;60.

A MICRO-SCALE APPROACH TO ARCHAEOLOGY

a clear line of sight to Monte San Pancrazio and provides a panoramic view of both the Conca Ternana and many access routes to northern and southern Umbria. However, the mountain peak was unfortunately used as a firing range and anti-aircraft station during the Renaissance and the Second World War. These human interventions have significantly altered the area's appearance and inevitably damaged its stratigraphy.

There is evidence of early human presence on the mountain, as flint arrowheads dating between the fourth and second millennium BCE have been found. However, it seems that the mountain was only inhabited from the sixth century BCE, when the fortified settlement of S. Erasmo occupied a spur. This settlement was the center of a larger system of fortified settlements on mountain peaks (ranging between 700 and 1000 meters in height) scattered along the southern slopes of the Monti Martani. These settlements are identified mainly by the presence of imposing fortifications. At S. Erasmo, the fortifications consist of a megalithic wall built with limestone blocks that runs for 160 meters and covers an area of approximately 7000 m². Archaic settlements have also been identified in the surrounding area of Monte Torre Maggiore, such as Maretta Bassa and Interamna.[41]

During the same period when these settlements were established, the summit of Monte Torre Maggiore was also being used as a place of worship. The Soprintendenza Archeologica dell'Umbria, led by Laura Bonomi Ponzi, conducted intermittent excavations of the mountain's peak from 1984 to 2006. Through these excavations, they were able to identify the development of the site as a place of worship, which occurred from the pre-Roman period to the fourth/fifth century CE.[42]

2.4.2   Sixth–Fourth Century BCE: Architectural and Spatial Distribution

From the sixth to the fourth century BCE, the sanctuary site did not have any permanent architectural structures. The original sacred area was likely only marked by a funnel-shaped pit and a connected channel (figure 9). When excavators discovered the pit in the *pronaos* of temple A (constructed in the third

---

41   The settlement of Maratta Bassa was used from the eightth century BCE to the fourth century BCE. Excavations carried out in the historic center of Terni (ancient Interamna) have shown that a settlement existed here as early as the seventh century BCE (Angelelli and Bonomi Ponzi 200, 11–12). The urbanistic development of Interamna occurred in the third century BCE, with the construction of walls and the definition of an urban street grid.

42   Bonomi Ponzi 1988; Bonomi Ponzi 1989; Angelelli and Bonomi Ponzi 2006, 118–130. The latter publication fully summarizes the results of these excavation seasons.

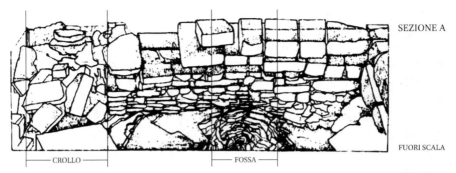

FIGURE 9   On the right: foundations of the third-century and the first-century temples (temples A and B). Notice the channel and the pit inside the *pronaos* of temple B (after Bonomi Ponzi 1988, 23, tav. v). On the left: section of the *pronaos* of temple A and of the funnel-shaped pit (after Bonomi Ponzi 2006, 116, fig. 6).

century CE), it was filled with sterile sand, leading them to interpret it as the foundation ditch or mundus of the sacred area.

2.4.3   Sixth–Fourth Century BCE: Votive Material

Ritual activity in these centuries is indicated by several fragments of *aes rude*, a gilded bronze object in the shape of a thunderbolt,[43] and bronze figurines (figure 10). These objects were recovered in disturbed layers throughout the sanctuary and in a well in the northwestern corner of the area, mixed with later material.

One hundred and fifty-six figurines of the EG type take up most of the assemblage (figure A60–65). One hundred and six of them represent males (figure A60–62), six represent female (figure A64–65), and forty-four depict warriors (figure A63).[44]

---

43   Bonomi Ponzi et al. (1995, 47) have suggested that this object may either have been deposited as *fulgur conditum* (buried after having been struck by lightning) or connected to Iuppiter Fulgurator, whose presence is attested at Interamna Nahars during the Roman period. However, the excavation has not yielded other indications of the burial of the *fulgur conditum* or of the deity to whom the sanctuary was dedicated. For the difficulty in identifying the incumbent deities based on the ex-votos in Italian sanctuaries, see Comella 1981, 717–803.

44   Males: MTM_73 MTM_74 MTM_75 MTM_76 MTM_77 MTM_84 MTM_85 MTM_98 MTM_99 MTM_100 MTM_101 MTM_104 MTM_105 MTM_109 MTM_112 MTM_113 MTM_114 MTM_115 MTM_116 MTM_117 MTM_118 MTM_120 MTM_121 MTM_123 MTM_124 MTM_125 MTM_126 MTM_127 MTM_128 MTM_135 MTM_137 MTM_139 MTM_145 MTM_146 MTM_147 MTM_148 MTM_149 MTM_150 MTM_151 MTM_152 MTM_153 MTM_154 MTM_156 MTM_157 MTM_158 MTM_163 MTM_164 MTM_166 MTM_168 MTM_172 MTM_173 MTM_174 MTM_175 MTM_178 MTM_179 MTM_180

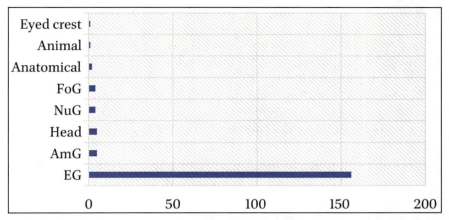

FIGURE 10   Graph showing the type distribution of the Monte di Torre Maggiore sanctuary's votive figurines between the late sixth and the fourth century BCE.

Five votive figurines belong to the Amelia Group type (AmG). Four depict a man striding forwards (figure A66–67), while the fifth portrays a warrior (figure A68).[45] These figurines are characterized by their heads, which have been filed on the front to create two flat surfaces that form an acute angle and end on the upper part with a curved edge. Small circles on the surfaces indicate the eyes and the mouth is represented by a cut at the base of the angle, which identifies the nose. The striding men are depicted with their right legs slightly bent and their left legs straight. Their left arms are raised with the palm facing upwards and the thumb stretched wide, while their right arms are bent downwards with an open hand and an outstretched thumb. The warrior is shown holding a shield on the left and a spear on the right.

Five votives represent schematic heads, and two depict anatomical parts (figure A69–72).[46] The heads (figure A69–70) are rendered in the same manner as the heads of figurines of the AmG type, while the anatomical parts consist of

---

MTM_182 MTM_183 MTM_185 MTM_190 MTM_191 MTM_192 MTM_193 MTM_194 MTM_195 MTM_196. Females: MTM_141 MTM_170 MTM_184 MTM_80 MTM_21 MTM_22. Warriors: MTM_78 MTM_81 MTM_91 MTM_92 MTM_102 MTM_103 MTM_106 MTM_107 MTM_108 MTM_110 MTM_111 MTM_119 MTM_122 MTM_129 MTM_130 MTM_131 MTM_132 MTM_133 MTM_134 MTM_136 MTM_138 MTM_140 MTM_142 MTM_143 MTM_144 MTM_155 MTM_159 MTM_160 MTM_161 MTM_162 MTM_167 MTM_169 MTM_171 MTM_197 MTM_198 MTM_23 MTM_24 MTM_25 MTM_26 MTM_27 MTM_28 MTM_29 MTM_30 MTM_97.

45   Striding men: MTM_16 MTM_17 MTM_18 MTM_19 MTM_20. Warrior: MTM_59.
46   Heads: MTM_63 MTM_64 MTM_72 MTM_66 MTM_67. Anatomical parts: MTM_65 MTM_68.

a left foot and a left hand (figure A71–72). The latter is shown opened, with the thumb outstretched. A break at the wrist does not allow us to reconstruct the original appearance of the figurines, which, like the other anatomical bronzes of the pre-Roman period, may have been supported by a spike or have been part of a larger figurine.

Four figurines of the NuG type represent warriors with a lozenge crest and the open arms (figure A73–74).[47] Four more warriors belong to the FoG type and are represented naked and striding forward (figure A75a and b).[48] Lastly, attested by one specimen is the eyed crest (figure A76) and the Animal type (figure A77–78).[49] To the latter belongs two bull figurines (one in bronze and the other in impasto rosso), whose heads are partially preserved.

2.4.4 Late Fourth–Early First Century BCE: Architectural Aspects and Spatial Organization

In the third century BCE, a temenos in *opus quadratum* (20 × 20.80 m) was laid around the area of the earlier *mundus* and organized in nine small utility rooms (ca. 16 m²). The center of this precinct was occupied by a temple (A), which incorporated elements of Etrusco-Italic temple architecture as well as that of Hellenistic type.[50]

On a tall podium in *opus quadratum* with travertine crown molding stood a rectangular temple oriented east-west (11.80 × 7.90 m), with *pronaos* (5.70 × 2 m) and *cella* (5.70 × 5.70 m). Fragments of columns around the temple and the impression left on the ground by a column's base suggested that the temple was surrounded by columns on all sides, unlike Etrusco-Italic temples. The entrance to the temple was through a flight of stairs that were still visible in front of the *pronaos*. Interestingly, the sixth-century BCE ritual pit was not obliterated by the temple's construction but was incorporated inside the *pronaos*, indicating its importance to the cult site.

In 2006, a circular well was discovered in the southwestern area of the sanctuary. It measured 1.27 × 1.33 meters and was made of limestone blocks without mortar. The well was filled with votive offerings and pottery from both pre-Roman and Roman periods. It is uncertain when the well was constructed, but a coin from the reign of Commodus found inside provides the *terminus*

---

47   MTM_95 MTM_82 MTM_83 MTM_93.
48   MTM_57 MTM_58 MTM_199 MTM_94.
49   Eyed crest: MTM_79. Animal: MTM_60.
50   For an overall study of Etrusco-Italic temple architecture, see Colonna 1985 and 2006. For a general overview of Hellenistic temple architecture, see Winter and Fedak 2016, 5–34.

FIGURE 11
Well identified in 2006 in the sacred area of Monte Torre Maggiore (courtesy of the Soprintendenza Archeologia Belle Arti e Paesaggio dell'Umbria).

FIGURE 12
Plan of the Monte di Torre Maggiore sanctuary with the two temples (after Bonomi Ponzi 2006, 113, fig. 5)

post quem of its obliteration. During excavations, fragments of travertine architectural and sculptural decoration were also uncovered, including lion-headed waterspouts and a female head inspired by Hellenistic art.

In the first century BCE, the sanctuary underwent a second renovation that included the construction of a new temple (B) made of *opus caementicium* and covered with limestone slabs. Temple B was oriented north–south and located northwest of temple A. The renovation also involved the extension of the temenos to the south, with additional facility rooms (figure 12). This second renovation seems to have been the final major refurbishment of the sanctuary, which continued to be used until the end of the third century CE, as evidenced by fragments of lamps and imperial coins found on the site.

2.4.5   Late Fourth–Early First Century BCE: Votive Material

The materials from this phase come primarily from the area between temples A and B and the facility rooms of the temenos: fragments of pottery and terra sigillata, black gloss bowls, plates, miniature vases, coins of the *as* and *semis* denomination, and a black gloss bowl with the name "PVPVN" which dates back to the end of the third or beginning of the second century BCE. Additionally, unspecified coins, a fusiform *balsamarium* made of glass, and

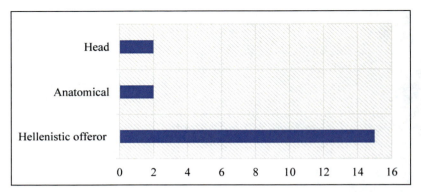

FIGURE 13   Graph showing the type distribution of the Monte di Torre Maggiore figurative votive offerings between the late fourth and the early first century BCE.

bronze figurines recognized by the excavators as Hellenistic worshipers were found. Anatomical terracotta pieces were also discovered during this phase (figure 13).

The votive figurines consist of fifteen specimens of the Hellenistic worshiper type, two terracotta heads, and two terracotta anatomical offerings. The Hellenistic worshiper type is attested by ten male and one female worshiper and four fragments of arms holding a patera, all dated to the third century BCE (figure A79–81).[51] The female worshiper wears a long chiton, wrapped under the breast, and a himation on the left shoulder, around the hips and hanging from the forearm. On her left arm she carries an acerra, and on her head is a diadem with several rays.

The terracotta anatomicals are dated to the Middle Republican period and represent a right hand and a foot (figure A82–83).[52] The hand (figure A82) is clenched into a fist and broken at the level of the wrist. The index finger seems to wear a ring. The foot is now lost, and only a picture of three fragments survives in the archaeological documentation. Two fragments belong to the platform on which the foot must have stood, while the other represents part of the big toe and the two closest to it (figure A83). Due to the poor state of preservation of both pieces, it is difficult to determine their exact age through stylistic comparison.

The two terracotta heads are mostly broken (figure A84–85). One specimen (figure A84) represents an individual whose gender is difficult to detect; the

---

51   Males: MTM_1 MTM_6 MTM_7 MTM_8 MTM_9 MTM_10 MTM_11 MTM_12 MTM_14 MTM_15. Female: MTM_13. Fragments with patera: MTM_2 MTM_3 MTM_4 MTM_5.
52   Hand: MTM_69. Foot: MTM_70.

only facial features preserved are half of the nose, mouth, chin, and face below the eyes. Despite the few anatomical details preserved, the resemblance of the chin and mouth to the male heads of the AI(i1)/ (i2) group from Tarquinia may suggest a more precise dating to the end of the third century BCE.[53] The second head (figure A85) is equally damaged; only its crown, with wavy hair parted at the center, and the left eye are preserved. The hairdo finds comparisons with some female heads of the BVI (a2) type from Tessennano, thus suggesting a dating to the beginning of the second century BCE.[54]

2.5 *Monte Moro Sanctuary*
2.5.1 Topographic Location
Monte Moro is a limestone upland mountain (696 m above sea level) located on the north bank of the Nera river, at the border between Umbrian and the Sabine territory. Prior to the Roman expansion into Umbria, the summit of Monte Moro was occupied by a sacred space. The southern slopes of the mountain were occupied by a settlement with a few structures made of dry stones that were possibly connected to natural water sources located further down the slopes.

The sanctuary was located in the Conca Ternana region and had a strategic position with regards to both the Umbrian and Sabine territories. It was situated in a location that overlooked the route connecting Spoletium in Umbria with Reate in Sabina, which passed through the Somma and Forca Sant'Angelo passes. Moreover, its location also created a strong visual link with the Monte Arrone peak sanctuary, situated on the left bank of the Nera river in Sabine territory.

In 1998, 2004, and 2010, the Soprintendenza Archeologica per l'Umbria, led by Liliana Costamagna, conducted archaeological excavations and surveys on the summit of the mountain to investigate structures that previous unauthorized excavations had uncovered.[55] Here, the excavators identified the presence of a sacred building whose stratigraphy had been entirely compromised by looters and reforestation activities. They were able to determine the timeline of the sacred area through ceramic analysis, which revealed that it was used from the fifth century BCE to the third century CE, when it seems to have been sub-

---

53   Söderlind 2002, 70–71.
54   Söderlind 2002, 180.
55   The results of the excavations are summarized by Sisani (2013, 132–134) in his latest publication on the *ager Nursinus*. The first season of excavations is published in: Costamagna 2002, 22–23. The report of the archaeological campaigns can be consulted in the Archivio della Soprintendenza Archeologia Belle Arti e Paesaggio dell'Umbria.

110 CHAPTER 5

jected to looting to remove construction materials. The area was only sparsely frequented in the fourth century CE.

2.5.2   Sixth–Fourth Century BCE: Architectural and Spatial Distribution
Based on a few fragments of bricks, limestone sherds, and pottery used as fill for a later sacred building and on the presence of archaic schematic votive bronzes, it is possible to hypothesize that an Umbrian sanctuary existed on the summit at least since the fifth/fourth century BCE.[56] However, nothing conclusive can be said of its original appearance and chronology, for the monumentalization of the area in the second century BCE required the leveling of the entire mountaintop and the use of any previous structure as excavation waste.

A pit, partially destroyed by looters, was found in 1998 on the eastern side of the later building and tentatively attributed to the pre-Roman sacred space. It is dug into the rock, lined with clay and rocks, and covered with small squared bricks. The excavators proposed that it may have been used as a cistern to collect rainwater or as a silo for storing food. Another pit from the second century BCE was found just east of it. Both pits were intentionally destroyed after the sanctuary site was abandoned in the third century CE and used as garbage pits for the architectural and votive materials accumulated at the sanctuary.

2.5.3   Sixth–Fourth Century BCE: Votive Material
The votive material from this phase comprises fragments of *aes rude* and bronze votive figurines (figure 14). This material has been found in two pits where it was mixed with material of the Roman period such as bronze nails, architectural elements, anatomical votives, and terracotta heads.

The bronze votive figurines consist of seven men belonging to the EG type (figure A86–88), five eyed crests (figure A89–90), two warriors of the FoG type (figure A91), two animal figurines—a horse and a fragment of an ox (figure A92–93)—and one schematic head with facial features that recall the rendering of the heads of the EG type figurines (figure A94).[57]

---

56   While Sisani (2013, 133) argues that no pottery of this period has been found on the excavation and casts doubts even on the chronology of the bronze figurines, the excavation reports I found in the Soprintendenza archive confirm the presence, although scant, of archaeological material of the fifth/fourth century BCE. On the basis of this evidence, I see no reason to doubt the existence of a sacred area on the summit during this period.

57   EG: MM_3 MM_4 MM_5 MM_6 MM_7 MM_8 MM_9. Eyed crests: MM_10 MM_11 MM_12 MM_13 MM_1. FoG: MM_1 MM_2. Horse: MM_16, ox: MM_17. Head: MM_15.

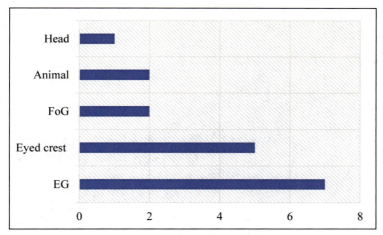

FIGURE 14   Graph showing the type distribution of the Monte Moro votive figurines between the fifth and the fourth century BCE.

2.5.4 Late Fourth–Early First Century BCE: Architectural Aspects and Spatial Organization

The sanctuary did not have an architectural form until the end of the second century BCE when the entire summit was leveled to create space for a building (figure 15). The new complex was 26 meters long and articulated into at least four rooms. The first (room A) is currently interpreted as the cult room. It runs northwest/southeast and measures 10 × 6 m. It was paved with concrete with small limestone and lithic inclusions; at the center of this room stood a rectangular structure lined with rock slabs set vertically into the bedrock. A large plastered pit was discovered south of room A and next to the previous pit, which may have been used as a silo.[58] An opening in the northern corner of room A connected it to room B, where the concrete floor is interrupted by large postholes and depressions related to the original setting of the room. On the northwestern side of the building, a small corridor granted entrance to both rooms. The 2010 excavation has established that the building extended southwest with more rooms, possibly used as service spaces.

Due to the lack of architectural materials, the building's decoration cannot be reconstructed with certainty. Two fragments of draped female figures have been tentatively attributed to the sanctuary's pediment decoration.

---

58 Both pits were no longer used in the late imperial period and were destroyed, becoming garbage pits.

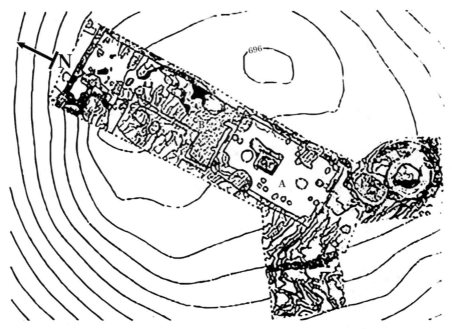

FIGURE 15   The Monte Moro sanctuary's structures (after Sisani 2013, 18 fig. 2).

2.5.5   Late Fourth–Early First Century BCE: Votive Material

The archaeological material dating to this phase consists principally of pottery, seven anatomical terracottas, and four heads (figure 16). These objects have been found in the pits mixed with other refuse material used to fill them.[59]

Nearly 3000 fragments of pottery have been found in the sanctuary area. Black gloss (paterae, cups, and plates) is the most attested pottery class, followed by unpainted pottery (tableware and cooking ware) and terra sigillata.

The anatomical terracottas are from the third–second century BCE and include several body parts such as two uteri, two hands, one nose, one foot, and one set of male genitals (figure A95–101).[60] The uteri (figure A95–96) are fragmented and have an ovoid body with a slight tapering towards the top, with striations representing musculature. The hands are also fragmented, with one specimen (figure A97) showing the second, third, and fourth finger of a

---

59   See *infra* for the other material found in the pit.
60   Uteri: MM23 MM24. Hand without palm: MM 21. Hand with palm: MM_22. Nose: MM_25. Foot: MM_19. Testicles: MM_26. The dating of both the anatomicals and the heads proposed by Sisani (2013, 137–140) suggests that their deposition may have pre-dated the monumentalization of the area.

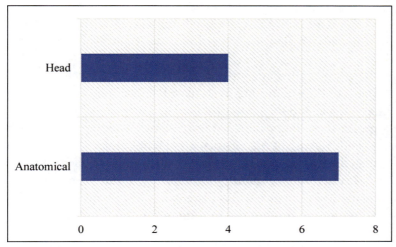

FIGURE 16 Graph showing the type distribution of the Monte Moro figurative votive offerings between the late fourth and the early first century BCE.

right hand without any visible anatomical details. The second specimen (figure A98) depicts the palm of a left hand without any fingers. The nose (figure A99) is larger than life-size, with small indentations indicating the nostrils. The votive foot (figure A100) shows only the second and third toes attached to each other with signs of footwear, most likely a sandal. Lastly, the male genitalia (figure A101) depict low-hanging testicles and a missing penis with a fracture line where it was attached.

Like the anatomical offerings, the votive heads date back to the third–second century BCE and are fragmented (figure A102–104).[61] One of the heads (figure A102) shows the left part of a male face with a smooth and rounded cheek and a straight mouth with separated lips. Another specimen (figure A103) includes three locks of forward-flowing hair and a fragment of the left eye and low eyebrow of a male figure. A third specimen (figure A104) is a small fragment of a veiled head's hairdo with no preserved facial features. The last specimen shows only the neck of a head.

2.6   *Monte Santo Sanctuary*

Located approximately 1 kilometer west of Todi, the sanctuary site is near Etruria and Umbria's border. The area's significance as a hub for commercial

---

61   MM_18 MM_19 MM_20 MM_28.

114   CHAPTER 5

exchange and a connection between the inland Apennine region and the Etruscan world is evident from the grave goods discovered at the pre-Roman settlement of Tuder, as well as the presence of the Tiber river in the vicinity.[62]

Based on the discovery of scattered artifacts on Monte Santo, such as a statue of Mars in the act of libation, parts of an inscribed honorary travertine column, and several small bronze figurines, it has been suggested that an archaic sacred place existed on the mountain.[63] Only a small amount of evidence is available regarding the use of the sanctuary on Monte Santo, which suggests that it was used during two periods: the fifth century BCE and the end of the first century BCE when Tuder became Colonia Iulia Fida Tuder. However, since no excavation has been conducted, it is not possible to determine if the sanctuary was in continuous use during these periods.[64]

2.6.1   Sixth–Fourth Century BCE: Architectural and Spatial Distribution
No excavation has been carried out on the mountain, and no architectural evidence is visible on the ground.

2.6.2   Sixth–Fourth Century BCE: Votive Material
In 1835, a local inhabitant of Todi noticed a bronze statue and a few travertine blocks of a column emerging from the ground on his property located on the western slopes of Monte Santo and carried out a private excavation of these objects. The statue, known as Mars of Todi after Francesco Roncalli's publication, is dated to the end of the fifth/beginning of the fourth century. It is 1.41 m high and depicts a warrior in armor, pouring a libation from a cup held in his extended right hand, while holding a spear with his left. An Umbrian inscription, carved in the Etruscan alphabet on the edge of the warrior's armor, suggests that the statue was given as a gift by Ahal Truitis, who could have been a local inhabitant. It is speculated that the statue was produced by a

---

62   See Chapter 4 for the pre-Roman necropoleis of Todi. It is also worth noting the presence of votive material found under the Chiesa della Visitazione di Santa Maria in Camuccia: Fabricotti 1969.

63   Bruschetti (2001, 155) briefly notes that black gloss pottery and architectural fragments were found on the hill's summit by the Soprintendenza Archeologica per l'Umbria. He does not provide any additional information, and, to my knowledge, these findings are neither displayed nor available in the archival records of the Soprintendenza.

64   For an overview and detailed summary of the finding of the statue and the Mars, see Roncalli 1973, 197. For an examination of the inscription carved on the statue, see Rocca 1996, 142 and Rix 2002, Um 1. The votive bronzes are published in Falcone Amorelli 1977 but without a historical contextualization of the sanctuary site.

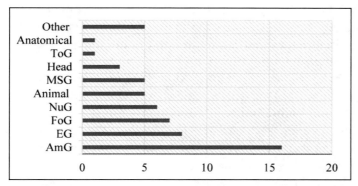

FIGURE 17   Graph showing the type distribution of the Monte Santo votive figurines between the fifth and fourth centuries BCE.

sculptural workshop in Volsinii, a trade center with the Umbrian territory known for its bronze sculptors.

Forty-nine bronze figurines may be related to the sacred area of Monte Santo (figure 17). In only one case is a provenance from the mountain known, while for the remaining objects, the only information available in the Museo Civico di Todi archive is that they were found in Todi. Notwithstanding the lack of provenance, a case can be made for the association of all these objects with Monte Santo. It is worth noting that other sanctuaries identified in this city—at the sites of la Rocca, S. Maria in Camuccia, Porta Catena, and the Cathedral—have been dated between the end of the fourth and the third century BCE, while the bronze figurines have been dated to the fifth century BCE.[65] Monte Santo seems, therefore, to be the only (known) temple that existed in the area of Tuder during the fifth century BCE where these votives could have been dedicated.

Sixteen figurines belonging to the AmG type make up the majority of Monte Santo votive figurines (figure A106–109). Three depict a warrior (figure A106), and the rest depict a man striding forward (figure A107–109). The EG type is represented by six male and two female figures (figure A109–113), the FoG type by six warriors (figure A114–116), and the NoG type by five warriors and one woman (figure A117–119). Five warriors belong to the Monte Santo type (MSG), whose characteristic features are chiseled eyes, a small tunic that leaves the genitalia uncovered, and a helmet distinguished by the narrow point and raised cheekpieces (figure A120–121). Only one of the Monte Santo warrior figurines

---

65   For sanctuaries at Todi, see Tascio 1989, 66–67.

116   CHAPTER 5

belongs to the ToG. Five figurines belong to the Animal type: three depict bulls and two horses (figure A122–123). Among the body parts, three figurines represent heads whose facial features stylistically recall the AmG (figure A124–126) and one a right hand (figure A234).[66]

Lastly, five figurines belong to the group "Other" (figure A 127–130). Even though they resemble some of the types identified by Colonna, the overall rendering of the body and features seems to indicate an original creation of an individual craftsman operating in the Todi area or directly on the sanctuary site. It is possible that a local craftsman re-utilized known casts and applied subtle changes in order to create unique figurines that perhaps were more in line with the preferences of the donor or the artist. MTS_23 and MTS_24 represent a warrior naked except for a helmet; the body is solid, the left arm lies on the left hip, and the right arm is either bent upward (MTS_23) or forward (MTS_24) in the act of holding a spear. The modeling of the body recalls Colonna's Maestro Rapino.[67]

MTS_7 shows a resemblance to Colonna's Chiusi type.[68] It represents a nude warrior in the act of striding forward with his left leg. He wears a helmet with a low crest and carries a shield on his left arm; his right arm is bent forward. The body is slender, and the facial features are roughly indicated.

MTS_45 portrays Hercules in the nude.[69] His right arm is raised in a club-wielding gesture, while his left arm is extended forward, and a lion's skin hangs from his left forearm. The protruding ears, nose, and bulging eyes are reminiscent of Colonna's Maestro "Le Arti" and Biel types.[70]

---

66 AmG warrior: MTS_10 MTS_11 MTS_12, AmG striding man: MTS_26 MTS_27 MTS_28 MTS_29 MTS_30 MTS_31 MTS_32 MTS_33 MTS_34 MTS_35 MTS_44. EG males: MTS_38 MTS_39 MTS_40 MTS_41 MTS_42 MTS_43; EG females: MTS_46 MTS_48. FoG warriors: MTS_8 MTS_9 MTS_13 MTS_14 MTS_15 MTS_16 MTS_17. NoG warriors: MTS_18 MTS_19 MTS_20 MTS_21 MTS_22. NoG woman: MTS_47. MSG: MTS_3 MTS_4 MTS_5 MTS_6 MTS_25. Bulls: MTS_49 MTS_50 MTS_53. Horses: MTS_51 MTS_52. Heads: MTS_72 MTS_73 MTS_75. ToG: MTS_2. Head: MTS_76.

67 Colonna 1970, 137–140.

68 Colonna 1970, 87–88.

69 Compared with other regions of central Italy, such as Etruria, Latium and Samnium, representations of Heracles are scarce in ancient Umbria; only two out of the sixteen sanctuaries analyzed in the present work have yielded votive offerings representing Heracles (Monte Santo and the Sanctuary of Cupra at Colfiorito). See Bradley 2005, 129–143 for a discussion on the cult of Hercules in Central Italy.

70 Colonna 1970, 145–146.

A MICRO-SCALE APPROACH TO ARCHAEOLOGY

2.6.3   Late Fourth–Early First Century BCE: Architectural Aspects and
         Spatial Organization

No architectural evidence belonging to this phase has been found on Monte
Santo. The column identified in 1835 is dated to the end of the first century BCE
when the entire region received Roman citizenship.[71]

2.6.4   Late Fourth–Early First Century BCE: Votive Material

Although several bronze figurines of Hellenistic worshipers are displayed in the
Museo Civico di Todi, none of them can be associated with certainty with the
Monte Santo sanctuary due to the lack of provenance.

3   Umbrian Valley

3.1   *La Rocca Sanctuary*

The cult site takes its name, "La Rocca," from the imposing medieval papal
fortress (Rocca Albornoziana) that occupies the entire summit. La Rocca is
located on the height of the Colle di Sant'Elia, a foothill of the Apennines
(452 m above sea level) in the town of Spoleto in east-central Umbria. Due
to its location at the head of a large, broad valley surrounded by mountains
and overlooking communication routes between the Umbrian valley and the
southern part of the region, the hill occupies a strategic geographical position
and has been continuously occupied since the Middle Bronze Age. Unfortunately, the major work of land leveling connected with the construction of the
Rocca Albornoziana has entirely compromised the archaeological record of the
ancient settlement's phases. Our knowledge of its development comes primarily from the dump layers accumulated along the hill's slopes.

The earliest signs of activity on Colle di Sant'Elia include pottery fragments, a
piece of a bronze fibula, spools, and loom weights, which suggest the existence
of a settlement that likely occupied the eastern and western slopes of the hill.
After the Bronze Age, archaeological findings indicate a gradual expansion of
the settlement. Iron Age activity is attested by postholes, both on the summit
of the hill and in the area of San Nicolò, located 3 km northwest of Colle S. Elia.
The presence of numerous fragments of bucchero found both on the hill and in
the modern centro storico, and the discovery of three necropoleis dating back

---

71   The column has been studied by Roncalli (1973). It has an attic base with two inscriptions
      and a 20 m high grooved shaft. The inscriptions preserved on the base of the column indi-
      cate that it was an honorary monument to the *duoviri quinquennales* of the colony: the
      patronus coloniae Q. Caecilius Atticus and C. Attius Bucina (*CIL* 11.4653a, 4652).

118   CHAPTER 5

to the seventh–sixth century BCE indicate that during the archaic period, the settlement had expanded and occupied the whole southwest slope of the hill.

Although a settlement existed before the Roman expansion, Spoletium appears in the historical record only after being established as a Latin colony in 241 BCE. The settlement was spread over an area of approximately 30 hectares and was organized on an orthogonal grid system, with *insulae* along the primary slope of the site. The terrain was purposely terraced to create regularity. The main street of the ancient village was maintained, regularized, and connected to the Via Flaminia, which acted as the *cardo* of the new settlement. When the colony was founded, the hill's summit was transformed into the citadel of the new city.

Although the construction of the Albornoziana Fortress leveled any preexisting structures, restoration and construction work carried out in the last thirty years on the slopes of the hill and inside the Fortress have yielded evidence of the existence of at least one sacred area used from the fifth century BCE to the fourth century CE.[72]

3.1.1 Sixth–Fourth Century BCE: Architectural and Spatial Distribution
No cult building of this period has been unearthed.

3.1.2 Sixth–Fourth Century BCE: Votive Material
The votive material attributed to a cult place in this phase consists of eleven bronze figurines (figure 18).[73] These have been found in disturbed layers during excavations in the Fortress' "Cortile delle Armi" and "Cortile ovest" and on the northern and southern slopes of the Rocca.

---

72   The analysis of the pottery typologies found on La Rocca shows that the area was only scarcely frequented in the imperial and the early medieval period; pottery fragments drop from more than 2000 pieces in the fourth–first century BCE to fewer than fifty in the first–fourth century CE: Ermini Pani 2011, 44. The first excavation results are published in Bruni et al. 1983 and De Angelis 1994. Pani et al. (2011) summarize all excavation seasons from 1993 to 2007. The sanctuary on La Rocca may not have been the only pre-Roman sanctuary. In 1986, a votive bronze figurine (inv. n. 390939), was found near the church of S. Niccolò. It remains unpublished but is displayed at the Museo Archeologico Nazionale di Spoleto. Its discovery opens up the possibility that another cult place existed in the area of the future Roman colony. For the earliest phases of occupation of the hill see also De Angelis 1994, 221–247. For the necropolis, see Museo Archeologico di Spoleto 2008, 11–15. For an overview of the colony of Spoletium, see Sisani 2007, 92–97 with previous bibliography.

73   Several fragments of pottery, such as impasto, black gloss, and bucchero, have been found during the excavation at La Rocca but have not been associated with the sacred area.

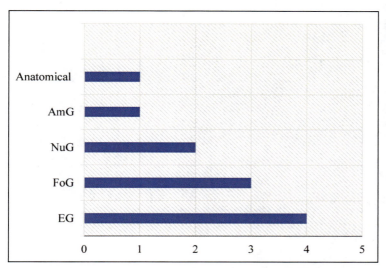

FIGURE 18   Graph showing the type distribution of the La Rocca sanctuary's votive figurines between the late sixth and the fourth century BCE.

The votive figurines consist of four male figures of the EG type (figure A131–133), three warriors of the FoG type (A3.134–135), two NuG figurines, a warrior (A3.136), and a striding male (A3.137), one striding male figure of the AmG (figure A138), and one anatomical specimen depicting an arm (A3.138).[74]

3.1.3   Late Fourth–Early First Century BCE: Architectural Aspects and Spatial Organization

Backfill layers on the hill's northern slope have yielded two fragments of Etrusco-Italic *antepagmenta* (figure 19) and two fragments of terracotta antefixes. These fragments can be attributed to the architectural and coroplastic decoration of the sacred building(s) on La Rocca during this phase.

The slabs appear to depict spiraling volutes,[75] while the antefixes show part of the lower body of a winged, draped female figure, identified by the excavators as the *Potnia theron* (Mistress of the Animals). This motif, believed to have originated in Faliscan territory in the fourth–third century BCE, became a common decorative motif on the antefixes of central Italian sanctuaries between

---

[74] EG: Rocca_4 Rocca_5 Rocca_6 Rocca_7. FoG: Rocca_1 Rocca_2 Rocca_3. NuG: Rocca_8 Rocca_9. AmG: Rocca_10. Anatomical: Rocca_11.

[75] For this type of revetment slabs, see *supra* 2.2. Pantanelli.

FIGURE 19 Architectural terracottas from La Rocca (after Ermini Pani 2011, fig. 20–23).

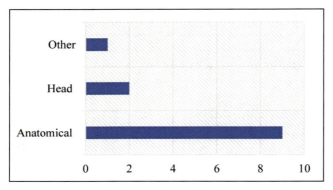

FIGURE 20 Graph showing the type distribution of the La Rocca figurative votive offerings between the end of the third and the early first century BCE

the third and the first century BCE. The goddess is traditionally represented as winged, draped, and flanked by two panthers.[76]

3.1.4   Late Fourth–Early First Century BCE: Votive Material

The material from this phase consists of several fragments of pottery, one third-century BCE Roman bronze coin of the *triens* denomination, nine anatomical votives, two heads, and one terracotta figurine of a bovine (figure 20). These objects were found in a modern landfill and a dump layer. The latter, based on

---

76   This type, known as classicizing, is widespread both in colonial and non-colonial areas of the peninsula. A list of sanctuaries with this type of antefix decoration is in Comella 1993, 66–67; Känel 2001, 35–36; Faustoferri and Lapenna 2014, 127.

A MICRO-SCALE APPROACH TO ARCHAEOLOGY 121

the *terminus post quem* provided by the presence of a fragment of sigillata italica and amphorae, appears to have been deposited in the first century CE.

Pottery is the most abundant category of material found at La Rocca. Common ware is the most frequent ceramic class (1796 fragments, mostly *ollae*), followed by black gloss (1027; some pieces are of local production), coarse ware (203) and grey pottery (9).

The anatomical terracottas are dated to the third/second century BCE and consist of two feet, two big toes, two fingers, two uteri, and one phallus (figure A3.140–142).[77] The feet are preserved in two fragments (A3.140): Rocca_13 represents a right foot with toes individually formed and separated from one another; the toenails are executed by means of incision and rise slightly off a small platform. A break runs through the entire left side of the foot, cutting off the big toe and a large part of the heel. Rocca_12 depicts the second, third, and fourth toes from a right foot on a high platform. They are attached to each other and marked by a groove in between. Rounded incisions indicated toenails. Rocca_14 and Rocca_5 show the big toe of a left foot, whose platform is partially preserved (A3.140). Rocca_16 represents a thumb whose shape is rendered realistically. It terminates in a break midway down. Rocca_21 shows an unidentifiable finger. It is long and thin and slightly curved in a way reminiscent of the joints of the finger. The tip is pressed, perhaps indicating a fingernail. It terminates at the bottom in a break (A3.140). Rocca_18 and Rocca_19 show an ovoid uterus (A3.141) slightly tapering toward the top to create a rounded point. Striations are visible along both fragments. The body of the organ rests on a flat and featureless bottom, the edges of which extend beyond it. Rocca_17 depicts part of a pair of low-hanging testicles (A3.142). An irregular break surrounds the entire fragments, cutting off half of the testicles. There is no trace of the penis attached initially to the piece.

The terracotta heads are dated to the third/second century BCE (figure A143).[78] Rocca_22, represents the oval face of a veiled female. The hair is swept back from the forehead and falls over the sides of the face, forming two lines of ringlets, completely covering the ears. The forehead is short, the eyes are narrow, and the nose is big with a rounded tip. The mouth is chipped off, and the chin is round and fleshy. A large break runs along the left edge of the face,

---

77   Feet: Rocca_13, Rocca_12. Fingers: Rocca_16, Rocca_21. Uterus: Rocca_18, Rocca_19. Male genitalia: Rocca_17. I was not allowed to view the anatomicals and the heads outside the case where they are displayed. The measurements of these objects and their inventory numbers, contained in Appendix 2, were kindly provided to me by Anna Riva, from the Museo Archeologico Nazionale di Spoleto.

78   Rocca_22, Rocca_20.

from the crown of the head to the cheek. A comparison with heads of the BIV type classified by Comella and dated between the fourth and the third century BCE may suggest a third-century BCE date for this head.[79] The second head, Rocca_20, is worn out and broken in multiple places; the only facial features preserved are the right eye, part of the nose, the mouth, parts of the cheeks, and the chin. The eye is shallow and framed by a low eyebrow. The upper eyelid is thin and plastic. The mouth is small, and the lips are even; the lower lip is slightly thicker with a soft undercut. Although the poor state of preservation prevents the identification of typologically similar heads, the resemblance of the chin and mouth to the male heads of the AI from Vulci, Tarquinia, and Tessennano suggests a dating to the second half of the third century BCE.[80]

Finally, Rocca_23 belongs to the group "Other," since it is an isolated find, and its presence in the region is limited to the sacred area on Colle S. Elia (figure A144). It represents a terracotta quadruped, most likely a bovine. The head is entirely cut off, and the features that remain after heavy wear do not show any details revealing what particular kind of bovine is represented. Although otherwise absent in Umbrian sacred contexts, terracotta animals are common in the western part of central Italy, southern Italy, and Sicily.[81]

3.2 *Monte Subasio Sanctuary*

The sanctuary site is located on the summit of the San Rufino hill, which represents the northernmost peak of Monte Subasio. The mountain is located 7 km east of Assisi (ancient Asisium) and, from a height of 1290 m above sea level, dominates the surrounding hills and valleys: on the western slopes are the towns of Assisi and Spello; on the east Nocera Umbra and Valtopina, in the northern territory of Gualdo Tadino; and on the south the city of Foligno. In antiquity, the mountain functioned as a regular stop for the summer transhumance that took place between the Umbria-Marche Apennines and the Ager Romanus via routes later retraced by the Via Flaminia.

The cult place was connected to a vast settlement area that occupied the slopes of Monte Subasio. The only settlement in the area that has been archaeologically investigated is Assisi. After an early occupation in the Bronze and

---

79 In particular, the heads from the Temple of Minerva Medica in Rome and Ariccia. Comella 1981, 783, fig. 19. In another publication (1982, 27), the author notes that, starting from the third century BCE, the type of hairdo with long ringlets framing the head is replaced by the one where the hair is gathered on top.

80 Söderlind 2000, 58–68.

81 Comella 1981, 767. On votive offerings of terracotta animals in central Italy, see Söderlind 2004. According to Comella 1981, this category of votive offerings is part of the Etrusco-Latial-Campanian (E-L-C) phenomenon. For this class of material, see also Appendix 1.

A MICRO-SCALE APPROACH TO ARCHAEOLOGY

Iron Ages, the central area of the modern town (Via Arco dei Priori) seems to have been continuously inhabited starting from the sixth century BCE. Some other settlements may have existed in the area, as suggested by the presence of bronze material dating from the Bronze Age to the seventh century BCE and grave goods in the form of jewelry of the sixth century BCE. On Colle San Rufino itself, a system of moats and earthwork ramparts was perhaps associated with a high settlement on the summit.

The archaeological record of the cult place located at the summit of Colle San Rufino is limited to a small number of votive offerings, likely due to the history of the site's excavation. In 1879, archaeologist Wolfgang Helbig reported the discovery of seventy-five votive figurines and fragments of handmade vessels made of brown clay near a sulphur spring in the locality of Torre Maser, on top of S. Rufino hill. Most of the figurines were coarse male figurines about 3 cm high. However, when Francesco Pennacchi, an official of the municipality of Assisi, excavated the area indicated by Helbig in 1923, he did not find any structural remains. No other excavations have been carried out since then. In 1984, when the votive assemblage from the hill was published by Monacchi, the votive figurines mentioned by Helbig had been lost, except for eight specimens.

Due to the disappearance of votive objects found in the nineteenth century and the lack of any excavation record, our knowledge of the Monte Subasio sacred area is extremely fragmented. However, based on Monacchi's publication, it appears that the area was in use from the end of the sixth century/beginning of the fifth century BCE until the third/second century BCE.[82]

3.2.1 Sixth–Fourth Century BCE: Architectural and Spatial Distribution

No cult building of this period has been unearthed.

3.2.2 Sixth–Fourth Century BCE: Votive Material

Bronze figurines seem to have been the only votive offerings found on the Colle S. Rufino (figure 21).

Although Helbig noted the presence of seventy-five votive figurines (see above), Monacchi was able to study only five of them: one male figure of the EG type (figure A145), one striding male of the AmG type (figure A146), and three figurines classifiable under the umbrella of the group "Other" (figure A147–149).[83]

---

82   The findings are published in Monacchi 1984. The objects viewed by Monacchi are today missing. For the nineteenth-century excavations, see Helbig 1880, 249 and Archivio Storico di Perugia: Assisi 1-6.

83   EG: CSRufino_2. AmG: CSRufino_8. Other: CSRufino_1 CSRufino_7 CSRufino_3. The mea-

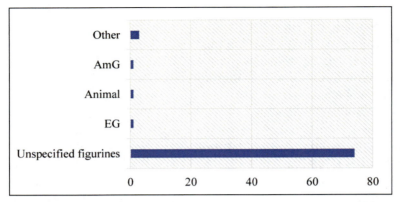

FIGURE 21   Graph showing the type distribution of the Monte Subasio votive figurines between the fifth and the fourth century BCE (the unspecified figurines are those mentioned by Helbig).

The first offering of this type (Other), CSRufino_1 represents a warrior figure with a miniature situla—a bucket-shaped vessel used for carrying liquids during religious ceremonies—attached to his left foot (A3.147). The warrior is depicted in a striding stance with the left leg forward, and the right arm lifted to throw a spear, while the left arm is bent to hold the shield. He wears a helmet with a fissure to hold the crest. The shoulder straps and the lower part of the greaves are decorated with small circlets. The iconography of the warrior belongs to the "Gruppo San Fortunato di Genga" ascribed by Colonna to northern Umbrian production and common in the Picenum region.[84] As for the situla, its miniature size and its association with a warrior figure have led Colonna to consider it as suggestive of the *lustratio agri*, a Roman ceremony described by Cato in *De Agricoltura* 141: farmers would address the god Mars with a prayer, beseeching him to "keep away, ward off, and remove" all kinds of catastrophes from their household, fields, and animals.[85]

---

surements in Appendix 2 for the offerings from Colle S. Rufino are those, often incomplete, noted by Monacchi. The inventory numbers for these objects reference the numbers given to them by Monacchi.

84   Colonna 1970, 48.
85   According to Cato (*Agr.* 141. 1–2), part of the formula for purifying the land was: *Mars pater, te precor quaesoque uti sies volens propitius mihi domo familiaeque nostrae, quoius re ergo agrum terram fundumque meum suovitaurilia circumagi iussi, uti tu morbos visos invisosque, viduertatem vastitudinemque, calamitates intemperiasque* **prohibessis defendas averruncesque**; *utique tu fruges, frumenta, vineta virgultaque grandire beneque evenire siris, pastores pecuaque salva servassis duisque bonam salutem valetudinemque mihi domo familiaeque nostrae.*

CSRufino_7 (A3.148) shows an elongated and rather flat figurine dressed in a tight, ankle-length dress with long sleeves; the surface of the dress is covered with a motif of incised circles that form parallel lines. The figure's left hand is bent to touch the side of the head, while the fingers of the right hand rest on the right hip. The facial features are coarsely rendered; the breast is signaled by incised circles. As Monacchi notes, although the figurine is stylistically in line with the Umbrian production of schematic offerings, its iconography recalls that of some Etruscan figurines found at Chiusi, interpreted as dancers.[86] The uniqueness of this object, as well as of CSRufino_1, suggests that they were most likely local products.

CSRufino_3 (A3.149) is an animal pendant with a hole through the center portion. The animal is schematically rendered, with no anatomical details. Pendants of this type are found most often in tomb context in Picenum.[87] Their presence among the materials of the Colle S. Rufino sacred area highlights the abovementioned cultural contacts between the two areas.

3.2.3 Late Fourth–Early First Century BCE: Architectural Aspects and Spatial Organization
No cult building of this period has been unearthed.

3.2.4 Late Fourth–Early First Centurys BCE: Votive Material
The material of this phase consists of three bronze figurines belonging to the Hellenistic worshiper type and dated to the third–second century BCE (figure A150).[88] Two represent the male worshiper type, and one is a fragment of an arm holding a patera.

4 Northern Umbria

4.1 *Monte Ansciano Sanctuary*
4.1.1 Topographic Location
The sanctuary is situated at the northern edge of a limestone mountain, standing 893 meters above sea level, in the northeastern region of Gubbio (formerly known as Iguvium). Positioned on the watershed between the Tyrrhenian and Adriatic coasts, the site holds strategic significance, with closer proximity to the

---

86 Maetzke 1957, 511; Richardson 1983, plate 193 figs. 562–563.
87 Monacchi 1984, 85–86, esp. note 50 for similar objects in Picene necropoleis.
88 CSRufino_4, CSRufino_5; arm with patera: CSRufino_6.

Adriatic. To the east lies the Gualdo Tadino Basin which, during Roman times and later, acted as a route for the Via Flaminia that ran from Rome to southern Umbria and then to the Adriatic through easy passes and valleys. The Apennines surround the site to the north and east. At the same time, the lower hills towards the south obstruct easy access from Perugia and the extensive former lake basins of central Umbria.

Bronze Age frequentation is attested in the area from 1100 BCE to 950 BCE. The presence of a drystone wall running around the summit, within which a midden accumulated—mostly bones and pottery but also a distinctive bronze fibula, daub, and blue glass beads—and a large oval posthole structure have led excavators to surmise that the summit served as an upland outpost, and that the majority of the population lived on the colluvial slopes below. During the same period, a similar settlement system existed on Monte Ingino, just northeast of Monte Ansciano, and a hut of the Late Bronze Age has been identified in the area of modern Gubbio, at the beginning of Via dei Consoli.

By the eighth century, occupation had shifted entirely from the summits of Monte Ansciano and Monte Ingino to the basin lying below them—the area of the Vescovado and S. Agostino—where a nucleated settlement and associated cemetery continued to be used until the Roman period. The material of this phase, mostly impasto pottery, suggests that these dwellings ceased to be used in the fourth century BCE when domestic structures and mortuary display became conspicuous in the area of Gubbio.

The Gubbio Project conducted a systematic excavation of the entire Gubbio valley from 1983 to 1987, which was published in 1988 and 1994.[89] Among their findings was evidence that the upper part of the Gubbio valley landscape had been intentionally made into a ritual space by the sixth century BCE. At Monte Ansciano, archaeologists discovered a sacred area likely in use from the sixth century BCE to the fourth–third century BCE, with occasional use continuing until the first century CE.

4.1.2   Sixth–Fourth Century BCE: Architectural and Spatial Distribution
The sacred area of this phase appears to have consisted of a simple drystone platform that capped a previous wall of the Bronze Age period (figure 22).

---

89   Stoddart and Whitley 1988, Stoddart and Malone 1994, Stoddart 2010, cf. Stoddart et al. 2012a and 2012b. The Gubbio valley may have hosted more than one sacred area. One bronze figurine was found on the Monte Ingino (Schippa 1987, 93) and two sporadic surface finds, published by Colonna (1970, 87; 105), come from Monte Loreto and Fratticciola Selvatica, on the northern and southern edges of the valley.

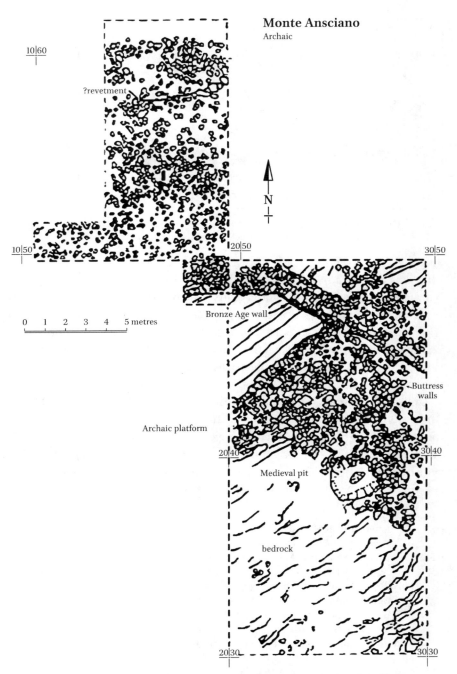

FIGURE 22 Plan of the sanctuary on Monte Ansciano (after Malone and Stoddart 1994, 146, fig. 5.2).

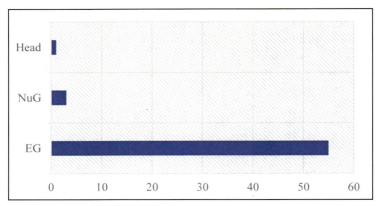

FIGURE 23   Graph showing the type distribution of the Monte Ansciano votive figurines between the fifth and the fourth century BCE.

4.1.3   Sixth–Fourth Century BCE Votive Material

Materials associated with this phase consist of one hundred and sixty-nine nails and some fragments of pottery, fifty-nine bronze figurines, and one fragment of a terracotta head (figure 23).[90] This material has been found mixed with earlier and later material in the upper soil layers of the excavations.

The votive figurines consist of thirty-five males (figure A151–154), twelve warriors (figure A155) and eight females (figure A156–158) of the EG type, three warriors of the NuG type (figure A159–160), and one head (figure A161).[91]

Unlike the Umbrian bronze votive heads of this period, the head from Monte Ansciano is made of clay. The face is characterized by large oval eyes and a mouth with closed lips. Fractures run right above the eyelids and along the left and lower part of the face; the nose is entirely chipped off. Despite the poor state of preservation of this artifact, the shape of the eyes and the mouth recalls specimens from Veii dated to the end of the sixth–early fifth century BCE.[92]

---

90   The pottery is unpublished and remains to date unstudied. One hundred and sixty-nine nails have been associated by the excavators with this phase.
91   EG males: MtAnsc_23 MtAnsc_24 MtAnsc_8 MtAnsc_9 MtAnsc_11 MtAnsc_4 MtAnsc_5 MtAnsc_6 MtAnsc_7 MtAnsc_14 MtAnsc_20 MtAnsc_21 MtAnsc_22 MtAnsc_26 MtAnsc_28 MtAnsc_29 MtAnsc_30 MtAnsc_33 MtAnsc_34 MtAnsc_35 MtAnsc_36 MtAnsc_37 MtAnsc_38 MtAnsc_39 MtAnsc_40 MtAnsc_41 MtAnsc_43 MtAnsc_44 MtAnsc_45 MtAnsc_47 MtAnsc_48 MtAnsc_49 MtAnsc_50 MtAnsc_51 MtAnsc_52.; EG warriors: MtAnsc_42 MtAnsc_53 MtAnsc_54 MtAnsc_55 MtAnsc_56 MtAnsc_57 MtAnsc_58 MtAnsc_59 MtAnsc_60 MtAnsc_61 MtAnsc_12 MtAnsc_13; EG females: MtAnsc_1 MtAnsc_2 MtAnsc_3 MtAnsc_18 MtAnsc_27 MtAnsc_31 MtAnsc_32 MtAnsc_46. NoG: MtAnsc_15 MtAnsc_16 MtAnsc_17. Head: MtAnsc_10.
92   Comparisons can be made in particular with the female head AII classified by Lucia Vagnetti (1971, 33; tav. V).

A MICRO-SCALE APPROACH TO ARCHAEOLOGY

4.1.4 Late Fourth–Early First Century BCE: Architectural Aspects and Spatial Organization

No cult building of this period has been unearthed.

4.1.5 Late Fourth–Early First Century BCE: Votive Material

Starting with the third century BCE, cult activity at Monte Ansciano seems to decrease. The only material evidence of this phase is represented by a coin of a very early Roman Republican issue and a bronze fragment depicting a patera (figure A162), most likely related to a figurine of the type Hellenistic worshiper.[93]

4.2 *Monte Acuto Sanctuary*

4.2.1 Topographic Location

The sanctuary is situated at a height of 926 meters on the summit of Monte Acuto, which is located on the right bank of the Tiber river in northwestern Umbria. From its peak, the mountain overlooks the surrounding territories, including the river and the Fratta plain situated on the border between the Etruscan and Umbrian territories.

This position of control over river and transit routes has been exploited since the Late Bronze Age. In this phase, a fortified settlement—identified on the ground by a ditch, an embankment of stone heaps, and fragments of bowls, handles (*a cornetti* and *a maniglia*), and impasto cooking ware—was built on the extreme limit of the crest in direct visual control of the Umbrian plains and territory. A series of fortified settlements on the lower mountain peaks at about 700 m above sea level (Monte Elceto di Murlo, Monte Civitelle, Cerchiaia, Monte Corona, Monte Santa Croce) gravitated to this axis of control. These settlements shared similar features of altitude and were equipped with circular or elliptical enclosures, whose local drystone elements are still visible on the ground.

After an apparent hiatus of hundreds of years, the summit of Monte Acuto was transformed into a sacred place starting from the sixth/fifth century BCE. Given its position, the sanctuary had a viewshed that enclosed other similar Umbrian sanctuaries in Umbria: from north to south, Gubbio (Monte Ansciano), Umbertide (Monte Acuto), Assisi (Monte Subasio, Monte Subasio), Terni (Monte Torre Maggiore), and Calvi dell'Umbria (Monte San Pancrazio). It seems, therefore, that the original purpose of utilizing the mountain for its elevated position was reiterated during the archaic period and accompanied by a sacred function. It is reasonable to imagine that the population of the sur-

---

93 MtAnsc_19.

FIGURE 24 Excavation plan of the Monte Acuto sanctuary. A: entrance; B: precinct; C: *sacellum*; D: votive pit (after Cenciaioli 1998, 46).

rounding territories used the sanctuary on Monte Acuto not only for religious purposes but also to find shelter and gather in moments of danger.

From 1986 to 1995, the Soprintendenza Archeologica dell'Umbria, led by Luana Cenciaioli, conducted investigations on the summit of Monte Acuto. These excavations revealed a cult site that was in use from the sixth to the fourth century BCE and was occasionally visited until the fourth century CE.[94]

Unfortunately, the area on top of Monte Acuto has suffered from degradation caused by both natural and human factors over time. Human activities, such as the installation of cell towers, have caused significant harm to the site. Furthermore, clandestine actions and looters have disrupted the stratigraphy and resulted in the loss of essential archaeological information.

4.2.2   Sixth–Fourth Century BCE: Architectural and Spatial Distribution

The sanctuary is characterized by a pseudo-rectangular enclosure (35×20 m) with a wall of about 3 m wide built with local stones without mortar. On the western side of the enclosure, a small drystone corridor led to the *sacellum*, built with two courses of drystone wall (figure 24). The presence of three small

---

94   For a topographic framework of the sanctuary and the excavation's results, see Cenciaioli 1992, 1996, 1998.

A MICRO-SCALE APPROACH TO ARCHAEOLOGY

channels cut into the rock of the rectangular foundation suggests that this area was dedicated to the sacrifice of animals, whose remains (bovine) have been recovered inside the votive pit. The latter (4 m deep and ca. 3.50 m wide) is dug into the rock south of the *sacellum*. Besides bones and votive figurines (below), the pit has yielded brick fragments—interpreted as the material of the structure's roof—one spindle, impasto clay, the base of a cup, and a ribbed handle related to a previous occupation of the area.

4.2.3 Sixth–Fourth Century BCE: Votive Material

Votive figurines represent the only type of offerings found at the Monte Acuto sanctuary. The excavation has retrieved 1600 specimens, of which I could analyze only one hundred and eighteen (figure 25). Sixty-nine of them have been recovered inside the votive pit, while the rest has been found spread across the entire excavation areas in disturbed layers.

The most common type of figurine is the EG (figure A163–166). At Monte Acuto this group comprises sixteen male figures (A3.163–164), twenty females (165–166), and six warriors (A3.167). Animal figurines (figure A168–172) are attested by twelve pigs (A3.168), ten sheep (A3.169), seven oxen (A3.170), two goats (A3.171), and three unidentifiable quadrupeds (A3.172). Thirteen human figures cut from thin sheets of bronze belong to the BS type (figure A173–174). The extreme approximation of their bodily features and poor state of preservation allows us only to identify two as men, while the rest remain unrecognizable. The NuG is attested by nine figurines of warriors (figure A175–176) and the AmG by six figurines representing a striding male (figure A177–178). Lastly, eleven votive figurines represent specific parts of the human body (figure A179–182): five heavily deteriorated heads (A3.179) with features that resemble the heads of the EG figurines, four legs (A3.180), one hand (A3.181), and one arm (A3.182).[95]

---

[95] EG males: MTA_21 MTA_22 MTA_23 MTA_24 MTA_25 MTA_26 MTA_27 MTA_28 MTA_29 MTA_30 MTA_31 MTA_32 MTA_39 MTA_40 MTA_41 MTA_42 MTA_43 MTA_44 MTA_45 MTA_46; EG female: MTA_10 MTA_11 MTA_12 MTA_14 MTA_15 MTA_16 (extremely schematic); MTA_47 MTA_48 MTA_49 MTA_50 MTA_51 MTA_52 MTA_53 MTA_54 MTA_55 MTA_56; EG warriors: MTA_17 MTA_18 MTA_19 MTA_56 MTA_57 MTA_58. Animals: MTA_59 MTA_60 MTA_61 MTA_62 MTA_63 MTA_64 MTA_65 MTA_66 MTA_67 MTA_68 MTA_69 MTA_70 MTA_71 MTA_72 MTA_73 MTA_74 MTA_75 MTA_76 MTA_77 MTA_78 MTA_79 MTA_80 MTA_81 MTA_82 MTA_83 MTA_84 MTA_85 MTA_86 MTA_87 MTA_88 MTA_89 MTA_90 MTA_91 MTA_92 MTA_93. NoG: MTA_1 MTA_2 MTA_3 MTA_4 MTA_5 MTA_6 MTA_7 MTA_8 MTA_9. BS: MTA_94 MTA_95 MTA_96 MTA_97 MTA_98 MTA_99 MTA_100 MTA_101 MTA_102 MTA_103 MTA_104 MTA_105. AmG: MTA_33 MTA_34 MTA_35 MTA_36 MTA_37 MTA_38. Heads: MTA_108

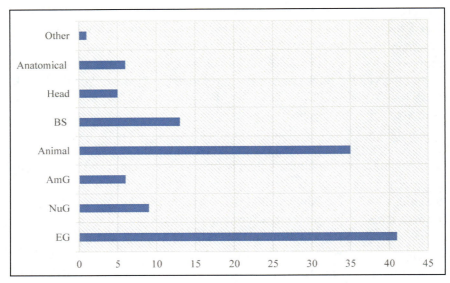

FIGURE 25 Graph showing the type distribution of the Monte Acuto sanctuary's votive figurines between the sixth and the fourth century BCE.

The excavation has also retrieved a situla in the shape of a basket (MTA_118). This vessel has a narrow foot and two small rings (broken on the upper part) attached to each handle, and, unlike the situla found at the Monte Subasio sanctuary (CSRufino_1), it is not hollow. If Colonna's interpretation of the connection between this miniature vessel and the god Mars is right,[96] it is possible that also in the case of Monte Acuto the object relates to the *lustratio agri*, the propitiatory ceremony dedicated to the god Mars in the hope that he will increase the abundance of fields and cattle. In this respect, the high number of animal figurines dedicated at this site may be a further indication of the practice of this type of purification ceremony.

4.2.4 Late Fourth–Early First Century BCE: Architectural Aspects and Spatial Organization

No interventions seem to have been made at Monte Acuto during this phase.

MTA_109 MTA_110 MTA_111 MTA_112 MTA_113. Arm: MTA_106; hand: MTA_107; legs: MTA_114 MTA_115 MTA_116 MTA_117.

96 Colonna 1970, 48.

A MICRO-SCALE APPROACH TO ARCHAEOLOGY 133

4.2.5 Late Fourth–Early First Century BCE: Votive Material

During this period, fragments of black gloss and sigillata italica, along with a miniature vase, have been found as the sole archaeological evidence from Monte Acuto. This apparent decline in use of the sanctuary continues during the imperial period, as attested by a group of coins of the second century CE and the fourth/fifth century CE.

5 Apennine Umbria

5.1 *Colle Mori Sanctuary*

5.1.1 Topographic Location

The sanctuary is situated at the summit of Colle Mori, which is located 743 meters above sea level and approximately 3 kilometers north of the modern town of Gualdo Tadino. The hill lies on the western side of the Umbria-Marche Apennines and is positioned only a few kilometers from the mountain passes of Fossato di Vico (740 m) and Scheggia (575 m). The surrounding landscape is characterized by mountains to the east, including Monte Serra, Monte Fringuello, and Monte Penna, and hills to the west. A plain stretches from north to south, bounded by mountains and hills.

The presence of iron and copper deposits in the area controlling important trans-Apennine routes encouraged human occupation since the Late Bronze Age (thirteenth century BCE). During this period, there seems to have been a protohistoric settlement on the summit of the hill. Archaeologists have found traces of circular hearths and a considerable number of objects, such as cups and ollae made of impasto, spindle whorls, loom weights, and bronze ornaments dated between the thirteenth and the ninth century BCE. Additionally, some evidence of Bronze Age occupation in the area has been discovered about two kilometers southeast of this settlement, where a valuable deposit of two golden discs, horse bits, and scalpels was found.

In the sixth century BCE, Colle Mori saw a resurgence of human occupation after a gap of four centuries. On the western slope of the hill, a small nucleated settlement covering a few hectares was discovered (figure 26). The settlement was built on artificial terraces, constructed with walls made of dry-laid limestone slabs, and positioned along the contour levels. The buildings on the terraces included both public and private structures, featuring three rooms and, in some cases, multiple floors.[97] The cemeteries of San Facondino, Malpasso,

---

97   For this settlement, see also Chapter 4.

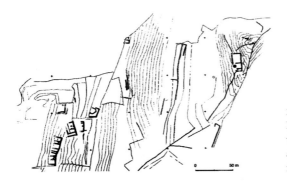

FIGURE 26
Plan of the Colle Mori Umbrian settlement. On the right: the sacred area (after Bonomi Ponzi 2010, 184 fig. 25).

Cartiere, and the sacred area on the summit of the hill were associated with the settlement. From the top of the hill, the sanctuary overlooked the entire valley and the access roads that straddled the Apennines.

The settlement, possibly occupied by the Tadinates mentioned in the Iguvine Tablets and attested in an inscription of the fourth century BCE,[98] was defended by a series of small fortified settlements that controlled access routes from the neighboring territories of Perugia and Gubbio, in addition to the Apennine routes towards the Adriatic Sea. The ceramic material, which covers cooking and food conservation needs, indicates that the settlement on the Colle Mori was occupied until the third century BCE before being abandoned, perhaps due to a fire. At the end of the third century BCE, following the abandonment of the Umbrian center, a new settlement was founded in the valley, southwest of the modern town of Gualdo Tadino and facing the Via Flaminia.

Our knowledge of the site is owed to the detailed fieldwork of Enrico Stefani and Laura Bonomi Ponzi. In 1921 and 1935, Stefani uncovered the remains of the necropolis of San Facondino and evidence of the sacred area on the summit of the Colle Mori. Between 1992 and 2002, Stefani's work was resumed by the Soprintendenza per i Beni Archeologici dell'Umbria under the direction of Bonomi Ponzi. This decade of archaeological investigation brought to light the existence of the Bronze Age and archaic settlement and clarified the phases of the sacred area on the summit of the hill.[99] The votive material suggests that the

---

98   The inscription, published by Rix (2002, Um 201) was found in 1996 on the slopes of the Colle Mori. It reads *tarina/ ei tuce st[ahu]* (I-stand (here) in-public/publicly for-the-Tadinates) and has been interpreted as the boundary marker of the settlement that occupied the summit of the hill. It attests that, at least in the fourth century, the Umbrians living on the hill referred to their settlement with a name and offers a confirmation of the later mention of this community in Tablet I of the Iguvine Tablets. The inscription is examined in Agostiniani et al. 2011, 54–55.

99   Stefani's excavation results are published in Stefani 1935. Some of the findings from the

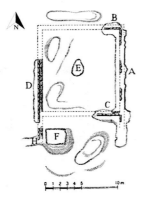

FIGURE 27
Plan of the *sacellum*: letters A, B, and C indicate the walls of the *cella*; E is the pit; F is the cistern inside the *pronaos* (modified after Stefani 1935, 156, fig. 2).

sacred area continued to be used even after the abandonment of the settlement on the slopes and was been frequented until at least the second century BCE.

5.1.2 Sixth–Fourth Century BCE: Architectural and Spatial Distribution

During this period, the sacred complex comprised a temple (measuring 11.90 × 10.70 m) with a rectangular *cella* and *pronaos*, which was almost precisely oriented according to the cardinal points (figure 27). The perimeter walls (A, B, C, D) were constructed using dry-laid and irregularly shaped limestone blocks. The regularly spaced openings on the walls were likely post holes that once supported the poles that held the structure of the walls. Inside the *cella*, there was a pit (E) where a bronze foot and a slab with two clumps were discovered, possibly related to a cult statue. Within the space of the *pronaos*, a 3 m deep pit (F) was dug and interpreted by the Soprintendenza's excavators as a cistern that was connected to the religious activity practiced on site.

5.1.3 Sixth–Fourth Century BCE: Votive Material

The votive material is composed of eight specimens of *aes rude*—noted by Stefani and now lost—six bronze figurines, and one terracotta head (figure 28). Except for two bronze figurines and the coins, which Stefani reports to have been found in the temple's *cella*, the offerings were found deposited inside the cistern together with a number of iron nails and four metal objects, three unidentifiable and one interpreted by the excavator as part of a door hinge.

Soprintendenza's excavation, mainly related to the settlements and the necropolis, are summarized in De Vecchi 2002, Bonomi Ponzi 2010, Micozzi 2014 (on the necropolis only), and Manconi 2017, 620–621. Unfortunately, the unpublished reports of the excavation season are absent from the archive of the Soprintendenza.

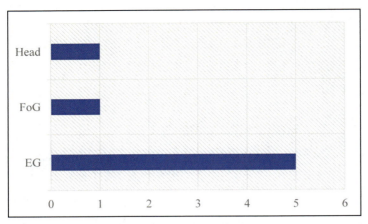

FIGURE 28   Graph showing the type distribution of the Colle Mori votive figurines between the sixth and the fourth century BCE.

The bronze figurines consist of five males of the EG type (figure A183–185) and one warrior of the FoG type (figure A186).[100] Although only the head of the latter is preserved, the original appearance can be reconstructed with the aid of a drawing produced by Stefani (A3.186).

The terracotta head is wheel-made and entirely in the round (figure A187).[101] Due to a large break running across the figure's mouth, the only features preserved are the lower lip, the chin, and the neck. The lips appear to be pursed in a faint "archaic smile," the chin is pointed, and the neck tapers at the center and widens at the bottom. The rendering of the smile and neck is clearly derived from Attic korai, or maiden figures, sculpted in Athens around 530–500 BCE. The closest central Italian parallel is a head (AIV according to Vagnetti's classification) from Veii that is dated around the end of the sixth to the beginning of the fifth century BCE.[102] It is likely that the terracotta head from Colle Mori was also made in the same timeframe.

5.1.4 Late Fourth–Early First Century BCE: Architectural Aspects and Spatial Organization

The cistern and the temple are paved in cocciopesto (figure 29).

---

100   EG: CM_5 CM_6 CM 7 CM_8 CM_9; FoG: CM_10_.
101   CM_1. Bonomi Ponzi (2010, 187) tentatively interprets the object as an acroterion. To be placed on roofs, however, statues in the round had to be attached to bases, and the bottom of the CM_1 is smoothly finished with no trace of having been attached to anything.
102   Vagnetti 1971, 32, tav. VII.

FIGURE 29 Colle Mori cistern clad in bricks (after Bonomi Ponzi 2010, 189, fig. 35).

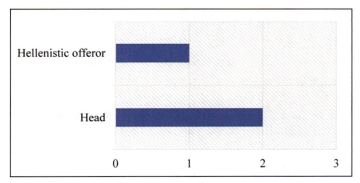

FIGURE 30   Graph showing the type distribution of the Colle Mori figurative votive offerings between the late fourth and the early first century BCE.

5.1.5   Late Fourth–Early First Century BCE: Votive Material

The materials from this phase comprise a black gloss miniature vase with Umbrian letters inscribed on the bottom and the outer wall, a black gloss plate, fragments of a black gloss cup, and three figurative votive offerings (figure 30). While the black gloss pottery is mentioned by Stefani as having been found alongside the eastern wall of the temple (D), the figurative votive offerings come from the cistern from inside the *pronaos*. These consist of one bronze figurine of the Hellenistic female worshiper type (figure A188) and two terracotta heads, all dated to the end of the fourth/third century BCE (figure A189–190).[103]

One head (A3.188) is represented in profile (left). The face is oval and slightly titled back. The hair is curly and combed tidily forward. A few locks stick out of

---

103   Hellenistic worshiper: CM_4; Heads: CM_2 CM_3.

138   CHAPTER 5

a hairband and rise above the center of the crown, and some cover the temple and the ear. The eye is oval and deep and the nose is straight and small. The mouth is straight. The overall effect is slightly androgynous, making it difficult to determine the gender. The soft lines and features of the head are reminiscent of some Etruscan heads classified as type AI by Söderlind, indicating a possible dating to the second half of the third century BCE.[104]

The second piece (A3.190) represents the back of a head rejoined from four pieces. The hair is simply represented with wavy incisions, and a diadem is visible on the top of the head, indicating that it is likely a depiction of a female head. However, due to the poor state of preservation and lack of details in the hairdo, it is difficult to precisely date this piece or compare it to other dated heads from central Italy.

5.2   *Cancelli Sanctuary*

5.2.1   Topographic Location

The sanctuary site is in the modern cemetery of Cancelli, 13 km east of Foligno (ancient Fulginae), on a mountain almost 1000 meters above sea level. It is situated in the heart of Apennine Umbria, along a mountain chain that marks the eastern boundary of the Umbrian valley, on the left of the river Menotre, a tributary of the Topino. The centrality of this site as a crossroads and crossing point is highlighted by the presence of a series of ancient paths that, originating in the Umbrian valley, converge at Cancelli.

Archaeological evidence suggests that human occupation of the area dates back to the sixth century BCE, with the establishment of a fortified settlement in the valley below the mountain, 910 meters above sea level. At the same time, a cult place was built halfway up the slope, in the locality of La Corte, 934 meters above sea level. On the hilltop, 1010 meters above sea level, a fortification with a moat and embankment was discovered, which was part of a larger system of fortified settlements strategically placed around the mountains surrounding Foligno. These fortifications served defensive and territorial control purposes, as they allowed for monitoring approach routes like the Via Plestina and the road leading to Cancelli. Other examples of such fortified settlements include the Monte Aguzzo (1100 meters above sea level), the two peaks of Monte Cologna, and the area of Acqua Santo Stefano.

The sacred area on the hill has been known since the late nineteenth century, but only in recent years has it been the focus of systematic archaeological campaigns.[105] In the summer of 2012 and 2013, the Soprintendenza per i Beni Arche-

---

104   Söderlind 2000, 145–145.
105   Michele Faloci Pulignani published a report in 1890 where he mentions the fortuitous find-

A MICRO-SCALE APPROACH TO ARCHAEOLOGY

ologici dell'Umbria, under the direction of Maria Laura Manca, and a team of high school students supervised by archaeologists Maria Romana Picuti and Matelda Albanesi, investigated the central and northern sectors of the modern cemetery of Cancelli. They uncovered an area of 20×8m that belonged to the ancient cult place.[106] The excavations revealed that the sacred place was in use from the sixth century BCE until the Augustan period, after which it appears to have been abandoned, possibly due to an earthquake. Fragments of lamps dated to the fourth/fifth century CE attest to occasional visitation of the area until the Late Antique period.

5.2.2   Sixth–Fourth Century BCE: Architectural and Spatial Distribution
No architectural remains belonging to this phase have been unearthed in the area.

5.2.3   Sixth–Fourth Century BCE: Votive Material
The materials associated with this phase of the site include various vessels for cooking and eating food, such as impasto ollae and cups, which were locally produced, as well as imported bucchero bowls and Faliscan overpainted black gloss cups and plates from Etruscan and Faliscan territory. A few miniature vessels, such as jugs and bowls in impasto or purified ware, bronze Etruscan vessels, one bronze fibula, one bronze pendant, loom weights, and twelve figurative votive offerings in bronze were also found (figure 31). These materials were discovered mixed with later objects in two layers of soil rich in charcoal, which are believed to be the layers that leveled and sealed the earliest architectural structures below.

Among the figurative votive offerings, the most frequently represented types are the FoG (figure A191–192), attested by three warrior figurines, and the EG, which includes the figure of one man (3.193), one woman (A3.194), and one warrior (A3.195). The other figurines consist of two bulls of the Animal type (figure A196), one warrior of the NoG type (figure A197), one bronze sheet depicting a male figure (figure A198), one "eyed crest" (figure A199), one schematic head (figure A210), and one schematic limb representing a left arm (figure A201).[107]

---

　　　　ings of some bronze votive offerings in the area of the modern Cancelli cemetery: Faloci Pulignani 1890, 315.
106   Manca et al. 2014.
107   FoG: Cancelli_3 Cancelli_9 Cancelli_12. NoG: Cancelli_13 Cancelli_14 Cancelli_16Animal: Cancelli_11 Cancelli 15; BS: Cancelli_1; Eyed crest: Cancelli_4; Head: Cancelli_5; Anatomical: Cancelli_6.

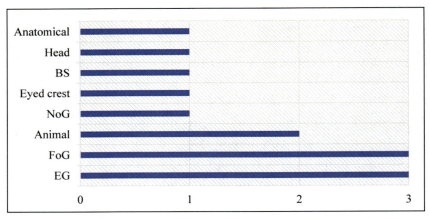

FIGURE 31   Graph showing the type distribution of the Cancelli votive figurines between the sixth and the fourth century BCE.

5.2.4 Late Fourth–Early First Century BCE: Architectural and Spatial Distribution

Although the complete layout of the sanctuary is not known, it is during this phase that it was monumentalized. The first phase of this construction, which occurred in the fourth–third century BCE, involved the creation of drystone walls that were aligned northwest/southeast and built directly on the bedrock. Additionally, a large container called a dolium was buried in the ground and filled with lime during this phase. While there are no comparisons available for such a use, the excavators believe that the lime was stored in the vessel for use in ritual activities.

These structures underwent a significant change sometimes during the second century BCE when they were rebuilt and rotated on a north–south/east–west axis. Three rooms (one has been excavated only partially) were built following the new orientation (figure 32). Two of them, equipped with *opus signinum* floors, show evidence of later alterations, such as the blocking and substitution of two openings with a drain, which also went out of use and was subsequently replaced by a drain with *opus reticulatum* inserts. The original function of these rooms is unknown, although the presence of the water channel suggests water-related rituals.

With respect to the architectural decoration of the complex during this phase, the excavation yielded a terracotta antefix and a small sandstone fragment belonging to the vegetal ornaments of a capital. The former, destroyed during the Second World War, depicts a female head surrounded by acanthus leaves. At the base of the antefix is a socle decorated with an ionic frieze with ovules and smooth listels. This motif, with human heads surrounded by a deco-

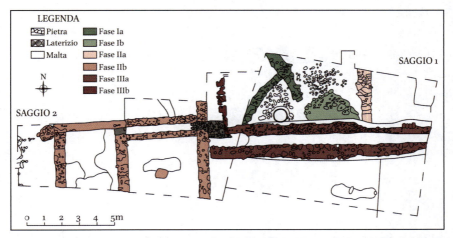

FIGURE 32 Plan of the excavation. The features in green belong to the first phase of the structure, while the ones in brown belong to the second-century BCE phase (after Manca et al. 2014, 31, fig. 10).

rative shell that begins at the base with a pair of acanthus leaves, has its origins in southern Italy in the area of Taranto and is believed to have been elaborated in Etruria around the fourth century BCE. A comparison with similar specimens found at Arezzo, Chiusi, Cortona, Perugia, and other centers of Apennine Umbria suggests a dating for the piece from Cancelli around the late third–second century BCE.[108]

5.2.5 Late Fourth–Early First Century BCE: Votive Material

The material from this phase consists of ceramics (one south-Etruscan or northern-Latial overpainted *kantharos* and small cups with black floral motif), a bronze bowl, one Roman Republican coin, one figurine of Hellenistic worshiper, one head, and one foot (figure 33).

The coin is a Republican *as* of the first century BCE and shows Janus on the obverse and three prows on the reverse. Ceramics are mostly represented by imported and locally produced black gloss pottery, a vast proportion of which includes plates, bowls, and cups. Miniature pottery is also abundant and includes amphorae, one of which has the letter *a* inscribed on the outer wall, and pitchers.

---

108   Picuti 2006, 205. A second antefix from Cancelli depicts a head between felines and can be attributed to the Julio-Claudian period.

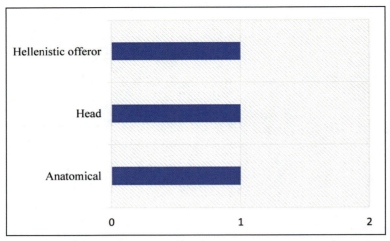

FIGURE 33 Graph showing the type distribution of Cancelli figurative votive offerings between the end of the fourth and the first century BCE.

The figurine of the Hellenistic worshiper type is unfortunately lost, but is preserved in one drawing produced by Michele Faloci Pulignani and published by Picuti (figure A 212), which shows the figure of a male wearing a long tunic and a rayed crown; in his right hand he holds a patera. The terracotta anatomical offerings have been both generically attributed by the excavators to the Republican period.[109] They are in an extremely poor state of preservation, with breaks that hinder a comprehensive understanding of the whole item.[110]

The foot is realized in a summary way without most anatomical details, except for a slight separation between the big toe and the other toes (figure A203). The toes are not separated and there is no indication of toenails. The foot rests on a rounded shoe sole that follows the contours of the foot. The poor state of preservation does not allow the object to be dated more precisely than to the Republican period. Furthermore, we cannot exclude the possibility that the foot was part of a statue rather than a votive offering on its own.

The head, which preserves traces of red paint on the orbital region and the crown, presents deeply carved eyes with their pupils plastically rendered and protruding eyebrows with sharp lines (figure A204). Overall, the hair and features are coarsely rendered. The few surviving typological properties seem to

---

[109] Cancelli_17 Cancelli 2.
[110] It is worth mentioning that the excavators do not provide a clear interpretation for these objects. In particular, they suggest that the head may be interpreted as an antefix but do not present any comparisons to make this interpretation sound.

correspond with Söderlind's AIX type and thus can be tentatively attributable to the second century BCE.[111]

5.3   *Campo La Piana Sanctuary*

5.3.1   Topographic Location

The sanctuary at Campo La Piana, like the sanctuary at Monte Pennino (5.4.4, below), is in the territory of Nocera Umbra (ancient *Nuceria*) located in the Umbrian Apennines some 20 km north of Foligno. This large area measures about 100 km² and lies on a hill flanked by the valleys of the rivers Topino and Caldagnola. The river valleys and the roads that run on both sides of Monte Pennino guaranteed a functional connection between the Tyrrhenian and the north-central Adriatic coast prior to the construction of the Via Flaminia. They connected the Nucerian territory with, on the one hand, the road system of the Colfiorito plateau and, on the other, the valley of the Potenza river in the modern Le Marche region. Such territorial organization was complemented since the sixth century BCE by the cult places identified at Campo La Piana and on Monte Pennino.

Traces of occupation in the Nuceria area begin during the Orientalizing period (eighth century BCE) and become more frequent in the archaic period (sixth/fifth century BCE). During this phase, the dominant settlement pattern was one of fortified villages set on hilltops. These settlements have been identified mainly through aerial photos and surveys (pottery, tiles, millstones fragments), and they appear to have been surrounded by moats and ramparts of stones and grouped around major topographical elements such as mountains, valleys or plains.

The necropoleis associated with the hilltop villages were laid at the bottom of the hill. Grave goods from the necropolis of Portone (second half of the eighth century to the end of the sixth century BCE) and Boschetto-Ginepraia (end of the seventh century to the early fifth century BCE) illustrate the existence of a wealthy aristocracy and lively trade with both the Tyrrhenian and the Adriatic coasts. Among the most remarkable grave goods are ceramic and metallic imported objects, such as Etruscan bronze basins and red-figure vases, fibulae and cups from Picenum, amber beads and glass paste, weapons, and precious ornaments in bronze, silver, and iron (bracelets, fibulae, pendants, decorated discs).

The Campo La Piana sanctuary was located near a transhumance route that, crossing the Subasio mountain, connected Asisium (modern Assisi) with Tad-

---

111   Söderlind 2002, 142–145.

FIGURE 34   Drawing of the walls identified by Ticchioni in loc. Campo La Piana. Letter D indicates the space where votive materials were found (after Brizio 1891, 309).

inum (modern Gualdo Tadino), and the Umbrian valley with the valley formed by the Topino river. The sanctuary was discovered and excavated in 1890 by a local resident, Pierleone Ticchioni, in the aftermath of the fortuitous discovery of votive bronzes, coins, and pottery. Edoardo Brizio, at the time "Ispettore dei Musei e degli Scavi presso la Direzione Generale degli Scavi di Antichità," was appointed to write a report of Ticchioni's investigation and examine the objects found on site.[112] Based on the coins he found, Brizio determined that the sanctuary was used from the fifth century BCE to the second BCE, and then again in the third century CE.

It is not possible to verify Brizio's assessment for two reasons. First, the area has not been investigated since 1890, and the documentation has thus not been updated. Second, apart from four figurines and two coins, the material has been irretrievably lost and was never documented.

5.3.2   Sixth–Fourth Century BCE: Architectural and Spatial Distribution
The complete layout of the cult place is not known. The excavation carried out by Ticchioni brought to light a wall in *opus quadratum* (wall A) which ran for ca. 50 m and was preserved for a height of 10 m. This wall intersected at an acute angle with a smaller wall in *opus incertum* (wall C; figure 34).

5.3.3   Sixth–Fourth Century BCE: Votive Material
A large quantity of votive material has been recovered in the sanctuary area. No quantitative data are available, and there has been no stratigraphic contextualization of the finds.

This material was found in the space between the two walls (D in the figure above) under a thick layer of ash. It is composed of fragments of *aes rude* and

---

112   Brizio 1891, 308–313. More in general on the Nuceria territory and the necropoleis, see Bonomi Ponzi 1985 and Albanesi and Picuti 2013.

A MICRO-SCALE APPROACH TO ARCHAEOLOGY

several figurative votive offerings, whose number and type remain unknown. Although Brizio records the presence of more than one hundred and fifty items—mostly figures of warriors and devotees but also two bronze heads— only four specimens survive (figure 35). These are four male figurines of the EG type (figure A205–206) and one clay head that falls under the broad umbrella of the group "Other" (figure A207).[113]

The clay head dates to the fourth century BCE and was part of a now-missing statuette. It represents an individual with rounded eyes, a large nose, and a wide mouth wearing a pointed hat. This peculiar hat provides an important clue that allows the identification of the subject. Scholars have recognized hats as identifying elements in Etruscan priestly costumes.[114] In particular, the pointed hat has been attributed to the haruspices, the diviners specializing in reading animal entrails to determine the will of the gods, whom the Romans used during the period of the Roman Republic and the Empire.[115]

Although the available evidence points to the presence of haruspices in Umbria from Etruria or trained there only in the first BCE,[116] our figurine may

---

113   CLP_1 CLP_2 CLP_3 CLP_4; other: CPL_5.
114   The hats had similar importance in the presentation of Roman *flamines*. For an extensive analysis of priestly dress and attributes in Etruria, see de Grummond 2006, 35–38; Gleba and Becker 2009, 184–191.
115   Information on the function and role of these priests during the Roman period comes from literary (Cic. *Div.* 1.92) and epigraphic sources (the well-known Constantine inscription from Spello of the fourth CE). In Roman sources, the haruspices appear as interpreters of *fulgura* (thunderbolts), *ostenta* (unusual happenings), and above all *exta* (entrails, especially liver). Iconographically, scholars have identified features of the costume of the haruspex in a bronze statuette of the fourth century BCE dedicated by Vel Sveitus and displayed in the Vatican Museums. It represents a clean-shaven figure wrapped in a fringed mantle fastened with a fibula wearing a tall hat, tied under the chin, that broadens into a fitted cap with a slight brim: Gleba and Becker 2009, 183–193 and 283 fig. 50; Turfa 2013, 539–556. Another depiction of a haruspex occurs on a mirror from Tuscania, dating to the third century BCE. In the scene represented here and interpreted as a sort of lesson in haruspicy, a beardless man wears a similar apical hat with a cord at the neck. For a discussion on this bronze mirror, see Turfa 2013, 540–541. See also Jannot 2005, 125–126; De Grummond 2006, 27–28.
116   A funerary epitaph (ET Um 1.7; *CIL* 11.6363) inscribed on a marble plaque dated to the last quarter of the first century BCE was found at Pesaro. The inscription, in Latin and Etruscan, recalls the role of the Etruscan native Cafate, who, with his part-Latin genealogy, was both haruspex and interpreter of thunderbolts. Another inscription (*CIL* 1.3378) found in Maevania (Bevagna) and dated to the Late Republican period mentions that the local senate had decreed the posting of this inscription in honor of Aulus Rubrius, a haruspex from Volsinii. Bonomi Ponzi (Feruglio et al. 1991, 86–87) notices that the name Rubrius appears in other inscriptions from Maevania but not in Volsinii. She therefore proposes that the haruspex came from Mevania but had been instructed in the art of haruspicy at Volsinii,

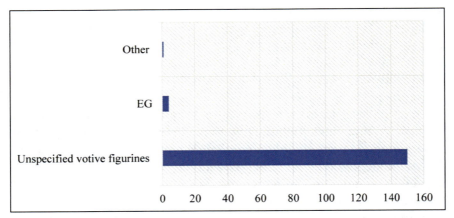

FIGURE 35   Graph showing the type distribution of the Campo La Piana votive figurines between the sixth and the fourth century BCE.

represent the dedication of such a priest (or his family member) who either was traveling or was asked to intervene at the Campo La Piana sanctuary in the region in the fourth century BCE. However, since Umbrian priestly attire is unknown, our figure arguably represented a local priest with uncertain functions.

5.3.4   Late Fourth–Early First Century BCE: Architectural and Spatial Distribution

No cult building of this period has been unearthed.

5.3.5   Late Fourth–Early First Century BCE: Votive Material

Like the pre-Roman material, objects of this phase have been found under the ash layers inside the walls. None of them have survived, and only scant information can be gathered from Brizio's account. He lists black gloss pottery, *fibulae*, glass beads, Greek and Roman coins, and figurative votive offerings. These are generically attributed to the Hellenistic and Republican periods on the basis of the votive type they represent: one female Hellenistic worshiper and two forearms (figure 36).[117]

and Haack (2002, 128) adds that this is the earliest known source that shows an Etruscan office translating to an Italian/Roman position.

117   CLP_8 CLP_9 CLP_10.

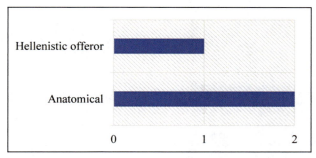

FIGURE 36   Graph showing the type distribution of Campo La Piana figurative votive offerings between the late fourth and the early first century BCE.

5.4 Monte Pennino Sanctuary

5.4.1 Topographic Location

The cult site is located on the peak of Monte Pennino (1590 m above sea level), on the border between the province of Macerata, in the region Le Marche, and the province of Perugia in Umbria. The high peak played a significant role as a passage between the eastern and northern regions of the Apennines, with roads connecting the Colfiorito basin, the Umbrian valley, and the Val Nerina on both sides of the mountain.

The existence of a sacred area on the mountaintop was first proposed after World War II by Pietro Staderini, an antiquities collector and resident of Nocera Umbra, who found several votive offerings and a pit dug into the rock. Using numismatic evidence, he suggested that the cult site existed on the mountain from the sixth century to the Late Republican period. However, without any archaeological investigation of the peak following Staderini's discovery, it is impossible to verify his information. The only documentation available on the sacred area is an account published by a priest, Gino Sigismondi.[118] Adding to the challenge, most of the votive offerings collected by Staderini have been lost or are in private possession, making it impossible to determine the exact location of the sanctuary, its layout, and the duration of its use. Based solely on the information provided by Sigismondi, it appears that ritual activity on the mountain took place from the sixth to the second or first century BCE.

---

118   Sigismondi 2009, 44–45.

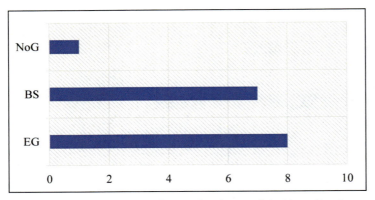

FIGURE 37   Graph showing the type distribution of the Monte Pennino votive figurines between the sixth and the fourth century BCE.

5.4.2   Sixth–Fourth Century BCE: Architectural and Spatial Distribution

In the absence of excavation, it is impossible to know if a cult building existed on the mountain.

5.4.3   Sixth–Fourth Century BCE: Votive Material

Part of the votive deposit was contained within a small pit (60 cm deep) found and excavated by Staderini. The material therein consists of a small iron blade, a pot, and remains of animal bones belonging to a rooster, a jackdaw, and a toad, interpreted as the remains of animal sacrifice.

Other material found scattered on the peak included an indefinite number of bronze votive figurines, only sixteen specimens of which survive, either displayed in a local museum or privately owned (figure 37).[119] These are eight male figures of the EG type, seven figurines of the BS type (figure A208), and one warrior of the NoG type.[120]

5.4.4   Late Fourth–Early First Century BCE: Votive Material

Some finds provide evidence for the use of the area during the Roman period. They include three Roman Republican *asses* and several fragments of painted pottery.

---

[119]   Unfortunately, however, only two are currently visible. The remaining part is owned by the Staderini family and not available to be studied.

[120]   BS: MTP_1 MTP_2 MTP_3 MTP_4 MTP_5 MTP_6 MTP_7; EG: MTP_8 MTP_9 MTP_10 MTP_11 MTP_12 MTP_13 MTP_14 MTP_15; NoG: MTP_16.

A MICRO-SCALE APPROACH TO ARCHAEOLOGY

5.5 Sanctuary of Cupra at Colfiorito

5.5.1 Topographic Location

The sanctuary site is located on the upland plateau of Colfiorito, between the towns of Foligno in Umbria and Camerino in Le Marche. It lies 200 meters north of the ancient settlement of Plestia. During the Pleistocene epoch, the plateau was covered by a large lake. By the Iron Age, the lake had receded, leaving behind two large basins. These basins are known as the marshes of Colfiorito (located to the south) and Lacus Plestinus (a lake in the plain of Casone to the north, which has since been drained).

The plain of Colfiorito, which was shaped by the marshes and lake, served as the sole passage connecting the eastern and western shores of the Italian peninsula. This made it a crucial crossing point for centuries, starting from prehistoric times, facilitating travel between the Tyrrhenian and Adriatic coasts, and establishing it as an important central Italic crossing point. Several communication roads, connecting Umbria with Etruscan, Sabine, and Picene territories, crossed the plateau, facilitating movement across the Apennines. In addition to its strategic location on supra- and interregional communication routes, the plain had direct visual communication with other Umbrian landmarks such as Monte Pennino, Monte Acuto, and Monte Torre Maggiore, all visible beyond the basin.

The plateau was likely inhabited on a seasonal basis from the Neolithic period, but evidence of permanent settlement dates back to the late ninth or early eighth century BCE. At first, three villages consisting of huts were established on the shores of the former upland lake basin (Lacus Plestinus, 700 meters above sea level), with each village approximately 500 meters apart from the others. The cemeteries of these settlements only contain inhumation burials, and they remained in use until the third century BCE.

At the end of the seventh century, occupation shifted to higher fortified positions, perhaps as a response to flooding in the lowland settlements. The new hillforts were situated at an altitude of approximately 800 to 1000 meters above sea level and were all surrounded by moats and stone ramparts. The fortifications could be either circular, elliptical, or arranged in artificial terraces that sloped downward toward the outermost fortification.[121] Some of the con-

---

121   The focus of this settlement system seems to have been the hillfort identified on Monte Orve. Here a 1300 m long wall circuit in polygonal masonry surrounds a series of terraces and a higher citadel. Besides Bonomi Ponzi's (2010, 176) mention of the discovery of bronze figurines and walls of a temenos, the results of the excavation of the Monte Orve *sacellum* remain unpublished, and the materials mentioned by Bonomi Ponzi unobtainable. From the survey of the Archive of the Soprintendenza, I was able to find only

150 CHAPTER 5

temporary grave goods from the lowland cemeteries consisted of weapons, drinking vessels, bronze discs, and luxury objects from Etruria, Greece, and southern Italy, all elements that point to the presence of wealthier individuals and families. The cult focus for the inhabitants of the Colfiorito plateau was the sanctuary of the goddess Cupra, situated on the shores of Lake Plestinus near the hillforts and their cemeteries. Because the sanctuary was established at the same time as the settlements, and due to its location, Bonomi Ponzi concluded that it was the territory's "federal" sanctuary.[122]

At some point in the third century BCE, the fortified settlements and the accompanying cemeteries were no longer being used, potentially due to the trans-Italian trade routes shifting onto a north–south axis with Rome as the center.[123] The population then moved back to the area of the Iron Age village, and by the end of the third century, the settlement of Plestia was established just 200 meters south of the Sanctuary of Cupra.

The excavation of the sanctuary, overseen by Anna E. Feruglio, started in 1962 and continued in 1966 and 1967. Feruglio found that the sacred space was utilized from the sixth to the first century BCE. However, the knowledge available on the sanctuary is not as extensive as the literature about the Colfiorito region and its cemeteries. Feruglio's findings have only been published as brief reports, and no extra documentation is available in the Soprintendenza's archives.[124] As a result, it is impossible to reconstruct with precision the sanctuary's archaeological phases or to have a clear idea of the amount and context of discovery of the votive material.

5.5.2 Sixth–Fourth Century BCE: Architectural and Spatial Distribution
During its earliest period of use, the sacred area does not seem to have been marked by any permanent architectural structure.

---

the report of the 2001 excavation, where it was possible to identify only three sides of the temenos and an east-west wall running for 11 meters N of the temenos. (Monte Orve 2001, Sergio Occhilupo, saggio 2, p. 2).

122 Bonomi Ponzi 1982, 142; 1985, 213; 2010, 179.

123 Roncalli and Bonfante 1991, 61.

124 The results of the excavations have been briefly summarized in Ciotti 1964, 99–112; Feruglio 1966, 306; Manca and Menichelli 2014. For an overview of the Colfiorito territory and its necropoleis from the Iron Age to the Roman period see in particular the results of the survey and excavation carried out by Bonomi Ponzi (1985 and 1997). See also Bomoni Ponzi 1982; 1998, 9–19; 2010,73–79. On the settlement of Plestia and the Roman *municipium* see Perna et al. 2011 and Manca and Menichelli 2014, 34–37.

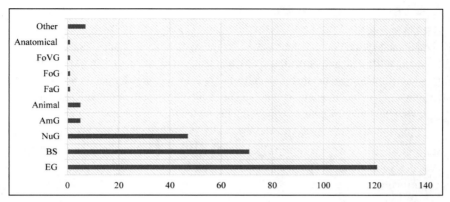

FIGURE 38   Graph showing the type distribution of the Sanctuary of Cupra votive figurines between the sixth and the fourth century BCE.

5.5.3   Sixth–Fourth Century BCE: Votive Material

Particularly noteworthy among the votive material of this phase is the presence of four bronze sheets dated to the fourth century and bearing a dedication to the goddess Cupra, the "mother of the Plestini."[125] I have already mentioned in Chapter 4 the importance of this epitaph for the study of ethnic identity. Here it is worth noting that these sheets represent the only archaeological evidence in the region linking a sanctuary site firmly to the goddess to whom it was dedicated.

Alongside the inscribed bronze sheets, the archaic and classical phase is attested by the presence of a wealth of Etruscan red figure pottery, large dolia, and two hundred and sixty bronze figurines (figure 38). Other materials mentioned by Feruglio but difficult to phase in the absence of available records include coins, spindles, and looms. All this material appears to have been found scattered around the sacred area.

The bronze figurines are represented by a wide array of votive types. Those of the EG type, sixty-nine males (figure A109–110) and fifty females (figure A111–112), make up most of the assemblage. The BS type is also well represented, with seventy-one specimens all depicting males (figure A213–214). The NoG type follows with seventeen figurines of females (figure A215–216) and thirty of warriors (figure A217–218). The remaining types are represented by a few figurines. The AmG type comprises five figurines of a male striding forward (figure A219–220), and the Animal type consists of two figurines representing a horse

---

125   On the significance of this inscription as an indication of local identity, see Chapter 4. In general, on this goddess, see Betts 2013 and Capriotti 2020 with previous bibliography.

(figure A221) and three oxen (figure A222). One figure of a warrior belongs to the type FoG (figure A223), one to the Fabriano (FaG; figure A224), and one to the Fossato di Vito (FoVG; figure A225). The FaG type warrior is represented striding forward with the right arm bent upward in the act of throwing a weapon. The body is slender and anatomical details are coarsely rendered; he wears a skirt of *pteruges* or leather straps, greaves, and a crested helmet with raised cheek-pieces. The FoVG type warrior similarly strides forward. He wears a high, thick belt, a large and flat crest, and is represented with his left arm bent upward in the act of throwing a weapon. The front of the helmet ends in an interrupted curve, and a crisscross pattern decorates the defensive skirt. A single anatomical offering, a bronze foot, was also present (figure A226).[126]

---

126   BS: CupraCF_2 CupraCF_3 CupraCF_4 CupraCF_5 CupraCF_6 CupraCF_7 CupraCF_8 CupraCF_9 CupraCF_10 CupraCF_11 CupraCF_12 CupraCF_13 CupraCF_14 CupraCF_15 CupraCF_16CupraCF_17 CupraCF_18 CupraCF_19 CupraCF_20 CupraCF_21 CupraCF_22 CupraCF_23 CupraCF_24 CupraCF_25 CupraCF_26 CupraCF_27 CupraCF_28 CupraCF_29 CupraCF_30 CupraCF_31 CupraCF_32 CupraCF_33 CupraCF_34 CupraCF_35 CupraCF_36 CupraCF_37 CupraCF_38 CupraCF_39 CupraCF_40CupraCF_41 CupraCF_42 CupraCF_4 3CupraCF_44CupraCF_45CupraCF_46 CupraCF_47 CupraCF_48 CupraCF_49 CupraCF_50 CupraCF_51 CupraCF_52 CupraCF_53 CupraCF_54 CupraCF_55 CupraCF_56 CupraCF_57 CupraCF_58 CupraCF_59 CupraCF_60 CupraCF_61 CupraCF_62 CupraCF_63 CupraCF_64 CupraCF_65 CupraCF_66 CupraCF_67 CupraCF_68 CupraCF_69 CupraCF_70 CupraCF_71 CupraCF_72. EG females: CupraCF_73 CupraCF_74 CupraCF_75 CupraCF_76 CupraCF_77 CupraCF_78 CupraCF_79 CupraCF_80 CupraCF_81 CupraCF_82 CupraCF_83 CupraCF_84 CupraCF_85 CupraCF_86 CupraCF_87 CupraCF_88 CupraCF_89 CupraCF_90 CupraCF_91 CupraCF_92 CupraCF_93 CupraCF_94 CupraCF_95 CupraCF_96 CupraCF_97 CupraCF_98 CupraCF_109 CupraCF_170 CupraCF_171 CupraCF_172 CupraCF_173 CupraCF_174 CupraCF_175 CupraCF_176 CupraCF_177 CupraCF_178 CupraCF_179 CupraCF_180 CupraCF_181 CupraCF_182 CupraCF_183 CupraCF_184 CupraCF_185 CupraCF_186 CupraCF_187 CupraCF_188 CupraCF_189 CupraCF_190 CupraCF_191 CupraCF_192. EG males: CupraCF_1 CupraCF_99 CupraCF_100 CupraCF_101 CupraCF_102 CupraCF_103 CupraCF_104 CupraCF_105 CupraCF_106 CupraCF_107 CupraCF_108 CupraCF_110 CupraCF_111 CupraCF_112 CupraCF_113 CupraCF_114 CupraCF_115 CupraCF_116 CupraCF_117 CupraCF_118 CupraCF_119 CupraCF_120 CupraCF_121 CupraCF_122 CupraCF_123 CupraCF_124 CupraCF_125 CupraCF_126 CupraCF_127 CupraCF_128 CupraCF_129 CupraCF_130 CupraCF_131 CupraCF_132 CupraCF_133 CupraCF_134 CupraCF_135 CupraCF_136 CupraCF_137 CupraCF_138 CupraCF_139 CupraCF_140 CupraCF_141 CupraCF_142 CupraCF_143 CupraCF_144 CupraCF_145 CupraCF_146 CupraCF_147 CupraCF_148 CupraCF_149 CupraCF_150 CupraCF_151 CupraCF_152 CupraCF_153 CupraCF_154 CupraCF_155 CupraCF_156 CupraCF_157 CupraCF_158 CupraCF_159 CupraCF_160 CupraCF_161 CupraCF_162 CupraCF_163 CupraCF_164 CupraCF_165 CupraCF_166 CupraCF_167. NuG: CupraCF_193 CupraCF_194 CupraCF_195 CupraCF_196 CupraCF_197 CupraCF_198 CupraCF_199 CupraCF_200 CupraCF_201 CupraCF_202 CupraCF_203 CupraCF_204 CupraCF_205 CupraCF_206 CupraCF_207 CupraCF_208 CupraCF_209 CupraCF_211

A MICRO-SCALE APPROACH TO ARCHAEOLOGY

Seven bronze figurines with zoomorphic features belong to the group "Other" (figure A227–230). The characteristic feature of these figurines is the body, schematically rendered as the EG type, with lower limbs ending with spikes. Unlike the EG type, however, the head and the upper limbs do not seem to depict a human figure but rather an animal. Six figurines (figure A227–229) present bird-like features: a small head, with round eyes and a horizontal slit as the mouth, a broad neck and flat upper limps with incisions that could represent feathers. The remaining one (figure A230) has short upper limbs and an almost monkey-like snout with protruding nose and mouth.[127]

In the absence of direct comparanda, it is difficult to hypothesize what these figurines aimed to represent. Perhaps the closest comparison for the type is with seventh-century BCE clay figurines from Cyprus representing standing males with a bull's head.[128] Following a tradition that originated in the Levant, where anthropomorphic clay masks were popular,[129] the masks from Cyprus have been interpreted as masks worn by priests or worshipers. It is possible that the zoomorphic features of the figurines from the Sanctuary of Cupra were also intended to depict a mask or a costume perhaps worn in connection with a specific local religious festival.

5.5.4 Late Fourth–Early First Century BCE: Architectural Aspects and Spatial Organization

Although the sanctuary's complete layout is unknown, during this phase it consisted of a temenos, wherein a small *sacellum* was erected. East of the *sacellum* there was a quadrangular basin, most likely a cistern (figure 39).

In terms of architectural decoration, the *sacellum* was covered with Etrusco-Italic architectural slabs depicting floral motifs such as palms, garlands, and

---

CupraCF_212 CupraCF_213 CupraCF_214 CupraCF_215 CupraCF_216 CupraCF_217 CupraCF_218 CupraCF_219CupraCF_220 CupraCF_221 CupraCF_222CupraCF_223 CupraCF_224 CupraCF_225 CupraCF_226 CupraCF_227 CupraCF_228 CupraCF_229 CupraCF_230 CupraCF_231 CupraCF_232 CupraCF_233 CupraCF_234 CupraCF_235 CupraCF_236 CupraCF_237 CupraCF_238CupraCF_239 CupraCF_240. FoG: CupraCF_210. FaG: CupraCF_248 FoVG: CupraCF_249. Anatomical: CupraCF_266.

127   Bird-like figurines: CupraCF_255 CupraCF_256 CupraCF_257 CupraCF_258 CupraCF_259; monkey-like figurines: CupraCF_260CupraCF_261.

128   Karageorghis 2012, 146.

129   Depictions of human figures wearing masks were common from the proto-historic Near East. Masks are exaggerated into an unrealistic size or shape or resemble human heads. Unlike the depiction of human heads, where anatomical details are not represented, masks are characterized by eyes and open mouths: Renfrew et al. 2018, 153.

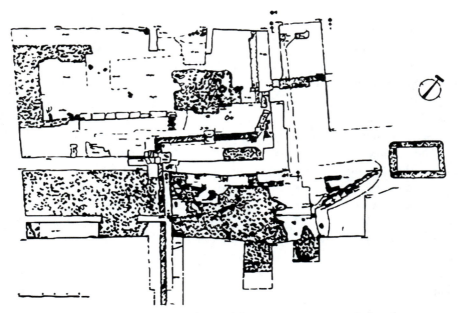

FIGURE 39 Plan of the Sanctuary of Cupra (after Bonomi Ponzi 2010, 180 fig. 21).

FIGURE 40
Revetment slab from the Sanctuary of Cupra (after Manca and Menichelli 2014, 27).

lotus flowers, as well as antefixes with male and female heads.[130] Of particular interest is a slab that shows a winged female figure riding a chariot, which is dated to the first half of the second century BCE; no similar examples are found in central Italic regions (figure 40).[131]

---

130 On Etrusco-Italic revetment slabs and antefixes with human head see *supra* in this chapter.
131 These fragments are briefly mentioned by Manca and Menichelli (2014, 26–27) but not elsewhere published or displayed.

A MICRO-SCALE APPROACH TO ARCHAEOLOGY 155

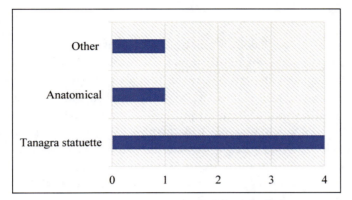

FIGURE 41   Graph showing the type distribution of the Sanctuary of Cupra figurative votive offerings between the late fourth and the early first century BCE.

5.5.5 Late Fourth–Early First Century BCE: Votive Material

A large quantity of pottery and six figurative offerings belong to this phase (figure 41). The ceramic material consists of Etruscan red figure pottery, overpainted Etruscan/Faliscan vases, and black gloss vessels. Five coroplastic objects are dated to the third-second century BCE and include one terracotta left foot and four heads of now-lost Tanagra statuettes. The terracotta foot terminates halfway up the calf in an irregular break. It is realized in a summary way without any attention to most anatomical details, except for the toes which are rendered through horizontal incisions (figure A231).[132] The Tanagra statuettes' heads have the hair gathered in a low bun; on the heads is a wreath of ivy leaves, with a circular element in the center. The faces have a small, fleshy mouth and a prominent nose. They wear large circular earrings (figure A232).[133]

One last figurine belongs to the "Other" type. It is dated to the third–second century BCE and represents Heracles (figure A233). The demigod is represented in the nude, with the left leg forward and the left arm bent and raised in the act of holding a spear/club. The lionskin is wrapped around his left forearm; on his head he wears a Phrygian cap.[134]

---

132   CupraCF_267.
133   CupraCF_262 CupraCF_263 CupraCF_264 CupraCF_265.
134   CupraCF_268.

6 Conclusions

This chapter presents a thorough and current examination of the archaeological findings related to Umbrian sanctuaries from the sixth century to the early first century BCE. Through this analysis, we are able to challenge two commonly held beliefs about the relationship between Umbrian sacred sites and Roman interference. The first assumption is that the presence of Romans resulted in a decline in the use of rural sanctuaries, particularly those located near Romanized regions. However, the evidence suggests that sanctuaries located in internal, Apennine areas were more likely to persist. The second assumption is that the presence of anatomical votives and terracotta heads is evidence of Roman influence and a shift in the Umbrian people's religious practices. However, the archaeological evidence from Umbrian sanctuaries contradicts these claims.

During the period between the sixth and fourth centuries BCE, anatomical parts and heads were commonly found in Umbrian sanctuaries, mostly made of bronze but sometimes also of terracotta, as the heads from Monte Ansciano and Colle Moro show. Their occurrence in Umbria shows that the practice of dedicating anatomicals before the fourth century was not limited to a few sites of the Adriatic Etruscan region (Marzabotto and Adria) and, therefore, should not be considered a sporadic phenomenon, as Turfa and Fenelli held.[135] A similar observation can be made for the presence of archaic heads. Their presence at Colle Mori and Monte Ansciano suggests that the dedication of clay heads was not limited to the areas of southern Eturia (especially Falerii and Veii). Most importantly, these votives demonstrate an earlier ritual practice of dedicating parts of the body and heads—one that existed in Umbria before the beginning of the Roman expansion at the end of the fourth century BCE. In approaching the change that followed the conquest, it therefore seems necessary to abandon the old paradigm that sees in the terracotta anatomicals of the Roman period a wholesale change in the religiosity of the Italic peoples connected to the spread of *romanitas* through the foundation of Roman colonies. In sum, the evidence of pre-Roman anatomical votive figurines from Umbrian sanctuaries shows a vital and widespread ritual practice during the sixth–fourth century BCE, rather than an isolated phenomenon limited to a few sites in northern Etruria.

---

135 Turfa 2004 359–336; Comella 1981, 767; cf. Appendix 1. As recently demonstrated (Zapelloni Pavia, 2024), the practice of dedicating anatomicals in bronze during the pre-Roman period was a widespread phenomenon that involved regions such as Umbria, Etruria, and Veneto.

A MICRO-SCALE APPROACH TO ARCHAEOLOGY 157

Second, the archaeological evidence shows that the use of rural sanctuaries and the distribution of terracotta votive heads and anatomicals during the period from the late fourth to the early first century BCE were not related to the political status of communities in relation to Rome. While the level of usage may have changed, all rural sanctuaries in the region were still being used at least until the end of the second century or early in the first century BCE. This includes not only sanctuaries located in Apennine areas but also those near more Romanized territories, such as the sanctuaries of Monte Torre Maggiore, Monte San Pancrazio, and Colle Mori. These sacred sites continued to be used during the Roman period and were even given monumental structures. In the next chapter, I test Bradley's hypothesis that the usage of Umbrian sanctuaries during this period may have been linked to their proximity to urban centers.[136]

Concerning the terracotta anatomicals and heads, their presence in Umbrian sanctuaries during the Hellenistic period is independent of the Roman presence in the region. These objects can be found in areas under direct Roman rule (La Rocca), but also in remote rural sanctuaries within a day's walk from a Roman praefectura (Monte Torre Maggiore, Monte Moro) or near a *civitas sine suffragio* (Cancelli and Sanctuary of Cupra), as well as in those areas that remained independent until the Social War (Monte San Pancrazio, Pantanelli). That the presence of anatomical votives has little to do with the Roman conquest is also supported by the absence of anatomical votives in areas geographically closer to colonies, where we might expect these artifacts to be more present. As Scopacasa rightly points out, neither heads nor anatomicals have been retrieved at the sanctuary of Monte Subasio, despite its proximity to areas where Roman citizens received plots of land in the third century BCE and to the Roman center of Forum Flaminii.[137] Similarly, the sanctuary of La Rocca, located in the Latin colony of Spoletium, did not yield significantly more anatomical votives than sanctuaries that were significantly far from colonized territories, such as Pantanelli and Monte Moro. All of this shows no intrinsic connection between terracotta anatomical votives and the Roman expansion and colonization, confirming Glinister's idea that their spread was a product of different variables.[138]

All this suggests the need to revisit the traditional interpretation of the role of sanctuaries in Umbria during the Roman period and the alleged cultural change indicated by the presence of anatomical votives and heads. Rather than viewing Umbrian sanctuaries from the perspective of one-way influences from

---

136 Bradley's argument is explained in Chapter 2.
137 Scopacasa 2015b, 9.
138 Glinister 2006a, 23–27.

Rome into central Italy, it is more useful to examine the context of the sanctuaries and their votive objects to identify broader patterns in cultural practices that spread through the region following Roman expansion. Points of reflection include: What is the significance of the deposition of anatomical votives and figurines before the fourth century BCE? What motives led to the frequentation and monumentalization of certain sanctuaries during the Hellenistic period? If anatomical votives and heads were already in use in Umbria prior to the fourth century BCE, what does their continued presence tell us about the ritual practices of the Umbrian peoples during the centuries of Roman conquest?

The upcoming chapter will delve into the questions raised in this chapter and interpret the data using a macro-scale approach that considers all of the sacred spaces of Umbria together. In the next chapter, I will propose a hypothesis to explain not only the continuation and monumentalization of Umbrian sacred places during the Roman period but also the continued use of anatomical votives and heads.

CHAPTER 6

Conclusions: A Macro-Scale Approach to the Archaeology of Umbrian Cult Places

1   Introduction

The sanctuaries of ancient Umbria provide a unique opportunity to examine the political, economic, and social changes during the Roman expansion. In Chapter 5, a comprehensive study of the material evidence collected from the sacred sites in the region challenged the commonly held belief that the expansion of Rome resulted in the decline of religious sites and the emergence of anatomical votives. By integrating the findings from the previous chapters, this concluding discussion reevaluates the traditional viewpoint on the usage of sanctuaries and anatomical votives during the Roman conquest. The argument suggests that local geographical and social factors influenced the persistence of religious practices at Umbrian sanctuaries. Furthermore, the custom of dedicating anatomical votives had already been prevalent in the region and was not a significant deviation from the established ritual practices of the Umbrian people. Additionally, the discussion provides broader conclusions regarding the cultural and socioeconomic patterns discernible in Umbrian sanctuaries during the archaic and Hellenistic periods.

To begin with, I examine the role of sacred spaces during the sixth to fourth century BCE before the Romans expanded their presence in the region. Based on the evidence that offerings were made locally and that specific figurines were associated with particular areas, coupled with the relatively low investment in votive offerings, it seems that the sanctuaries were closely linked with the local communities. These findings support Bradley's argument that ancient Umbria had a sense of community identity rather than a broad Umbrian ethnic identity, which contributes to the ongoing debate about the formation of ethnicity in the region. Next, I explore the possible significance of the ritual deposition of archaic figurines in Umbrian sacred sites. The prevalence of archaic anatomical votives in almost all sites presented in this study suggests that Glinister's interpretation of anatomical votives during the Roman period could be extended to pre-Roman times. I propose that the deposition of figurines and anatomical objects served as a ritual for promoting well-being for both individuals and the community. The figurines of warriors and Heracles represent stability and protection and may be associated with the requests made to the

© CHARLES UNIVERSITY, FACULTY OF ARTS, PRAGUE, 2025 | DOI:10.1163/9789004712171_007
This is an open access chapter distributed under the terms of the CC BY-NC-ND 4.0 license.

gods. Similarly, generic figurines of humans and animals draw attention to the source of the request for well-being, the individual, the community, and their livelihoods. By focusing on the ritual act of offering votives instead of their possible socio-economic implications, I detach these objects from their association with the particular social class that offered them, which, as previously discussed in Chapter 3, cannot be determined.

The evidence shows that while all the sanctuaries in Umbria continued to be visited during the late fourth–early first century BCE, the votive offerings indicate that some, particularly those located at higher elevations or near urban areas, experienced a decrease in usage. This trend may be linked to larger social changes in the region, such as the abandonment of hilltop settlements and the emergence of temple construction in some Umbrian towns. The decision by communities to relocate closer to roads and commercial hubs may have contributed to the decrease in visitation at the Monte Acuto sanctuary. Additionally, the establishment of new religious buildings at Iguvium and Asisium, as suggested by Bradley, could have led to a reduction in the frequency of religious activities at the Monte Subasio and Monte Ansciano sanctuaries.

As we examine the design of sanctuaries, we observe that the level of investment in these sacred sites increased in the late fourth and third centuries BCE. This is evident from the expansion and renovation of religious complexes, indicating a growing interest among individuals and groups in promoting building activities. This trend may be associated with a new political scenario emerging after Rome established its control over the peninsula and the wider central Mediterranean region. As recent work by scholars such as Terrenato and Colivicchi has rightly underscored, public munificence becomes an important part of central Italian aristocrats' political agenda, which could intertwine with the expansionistic plans of elite factions from Rome.[1] The possibility of eventually receiving Roman citizenship and thus entering the new global political arena initiated by Rome must have been an alluring perspective for the allied elites who aimed at having a stake in the electoral and decision process in Rome, and, as was the case for many other Italians, influencing new legislation. Therefore, the negotiation and interaction between the dominant elites in Umbria and Rome aimed at strengthening their own private status and may have been the driving force behind the monumentalization of Umbrian sanctuaries.

Similar dynamics, in which local practices mingle with and are shaped by the contemporary socio-political environment, are visible in the Umbrian votive deposits. Instead of being considered as evidence of a ritual change moti-

---

1 Terrenato 2019, 240.

CONCLUSIONS   161

vated by the use of foreign models, the adoption of terracotta for molding into anatomical shapes should be seen as a technical improvement on a long-lived ritual practice and part of a fashion that, alongside the use of Hellenistic figurines of worshipers and miniature vessels, was widespread throughout the Italian peninsula as well as in Greece.

By tracing the development of Umbrian sanctuaries from the archaic (sixth–fourth century BCE) to the Hellenistic period (late fourth–early first century BCE), this study elucidates the complex ways in which indigenous populations responded and adapted to the new socio-political realities that accompanied Roman hegemony and to more intense cultural borrowing from other regions of the peninsula and the Greek world. The interplay between new architectural models, materials and artifacts, and local religious traditions fittingly follows the substance of White's Middle Ground theory, where different cultural backgrounds create new cultural structures.[2] The influences recognizable in the material evidence from Umbrian sanctuaries are connected, however, to the interaction between locals and Romans and the broader context of the Italic peninsula and the Mediterranean.

2   Umbrian Pre-Roman Sanctuaries in Context

2.1   *Topographical Aspects*
As the topographical information presented in Chapter 5 shows, Umbrian sanctuaries were located in a variety of positions, mostly in accordance with prominent landscape features and near fortified or inhabited areas. The most common setting is the mountain peak. The sanctuaries of Monte Torre Maggiore, Monte Ansciano, Monte Ingino, Monte San Pancrazio, Monte Pennino, Monte Moro di Montefranco, Monte Subasio, and Cancelli are located on summits whose height varies from 1000 to ca. 1600 meters. Some sanctuaries were associated with other types of natural phenomena, such as caves (Grotta Bella sanctuary), lakes or other bodies of water (Sanctuary of Cupra at Colfiorito, Monte Moro, Monte Subasio),[3] or hills (Colle Mori sanctuary). Some were located in or

---

2   It is important to note, however, that, unlike White's model, where interactions between Algonquian tribes of the Great Lakes and French settlers happened *ex novo*, Romans and Umbrians were close neighbors who had shared similar material culture since the Orientalizing period.

3   On the importance of the presence of water in Umbrian and Etruscan sanctuaries see Giontella 2006. For the religious significance of water in the selection of Roman and Greek sacred spaces, see R. Bradley, 2000. As Moser (2019, 48) rightly points out, water had also a very prac-

162   CHAPTER 6

near settlement sites (Colle Mori, Pantanelli, Monte Torre Maggiore, Monte San
Pancrazio, Monte Moro, Monte Subasio, Monte Ansciano and La Rocca sanctu-
aries) and in the vicinity of one or more hillforts (Monte Torre Maggiore, Cupra,
Cancelli).[4]

Besides this proximity to natural landmarks, settlements, and hillforts, a distinctive feature of some Umbrian cult places, such as the Colle Mori, Monte
Ansciano, Monte Acuto, Grotta Bella, and La Rocca sanctuaries, is their location
in areas of long-abandoned Bronze Age sites (twelfth to tenth century BCE),
whose use is attested by the presence of vessels, ornaments, spools, and loom
weights. The link between Umbrian archaic sanctuaries and earlier sites has
been noted by Bradley and Stoddart, who reasonably connected it to similar
situations in Greece and Latium, where it was not unusual to legitimize the
sacralization of a place by appealing to its antiquity.[5] At Palaikastro, on Crete,
for example, the memory of an earlier association of the place with a cult for
a Bronze Age deity is believed to have prompted the building of a temple in
later times.[6] Similarly, at Lavinium a mound covering a tomb of the seventh
century BCE was re-used as the "heroon of Aeneas" at the end of the fourth
century BCE, and at Setia an archaic sanctuary was placed in the location of an
earlier Bronze Age cult place.[7]

Although the available evidence does not enable us to determine the specific
functions of the earlier Umbrian Bronze Age sites (religious/domestic, etc.),
comparisons with elsewhere in Italy and Greece enable us to infer with a certain degree of confidence that the memory of earlier site occupation played an
important role in the establishment of archaic cult places in the region in the
sixth/fifth century BCE, and perhaps even served to legitimize their sacralization.

2.2   *Architectural Aspects*

Generalizing about the original appearance of pre-Roman Umbrian sanctuaries is difficult due to incomplete excavation and documentation.[8] However,

---

   tical use as an integral component of the ritual connected to the purification before and after
   the sacrificial slaughter of animals.
4 It is difficult, however, to draw conclusions about the topographic relationship between
   sacred spaces and hilltop centers, for the latter have scarcely been investigated and their internal organization is not well known; in this respect, see Chapter 4.
5 Bradley 1997, 114; Bradley 2000a, 63; Stoddart 1994, 152.
6 Van Dyke and Alcock 2008, 98.
7 Sommella 1971–1972, 47–74; Nijboer 2001, 81.
8 The sanctuaries of La Rocca, Pantanelli, Monte San Pancrazio, Campo La Piana, Colle San
   Rufino, Monte Santo, and Monte Pennino have been only partially investigated and never or

CONCLUSIONS   163

based on the full excavation and documentation of nine sanctuaries (Monte
Acuto, Monte Ansciano, La Rocca, Monte Torre Maggiore, Colle Mori, Monte
Moro, Grotta Bella, Cancelli, and Colfiorito), it appears that there was no
standard layout or organization, and that each community's sanctuary was
designed to meet their unique ritual and practical needs. Similar to other
archaic sanctuaries in the region, most Umbrian sacred places were open-air
and sometimes included a bedrock pit, with only a few having any type of building.[9]

Among the nine fully excavated and documented Umbrian sanctuaries, only
Monte Acuto, Colle Mori, and Monte Ansciano featured some kind of architectural structure to delineate the sacred area. A drystone wall marked the
boundary at Monte Acuto and Colle Mori, while at Monte Ansciano, a platform made of limestone dumps served this purpose.[10] The majority of Umbrian
sanctuaries, however, showed little or no evidence of human intervention.[11]
While Colfiorito and Cancelli appeared to have no human-made features during the archaic period, sanctuaries such as Monte Acuto, Monte Torre Maggiore,
Monte Moro, and Colle Mori shared the presence of a pit dug directly into the
bedrock, which served either a religious or practical function.[12] The circular pit
at Monte Acuto was likely used for sacrificial purposes, while the one at Monte
Torre Maggiore was interpreted as the foundation ditch of the sacred space.
The pit at Colle Mori served as a well for cult-related functions, and the one
at Monte Moro functioned as a cistern to collect rainwater or as a silo for food
storage.

From the known examples of religious places in Umbria, it seems that, unlike
the neighboring regions of Etruria and Latium that developed in the sixth
century BCE "a separate architectural language for cult buildings" (e.g., podia
and altars),[13] Umbrians felt no need to separate cult areas visually from their
surroundings. Rather than manmade structures, the distinguishing features
of Umbrian sanctuaries were their topographical locations and, at times, the

---

       only roughly recorded. We cannot therefore exclude entirely the possibility that they may
       have had permanent architectural features during the archaic period.
9   A list of open-air rural Italic shrine is in Bradley and Glinister 2013.
10   It is of course possible that drystone precincts may have been weathered down and thus
       become unrecognizable to archaeologists. Clandestine and inadequately documented
       excavations also contribute to the difficulties of reconstructing the earliest layout of
       Umbrian cult places.
11   As Bradley notes (1987, 114), the natural cave setting at Grotta Bella may have rendered the
       presence of hand-made structure superfluous.
12   A pit is also mentioned by Staderini on Monte Pennino. See Chapter 5.
13   Potts 2015, 45.

presence of a pit that served various ritual needs. The functional spatial organization and permanent architecture of Umbrian cult places were provided only after the fourth century BCE, mostly as a result of elite munificence within the new political network established by Roman expansion.

2.3 *Function of Pre-Roman Sanctuaries*

As the evidence presented above shows, most Umbrian sanctuaries were topographically associated with particular settlements. Even those that appear to have been located away from inhabited settlements, such as the Grotta Bella, Campo La Piana, and Monte Pennino sanctuaries, are sited in areas where hilltop fortified villages have been detected.

Scholars have long attempted to explain the relationship between these settlements and sacred spaces. Owing to the popularity of the *pagus-vicus* model,[14] they have generally assumed that, in the absence of "real" urban units, such as those in Latium or Etruria, Umbrian sanctuaries functioned as civic, political, and economic centers. However, when we look at the material evidence, this interpretation can be hardly proved.

As I have discussed, Bradley rightly points out that the *pagus-vicus* model is inherently flawed, for it revolves around an ideal dichotomy between urban and non-urban, and it does not take into consideration that Umbrian centers may have functioned as self-sufficient even in the absence of cities like those in Latium and Etruria. Furthermore, it is virtually impossible to establish with certainty what type of political and administrative connections existed between cult places and inhabited centers. The main complication is that, with the exception of Colle Mori and Colfiorito, the settlements (whether hilltop or not) and their internal organization are not well known. Moreover, in cases such as Monte Moro and Grotta Bella, the presence itself of a settlement is based on pure conjectures and surmises rather than archaeological evidence. Without concrete archaeological data to support the *pagus-vicus* model, the role of sanctuaries as political and economic centers can only remain speculative.

Upon reviewing the published material, Bradley put forth an alternative interpretation of the function of Umbrian sanctuaries that does not frame them within the conventional *pagus-vicus* model but considers them as poles of aggregation for local communities. Specifically, he notes that the number of sanctuaries within the Umbrian territory and the presence of local votive offerings "strongly suggest that sanctuaries were closely related to particular com-

---

14   See Chapter 2.

CONCLUSIONS

munities."[15] Indeed, as the presence of metal slugs at the sanctuaries of Monte Torre Maggiore and Grotta Bella shows,[16] it was possible for metal workshops to produce and sell votive offerings directly *in situ*. In addition, the proximity of sanctuaries to inhabited centers and the presence of casting workshops manufacturing votive figurines suggest that the activities at the sanctuary were integral to local community life. Bradley also notes that the low level of investment in votive offerings indicates that people from all levels of society participated in these sanctuaries. The examination of all votive figurines from Umbrian sanctuaries supports Bradley's observations.

The two graphs presented in figures 6.1 and 6.2 compare the votive offerings from different Umbrian cult places. The first graph shows the number of votive offerings for each sanctuary, while the second graph shows the percentage of each votive type in relation to the total number of figurines dedicated at a particular sanctuary. The graphs reveal that the most commonly dedicated figurines in Umbrian sanctuaries are the less elaborate types, which are characterized by coarse rendering of anatomical details and minimal attention to the plastic cogency of the object. Among these types, the Esquiline Group (colored light blue in the graphs) is the most prevalent, followed by simple figurines made from bronze sheets (red), schematic-eyed crests (orange), and the Foligno and Amelia Groups (purple and dark green respectively).

Of similar, small economic value are the votive offerings of the type "Other" (salmon color in the graphs), distinguished by an overall simplified outline and an extremely small size. These characteristics apply to bronze specimens and those made from lead and found at the Grotta Bella and Pantanelli sanctuaries. As pointed out by Monacchi with respect to Grotta Bella, the mass production and small size of lead figurines provided a particularly inexpensive and easy way to shape the character of the rituals, just like the figurines of the Esquiline Group and the Nocera Umbra Group.[17] Only in the case of Mars with the attached situla from Assisi (CSRufino_1; figure A147) can we imagine that the object's dedication could have resulted from a more substantial economic expenditure.

The percentage graph (figure 43) reveals that larger and more sophisticated figurines, such as those of the Fabriano, Fossato di Vico, and Todi types (or the "Mars of Todi," not shown in the graph), are practically absent from Umbrian sanctuaries. In fact, no more than two specimens of each type have been discovered in the region, with two figurines (one belonging to the Fabriano type

---

15   Bradely 2000a, 67.
16   See Chapter 5.
17   Monacchi 1988, 82.

and the other to the Fossato di Vico type) found at the Sanctuary of Cupra, and one figurine of the Todi type found at Monte San Pancrazio and another at Monte Santo. Unlike contemporary necropoleis, sanctuaries did not appear to be viewed as suitable places for expensive dedications intended to glorify or display the social status of the donor.[18] Instead, the small investment in votive figurines suggests that the act of dedicating these objects was accessible to various strata of the community and that individuals acted collectively in the sacred realm, regardless of their position in society. The modest expenditure on these objects and the possibility for virtually the entire community to participate in the practice of dedicating votive figurines underscore the connection between inhabited centers and sacred spaces. As Bradley points out, it is feasible that the use of local sanctuaries may have strengthened a sense of belonging to specific communities and may have played a role in shaping community identity.

The presence of figurines categorized as "Other" adds to the evidence of the use of sanctuaries by individual communities. These figurines are unique to specific cult places and have no comparisons elsewhere in central Italy. The zoomorphic figurines from the Sanctuary of Cupra at Colfiorito, the warrior figures from Monte Santo (Tuder), and the lead figurines from Pantanelli and Grotta Bella (near Ameria) suggest an appreciation for a particular aesthetic that allowed the worshiping community to distinguish itself.[19] As these figurines are found only at specific Umbrian sanctuaries, it is likely that the use of the sacred space was focused on the surrounding communities. In addition to dedicating the more common types of votive offerings, these communities sought to emphasize their uniqueness.

It is interesting to note that these areas where the unique figurines were found also yielded some of the earliest evidence of the names of individual groups in Umbria. For example, the fourth-century inscription from Colfiorito records the ethnic name *pletinas*, while third-century BCE bronze and lead coins from Tuder and Ameria have the local ethnics *tutere*, and *amer/ameri*.[20]

---

18   It is crucial to note that due to the compromised exploration of certain Umbrian sanctuaries, the variety of votive offerings uncovered may not offer a complete representation. As a result, we cannot dismiss the possibility that prestigious dedications might have been more prevalent than suggested by the limited findings in the archaeological record.

19   On Grotta Bella and how this cult place strengthened a sense of belonging to specific communities and played a role in the formation of community identity, see Zapelloni Pavia and Larocca 2023.

20   Bradley 2000a, 24–25, adds that coins bearing the name **ikuvins** are further evidence of ethnic community in the third century BCE.

CONCLUSIONS

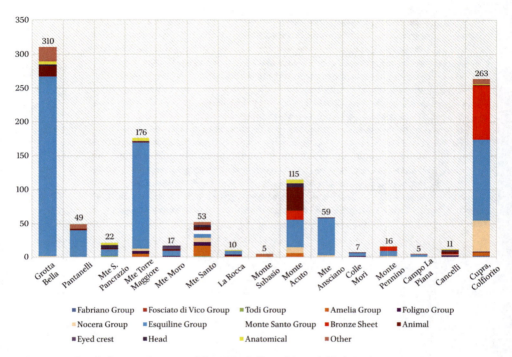

FIGURE 42 Graph showing the types of figurines dedicated in each Umbrian sanctuary.

This suggests that the use of local figurines may have been associated with the emergence of distinctive regional groups during the Republican period.

Overall, the evidence from the votive figurines dedicated at Umbrian sanctuaries supports Bradley's argument that these spaces were linked to the individual communities that occupied the area near them. While it is possible that worshipers from other parts of the region could dedicate objects, as the presence of the animal pendant—characteristic of the Picene area—from Monte Subasio shows (CSRufino_3; figure A149), it appears that local groups were the main users of these sacred spaces.[21] Their participation in the ritual activities of dedicating votive offerings may have strengthened their sense of belonging to a particular community and eventually contributed to the formation of regional identities during the Middle Republican period.

---

21 In this respect, it is worth noting that extra-urban sanctuaries have served as venues for consolidating political links between different communities that nonetheless speak the same language. See, Marroni 2012; Terrenato 2019.

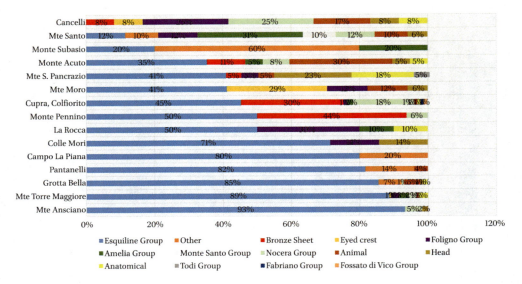

FIGURE 43 Graph showing the percentage of votive figurines dedicated in each Umbrian sanctuary

2.4 Towards an Understanding of the Ritual Function of Umbrian Votive Offerings

The archaic votive figurines found in Umbrian sanctuaries can be categorized into four groups based on their subjects (see figure 44).[22] The first and most common group includes male and female figures that may represent worshipers, according to Colonna's interpretation. The second group, found in thirteen out of fifteen sanctuaries, features warrior figurines depicted in an attacking stance, holding a shield and a spear. The third group, found in ten sanctuaries, consists of body parts and heads. Lastly, the fourth group is represented by a single example of the deity Heracles.

As Chapter 3 highlights, scholars have traditionally interpreted these votive figurines in the context of the socio-economic life of archaic Umbrian communities. They have analyzed the figurines' refinement and iconography, attempting to link them to specific social classes of worshipers who may have dedicated them. However, this approach has limitations, as I have previously discussed. While the figurines' size, quality, and production may suggest the level of investment put into their dedication, we cannot accurately determine the wealth of the individuals who donated them. In this section, I shift the focus from the

---

22 These groups comprise the figurines from all the Umbrian sanctuaries presented and belonging to the typologies described in Appendix 1.

CONCLUSIONS

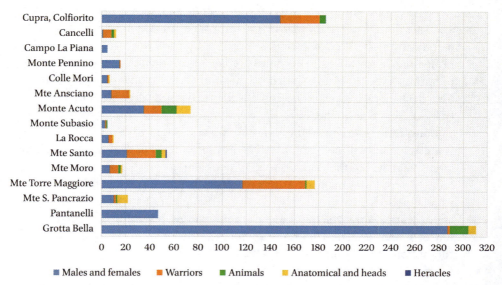

FIGURE 44 Graph showing the groups of votive figurines dedicated in each Umbrian sanctuary.

socio-economic connotations of these figurines to their ritual significance. To achieve this, I adopt Glinister's interpretation of anatomical terracottas from the Roman period and apply it to these archaic offerings.

In Chapters 2 and 5, I demonstrated that the conventional belief linking the diffusion of anatomical terracottas throughout the Italic peninsula to Roman domination is unfounded. To challenge the conventional assumption that votive terracottas reflect an "obsession with health and fertility" that arose from Roman conquest, Glinister argues that anatomical terracottas were dedicated to various deities and that only a small number of them were specifically associated with "health."[23] Secondly, Glinister emphasizes that the existence of anatomical votives in pre-Roman sanctuaries demonstrates that this type of votive predates the diffusion of Asclepius' healing cult, which has been associated with the spread of anatomical terracottas. Additionally, shrines dedicated to Asclepius are scarcely attested in the peninsula during the fourth and third centuries BCE. While some anatomical votives from Latium and Etruria may indicate specific concerns for health and bodily ailments, most do not clearly connect with healing. In fact, the depiction of body parts such as open torsos or internal organs is limited to Latin and Etruscan areas, such as the polyvisceral plaques found in Veii, Fregellae, Pozzarello, and the Manganello sanctuary at

---

23   Glinister 2006b, 93.

Cerveteri, or the internal organs from Tarquinia, Veii, Gravisca, Ponte di Nona, and Lavinium.[24] Given these insights, Glinister's proposal that anatomical terracottas from the Roman period are likely connected to a ritual of well-being rather than medical health becomes even more compelling. This broader interpretation of the ritual linked to the dedication of these votives suggests a desire for a healthy, peaceful, and prosperous life both physically and morally, rather than solely a focus on healing.

Considering the constancy and tradition associated with ritual practices, it is unlikely that well-being rituals were only introduced to the Italian peninsula after the arrival of the Romans in a particular area.[25] It is more plausible that local communities expressed their desire for happiness and comfort through ritual practices prior to significant cultural interactions with Rome in the fourth century BCE. Moreover, the presence of bronzes representing body parts in six out of fifteen archaic Umbrian sanctuaries, as shown in figure 42, supports the notion that Glinister's interpretation of well-being rituals should not be restricted to the Roman period. It is conceivable that figurines from the sacred shrines of the region were associated with the same ritual of well-being as the one identified by Glinister in anatomical terracottas from the Roman period.

This raises the question of whether the votives from Umbria were intentionally created for their ritual function or whether their function emerged after their production through social relationships. Recent posthumanist studies have shown that human-made objects can shape religious tradition, suggesting that the objects themselves can lend themselves to their ritual function. This aligns with Alfred Gell's view that objects may assume a function once they become enmeshed in social relationships, rather than being created with a specific purpose in mind.[26] Indeed, the abovementioned groups of votives represent the basic recognizable figures through which worshipers could identify themselves and their environment: the warrior, identifiable also with Mars, who, as Sigismondi argues,[27] for Italic populations had the two-pronged function of being able to protect people, animals, and crops from nature's plagues; female and male figures; animals, which constituted the basis of the Umbrian economy; and, finally, heads and parts of the body, which, through synecdoche, may stand for the whole male or female figure. The dedication of these categories of votives may be related to the complex concept of personhood applied

---

24   Turfa 1994; de Grummond and Simons 2006, 90–115; Recke 2013; Hughes 2017.
25   Kyriakidis 2007, 15–16.
26   Gell 1988.
27   Sigismondi 1979, 48.

CONCLUSIONS

to archaeology by Chris Fowler and recently used by Emma Graham.[28] In summary, heads and parts of bodies are a "visual abbreviation of the whole being of a suppliant," and animal votive figurines are representative of the divisible part of a dividual human being (defined as the part of the self that can be detached and entrusted to the care of the gods), for they represent the things which people "grow, cultivate, and, most vitally, exchange."[29] As Graham argues with respect to anatomical and animal votives, these votive offerings represent bodies, their extension, and the base of their subsistence. They can be considered a prime means of dedication to an intangible divine power.

In his investigation of objects' effect on people, Gosden demonstrates that an artifact's form displayed *en masse* can suggest thought and mental representation.[30] This means that artifacts influence how people use them and that their use may have nothing to do with the human intention that created them. It is, therefore, possible that these figurines, made because they represented a familiar and recognizable association with the everyday life of worshipers, used together and displayed in the specific context of the sanctuary, influenced the meaning of the ritual they came to represent. As Glinister noted,[31] Italic and Roman religions were concerned with the gods' close interaction with humans and control of human fates, individual and collective. The images of worshipers and animals displayed in the sacred areas of the region contributed to creating a ritual whose teleological aim was the overall prosperity of the community and the worshipers. Although limited to one case, we can read the same association in the warrior group and in the figure of Heracles, as both the soldiers and the deity evoke the maintenance of stability and more general protection.

---

28   Fowler 2004; Graham 2017. Personhood, as defined by Fowler (2004, 4) is "the condition or state of being a person, as it is understood in any specific context. Persons are constituted, de-constituted, maintained and altered in social practices through life and after death. This process can be described as the ongoing attainment of personhood. Personhood is frequently understood as a condition that involves constant change, and key transformations to the person occur throughout life and death. People may pass from one state or stage of personhood to another. Personhood is attained and maintained through relationships not only with other human beings but with things, places, animals and the spiritual features of the cosmos. Some of these may also emerge as persons through this engagement. People's own social interpretations of personhood and of the social practices through which personhood is realized shape their interactions in a reflexive way, but personhood remains a mutually constituted condition."

29   Graham 2017, 51.

30   Gosden 2005.

31   Glinister 2006b, 94.

172 CHAPTER 6

It is interesting to note that bronze figurines are not the only evidence of this concern in Umbria. The Iguvine Tablets also highlight the well-being of the Iguvine community. For example, Tablet I.1.5 reads: "Commence this ceremony by observing the birds, those from in front and those from behind. Before the Trebulan Gate sacrifice three oxen to Jupiter Grabovius. Present grain-offerings, place the ribs on a tray, sacrifice either with wine or with mead, for the Fisian Mount, for the state of Iguvium."[32] These tablets mention a ritual that, according to Bradley,[33] remains invisible in the archaeological record of Umbrian sacred spaces. However, when we turn our attention to Umbrian sanctuaries, the votives of humans, animals, parts of the body, warriors, and animals represent additional evidence of the presence of rituals of well-being, whose importance over time is emphasized by the presence of the Tablets during the Roman period in the Umbrian town of Iguvium.

From this point of view, the anatomical votives that are part of the votive assemblages of Umbrian sanctuaries during the Roman period do not represent a novelty. As we have observed, not only were anatomical bronze votives already in use in Umbria during the archaic period, but, together with male, female, warrior, and animal figurines, they were used for the same ritual of well-being. In the next section, I will return to this point about the presence of anatomical votives after the fourth century BCE.

2.5 Display of Votive Offerings

Due to the limited information available regarding the original placement of these votive objects, as they were discovered in a secondary deposition, spread out across the area, inside pits, or cisterns, it is challenging to determine where they were exhibited within any given sanctuary. Nonetheless, it is possible to propose some hypotheses regarding the duration and manner in which these objects were exhibited. The previous chapter's material survey indicates that almost all figurine types have sharp points on their lower surface. Bradley suggests that this characteristic may suggest that "they were intended for display, probably affixed to a wooden surface."[34] The aforementioned hypothesis becomes even more compelling when taking into account the discovery of numerous nails at sites like the Monte Ansciano and the Colle Mori sanctuaries.[35] These nails may have been employed to fasten several wooden planks together and/or attach them to the walls or platforms of the temple. Alter-

---

32   For the full English translation of this text, see Poultney 1958.
33   Bradley 2000a, 75.
34   Bradely 2000a, 72.
35   Malone and Stoddart (1994, 145) suggest that the nails were used to attach the offerings

CONCLUSIONS 173

natively, in the absence of any built structure, they could have been used to secure the wooden planks somewhere within the sacred perimeter of the area. In this respect, the discovery of 169 nails at Monte Ansciano suggests that they might have been used to attach a wooden plank to a specific location within the sacred area. Furthermore, it is plausible that the bronze figurines were first attached to a stone base and then displayed on a wooden platform, as suggested by some Etruscan and Venetic figurines of the same period, which have been found to be still attached to their original supports.[36]

The presence of a hole on the surface of a bronze sheet figurine from Monte San Pancrazio (MSP_12; figure A57) suggests that there may have been an alternative method of displaying the figurine.[37] Perhaps pierced figurines of this type were suspended for display either on trees, in a manner akin to the display of ox and cow masks on Cyprus, or on walls, like the fifth-century clay offerings from Corinth or the anatomical arm in bronze from Lagole, located in the Veneto region.[38] This solution may have been particularly appropriate for the thin offerings made from bronze sheets or lead, as the preservation status of these materials does not provide any indication about their display. Given

---

directly to the wooden plank. I agree with Bradley (1987, 199) that this interpretation does not seem likely, because most bronze votives do not show any possible nail holes.

36   In Etruria, the supports used for displaying figurines were typically stone bases often inscribed with information such as donors' names, affiliations, and the divinity to whom the figurines were dedicated. At certain sites, like Campo della Fiera near Orvieto, these stone bases could support up to eight figurines at once (Stopponi 2011, 33–35). In some cases, the bases have been found without the figurines that they originally held; at Pasticcetto di Magione, pieces of the lead used to fix the figurines to their base have been found within the votive deposit (Roncalli 1989, 122, 4.32) and at Marzabotto molded travertine bases with traces of lead and small holes for the placement of one or two figurines are associated with the votives found at Fontile Sanctuary. The preserved bases are deliberately disproportionately shaped in relation to the size of the votive figurines in order to adapt their display to the architecture of the monumental complex while at the same time making the votive offerings visible from afar (Gualandi 1973, 63 and 1983,42; Mansuelli 1983, 48–49). Similarly attached to stone bases were the bronze figurines from the Venetic sanctuaries such as the Sanctuary of Raetia (Este), where bases, ca. 50 cm in height, are sometimes molded and accompanied by a dedication to Reitia (Chieco Bianchi 2002, 21), or the Sanctuary at San Pietro Montagnon (between Padua and Este), where remains of figurines held by lead to a base have been recovered (Dämmer 1986, 65). In one isolated case in the Venetic area, at Lagole, a bronze foot is pierced at the top suggesting the possibility that it could have been hung in the sanctuary area (Fogolari and Gambacurta 2001, 153 n. 82).

37   A few examples of the same type from Satricum and Segni (near Rome) also have small holes similar to that of the specimen from Monte San Pancrazio: Colonna 1970, tav. 46–47.

38   Ohnefalsch-Richter 1893, 257 (Crete); Lesk 2002 (Corinth); Gambacurta, and Fogolari 2001, 150 n. 82 (Lagole).

the extreme thinness of the lead figurines, it is unlikely that they could have been affixed to wood without sustaining irreparable damage.

Once fixed on the wooden planks or hung in the sanctuaries, votive figurines were likely visible until they were too numerous to display. In Umbria, four sanctuaries have provided evidence of where the figurines were placed after they were removed from view. Keeping up with a practice seen in the Greek world and elsewhere in the Italic peninsula,[39] some votives (such as those from Pantanelli and Monte Acuto) were placed in pits, while others (such as those from Monte Torre Maggiore and Monte Moro) were deposited in wells and cisterns once these structures were no longer in use. For example, at Monte Torre Maggiore, it is possible to determine the duration of time that the archaic votive figurines were displayed before being discarded. Some of these objects, mixed with pottery, an *aes rude*, and an imperial *balsamarium*, were found in a layer that filled the well in the northwest corner of the sanctuary area. Although we do not know the construction phase of the well, an imperial coin of Commodus found therein provides us with a *terminus post quem* of its obliteration. This datum suggests that the well fell out of use at the end of the second century CE, after which it was used as a refuse pit for some of the many objects that accumulated in the sanctuary over the centuries. Thus we can surmise that, at least in the case of Monte Torre Maggiore, the figurines continued to be displayed for many centuries after their first deposition and that they were displayed alongside the other votives that began to be dedicated in the centuries following the fourth century BCE.[40]

---

39 Larson 2007, 82; Bradley and Glinister 2013, 178. For votives found in wells and cisterns in Italy, see Glinister (2000) with respect to Falerii and Heldring (2007) for Satricum.

40 The partial reuse of older votive offerings has been recognized in sacred areas of southern Italy, as well as in Sicily and at the Faliscan sanctuary of Monte Li Santi-Rote at Narce, and could relate to the practitioners' desire to keep alive through the centuries the essence of a cult: De Lucia Brolli 2018, 65 with previous bibliography. Following this idea and with respect to the new data from the sanctuary of Bagno Grande (Casciano, Tuscany), De Lucia Brolli (in Mariotti-Tabolli 2021, 229) suggests that the bronze votives belong to an earlier phase of the sanctuary and were reused in the Hellenistic period, perhaps after the interception of an earlier deposit during the restoration of the area.

CONCLUSIONS   175

3   Umbrian Sanctuaries between the Late Fourth and the Early First
         Century BCE

3.1   *Votive Offerings in the Hellenistic Period*
In Chapter 5, we learned that Umbria's votive assemblages during the archaic
period mainly consisted of bronze figurines and occasionally *aes rude* pieces.
This pattern was also seen in other central Italian regions. However, in the Hellenistic period, the assemblages became more varied, including terracotta body
parts, heads, Hellenistic worshiper type bronze figurines, miniature vases, and
unguentaria. It is important to note that the number of figurative votive offerings significantly decreased during the Hellenistic period compared to the pre-
Roman era, and the production of locally made bronze figurines, predominant
in the pre-Roman period, came to a halt. This information should be considered
before exploring the figurative votive offerings commonly found in the region's
sanctuaries during this period.

Three reasons could be behind this change. First, the decline in the dedication of figurative votives can be partially explained by the Umbrians' adoption
of a wider array of votive objects typical of much of central Italy. As Bradley
notes,[41] the connectivity brought about by the Roman expansion, in particular by means of the opening of new trade and communication routes across
the peninsula, facilitated the acquisition and dedication of objects of more
imported material, not only molded terracottas but also miniature vases, *balsamaria*, and black gloss and terra sigillata wares. With the opening of new
trade and communication routes across the peninsula, some routes declined,
such as those across the Apennines from Volsinii, which was sacked by Rome
in 264 BCE. Since the raw material used to produce Umbrian bronze figurines
came from the Etruscan *colline metallifere*,[42] it is possible that the decline of
this trade route affected the local production of bronze offerings.

Bradley suggests that another possible explanation for the decline in the
quantity of votive offerings may reside in "the greater focus of life on city sites,"
apparent as early as the end of the fourth century BCE.[43] This phenomenon
coincided with the new political situation that opened up for local elites, who
could now pursue public recognition, profitable connections with Roman aristocrats, and a role in the Roman imperial machinery through actions of public
munificence. In this context, it is reasonable to assume that the resources of

---

41   Bradley 2000a, 176–177.
42   Stoddart 2013, 111.
43   Bradley 2000a, 173.

individuals across the regions were increasingly directed towards public architecture in city centers and the monumentalization of buildings, rather than investing in votives to be displayed in rural sanctuaries.

Lastly, it is worth noting that as the number of votive offerings decreased during this period, a large quantity of pottery appeared in Umbrian sanctuaries. In some cases, where excavation reports allowed the evaluation of pottery forms, such as Monte Moro and La Rocca, it was observed that the most commonly represented shapes were paterae, ollae, plates, cups, and bowls. While a patera is an offering dish used for sacrifices, the other pottery forms identified are drinking and eating vessels that may not have been made exclusively for votive purposes. These shapes were generally the same as those found in burials and settlements, and related to commensality, including cooking, drinking, and feasting.[44] The increased prevalence of pottery shapes related to feasting and banquets in Umbrian sanctuaries during the Hellenistic period could be attributed to a clearer diversification of activities within the sacred sphere, including dedications to the gods, drinking, and banqueting, both ritual and non-ritual.

3.2   *Anatomical Votives Revisited*

With respect to the dedication of figurative votive objects, anatomical votives and heads, present at eight out of the twelve Umbrian sanctuaries that continued to be used during the late fourth–early first century BCE, are the most ubiquitous (figure 45). Also widespread is the Hellenistic worshiper votive type, while the types Animal, Tanagrine, and Other are attested only at one sanctuary each.

Although the Hellenistic worshiper votive type has been rightly seen as part of the more homogenized central Italian cultural koine, the presence of heads and anatomical votives has been regarded as prime evidence of the cultural Romanization of the Umbrian community and a wholesale change in the religiosity of the local peoples. In line with some recent critiques of this assumption,[45] I have shown in the previous chapter that the link between their presence and the progression of the Roman conquest in Umbria is untenable.

To summarize some of the counterarguments, the presence of anatomical heads and body parts in Umbrian sanctuaries is not necessarily tied to the political status of communities in relation to Rome. As the graph above shows

---

44   Perego and Scopacasa 2016, 35.
45   Most notably put forth by Glinister 2006a and 2006b.

CONCLUSIONS

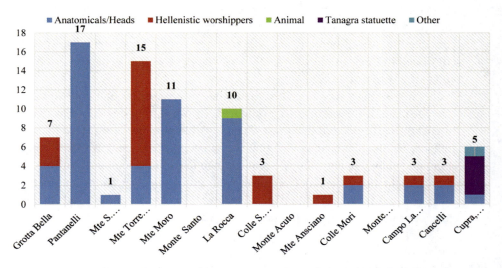

FIGURE 45 Graph showing the groups of figurative votive objects dedicated in each Umbrian sanctuary.

(fig. 45), they can be found both in areas under direct Roman control, such as La Rocca, and in independent or rural areas (Monte San Pancrazio, Pantanelli, Grotta Bella, Monte Torre Maggiore, Monte Moro), as well as near a *civitas sine suffragio* (Cancelli and the Sanctuary of Cupra at Colfiorito). Additionally, the tradition of dedicating anatomicals and heads is not a new practice that suddenly emerged in the late fourth or early third century but rather a long-established tradition in the region dating back to the sixth century BCE, with offerings made mostly in bronze and, in some cases, in terracotta.[46] From this point of view, the anatomical votives that are part of the votive assemblages at Umbrian sanctuaries during the Hellenistic period do not represent a novelty, as Comella and Turfa have argued.[47] As we have observed, not only were anatomical bronze votives already in virtually all sanctuaries of the archaic period, but, together with male, female, warrior, and animal figurines, they were used for the same ritual of well-being that Glinister associates with the anatomical votives of the Hellenistic period.

When we disregard the notion that the existence of anatomical votives and heads is linked to Roman influence and consider the evolution of the material artifacts found in Umbrian sanctuaries over time, there is no evidence to support the belief that the anatomical votives and heads of the Hellenistic

---

46 See figures A171 (Monte Ansciano) and A3.179 (Colle Mori) in Appendix 3.
47 Turfa 2004, 359–336; Comella 1981, 767.

period were associated with a novel ritual practice. Rather, the evidence points towards the same ritual practice of dedicating anatomical votives and heads connected to a well-being ritual, which originated in the archaic period and continued in the Hellenistic era. The only change was in the material used to create the votive offerings.

It is increasingly recognized in the archaeology of ritual that constancy is a key feature of long-term ritual practices. However, this does not necessarily mean that the material expressions of a ritual remain constant over time. Instead, researchers have shown that the same ritual can be performed using different materials, and that material change does not necessarily indicate a change in the ritual itself. In the case of anatomical votives in Umbrian sanctuaries, the shift from bronze and lead figurines to terracotta anatomical votives does not imply a change in the underlying ritual practice of offering anatomical votives for well-being. Rather, it suggests a shift in the available materials and technologies used to produce such votives.[48] Many of the contributions in the recent book edited by Stek and Burgers[49] successfully show that it was not uncommon in cult places of the Italic peninsula to add new votives to rituals that were already in existence.

The anthropologist Anthony Cohen has suggested that during phases of significant social and spatial change, groups tend to emphasize and enhance old community borders through reinterpreting the past in a ritual context.[50] This may explain why a ritual practice persists but its votive form evolves over time. In the case of Umbrian sanctuaries, the practice of dedicating anatomical votives and heads was likely connected to a ritual of well-being that began in the archaic period and continued into the Hellenistic period. However, as the social and political landscape changed with the Roman conquest, the material expression of the ritual may have evolved to reflect new social and cultural realities. The ability of ritual to articulate group identity and promote group cohesion, trust, and cooperation has been discussed in archaeology through various perspectives. Colin Renfrew has emphasized that the experience of ritual activity creates links between people and defines the membership of certain groups.[51] This process may have had a stronger impact on colonies, where local and Roman people of varying statuses were included as founding mem-

---

48 Kyriakidis 2007, 9–23. Conversely, the author points out that the presence of the same material evidence for ritual practices does not necessarily reflect a continuity of the associated belief.

49 Stek and Burgers 2015, 97–113.

50 Cohen 1985, 87.

51 Renfrew 2007, 109–123.

CONCLUSIONS   179

bers,[52] but the winds of change brought about by new settlers in the region must have been influential for independent Umbrian communities as well. By reinforcing shared values and beliefs, the continuation of the well-being rituals during the Hellenistic period helped the local people define their communities' identity after the Roman conquest and the formation of new cultural and political settlements.

As previously noted, anatomical bronzes were present in Umbrian pre-Roman cult places, but during the Hellenistic period they were replaced by terracotta votives. It remains unclear why locals chose terracotta votives for their well-being ritual instead of the bronze figurines they were accustomed to. However, we can suggest three possible reasons, all of which could be valid simultaneously. The first reason is that offering body parts instead of full bodies may have been more effective in conveying the message of the ritual, as the anatomical votives represented an extension of the corporeal body. This approach would have been more immediate and effective in achieving the ritual's aim of promoting contentment and wellness for the individual or group. The second reason for the selection of anatomical terracottas as votives may be efficiency. Anatomical terracottas were often produced using a mass-production technique with molds, traveling workshops, or specialized artisans. They were usually made of coarse fabrics and required little reworking or retouching, making them easy to produce and transport.[53] Compared to bronze figurines, anatomical votives and heads were stock productions and relatively easy to produce, and this made them more convenient for craftsmen and worshipers of different socio-economic statuses, given their overall low cost.[54] To draw from Freeman's reaction to Millett's book, the adoption of Roman goods often had a lot to do with the "arrival of new, technologically better and cheaper goods" and "does not prove a desire to be seen as Roman."[55] Additionally, the large number of anatomical votives found throughout Central Italy and Greece during the

---

52   Bispham, 2006, 91; Bradley 2006a; Coles 2009; Glinister 2015 (esp. fn. 39 on the incorporation of the existing population, also as magistrates, in the colonies); Scopacasa 201, 47–50. Coles (2009, 167–168), in particular, has examined how cult and sacred spaces aided the integration of diverse social and ethnic groups in newly founded colonies. At Fregellae, for example, the placement of extra-urban sanctuaries along the Via Latina helped define community cohesion and boundaries.

53   Fenelli, 1975a, Comella, 1981, 793–794. Evidence of clay molds from Campania (Valle d'Ansanto and Paestum) seems to suggest that some producers may have worked directly on the sanctuary site: see Rainini 1976 (Valle D'Ansanto) and Ammerman 2002, 15–22 (Paestum).

54   Scopacasa 2015b, 7.

55   Freeman 1993, 444.

Middle Republican period indicates that they were popular and in line with contemporary demands for votive objects. However, it is important to note that considering these objects fashionable does not imply their Roman origin, especially since the earliest anatomical terracottas were not even found in Rome.[56]

A question remains as to why a worshiper dedicated one particular part of the body instead of another. Glinister and Recke suggest that worshipers may have dedicated specific body parts as a more specific request for certain needs, such as terracotta genitalia for fertility or to mark puberty, feet for journeys or pilgrimage, eyes to be seen by the divinity, hands for prayer, and so on.[57] Similarly, as suggested by Scopacasa,[58] the presence of lower limbs may have expressed a concern about body parts regarded as essential for mobility and manual labors. Additionally, the availability of certain votives at a given sanctuary and local factors related to the cult may have influenced the choice of a particular anatomical votive. Although the specific significance of each individual anatomical votive is unclear, the fact that a wide range of body parts were dedicated in Umbria and throughout Central Italian sanctuaries indicates that the form of the votive played a significant role in the worshiper's decision to make a vow.[59]

In conclusion, if we are to attribute any Roman influence to the prevalence of anatomical terracottas in Umbrian pre-Roman cult sites, it would likely be due to the development of a new road network that allowed for easier transportation of goods and ideas.[60] A new road network crossing central Italy may have created the preconditions for spreading this new material into colonial and non-colonial areas. Traders and artisans from different parts of the Mediterranean could now easily reach this central region without the difficulty of crossing the Apennines. However, if roads and freer trade may have facilitated their diffusion, the presence of anatomical terracottas in Umbria is most likely linked

---

56   See the discussion in Chapter 2.

57   Glinister 2006b, 12; Recke 2013, 1076.

58   Scopacasa 2015, 19–20. In his analysis, Scopacasa focuses on the published material about anatomical votives from Apennine sanctuaries, with only the Umbrian sanctuaries of Monte Acuto, Monte Subasio, and Grotta Bella featuring in his list. In comparison to Tyrrenian and Daunian sanctuaries, here he notices a higher prevalence of lower and upper limb votives, which he regards as the "Apennine preference." However, in Umbria this does not seem to be the case as the anatomical terracottas depict a broader range of body parts and organs.

59   We should also consider the possibility that the choice of a votive form was limited by the availability of votive offerings on sale at a given sanctuary.

60   Glinister 2006b, 26. In this respect, nobody should be surprised that, as noted by Gentili (2005), the earliest anatomical terracottas at Carsoli are dated to the middle of the fourth century BCE, some fifty years before the foundation of the colony in 298 BCE.

CONCLUSIONS

181

to reasons other than Roman imposition of new cultic material evidence, such as convenience, fashion, and earlier local customs of dedicating such objects.

3.3 Continuity and Abandonment of Pre-Roman Cult Places

In the previous chapter, I challenged the traditional assumption that the continuation of Umbrian sanctuaries was linked to the Roman presence in the region. I demonstrated that pre-Roman Umbrian sanctuaries were still in use after the end of the fourth century BCE, regardless of the political status of communities in relation to Rome. However, I also found that compared to previous centuries (sixth/early fourth century BCE), there was a significant decrease in the material evidence for ritual activity (figurative offerings, pottery, coins) in some sanctuaries (Monte Acuto, Monte Subasio, Monte San Pancrazio, Monte Santo, Monte Ansciano) between the end of the fourth and the beginning of the first century BCE. This suggests a decline in the level of frequentation of these sanctuaries. In contrast, the archaeological data from the sanctuaries of Grotta Bella, Monte Torre Maggiore, Colfiorito, La Rocca, Campo La Piana, Monte Pennino, Cancelli, and Pantanelli did not show a significant decrease. In this section, I examine the level of use of Umbrian sanctuaries and propose possible reasons for the decline in use of some of them.

Before we explore this matter further, it is crucial to assess the credibility of the archaeological evidence available. As previously stated, the excavation of most Umbrian sanctuaries has been incomplete (such as Pantanelli, Monte San Pancrazio, Monte Subasio, Campo la Piana, Monte Pennino, and Monte Santo), and the information collected has been either insufficient (Pantanelli, Campo La Piana) or entirely absent (Monte San Pancrazio, Monte Pennino, Monte Subasio, Monte Santo).[61] As a consequence, our knowledge of the archaeological material from these sanctuaries is extremely limited; except for the little information from the archaeological reports, it relies either on later studies of specific classes of objects, as is the case for Monte Santo and Monte Subasio, or on the presence of a selection of bronze figurines, whose original number is unknown, in the local museums of the region. Thus, the changing proportion of votive offerings between the archaic and Roman periods in these sanctuaries does not indicate the site's overall use.

To gain a better understanding of the frequency of use of Umbrian sanctuaries, it is necessary to examine the ones that have been recently and thoroughly excavated. The rural sanctuaries of Grotta Bella, Monte Ansciano, Monte Torre

---

61   I found no records of this excavation in the Archaeological Archives of the region and in the depot of the Soprintendenza Archeologia Belle Arti e Paesaggio dell'Umbria.

Maggiore, Monte Acuto, Colle Mori, Monte Moro, La Rocca, and Colfiorito provide more representative data. Among these sanctuaries, Monte Acuto, and Monte Ansciano show a near absence of votive material dating from the late fourth to the early first century BCE, suggesting a halt in their activity during that period. The only evidence of cult activity during the beginning of the third century BCE at Monte Ansciano is a coin of a very early Republican issue and a fragment of a figurine belonging to the Hellenistic worshiper type. Similarly, Monte Acuto only shows evidence of activity during the late fourth to the early first century BCE in the form of fragments of black gloss and sigillata italica, as well as a miniature vase.

Bradley has offered a possible explanation for the reduced frequentation at the Monte Ansciano sanctuary.[62] He notes that the apparent ending of ritual activity on Monte Ansciano is paralleled by the beginning of temple activity at Iguvium, which is attested for the Hellenistic period by a number of architectural terracottas found in the city center.[63] It is highly likely that the construction of a new sacred space in the general area resulted in a reduction of ritual activity at an archaic cult place, as evidenced by other excavated sanctuaries in close proximity to Umbrian centers that continued to witness cult activity during the same period. Sanctuaries such as Colle Mori, Colfiorito, and Cancelli were situated close to urban centers like Monte Ansciano, but unlike Iguvium, no new sacred buildings were erected in these centers until the beginning of the first century BCE. The emergence of new temples at Iguvium after the fourth century BCE may have attracted the local community that previously worshiped at Monte Ansciano, resulting in a significant decline in its attendance.[64]

There needs to be a different explanation as to why there was a decline in ritual activity at the sanctuary on Monte Acuto, as it was not located near major settlements during the Hellenistic period, unlike Monte Ansciano. As Bonomi Ponzi points out, surface surveys in the territory surrounding Umbrian high-peak settlements testify to a significant decrease in the number of sites early in the Roman period.[65] She observes that the trend of abandoning high

---

62   Bradley 1997, 122.

63   Sisani 2001, 42; Strazzulla 1981, 186.

64   Although the few surviving votive offerings at Monte Subasio (near Assisium) in the third century BCE may not represent the original votive corpus, Bradley (1987, 125) hypothesizes a similar trend for this sanctuary. At Assisium, as at Iguvium, there is evidence of the development of a temple within the settlement.

65   Bonomi Ponzi 1989, 23. A similar phenomenon is observed in Samnium by Battiloro 2018, 165–168.

CONCLUSIONS 183

peaks after the fourth century BCE coincided with people moving towards marketplaces closer to the main commercial routes and paying more attention
to lowland, sub-Apennine settlements. This pattern is similar in other parts
of the peninsula, where during this time, Iron Age villages that were well-
defended moved towards sites that were more suitable for cultivation and communication. Additionally, Fracchia's surveys of Roman Republican settlements
in southern Italy demonstrate that areas closer to major road systems had a
greater incidence of survival, and the sites that flourished over time were those
that served nearby markets, such as villas or village.[66] Therefore, it is likely that
the new socio-economic reality influenced the decrease in ritual activity during the Hellenistic period on Monte Acuto, which was isolated from populated
areas and not connected to major roads. The reason why other hilltop sanctuaries such as Monte Torre Maggiore and Monte Moro did not experience a
significant decline in activity due to the new settlement patterns could be that
they were located near major commercial routes (the Via Flaminia for Monte
Torre Maggiore and a branch of the Via Salaria for Monte Moro) and urban settlements (such as Carsulae and Interamna Nahars, which were respectively 6
and 17 km away from Monte Torre Maggiore; Interamna Nahars and Spoletium
were approximately 14 and 18 km away from Monte Moro). A similar situation
can be seen with the sacred cave of Grotta Bella, where the continuous use of
the space for rituals may have been facilitated by its easy access from the Via
Amerina.

Although the available data do not allow us to have a complete picture of
the level of frequentation of Umbrian sanctuaries, the analysis of the evidence
from a few well-excavated cases suggests that sanctuaries continued to be visited during the Hellenistic period. It is plausible to hypothesize that, in the few
cases where the evidence points to an apparent cessation of ritual activity, factors such as the construction of new temples in nearby settlement areas and the
concentration of the economic life away from mountainous areas and towards
commercial routes played a role in the progressive abandonment of a sacred
area. Conversely, the evidence shows that sanctuaries located in areas closer to
roads had a greater survival incidence, and those sites would flourish until the
Imperial period.

The continuation of ritual activity at the La Rocca sanctuary demands separate consideration because it is distinct from other Umbrian sanctuaries in
two ways. Firstly, this sanctuary is in an urban context, unlike the other rural
sanctuaries previously discussed. Secondly, it is the only Umbrian, pre-Roman

---

66   Fracchia 2013.

184   CHAPTER 6

cult place that, in this period, sat within the area of a Latin colony (Spoletium). Although I demonstrated that overall there does not seem to be a link between the continuation of an Umbrian sanctuary and the political status of nearby communities' relationship to Rome, Stek and Perna have made a case for the correlation between urban cult places and Roman colonization and incorporation.[67] Significantly, Stek points out that the religious, social, and economic power of pre-Roman cult places represented an "important attraction for Roman expansion."[68] Similarly, Perna notes that the continuation of ritual activity at pre-Roman urban sanctuaries in Picenum after the foundation of colonies and *municipia* may have been the result of the conscious choice to use the importance of cult places as an element of syncretism between local and Roman cultures. Despite the presence of new sacred places built after the foundation of the Latin colony of Spoletium, it seems plausible that the Umbrian sanctuary at La Rocca continued to represent power on a tangible level in socio-economic and religious terms. The fact that, as Glinister points out, "collective cults enhanced an already dynamic interactive process, integrating different groups into society,"[69] makes it possible that the La Rocca sanctuary served as a facilitator for cultural contact between the new settlers and local people.[70] Another factor that could have helped in building a new community is the tradition of dedicating anatomicals, which was familiar to both colonists from Rome and local Umbrian peoples. Furthermore, the similarities between Roman and local cults might have played a role in integrating different groups into a cohesive community.[71]

3.4   *Monumentalization of Umbrian Sanctuaries: Architectural Features*
During the Roman conquest of Umbria, the region was made up of many politically independent communities, which had specific settlements and sanctuar-

---

67   Stek 2017, Perna 2013.
68   Stek 2017, 286.
69   Glinister 2015, 154.
70   See fn. 513 for references on the inclusion of locals and foreigners in a new colony.
71   Glinister (2015, 151) mentions how the structural equivalences between Italic and Roman cults such as similar concepts of delimiting sacred spaces, the importance of the natural world for the divine, the presence of common gods to whom to dedicate prayers, vows, and rituals, helped the merging of religious traditions and patterns. At the same time, she stresses, the distinctive background of colonial founders, the presence of locals of different statuses, and the permeability which came from the possibility of acquiring links with nearby colonies or receiving new incomers at a later stage are all factors that facilitated "the development of colonial distinctiveness in the religious sphere" (153) and further enhanced a multi-cultural and hybrid colonial landscape.

CONCLUSIONS   185

ies, as previously explained. Starting from the end of the fourth or the beginning of the third century BCE, Umbrian allied communities and Latin centers initiated significant construction projects. The Latin colony of Spoletium and the allied centers of Ameria, Asisium, and possibly Urvinum Hortense had massive defensive walls constructed around the mid-third century BCE; new temples are built at Spoletium, Iguvium, Urvinum Hortense, Asisium, Vettona, and Mevania; stone walled buildings are erected at Hispellum,[72] and an inscription from Fulginiae attests to the presence of work concerned with the management of water supplies.[73] As Bradley puts it, during this phase, towns began to "gain monumental physical dimension to complement their political identity."[74]

Between the end of the fourth and the second century BCE, this trend of intense building activity also affected some rural sanctuaries of the region; complexes underwent phases of complete restructuring, involving the construction of buildings in areas previously marked by no permanent architectural structure. Although the available published material is limited and complete publications are lacking, it is clear that some individuals or groups invested in enhancing sacred buildings during this phase. Surviving evidence indicates that Umbrian sanctuaries were embellished with different architectural solutions mainly borrowed from contemporary Italic and Hellenistic templar architecture.

Architectural evidence for the monumentalization of Umbrian sacred buildings during the Hellenistic phase comes from the sanctuaries at Monte Moro, Monte Torre Maggiore, Cancelli, and Monte San Pancrazio. However, at Cancelli and Monte San Pancrazio, there is limited archaeological evidence available, which makes it difficult to reconstruct the original appearance of the buildings. Therefore, only a few inferences can be drawn from the available data. At Cancelli, the surviving evidence suggests that the building consisted of at least three rooms partially covered in *opus signinum*, and a water-related drain. Monte San Pacrazio's sacred area was bounded by a Hellenistic porticus, intersected by a water channel. The archaeological evidence from Monte Moro and Monte Torre Maggiore is less fragmented and allows for a better reconstruction of the original appearance of these sanctuaries. At Monte Moro, the sacred complex was organized around three main rooms, with the central one likely serving as the main cult room. Additional rooms to the south formed an

---

72   Architectural decorations were also found at Civitalba, near Sentinum in the modern Le Marche region. Although this area lies outside the area covered by this work, it still belonged to the ancient region of Umbria.
73   For a discussion of the dates of these building constructions, see Bradley 2000a, 158–170.
74   Bradley 2000a, 158.

L-shaped space around an unpaved and open area. At Monte Torre Maggiore, the architectural layout and decoration are preserved. A precinct bounded the sacred area, and a rectangular temple made of large limestone blocks, oriented east-west, with a *pronaos*, *cella*, and columns all around it, was built on top of a tall podium in *opus quadratum*.

The available evidence suggests that most Umbrian sanctuaries followed Etrusco-Italic decorative forms. While Monte Torre Maggiore has yielded lion-headed waterspouts and a female head directly inspired by Hellenistic art, the *antepagmenta* and antefixes discovered at the sites of Pantanelli, Cancelli, Colfiorito, and La Rocca conform to decorative motifs that were popular in contemporary sanctuaries of Latium Alatri, Anagni, Minturnae, southern Etruria (Civita Castellana), and Samnium (Pietrabbondante).[75]

Umbrian sanctuaries had no standard architectural and planimetric style during the Hellenistic period. The available evidence suggests that the few cases that can be reconstructed either followed the Hellenistic tradition (Monte San Pancrazio) or combined the axiality of Etrusco-Italic architecture with decentralized rooms (Monte Moro) or elements of the Hellenistic tradition in a local manner (Monte Torre Maggiore). At Monte Torre Maggiore, various architectural models are used, including the Hellenistic temple plan with columns on all sides, which matches the remaining decorative elements, such as the lion spouts and a statue's female head. These Hellenistic features are combined with local elements, such as locally carved limestone blocks and the frontality of the high-podium temple style that is typical of the Etrusco-Italic canon. The skill to manipulate different architectural canons and experiment with variations in a local fashion has been noticed by Battiloro and Scopacasa in Lucania and Samnium and framed within the context of what Ranuccio Bianchi Bandinelli named "Italic Hellenism," which entailed the assimilation of Greek cultural forms into the Italic decorative and stylistic traditions.[76]

After an initial phase, spanning from the middle of the fourth to the middle of the third century BCE, during which the spread of Hellenistic culture in central Italy was largely due to the contacts that Italic communities had with Greece, southern Italy, and Sicily, Hellenistic iconographic models came to be widely used as a "language of power" in other parts of the peninsula

---

75 For Latin and Faliscan examples, see Andren 1940; for Samnium, Scopacasa 2015a, 265.

76 Battiloro 2018, 203–207; Scopacasa 2015, 115–119 and 262–270; Bianchi Bandinelli 1970, 11. For an overall picture of Italic Hellenism in Italy see Haumesser 2017, 645–665; Coarelli 1970–1971, 254–255; Torelli 1983; La Rocca 1996; Wallace-Hadrill 2008, 99. For Samnium see also: La Regina 1976; Tagliamonte 2005, 189–201.

CONCLUSIONS   187

as Italy became more integrated into the economic and cultural networks with the Hellenistic East. This phenomenon affected various regions, including the Samnite and Lucanian areas, where pre-Roman cults were revitalized through the use of monumental religious complexes, such as the sanctuary of Rossano di Vaglio, or through the construction of new buildings and complementary structures, as seen most notably at Pietrabbondante.[77] Although the new architectural stimuli and influence in Umbria took less dramatic forms compared to their Samnite and Lucanian counterparts, they were still part of the same cultural trends. In other words, during the Hellenistic period, the architectural layout of Umbrian sanctuaries resulted from the adoption of new architectural trends that were common to all Italic communities. This was a consequence of an increased dialogue between the Italian peninsula and the eastern Mediterranean, as well as the integration of local and Italic traditions.

The transformations that occurred in Umbrian sanctuaries during the Hellenistic period raise questions about the promoters of their monumentalization during the last centuries of the Republic. This was a time when hilltop centers were abandoned, and Umbrian society was redefining itself under the influence of Roman preeminence in Italy and the Mediterranean.

3.5   *Monumentalization of Umbrian Sanctuaries: Possible Agents*

As previously mentioned, much of the public munificence visible during the Hellenistic period must be understood in the context of the relationship between Rome and its Italian allies. Gosden has recently stressed that in the context of Rome's expansionism from its central Mediterranean base, "the possibilities of local participation in the new broader culture were attractive to many,"[78] an idea that Terrenato has further elaborated. As he has underscored,[79] Roman and Italic elite networking and negotiations played an important part in this interconnectedness. On the one hand, having local contacts was beneficial to Roman aristocrats trying to advance their specific agendas, such as the dominance of the local community, maintenance of the established order, control of the political brokerage between the community and the center of power, and the piloting of tribal formation and composition. On the other hand, the support of powerful Roman friends would facilitate the careers of Italic elite members, either in their own cities or in Rome itself. In short, Terrenato's model

---

77   For a discussion of the architecture of these sanctuaries see Battiloro 2018, 188–196; Scopacasa 2015a, 262–270.

78   Gosden 2004, 110.

79   Terrenato 2014 and 2019.

goes beyond the classic dichotomy between Romans and Italians and suggests that the integration process may have been the result of a broad network of factional projects.

In central Italy, archaeological, epigraphical, and prosopographical material from some Etruscan, Latin, and Campanian polities provides evidence for factionalism in the context of Italic integration with Rome.[80] Caere is a particularly illustrative case of the types of contact between peer groups in Rome and the Italic regions of the peninsula. Here, contacts between local elite members and those in Rome are attested as early as the fourth century BCE[81] and intensified in the third century, when two members of the Roman family of the Genucii added to their name the appellative Clepsina, represented in Etruria at Tarquinia, Tuscania, and Caere. In order to strengthen the family ties with this region, C. Genucius Clepsina dedicated an underground cultic building in Caere and, likely due to his connection with the area, played a role in facilitating the interactions and negotiations between this city and Rome in the second decade of the century.[82]

Coles has also observed a similar dynamic of interwoven personal interests among local and Roman aristocrats in the Latin colonies of Latium and Campania.[83] Specifically, she demonstrates that the impetus to found a colony was driven by a desire for a combination of benefits, including a closer tie to regions of personal concern, clientele, and political and economic advancement. Coles notes that given these ties between specific geographical areas and the interests of colonial officials, it is not difficult to imagine the benefits this group would have gained—particularly in terms of personal networks and assistance up the *cursus honorum*—by monumentalizing traditional religious landmarks.

In the Umbrian region, which gradually became part of the Roman expansionistic network through local alliances, the establishment of colonies, and the formation of *civitates sine suffragio*, evidence of elite agendas and faction-

---

80   Terrenato (2014 and 2019) provides a lengthy and accurate review of central Italian examples of elite private agendas in the context of Roman expansion. Among the most noteworthy cases, we can mention the involvement of some members of the Latin family of the Plautii with the rebellion at Privernum and long-distance aristocratic connections between Rome and local elites from Arezzo (the Cilnii for example) or from Capua.

81   As reported by Livy (9.36.2–4), in the fourth century members of the Fabii, attested at Caere since the late seventh century BCE, were educated here to learn the Etruscan language. Furthermore, in the same century a Latin woman who resettled in Rome and held important political offices married a member of the powerful family of the Matuna in Caere: Terrenato 2018, 121.

82   Colivicchi 2015.

83   Coles 2009.

CONCLUSIONS

189

alism can be seen in two notable cases mentioned in Chapter 4. In the context of the foundation of the colony of Nahars, Livy recounts how two townsmen betrayed the pre-Roman city to the Romans. At Asisium, Nero Babrius chose to commemorate his offices in two inscriptions: one in Umbrian using Latin script and the other in Latin language and script. These examples illustrate the presence of personal interests and factionalism among local and Roman aristocrats and how they influenced the development of the region.

In this varied and hybrid political scenario, where competition for a successful position within the nascent empire must have been particularly intense among the elites, it is difficult to pinpoint specific agents for the monumentalization of Umbrian sanctuaries. It is likely that the monumentalization of Umbrian sanctuaries during the Hellenistic period was the result of a complex interplay between local and Roman elites with intertwined interests. Rather than being solely driven by economic investment, the embellishment of local temples would have brought benefits to both Roman and local elites by extending their networks of clientele and providing access to new territories for political career advancement. In this competitive political scenario, both Umbrian and Roman agents sought to assert themselves, and public munificence was a valuable tool for achieving this goal.

4 Conclusion and Looking Forward

The discussion focused on the analysis of the data presented in Chapter 5, contextualizing it within the broader development of cult places in Umbria from the archaic to the Hellenistic periods. Four central themes of this study were explored: (1) the function of archaic Umbrian sanctuaries, (2) the significance of the votive practice of dedicating bronze figurines during this time, (3) the continuation and embellishment of sacred places, and (4) the emergence of anatomical terracottas in the Hellenistic period. The traditional *pagus-vicus* model and the political status of local communities in relation to Rome fail to fully account for the function of ancient sanctuaries and their decline following Roman expansion into the region. As an alternative approach, the analysis closely considered cult places' topographical features and votive deposits.

By examining the topographical relationship between sanctuaries and nearby inhabited areas and identifying common votive figurines and locally made offerings, it becomes evident that archaic sanctuaries in Umbria were closely linked to the communities that inhabited the surrounding areas. The presence of unique figurines found only at specific Umbrian sanctuaries indicates that these sacred places were utilized by distinct communities that sought to emphasize their individuality. During the Hellenistic period, the decline in ritual activities at two of the sixteen sanctuaries studied was due to factors such as the construction of new temples in nearby settlements and the shift of economic activity away from high elevations and towards commercial routes.

The votive figurines found in Umbrian sanctuaries have been central to my interpretation of the associated deposition ritual. By examining these figurines, we can gain insight into the cultural continuity, modifications, and reinterpretations that occurred as a result of the Roman expansion. The ritual that was practiced in Umbrian cult places from the archaic period onwards was likely aimed at promoting the wellness of individuals and communities. Moreover, I have argued that the function of the figurines was not predetermined during their creation. Rather, the materiality of the figurines, along with their association with the sacred sphere and identification data, may have dictated the well-being ritual that was associated with them. The continuity of the votive ritual in Umbrian sanctuaries during the Roman period is demonstrated by the presence of anatomical terracottas and heads. This continuity also reveals the selective adoption and adaptation of foreign cultural elements, as discussed in Wallace-Hadrill's code-switching model. In Umbria, the tradition of anatomical votives, common on the Tyrrhenian coasts of Latium and Etruria, was applied to archaic ritual in a selective manner. The presence of archaic votive offerings in Hellenistic sanctuaries further suggests the tangible connection between worshipers and the local past. Additionally, the offering of body parts and heads, familiar to the Umbrians and Roman settlers, may have facilitated the formation of new communities by acting as a point of contact between them.

In addition to the presence of more varied votive assemblages, containing heads and anatomicals alongside figurines of Hellenistic worshipers, miniature vases, and coins, the architectural embellishment of some Umbrian sanctuaries also indicates the adoption and adaptation of wider cultural trends that were prevalent in the Italic peninsula during the Hellenistic period. The use of local, Etrusco-Italic, and Hellenistic elements in these embellishments suggests that the region was open to new artistic stimuli, similarly to what was happening in other parts of the peninsula, such as Samnium and Lucania. Regarding the agents involved in this refashioning of Umbrian religious landmarks, it is likely that local as well as Roman elites were equally interested in using public munificence to pursue their political goals. This is supported by the competitive political scenario of the time, where alliances between elites were key to personal success and a public career.

In such an account of the change that happened in the cult places of the region after the Romans began their expansion, there is little space for a system-

CONCLUSIONS 191

atic imposition of Roman culture onto the region's local people. The conquest of the region did not happen in the unilateral model of the imposition of one culture on another, but rather in a middle ground, a space "in between and within which peoples interact,"[84] where the encounter between different cultural traditions created new cultural structures. This middle ground, shared by the Umbrians and Romans and influenced by the broader Hellenistic koine of the Mediterranean, allowed for the continuation of the tradition of dedicating anatomical votives and heads, which mingled with new offering types and a variety of architectural solutions that transformed the sacred areas into monumental structures. Furthermore, the use of a new material, terracotta, made the creation of votive offerings more affordable and accessible.

The type of approach advocated in this study—that sanctuaries and their votive deposits need to be studied simultaneously as components of a larger regional sacred landscape and with an eye toward each site specificity and its development from the archaic to the Hellenistic periods—can be fruitfully applied to the study of the sanctuaries of other regions. In the context of the Italic peninsula, this detailed analysis has been successfully conducted in Lucania and Samnium but is lacking in other regions of Central Italy, such as Picenum and Latium. By comparing the material culture, ritual practices, and historical contexts of different regions, scholars can identify commonalities and differences in the ways that local communities responded to cultural contact and change. This can contribute to a more nuanced understanding of the diversity and complexity of ancient Italian societies, as well as the ways in which cultural traditions were adopted, adapted, or rejected in different regions and contexts. As the example of Umbria shows, once a more complete picture of Italic sacred places is achieved, we can re-evaluate Rome's impact on the sacred sphere of the peninsula.

---

84   Lyons and Papadopoulos 2002, 158.

Appendix 1: Types of Umbrian Figurative Votive Offerings

The typology of votive figurines is largely based on Colonna's classification and my own grouping of the votives not considered by him.[1] In this Appendix, for each type I present a description,[2] the average measurements, the areas of distribution, and when applicable, I briefly outline the scholarly framework of their interpretation.

1 Sixth–Fourth Century BCE

1.1 *Fabriano Group (FaG; figure A234)*[3]

This type of figurine belongs to north Umbrian production and comprises elongated figures of warriors characterized by course anatomical details of both the body and the face. These figures are depicted wearing a defensive skirt and a tall crest with raised cheekpieces, while some have additional greaves. The eyes are depicted with a circular punch, and the mouth with a small horizontal line.

The height varies from 14 to 25 cm. Figurines of this type have been found at Sassoferrato,[4] Fabriano,[5] and Colfiorito (Sanctuary of Cupra).

1.2 *Fossato di Vico Group (FoVG; A3.235)*[6]

This type of figurine belongs to the north Umbrian production and represents warriors. These figures are characterized by skeletal elongation, and wear a cuirass with a thick belt, a helmet with an interrupted curve, and a defensive skirt (*pteruges*) decorated with X lines and a crisscross pattern.

The height of these figurines varies from 20 to 32 cm. Besides two specimens from Fossato di Vico[7] and Colfiorito (Sanctuary of Cupra), figurines of this type lack provenance.

---

1 Colonna 1970.
2 The acronyms within parentheses refer to the abbreviation of the votive types used both in Chapter 5 and in Appendix 2. The figure number within parentheses refers to the photo catalog in Appendix 3.
3 Colonna 1970, 39–40.
4 Colonna 1970, 39 n. 48.
5 Colonna 1970, 39 n. 47.
6 Colonna 1970, 42–48.
7 Colonna 1970, 43 n. 61.

© CHARLES UNIVERSITY, FACULTY OF ARTS, PRAGUE, 2025 | DOI:10.1163/9789004712171_008
This is an open access chapter distributed under the terms of the CC BY-NC-ND 4.0 license.

1.3 *Todi Group (ToG; A3.56)*[8]

This type of figurine belongs to the southern Umbrian production and depicts warriors. The figurines share several characteristics, including the indication of eyelids in the modeling of the face, a softly modeled body, a helmet with raised cheekpieces, and a large crest rising directly from the cap. They also wear a leather cuirass with hinged shoulder guards, a belt, and greaves. Furthermore, the armor and the helmet are intricately decorated with geometrical motifs.

The height varies from 18 to 24 cm. Due to the size and sophisticated rendering of the figurines of this group, Colonna defines it as "the most noticeable episode of the southern Umbrian school."[9] Figurines of this type have been found in the Sabine area at Ancarano[10] and in Umbria at Calvi dell'Umbria (Monte San Pancrazio sanctuary) and Todi (Monte Santo).[11] The latter is considered by Colonna the most likely place for the manufacture of these figurines.

1.4 *Amelia Group (AmG; A3.66–68; A3.106–109; A3.138; A3.146; A3.187–188; A3.229–230)*[12]

This type of figurine belongs to the southern Umbrian production and consists of warriors, striding men, and male and female worshipers. The most unique feature of these figurines is their heads, which are filed at the front to create two flat surfaces that form an acute angle and end on the upper part with a curved edge. The eyes are represented with small circles, and the mouth is indicated with a cut at the base of the angle, which serves as the nose. The naked bodies of the figurines have nipples and navels that are incised with circles, while the men have protruding genitals. The striding men have their right leg slightly bent and their left leg straight, while their left arm is raised with the palm facing upwards and the thumb stretched wide. The right arm is bent downwards with an open hand and a stretched-out thumb. The lower limbs of the figurines end with spikes.

The height of the figurines varies between 5 and 10 cm. In Umbria, specimens have been found at Todi (Monte Santo),[13] Umbertide (Monte Acuto),[14] Spoleto (La Rocca), Assisi (Colle S. Rufino),[15] and Colfiorito (Sanctuary of Cupra).[16] Out-

---

8	Colonna 1970, 76–79.
9	Colonna 1970, 80.
10	Colonna 1970, 77 n. 176 and 177.
11	Colonna 1970, 78 n. 180 (Calvi dell'Umbria); Colonna 1970, 78–79, n. 181 (Todi).
12	Colonna 1970, 90–93.
13	Falcone Amorelli 1977, tav. 90 i/l.
14	Cenciaioli 1991, 214, 216, and 226.
15	Monacchi 1986, tav. 39d–e.
16	Colonna 1970, 94 n. 253.

TYPES OF UMBRIAN FIGURATIVE VOTIVE OFFERINGS 195

side the region, figurines of this typology come from the Sabine (Ancarano) and Etruscan (Fiesole) areas, and from Rome (Via Magenta).[17] A few examples have also been found beyond the Alps, in Switzerland (at Bessonens and Sembracher) and France (at Menthon-Saint-Bernard).[18] The abundance of this type at Todi has led Colonna to hypothesize that this was the center of manufacture.

1.5   *Foligno Group (FoG; A3.55; A3.91; A3.144–155; A3.196; A3.201–202; A3.233)*[19]

This type of figurine belongs to the southern Umbrian schematic production and consists of warriors and striding men. Both are depicted as naked and striding towards the left, with the warriors being depicted with crests on their heads. The punched roundels are used to represent the eyes, nipples, and navel, while the mouths are depicted with a small slit. The legs of the figurines end with pointed feet.

The height of the figurines of the Foligno group varies between 7 and 10 cm. Specimens have been found in Terni (Monte Torre Maggiore),[20] Montefranco (Monte Moro),[21] Todi (Monte Santo),[22] Calvi dell'Umbria (Monte San Pancrazio), Spoleto (La Rocca), Gualdo Tadino (Colle Mori),[23] and Foligno (Cancelli and the Sanctuary of Cupra).[24] Outside this region, figurines of this type come from the Etruscan area (Fiesole), northern Italy—Altino (Veneto) and Aquileia (Friuli-Venezia Giulia)—and Spain (Ampurias).[25] The abundance of this type at Todi has led Colonna to hypothesize that this was the center of manufacture of the FoG.

1.6   *Nocera Umbra Group (NuG; A3.15–16; A3.73–75; A3; 117–119; A3.136–137; A3.159–160; A3.175–176; A3.197; A3.215)*[26]

This type of figurine belongs to southern Umbrian schematic production and includes flat figurines of both warriors and females. The warriors in this group

---

17   Colonna 1970, 93 n. 247 (Ancarano); Colonna 1970, 93 n. 245 (Fiesole); Colonna 1970, 93 n. 244 (Rome).
18   Tabone 1995–1996, 217.
19   Colonna 1970, 96–97.
20   Bonomi Ponzi 1989, 20 fig. 4.
21   Sisani 2013, 134 n. 32.
22   Falcone Amorelli 1977, tav. 90 a/h.
23   Colonna 1970, 99 n. 280.
24   Manca et al. 2014, 55. n. 31 (Cancelli); Colonna 1970, 96 n. 264 (Sanctuary of Cupra).
25   Colonna Tabone G.pP. 1995–1996, 217 (Altino and Aquileia); Colonna 1970, 99 n. 281 (Ampurias).
26   Colonna 1970, 100–103.

are typically depicted with a lozenge crest and open arms. On the other hand, the female worshipers have open arms, and grooves indicate their hands. They also have different types of *tutulus* (a type of headdress) on their heads.

The height of the figurines is between 5 and 13 cm. In Umbria, specimens have been found at Amelia (Grotta Bella),[27] Terni (Monte Torre Maggiore), Todi (Monte Santo),[28] Umbertide (Monte Acuto),[29] Spoleto (La Rocca),[30] Gubbio (Monte Ansciano),[31] Foligno (Cancelli and Cupra Sanctuary),[32] and Monte Pennino. Outside the ancient region, figurines of the NuG type have been found in Sabine and Etruscan areas (Ancarano, Nocera Umbra, and Orvieto) and in northern Italy at Villazzano (Trentino-Alto Adige) and Altino (Veneto).[33]

1.7   *Esquiline Group (EG; A3.1–10; A3.44–49; A3.60–65; A3.86–88; A3.110–113; A3.131–133; A3.145; A3.151–158; A3.163–167; A3.193–195; A3.205–206)*[34]

This type of figurine, defined by Richardson as a typically Umbrian phenomenon,[35] belongs to southern Umbrian schematic production. The group consists of male and female worshipers as well as warriors, all with a flat, narrow body, outstretched arms and legs, and spikes at the end of their legs. The arms have transverse grooves to indicate fingers, while the long and narrow head has eyes marked by two grooves and a cut to indicate the mouth. Male figures are naked with genital protuberance, while females wear a long, tight tunic. Warriors are recognizable by the high crest on their needle-sharp head and a hole in the right arm to insert a weapon. Some figurines in this group are so schematized that they resemble the shape of a star.

The height varies from 2 to 6 cm. Specimens of the EG type have been found abundantly in the region of Umbria at Amelia (Grotta Bella and Pantanelli),[36] Todi (Monte Santo),[37] Umbertide (Monte Acuto),[38] Calvi dell'Umbria (Monte

---

27   Arena 1981–1982, tav. 18; Monacchi 1988, tav. 35c.
28   Falcone Amorelli 1977, 171 e and g/i.
29   Cenciaioli 1991, 217–219.
30   Costamagna et al. 2011, 41 fig. 6.
31   Malone and Stoddart 1994, 150 nn. 37 and 44–45.
32   Manca et al. 2014, 56 n. 32 (Cancelli).
33   Colonna 1970, 101 n. 298 (Orvieto); Colonna 1970, 102, n. 303 (Ancarano); Colonna 1970, 102–103 n. 306 (Nocera Umbra); Tabone 1995–1996, 217–218.
34   Colonna 1970, 103–105.
35   Richardson 1983, 162.
36   Monacchi 1988, tav. 35 a/b.
37   Falcone Amorelli 1977, 174–175.
38   Cenciaioli 1991, 215–217 and 219–220.

TYPES OF UMBRIAN FIGURATIVE VOTIVE OFFERINGS

197

San Pancrazio), Gualdo Tadino (Colle Mori),[39] and Foligno (Cancelli and Cupra Sanctuary).[40] The type is also attested in the Picene (San Severino Marche, Pievetorina, and Pioraco),[41] Sabine (Ancarano di Norcia and Forma Cavaliera),[42] Etruscan (Bettona, Maggione, and Orvieto),[43] Aequian (Carsoli),[44] and Roman (Rome, Piazza dell'Esquilino)[45] areas. A few examples have been also found beyond the Alps, in northern Italy (at Vertova in the Lombardy region), Austria (Zollfeld), and Hungary (Keszthely and Szombathely).[46]

1.8 *Montesanto Group (MSG; A3.120–121)*[47]

This type of figurine belongs to the southern Umbrian schematic production and includes only figures of warriors. The type is characterized by the repetition of the ToG costume but without greaves. The facial features are geometric, with a sharp nose, eyes represented by carved circles, and a small horizontal gash indicating the mouth.

The height of these figurines ranges between 11 and 14 cm. Besides those from Todi (Monte Santo),[48] the figurines of this group lack provenance.

1.9 *Bronze Sheets (BS; A3.57; A3.173–174; A3.198; A3.213–214)*[49]

Figurines belonging to this type are cut from bronze sheets and characterized by extremely flat and elongated bodies. These almost resemble a long strip where limbs and head are the only anatomical details; when preserved, the genitals hang between the legs of the male types.

The height of these figurines can vary from 3 to 55 cm. Given the presence of this type of figurines in several sanctuary contexts of Roman (Campidoglio and Sant' Omobono)[50] and Latin (Tivoli, Sermoneta, Satricum, Segni, and Norba)[51]

---

39 De Vecchi 2002, 57 n. 54.
40 Manca et al. 2014, 56 nn. 34–36.
41 Bittarelli 1987, 588.
42 Schippa, 1979, 204 and Sisani 2013, 148–149 (Ancarano); Sisani 2013, 128–129 (Forma Cavaliera).
43 Colonna 1970, 105 n. 320 (Orvieto); Bruschetti 1989 (Magione); Scarpignato 1989 (Bettona).
44 Colonna 1970, 105 n. 321.
45 Colonna 1970, 103 n. 307.
46 Tabone 1995–1996, 218–219.
47 Colonna 1970, 71–72.
48 Falconi Amorelli 1977, 167–168.
49 Colonna 1970, 107–114.
50 Colonna 1970, 107 n. 326 (Campidoglio); Colonna 1970, 108 n. 329.
51 Colonna 1970, 107 n. 328 (Sermoneta); Colonna 1970, 107 n. 327 (Tivoli); Perrone 1994 (Norba); Gnade 2007, 112 n. 67 and Colonna 1970, 109 nn. 331–332 (Satricum); Colonna 1970, 109 n. 333.

areas, Colonna hypothesized that their production began in Rome. In Umbria, the BS type is attested at Calvi dell'Umbria (Monte San Pancrazio), Umbertide (Monte Acuto),[52] Foligno (Cancelli),[53] and Colfiorito (Sanctuary of Cupra). Outside the region, a few figurines have been found in the Aequian and Sabine areas (Carsoli and Ancarano),[54] in Picenum (Montefortino di Arcevia),[55] and Etruria (Bagnolo S. Vito).[56]

1.10 Animals (A3.11–14; A3.58; A3.77–78; A3.92–93; A3.122–123; A3.168; A3.196; A3.121–122)

This type consists of bronze figurines depicting various animals such as pigs, goats, bulls, cows, and horses. The execution of these figurines is similar to that of schematic human figurines as they were cast and then hand-finished on the edges. Most of the time, these figurines are highly stylized, and it can be challenging to identify the exact animal being represented. The bodies are flattened and elongated, and the legs end in pointed feet. When there are anatomical details, they are rendered with punched circles for the eyes and notches or grooves for the mouth and fur.

The height varies from 2 to 6 cm. In Umbrian territory, votives of this type have been found at Grotta Bella,[57] Todi (Monte Santo),[58] Calvi dell'Umbria (Monte San Pancrazio), Monte Torre Maggiore,[59] Monte Moro,[60] Foligno (Cancelli),[61] Umbertide (Monte Acuto),[62] and Colfiorito (Sanctuary of Cupra). Outside this region, specimens come from Etruscan (Pasticcetto di Magione, Cortona, and Colle Arsiccio)[63] and Sabine (Ancarano)[64] areas. Since the level of schematization is close to the schematic rendering of the figurines of the EG type, it is possible that the bronze animal figurines were also a southern production, as suggested by Cenciaioli.[65]

---

52 Cenciaioli 1991, 229 nn. 4.33 and 4.34.
53 Manca et al. 2014, 57 n. 37.
54 Colonna 1970, 110 n. 334 (Carsoli); Colonna 1970, 110 nn. 336–337.
55 Colonna 1970, 111 n. 340.
56 Tabone 1995–1996, 220, tav. 54 1–4.
57 Monacchi 1988, 79–81.
58 Falcone Amorelli 1977, 183.
59 Bononi Ponzi 1989, 26; 2006, 116.
60 Sisani 2013, 136.
61 Manca et al. 2014, 57–58.
62 Cenciaioli, 1991, 223–224.
63 Bruschetti 1987–1988, 52–59; 1989, 121–122 (for Pasticcetto di Magione and Cortona); Maggiani 2002, 280 (Colle Arsiccio).
64 Schippa 1979.
65 Cenciaioli 1991, 223.

TYPES OF UMBRIAN FIGURATIVE VOTIVE OFFERINGS 199

1.11 Eyed Crests (*A3.54; A3.76; A3.89–90; A3.199*)
This type comprises small bronze filed crests that are commonly considered a simplified version of the warrior figure.[66] These crests stand on spikes and feature two grooves made with a punch to resemble eyes.

The height varies between 2 and 4 cm high. This type is widespread in southern Umbria (Monte San Pancrazio, Monte Moro, and Monte Torre Maggiore)[67] and limited to one sanctuary in the Apennine area (Sanctuary at Cancelli).[68]

1.12 Archaic Heads (*A3.21–22; A3.53; A3.69; A3.94; A3.124; A3.161; A3.179; A3.187; A3.200*)
This type consists of bronze figurines that depict human heads with an extremely geometric execution, making gender distinction difficult.[69] The heads are faceted, with details added using a burin or a circular punch, and bear a striking similarity to those of the Esquiline Group and Amelia Group, suggesting that some of the same casts may have produced them. The bottom of the heads features a sharp spike.

The height of the figurines varies from 2.5 to 4 cm. This type of figurine is attested throughout the Umbrian territory, including at locations such Amelia (Grotta Bella), Umbertide (Monte Acuto), Calvi dell'Umbria (Monte San Pancrazio), Terni (Monte Torre Maggiore),[70] Montefranco (Monte Moro),[71] Todi (Monte Santo),[72] Gualdo Tadino (Colle Mori), and Foligno (Cancelli).[73] Outside Umbria, this type of schematic bronze head has been found in Etruscan territory at Arna and Bettona.[74] It is worth noting that more realistic heads with elaborated anatomical features have been discovered at Fonte Veneziana and the Lake of the Idles (Arezzo), as well as in Fiesole.[75]

---

66 Bonomi Ponzi 2006, 115; Sisani 2013, 136.
67 Costamagna 1998, 9 and Sisani 2013, 136 (Monte Moro).
68 Manca et al. 2014, 56 (Cancelli).
69 In two cases, MtAnsc_10 (figure A161) and CM_1 (figure A187), the archaic heads are made of terracotta.
70 Bononi Ponzi 1989, 22.
71 Costamagna 1999, 9; Sisani 2013, 136.
72 Falcone Amorelli 1977 tav. 94a–f and h.
73 Manca at al. 2014, 57 fig. 39.
74 Feruglio 2001, 235 (Arna); Roncalli 1989, 125 (Bettona).
75 In the Arezzo territory, for the heads from Fonte Veneziana, see Villucchi et al. 2001, 123 (n. 20–21), 127 (nn. 38–39), for those from Lake of the Idles, see Trenti 2013, 121–121. For the heads from Albagino, see Nocentini et al. 2018, 98. For the heads in Fiesole, see Mingazzini 1932, 469 and 471–473.

APPENDIX 1

1.13 *Archaic Anatomicals (A3.17–20; A3.50–52; A3.139; A3.201; A3.226; A3.234)*

This type consists of bronze representations of limbs, including legs, feet, hands, and arms. The figurines are depicted schematically, with little attention paid to anatomical details. The arms are portrayed outstretched with hands indicated by small incisions to represent the fingers. The legs are extremely thin, with little distinction between the upper and lower parts, and the feet are similarly rendered with minimal anatomical detail, except for slight swellings on both sides of the ankle to represent the ankle bones. As with the other bronze votive types mentioned earlier, these figures stand on tall spikes.

The height of the specimens of this type varies from 2 to 8 cm. In Umbria, they have been found at Amelia (Grotta Bella), Calvi dell'Umbria (Monte San Pancrazio), Terni (Monte Torre Maggiore), Umbertide (Monte Acuto),[76] Spoleto (La Rocca), Foligno (Cancelli),[77] and Colfiorito (Sanctuary of Cupra). Outside the ancient Umbrian territory, the presence of bronze anatomical votives has been noticed in Venetic sanctuaries at Este, Villa di Villa, Lova, and San Pietro Montagnon, and in Etruscan sanctuaries at Marzabotto, Arezzo (Fonte Veneziana), Monte Falterona (Lake of the Idols), Fiesole, Magione, Arna, and Bettona.[78]

2 **Late Fourth–Second Century BCE**

2.1 *Hellenistic Worshiper with a Rayed Crown (A3.36; A3.79–80; A3.150; A3.162; A3.188; A3.202)*

This type comprises bronze figurines representing male and female worshipers. The male figurine is depicted wearing a knee-length tunic and holding a patera

---

76 Cenciaioli 1991, 225.

77 Manca at al. 2014, 57 fig. 41.

78 For the Veneto region, see Maioli and Mastrocinque 1992, table 22 (Villa di Villa); Chieco Bianchi 2001, table 54 (Este); Groppo 2011, 98 (Lova); Dämmer 1986, table 17 (San Pietro Montagnon). For the Etruscan area, see Gualandi 1974, 63 and Miari 2001, table 37 (Marzabotto); Villucchi et al. 2001, 125 (Fonte Veneziana); Nocentini et al. 2018, 65 and Fedeli 2007, 52–53 (Lake of the Idles); Orlandini Passigli 1990, 91 (Fiesole); Roncalli 1989, 122–123 (Magione); Feruglio 2001, 235 (Arna); Roncalli 1989, 126 (Bettona). Unlike the abovementioned anatomical votives, at Servirola Sanpaolo and Adria anatomical bronzes representing legs are surmounted by an animal figurine representing a duck, interpreted as a solar symbol, see Gualandi 1974, 40–68 and Turfa 2004, 360. For an overview of all anatomical votives in bronze from the pre-Roman period (including unpublished specimens), see Zapelloni Pavia, forthcoming.

TYPES OF UMBRIAN FIGURATIVE VOTIVE OFFERINGS   201

in his right hand and an acerra in his left. He wears a crown with either three or five leaves on his head.[79] The female figurine wears a long chiton that reaches her feet, draped under her breasts, and a himation that covers her left shoulder and wraps around her hips. She carries either an acerra or focaccia bread on her left arm and wears a diadem with several rays or a crown/diadem on her head.

Both female and male worshipers originally stood on a small cubic travertine base, which is preserved in one specimen from Grotta Bella (GB_285; figure A36) and from Monte Torre Maggiore (MTM_6; A3.80). Galestin suggests that several workshops may have been active in the region during the third and second centuries BCE due to the slight stylistic differences among the Umbrian Hellenistic figurines. It is also possible that the figurines were manufactured near or at the sanctuary where they were deposited.[80]

This type is influenced by the Hellenistic style, which began to spread gradually throughout many parts of Italy in the third century BCE. This style was introduced to central Italian areas through the Greek centers of Southern Italy.[81] As contacts between the Italians, the Romans, and the Greeks from Greece and Asia Minor increased in the second century BCE, Greek artists began to work in cities such as Rome, Volterra, and Ancona. This led to a greater influence of Hellenistic art in the region. As a result, figurines of Hellenistic worshipers with a rayed crown became widespread in the peninsula as part of the artistic koine of Latium, Etruria, and Umbria in central Italy.[82] In Umbria, this type is attested at Amelia (Grotta Bella),[83] Terni (Monte Torre Maggiore), Assisi (Monte Subasio),[84] Gubbio (Monte Ansciano), Gualdo Tadino (Colle Mori),[85] and Foligno (Cancelli).[86] Outside this region, figurines of this type have been found in Latin (Nemi),[87] Etruscan (Chiusi, Colle Arsiccio,

---

79   Interpreted by Manfrini and Argno (1987, 67–68, fig. 55) as the god Bacchus because of the presence of the ivy crown.

80   As Galestin (1987, 168) suggested for Latium and Etruria as well. For all the stylistic variations of the Hellenistic worshiper type, see Galestin 1987, 77–118.

81   Galestin 1987, 93.

82   An in-depth study on this type of votive is absent. For the presence of the type in Latin context, see Demma 2019, 275–277. For specific Etruscan contexts, see Haynes 1960, 34–38; Monacchi 1988, 88; Roncalli 1989, 138; Marini et al. 2002, 382; Trombetta and Bruschetti 2002; Bonfante et al. 2015, 179.

83   Monacchi 1988, 88, tav. 38d–e.

84   Monacchi 1986, 86–87, tav. 29a–c.

85   De Vecchis 2002, 57 n. 55.

86   Lost but published in Picuti 2009, 9.

87   Haynes 1960.

202   APPENDIX 1

and Caligiana di Magione),[88] Picenate (Monte Rinaldo),[89] and Aequian (Carsoli) areas.[90]

2.2   *Terracotta Heads (A3.59; A3.84–85; A3.1–2–104; A3.189; A3.143;*
       A3.204) and Anatomical Terracottas (A3.34; A3.43; A3.82–83;
       A3.95–101; A3.140–142; A3.203; A3.231)

Terracotta heads and anatomical votives belong to the Etrusco-Latial-Campanian group (ECL), which was first classified by Comella in 1981. These votives
have been linked to the process of Romanization and the offering of parts of
the body often associated with healing cults.[91]

As early as the end of the sixth century BCE, the practice of dedicating heads
as votive offerings was identified in Veii and Falerii.[92] Torelli suggests that this
custom in Etruria was influenced by similar practices in Magna Graecia associated with the chthonic cults of Demeter and Kore.[93] The practice began to
spread to other regions, including Caere, Capua, Teano, and Carsioli, during the
fifth century BCE. Eventually, the practice reached Rome and central Italy during Rome's expansion,[94] following the "direttrici della conquista romana" and
becoming a distinctive feature of Romanization.[95] These votive offerings are

---

88   Maetzke 1957, 500 fig. 22 (Chiusi); Calzoni 1947, 45–47 (Colle Arsiccio).
89   Giorgi 2020, 150–151.
90   Cederna 1951, 193–300, fig. 9–10.
91   In addition to terracotta figurines of worshipers, the ECL group also comprised figurines
      of animals, buildings, and swaddled infants. The ECL group is discussed by Comella
      (1981, 758), Fenelli (1975), Turfa (1994), Torelli (1999), de Cazanove (2000), and Lesk 2002.
      Recently, the presence of anatomical votives in Apennine and Abruzzo regions has led
      scholars to question the belief that the practice of dedicating ELC-type votives spread
      solely due to Roman expansion, as argued by Glinister (2006, 23–26). For further discus-
      sion about this group of votives, and in particular anatomical votives, see Chapter 2.
92   Heads of the sixth century BCE have been found in the Campetti deposit at Veii: Comella
      and Stefani 1986, 19; Comella 1997, 335. At Falerii, votive heads dating from the fifth cen-
      tury BCE are present in the sanctuaries of Celle and Vignale and in votive deposits at the
      Nifeo Rosa: Comella 1986, Blanck 1990. At Narce, votive heads of the first half of the fifth
      century BCE have been found in the suburban sanctuary of Monte Li Santi-Rote: De Lucia
      Brolli and Tabolli 2015.
93   Torelli (1990, 440) and Comella (1981, 772–775) suggest that the Campetti sanctuary at Veii
      was associated with the cult of Demeter not only because of some similarities between
      the Etruscan heads and some southern Italian votives in Greek style associated with this
      cult but also because it resembles some Sicilian sanctuaries dedicated to cthonic deities.
94   Comella 1981, 772–775.
95   Steingraber 1980, 247; Torelli 1981. According to Pensabene (1979, 218), the presence of
      the veiled heads is a characteristic of votive deposits from Rome and Latin colonies, for
      the presence of the veil was common during the *Romanus ritus* for sacrificing with the
      head covered. On the contrary, the absence of the veil should be connected with the

TYPES OF UMBRIAN FIGURATIVE VOTIVE OFFERINGS 203

believed to be forerunners of the terracotta heads that are part of the Etrusco-Latial-Campanian group.

Antomical votives are shaped like parts of the internal or external human body and represent the most conspicuous type in the Etruscan-Latial-Campanian group. Similar to the terracotta heads, since the spread of the anatomical terracotta tradition coincided with the expansion of Rome, its widespread adoption has been linked to the Roman conquest of Italy, in particular through the areas occupied by Latin colonies.[96]

2.3 *Tanagra Figurines (A3.232)*

This type consists of figurines of women, typically depicted standing, though sometimes seated. They wear tightly fitted and intricately folded garments and are often shown wearing high conical sun-hats with broad brims and carrying fans. The figurines are represented in an endless variety of poses, with their attire similarly diverse. Given that many specimens are depicted holding offerings, it is likely that these figurines represent worshipers engaged in religious rituals and public festivals, or in specific moments of their lives, such as purification rites before a wedding, puberty, or prenuptial rites.[97]

This type of figurine originated in Athens in the second half of the fourth century BCE and later became more widespread in the Italic peninsula as part of the Hellenistic cultural exchange. During the third century, this style spread from Magna Graecia, particularly Tarentum, to Samnium, Lucania, Latium, Etruria, and the Marrucine territory.[98] In Umbria, their presence is limited to the site of the Sanctuary of Cupra at Colfiorito.

2.4 *Other (A3.24–33; A3.39–42; A3.127–130; A3.147–149)*

This group consists of votive offerings that cannot be classified within any known figurative type and/or are limited to one or two Umbrian sanctuaries. In the pre-Roman period, figurines belonging to this group include: 1) male and female lead figurines found at Grotta Bella and Pantanelli in Amelia; 2)

Greek ritual practice, adopted by the Etruscans, of sacrificing with the head not draped. However, veiled female heads of the Etrusco-Latial-Campanian type are present in pre-Roman contexts, such as Pietrabbondante and Montefortino, and cast serious doubts on the "Romanness" of these artifacts (Glinister 2006, 15).

96 Cf. Chapter 2, in particular the bibliography in fn. 58.

97 James and Dillon 2012, 233; Graepler 1994, 283.

98 On the diffusion of the Tanagra figurines in the Mediterranean, see the latest work on this topic by Jeammet and Aravantinos (2010) with previous bibliography. For Samnium and Lucania, see Scopacasa 2015, 261–262; Battiloro 2018. For this type in the area occupied by the Marrucini, see Strazzulla 2012.

a zoomorphic pendant, a warrior attached to a situla, and a dancing figurine found at Colle S. Rufino in Assisi; and 3) the zoomorphic figurines found at the Sanctuary of Cupra in Foligno. For the Roman period, the figurines that belong to this group are: 1) a terracotta figurine of a bovine found at the La Rocca Sanctuary; and 2) a figurine depicting Hercules found at the Sanctuary of Cupra in Colfiorito.

Appendix 2: Tabulated Catalog of Umbrian Figurative Votive Offerings

This catalog goes beyond the published reports and attempts to provide a comprehensive re-examination of all the votive figurines, including many currently unpublished. At present, such a task has been achieved for three particular types of artifacts: figurines of humans, animals, and anatomical parts in bronze, lead, or terracotta. For other votives, such as pottery and coins, such an inventory remains a major desideratum. For the present, the tabulated catalog allows us to see the patterns of dedications, but also to bring some order to the current haphazard state of the published evidence, scattered over numerous publications, museums, and depots.

For the sake of completeness, the catalog includes pieces that are no longer available for study. These have been lost, and no images seem to exist for most of them. Museum records and previous scholarship is used to provide as exhaustive a record as possible. The recordings referred to are freely available online at https://doi.org/10.6084/m9.figshare.27102598.

1   Criteria for Classification

The data are presented in a quantitative form, covering the archaic and Hellenistic periods (sixth to early first century BCE). The entry of each votive object starts with a catalog number, always preceded by the abbreviation of the site name,[1] followed by the votive type.[2] A list and description of the possible votive types can be found in Appendix 1. Under the label "other" are grouped the exceptions to the norm, namely figurines that differ slightly from known types and/or figurines that are unique to specific sanctuaries.

---

1   The sanctuary sites are abbreviated as follows: GB for Grotta Bella, PTN for Pantanelli, MSP for Monte San Pancrazio, MTM for Monte Torre Maggiore, MM for Monte Moro, MTS for Monte Santo, Rocca for La Rocca, CSRufino for the sanctuary on Monte Subasio, Mt Ansc for Monte Ansciano, MTA for Monte Acuto, CM for Colle Mori, CLP for Campo la Piana, MTP for Monte Pennino, Cupra for the Sanctuary of Cupra at Colfiorito.
2   The votive types are abbreviated: EG stands for Esquiline Group, NuG for Nocera Umbra Group, FoG for Foligno Group, ToG for Todi Group, AmG for Amelia Group, MSG for Monte Santo Group, BS for bronze sheet, EC for eyed crest, AAnat for archaic anatomical, AH for archaic head, Anat for anatomical of the Hellenistic period, HellWorsh for Hellenistic worshiper.

© CHARLES UNIVERSITY, FACULTY OF ARTS, PRAGUE, 2025 | DOI:10.1163/9789004712171_009

This is an open access chapter distributed under the terms of the CC BY-NC-ND 4.0 license.

1.1 Date

In Umbria it is impossible to date bronze and terracotta figurines based on stratigraphy. This is because they were either buried in votive pits without external datable evidence or scattered in the area near sanctuary sites. Most scholars rely on Colonna's and Richardson's studies of bronze offerings and adhere to their suggested chronology of sixth–fourth century BCE for the votives of the archaic sanctuaries.[3] As for the terracotta votives, they are generally ascribed to the third–first century BCE, based on similarities with those of Latium, Campania, and Etruria.[4]

1.2 Measurements

The measurements are given in centimeters. The first number refers to the maximal height and the second number to the width of the object.

1.3 Preservation

The missing parts are accounted for. If more than 50% of the object could be estimated to be missing, the object is defined as a fragment (only the identifiable ones have been cataloged). The categories of preservation are good, fair, poor, and fragment.

1.4 Sanctuary Site

Refers to the sacred space where the votive figurines have been found.

1.5 Find Spot within Site

Refers to where on site the object was found. Votive figurines retrieved on the surface without a proper archaeological investigation are signaled as fortuitous finds. For objects retrieved from archaeological excavation, the available excavation reports record them as generically found in pits and/or in disturbed layers across the sacred areas and thus hinder the possibility of knowing where each figurine was found. For this reason, in most cases the find spot is indicated as a deposit/ disturbed layer, and only when available I provide the SU of the find spot. When none of this information from the available publications and archival documents is available, the find spot is signaled as NA (not available).

---

3 Colonna 1970, Richardson 1983.
4 Monacchi 1988.

TABULATED CATALOG OF UMBRIAN FIGURATIVE VOTIVE OFFERINGS   207

1.6   *Location of the Object*
Refers to where the object is displayed (museums) or stored (depots). The names of museums and depots are shortened with the following acronyms: CAOS (Centro Arti Opificio Siri, Terni); Dunarobba (Centro di Paleontologia Vegetale della Foresta Fossile di Dunarobba); MAC (Museo Archeologico di Colfiorito); MANS (Museo Archeologico Nazionale di Spoleto); MANU (Museo Archeologico Nazionale dell'Umbria); MANUdep (Magazzini del Museo Archeologico Nazionale dell'Umbria); MANoU (Museo Archeologico Nocera Umbra); MAU (Museo Archeologico Antichi Umbri – Polo Museale Gualdo Tadino); MCA (Museo Civico di Amelia); MCT (Museo Comunale di Todi); MCU (Museo di Santa Croce Umbertide); MSAP (Magazzino della Soprintendenza Archeologica Perugia); Pconsoli (Museo Civico Palazzo dei Consoli di Gubbio); PzTrinci (Museo della città di Palazzo Trinci, Foligno).

1.7   *Inventory Number*
Refers to the inventory number that the Soprintendenza ABAP dell'Umbria and the Polo Museale dell'Umbria have associated with the artifacts.

1.8   *Photo Number*
Refers to the number associated with the images of the votive figurines presented in Appendix 3.

1.9   *Bibliography*
Previously published literature mentioning the object. All the objects that do not have a bibliographic reference are unpublished.

1.10   *Comparanda*
Essential bibliography of stylistically analogous types.

Appendix 3: Catalog of Umbrian Figurative Votive Offerings

This appendix contains the photos of the figurative votive offerings discussed in the book and cataloged in Appendix 2. They are divided by location and votive type (described in Appendix 1) and presented in the same order as in the description of Umbrian sanctuaries in Chapter 5. In order to facilitate the link between Appendices 2 and 3, each photo is complemented by the number assigned to the object in the tabulated catalog. Not all the objects have a figure. Given the repetition of most objects' types, a selection of exemplificative photos for each sanctuary context is presented. If not otherwise specified, all the pictures have been taken by the author with the kind permission of the Soprintendenza ABAP dell'Umbria and of the Polo Museale dell'Umbria.

1 Grotta Bella

1.1 *Esquiline Group*

FIGURE A1
Schematic representation of a man (inv. n. 41; by permission of the Soprintendenza ABAP dell'Umbria).

CATALOG OF UMBRIAN FIGURATIVE VOTIVE OFFERINGS 209

GB_2

FIGURE A2
Schematic representation of a man (inv. N. 50306; by permission of the Soprintendenza ABAP dell'Umbria).

GB_3

FIGURE A3
Schematic representation of a man (inv. N. 50709; by permission of the Soprintendenza ABAP dell'Umbria).

GB_4

FIGURE A4
Schematic representation of a man (inv. N. 50351; by permission of the Soprintendenza ABAP dell'Umbria).

APPENDIX 3

GB_5

FIGURE A5
Schematic representation of a female figure (inv. N. 50709; by permission of the Soprintendenza ABAP dell'Umbria).

GB_6

FIGURE A6
Schematic representation of a warrior (inv. N. 50227; by permission of the Soprintendenza ABAP dell'Umbria).

GB_12

FIGURE A7
Schematic representation of a warrior (inv. N. 50744; by permission of the Soprintendenza ABAP dell'Umbria).

CATALOG OF UMBRIAN FIGURATIVE VOTIVE OFFERINGS 211

FIGURE A8
Schematic representation of a female figure (inv. N. 50311; by permission of the Soprintendenza ABAP dell'Umbria).

FIGURE A9
Schematic representation of a female figure (inv. N. 50309; by permission of the Soprintendenza ABAP dell'Umbria).

FIGURE A10
Schematic representation of a female figure (inv. N. 50707; by permission of the Soprintendenza ABAP dell'Umbria).

1.2 Animals

FIGURE A11
Schematic representation of a bovine (inv. N. 50770; by permission of the Soprintendenza ABAP dell'Umbria).

FIGURE A12
Schematic representation of an ox (inv. N. 50417; by permission of the Soprintendenza ABAP dell'Umbria).

FIGURE A13
Schematic representation of a sheep (inv. N. 50419; by permission of the Soprintendenza ABAP dell'Umbria).

GB_251

FIGURE A14
Schematic representation of an unidentifiable animal, likely a ferret (inv. N. 50724; by permission of the Soprintendenza ABAP dell'Umbria).

1.3 Nocera Umbra Group

GB_252

FIGURE A15
Schematic representation of a warrior (inv. N. N/A; by permission of the Soprintendenza ABAP dell'Umbria).

GB_253

FIGURE A16
Schematic representation of a warrior (inv. N. 50785; by permission of the Soprintendenza ABAP dell'Umbria).

1.4 Archaic Anatomicals

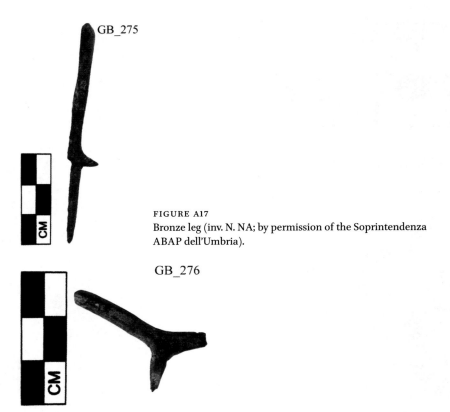

FIGURE A17
Bronze leg (inv. N. NA; by permission of the Soprintendenza ABAP dell'Umbria).

FIGURE A18 Bronze arm (inv. N. NA; by permission of the Soprintendenza ABAP dell'Umbria).

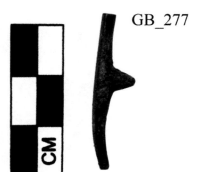

FIGURE A19
Bronze leg (inv. N. NA; by permission of the Soprintendenza ABAP dell'Umbria).

CATALOG OF UMBRIAN FIGURATIVE VOTIVE OFFERINGS 215

GB_278

FIGURE A20
Bronze foot (inv. N. 114336; by permission of the Soprintendenza ABAP dell'Umbria).

1.5   *Archaic Heads*

GB_279

FIGURE A21
Schematic head (inv. N. 50425; by permission of the Soprintendenza ABAP dell'Umbria).

GB_280

FIGURE A22
Schematic head (inv. N. 50423; 50424; by permission of the Soprintendenza ABAP dell'Umbria).

FIGURE A23
Schematic head (inv. N. 50423; 50424; by permission of the Soprintendenza ABAP dell'Umbria).

1.6 *Other*

FIGURE A24
Lead schematic representation of a warrior (inv. N. 50436; by permission of the Soprintendenza ABAP dell'Umbria).

FIGURE A25
Lead schematic representation of a warrior (inv. N. 50430; by permission of the Soprintendenza ABAP dell'Umbria).

CATALOG OF UMBRIAN FIGURATIVE VOTIVE OFFERINGS 217

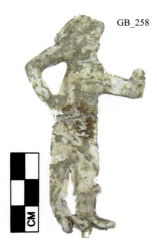

FIGURE A26
Lead schematic representation of a female (inv. N. 50704; by permission of the Soprintendenza ABAP dell'Umbria).

FIGURE A27
Lead schematic representation of a female (inv. N. 50431; by permission of the Soprintendenza ABAP dell'Umbria).

FIGURE A28
Lead schematic representation of a female (inv. N. 50433; by permission of the Soprintendenza ABAP dell'Umbria).

FIGURE A29   Lead *episema*. One side represents an arm fastened to the shield; the other depicts three men under a tree (inv. N. 50435; by permission of the Soprintendenza ABAP dell'Umbria).

FIGURE A30   Lead *episema*. One side represents an arm fastened to the shield; the other side depicts three men under tree (inv. N. 50437; by permission of the Soprintendenza ABAP dell'Umbria). On the right: drawing of the side of the shield with the three men.

FIGURE A31   Lead *episema*. One side represents an arm fastened to the shield; the other side depicts three men under a tree (inv. N. 50440; by permission of the Soprintendenza ABAP dell'Umbria).

CATALOG OF UMBRIAN FIGURATIVE VOTIVE OFFERINGS 219

FIGURE A32
Lead *episema* with *gorgoneion* (after Monacchi 1988, tav. 36 inv. N. 108773).

FIGURE A33   Lead *episema*. One side represents an arm fastened to the shield, the other a radiating sun (inv. N. 50440; by permission of the Soprintendenza ABAP dell'Umbria).

1.7   Anatomical Terracottas

FIGURE A34
Terracotta breast (inv. N. NA; by permission of the Soprintendenza ABAP dell'Umbria).

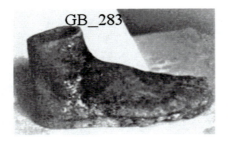

FIGURE A35
Terracotta foot (after Monacchi 1988, tav. 36; inv. N. NA).

1.8 Hellenistic Worshiper

FIGURE A36
Worshiper holding a patera and standing on a base (inv. N. 3038; by permission of the Soprintendenza ABAP dell'Umbria).

FIGURE A37
Worshiper holding a patera (inv. N. 50225; by permission of the Soprintendenza ABAP dell'Umbria).

GB_318

FIGURE A38
Worshiper with outstretched arms (inv. N. 50304; by permission of the Soprintendenza ABAP dell'Umbria).

2   Pantanelli

2.1   *Other*

PTN_1

FIGURE A39
Lead schematic representation of a warrior (inv. N. NA; by permission of the Soprintendenza ABAP dell'Umbria).

PTN_2

FIGURE A40
Fragment of a lead figurine representing a human figure (inv. N. NA; by permission of the Soprintendenza ABAP dell'Umbria).

PNT_3

FIGURE A41
Lead *episema* with *gorgoneion* (inv. N. NA; by permission of the Soprintendenza ABAP dell'Umbria).

PNT_4

FIGURE A42
Lead *episema* with zigzag and knobs motif (inv. N. NA; by permission of the Soprintendenza ABAP dell'Umbria).

2.2 *Anatomical Terracottas*

PTN_8

FIGURE A43   Terracotta foot (inv. N. 124019; by permission of the Soprintendenza ABAP dell'Umbria).

CATALOG OF UMBRIAN FIGURATIVE VOTIVE OFFERINGS 223

3 Monte San Pancrazio

3.1 *Esquiline Group*

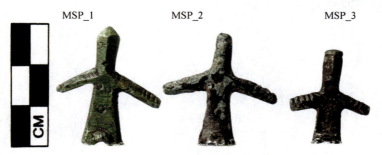

FIGURE A44 Highly schematic male figures (from left to right: inv. NN. 721816, 721817, 721818; by permission of the Polo Museale dell'Umbria).

FIGURE A45
Highly schematic male figure (inv. N. 721836; by permission of the Polo Museale dell'Umbria).

FIGURE A46
Highly schematic female figure (inv. N. 721862; by permission of the Polo Museale dell'Umbria).

FIGURE A47
Highly schematic female figure (inv. N. 721863; by permission of the Polo Museale dell'Umbria).

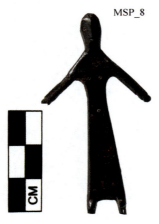

FIGURE A48
Highly schematic female figure (inv. N. 721861; by permission of the Polo Museale dell'Umbria).

FIGURE A49
Highly schematic female figure (inv. N. 721860; by permission of the Polo Museale dell'Umbria).

3.2 Archaic Anatomicals

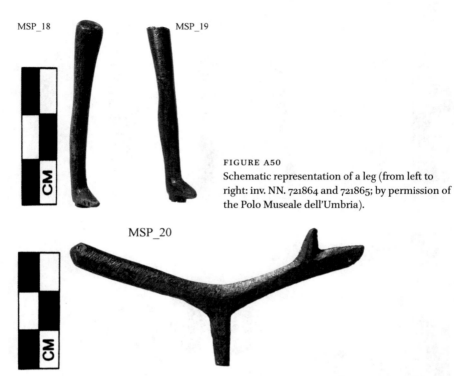

FIGURE A50 Schematic representation of a leg (from left to right: inv. NN. 721864 and 721865; by permission of the Polo Museale dell'Umbria).

FIGURE A51 Schematic representation of an arm (inv. N. 721820; by permission of the Polo Museale dell'Umbria).

FIGURE A52 Schematic representation of an arm (inv. N. 721821; by permission of the Polo Museale dell'Umbria).

3.3 *Archaic Heads*

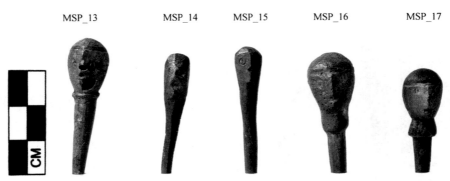

FIGURE A53   Schematic heads (from left to right: inv. NN. 721875–79; by permission of the Polo Museale dell'Umbria).

3.4 *Eyed Crests*

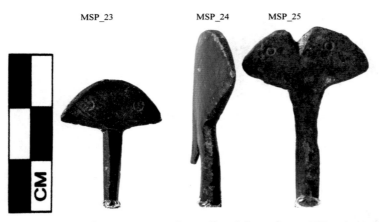

FIGURE A54   Schematic crests with eyes (from left to right: inv. NN. 721872–74; by permission of the Polo Museale dell'Umbria).

CATALOG OF UMBRIAN FIGURATIVE VOTIVE OFFERINGS 227

3.5 *Foligno Group*

MSP_10

FIGURE A55
Highly schematic warrior figure (inv. N. 721867; by permission of the Polo Museale dell'Umbria).

3.6 *Todi Group*

MSP_11

FIGURE A56
Schematic warrior figure (after Colonna 1970, tav. LII–LIII).

3.7 Bronze Sheets

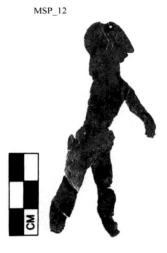

FIGURE A57 Schematic figure turned sideways (inv. N. 721871; by permission of the Polo Museale dell'Umbria).

3.8 Animals

FIGURE A58 Schematic figure of an ox (inv. N. 721819; by permission of the Polo Museale dell'Umbria).

CATALOG OF UMBRIAN FIGURATIVE VOTIVE OFFERINGS 229

3.9 *Terracotta Heads*

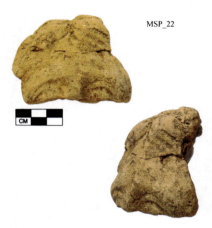

FIGURE A59
Terracotta half-head (inv. N. 721815; by permission of the Polo Museale dell'Umbria).

4 Monte Torre Maggiore

4.1 *Esquiline Group*

FIGURE A60
Highly schematic male figure (inv. N. NA; by permission of the Soprintendenza ABAP dell'Umbria).

FIGURE A61 Extremely schematic male figure (inv. N. NA; by permission of the Soprintendenza ABAP dell'Umbria).

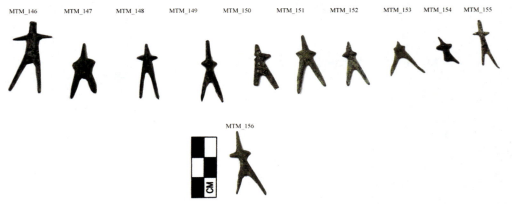

FIGURE A62 Extremely schematic male figures (from left to right: inv. NN. 209173, 209133; by permission of the Soprintendenza ABAP dell'Umbria).

FIGURE A63 Extremely schematic warrior figures (from left to right: inv. NN. 209173, 209133; by permission of the Soprintendenza ABAP dell'Umbria).

MSP_22

FIGURE A64
Highly schematic female figure (inv. N. 721809; by permission of the Polo Museale dell'Umbria).

MSP_23

FIGURE A65
Highly schematic female figure (inv. N. 721809; by permission of the Polo Museale dell'Umbria).

4.2   *Amelia Group*

MTM_16

FIGURE A66
Schematic figure of a striding male (inv. N. 721805; by permission of the Polo Museale dell'Umbria).

FIGURE A67
Schematic figure of a striding male (inv. N. 721808; by permission of the Polo Museale dell'Umbria).

FIGURE A68
Highly schematic figure of warrior (inv. N. 721807; by permission of the Polo Museale dell'Umbria).

4.3   *Archaic Heads*

FIGURE A69
Schematic head (MTM_63: inv. N. 721806; by permission of the Polo Museale dell'Umbria. MTM_64: inv. N. NA; by permission of the Soprintendenza ABAP dell'Umbria).

MTM_64

FIGURE A70
Schematic head (MTM_63: inv. N. 721806; by permission of the Polo Museale dell'Umbria. MTM_64: inv. N. NA; by permission of the Soprintendenza ABAP dell'Umbria).

MTM_65

FIGURE A71
Bronze hand (inv. N. 273867; by permission of the Soprintendenza ABAP dell'Umbria).

MTM_68

FIGURE A72
Schematic representation of a foot (inv. N. 313; by permission of the Soprintendenza ABAP dell'Umbria).

4.4 Nocera Umbra Group

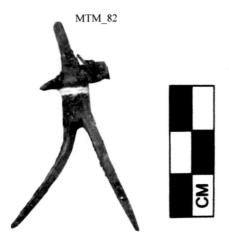

FIGURE A73
Schematic representation of a warrior (inv. N. 94422; by permission of the Soprintendenza ABAP dell'Umbria).

FIGURE A74
Schematic representation of a warrior (inv. N. 209104; by permission of the Soprintendenza ABAP dell'Umbria).

CATALOG OF UMBRIAN FIGURATIVE VOTIVE OFFERINGS 235

4.5 Foligno Group

MTM_57

FIGURE A75
Schematic representation of a warrior (inv. N. 113484; by permission of the Soprintendenza ABAP dell'Umbria).

MTM_58

FIGURE A75B
Schematic representation of a warrior (inv. N. 94420; by permission of the Soprintendenza ABAP dell'Umbria).

4.6   *Eyed Crests*

MTM_79

FIGURE A76
Schematic crest with eyes (inv. N. 113414; by permission of the Soprintendenza ABAP dell'Umbria).

4.7   *Animals*

MTM_60

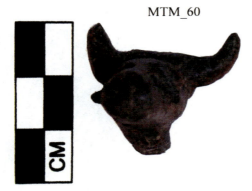

FIGURE A77
Schematic head of a bull (inv. N. 338233; by permission of the Soprintendenza ABAP dell'Umbria).

MTM_61

FIGURE A78
Schematic head of a bull (inv. N. 94429; by permission of the Soprintendenza ABAP dell'Umbria).

CATALOG OF UMBRIAN FIGURATIVE VOTIVE OFFERINGS 237

4.8 *Hellenistic Worshipers*

FIGURE A79
Male worshiper holding a patera (inv. N. 721804; by permission of the Polo Museale dell'Umbria).

FIGURE A80
Male worshiper holding a patera. Still visible underneath the figurine's feet are the traces of the cubic travertine small base that supported the figurine (inv. N. 209160; by permission of the Soprintendenza ABAP dell'Umbria).

FIGURE A81
Female worshiper holding an acerra (inv. N. 212196; by permission of the Soprintendenza ABAP dell'Umbria).

4.9 Anatomical Terracottas

MTM_69

FIGURE A82
Hand wearing a ring (inv. N. NA; by permission of the Soprintendenza ABAP dell'Umbria).

MTM_70

FIGURE A83
Fragments of a foot (modified after Bononi Ponzi 1989, 26 fig. 21).

4.10 Terracotta Heads

MTM_71

FIGURE A84
Fragments of a male head (inv. N. 341470; by permission of the Soprintendenza ABAP dell'Umbria).

MTM_72

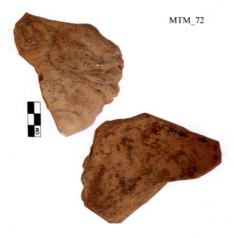

FIGURE A85
Fragments of a female head (inv. N. 209163; by permission of the Soprintendenza ABAP dell'Umbria).

5 Monte Moro

5.1 *Esquiline Group*

MM_3

FIGURE A86
Highly schematic male figure (inv. N. 183026; by permission of the Polo Museale dell'Umbria).

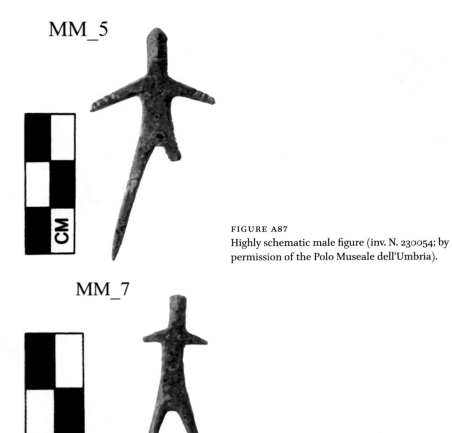

FIGURE A87
Highly schematic male figure (inv. N. 230054; by permission of the Polo Museale dell'Umbria).

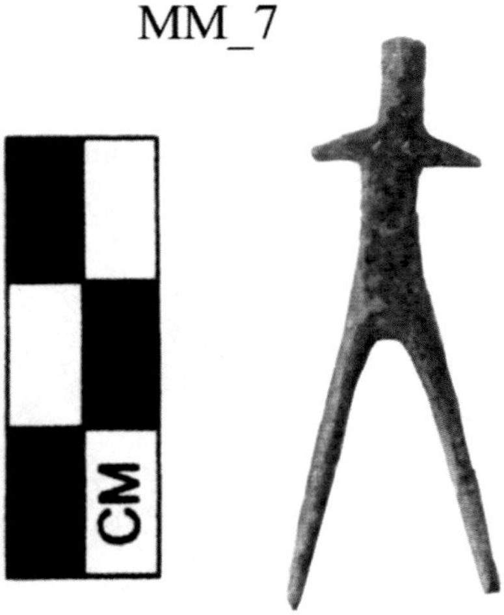

FIGURE A88
Highly schematic male figure (inv. N. 230054; by permission of the Polo Museale dell'Umbria).

CATALOG OF UMBRIAN FIGURATIVE VOTIVE OFFERINGS 241

5.2 *Eyed Crests*

MM_10

FIGURE A89
Schematic crests with two eyes (from left to right: inv.
NN. 183031 and 183034; by permission of the Polo Museale
dell'Umbria).

MM_11

FIGURE A90
Schematic crests with two eyes (from left to right: inv.
NN. 183031 and 183034; by permission of the Polo Museale
dell'Umbria).

5.3 *Foligno Group*

MM_1

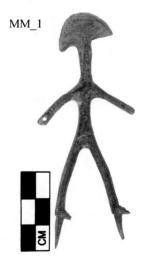

FIGURE A91
Highly schematic warrior figure (inv. N. 230034; by permission
of the Polo Museale dell'Umbria).

5.4 Animals

MM_16

FIGURE A92 Schematic figure of a horse (inv. N. 230045; by permission of the Polo Museale dell'Umbria).

MM_17

FIGURE A93
Schematic figure of an ox (inv. N. 230023; by permission of the Polo Museale dell'Umbria).

5.5 Archaic Heads

MM_15

FIGURE A94
Schematic head (inv. N. 230026; by permission of the Polo Museale dell'Umbria).

5.6 Anatomical Terracottas

MM_23

FIGURE A95   Fragment of a uterus (inv. N. 232367; by permission of the Polo Museale dell'Umbria).

MTM_24

FIGURE A96   Schematic head (inv. N. 232368; by permission of the Polo Museale dell'Umbria).

MM_22

FIGURE A97
Fragment of a right hand (inv. N. 232345; by permission of the Polo Museale dell'Umbria).

MM_21

FIGURE A98
Fragment of a left hand (inv. N. 183019; by permission of the Polo Museale dell'Umbria).

MM_25

FIGURE A99
Fragment of a nose (inv. N. 232369; by permission of the Polo Museale dell'Umbria).

MTM_27

FIGURE A100
Fragment of a foot (inv. N. 232376; by permission of the Polo Museale dell'Umbria).

CATALOG OF UMBRIAN FIGURATIVE VOTIVE OFFERINGS 245

MTM_26

FIGURE A101
Fragment of male genitalia (inv. N. 232374; by permission of the Polo Museale dell'Umbria).

5.7 *Terracotta Heads*

MTM_18

FIGURE A102
Fragment of male head (inv. N. 232366; by permission of the Polo Museale dell'Umbria).

MM_20

FIGURE A103
Fragment of male head (inv. N. 232375; by permission of the Polo Museale dell'Umbria).

MM_19

FIGURE A104 Fragment of hairdo of a veiled head (inv. N. 232373; by permission of the Polo Museale dell'Umbria).

MM_28

FIGURE A105 Base of terracotta head (inv. N. 232370; by permission of the Polo Museale dell'Umbria).

CATALOG OF UMBRIAN FIGURATIVE VOTIVE OFFERINGS 247

6 Monte Santo

6.1 *Amelia Group*

MTS_11

FIGURE A106
Highly schematic warrior figure (inv. N. 342; by permission of the Soprintendenza ABAP dell'Umbria).

MTS_27

FIGURE A107
Schematic figure of a striding male (inv. N. 358; by permission of the Soprintendenza ABAP dell'Umbria).

MTS_30

FIGURE A108
Schematic figure of a striding male (inv. N. 348; by permission of the Soprintendenza ABAP dell'Umbria).

MTS_32

FIGURE A109
Schematic figure of a striding male (inv. N. 325; by permission of the Soprintendenza ABAP dell'Umbria).

CATALOG OF UMBRIAN FIGURATIVE VOTIVE OFFERINGS 249

6.2 *Esquiline Group*

MTS_42

FIGURE A110
Highly schematic male figure (inv. N. 349; by permission of the Polo Museale dell'Umbria).

MTS_39

FIGURE A111
Highly schematic male figure (inv. N. 356; by permission of the Polo Museale dell'Umbria).

MTS_48

FIGURE A112
Highly schematic female figure (inv. N. 382; by permission of the Polo Museale dell'Umbria).

FIGURE A113
Highly schematic female figure (inv. N. 382; by permission of the Polo Museale dell'Umbria).

6.3   *Foligno Group*

FIGURE A114
Schematic warrior figure (inv. N. 332; by permission of the Soprintendenza ABAP dell'Umbria).

CATALOG OF UMBRIAN FIGURATIVE VOTIVE OFFERINGS 251

MTS_13

FIGURE A115
Schematic warrior figure (Inv. N. 334; by permission of the Soprintendenza ABAP dell'Umbria).

MTS_16

FIGURE A116
Schematic warrior figure (inv. N. 333; by permission of the Soprintendenza ABAP dell'Umbria).

6.4 *Nocera Umbra Group*

MTS_18

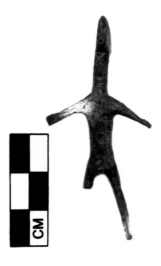

FIGURE A117
Schematic warrior figure (inv. N. 330; by permission of the Soprintendenza ABAP dell'Umbria).

MTS_22

FIGURE A118
Schematic figure of a warrior (inv. N .322; by permission of the Soprintendenza ABAP dell'Umbria).

CATALOG OF UMBRIAN FIGURATIVE VOTIVE OFFERINGS 253

MTS_47

FIGURE A119
Schematic female figure (inv. N. 380; by permission of the Soprintendenza ABAP dell'Umbria).

6.5   *Monte Santo Group*

MTS_3

FIGURE A120
Schematic female figure (inv. N. 337; by permission of the Soprintendenza ABAP dell'Umbria).

MTS_25

FIGURE A121
Schematic female figure (inv. N. 302; by permission of the Soprintendenza ABAP dell'Umbria).

6.6   *Animals*

MTS_53

FIGURE A122   Schematic figure of a bull (inv. N. 392; by permission of the Soprintendenza ABAP dell'Umbria).

CATALOG OF UMBRIAN FIGURATIVE VOTIVE OFFERINGS

MTS_52

FIGURE A123 Schematic figure of a horse (inv. N. 396; by permission of the Soprintendenza ABAP dell'Umbria).

6.7   *Archaic Heads*

MTS_72

FIGURE A124
Schematic head (inv. N. 385; by permission of the Soprintendenza ABAP dell'Umbria).

MTS_73

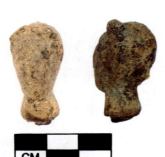

FIGURE A125
Schematic head (inv. N. 310; by permission of the Soprintendenza ABAP dell'Umbria).

MTS_75

FIGURE A126
Schematic head (inv. N. 319; by permission of the Soprintendenza ABAP dell'Umbria).

MTS_76

FIGURE A234
Right hand (inv. N. 316; by permission of the Soprintendenza ABAP dell'Umbria).

6.8 Other

MTS_23

FIGURE A127
Schematic warrior figure (inv. N. 303; by permission of the Soprintendenza ABAP dell'Umbria).

CATALOG OF UMBRIAN FIGURATIVE VOTIVE OFFERINGS 257

FIGURE A128
Schematic warrior figure (inv. N. 308; by permission of the Soprintendenza ABAP dell'Umbria).

FIGURE A129
Schematic warrior figure (inv. N. 307; by permission of the Soprintendenza ABAP dell'Umbria).

FIGURE A130
Schematic Heracles (inv. N. 304; by permission of the Soprintendenza ABAP dell'Umbria).

7 La Rocca

7.1 *Esquiline Group*

ROCCA_4

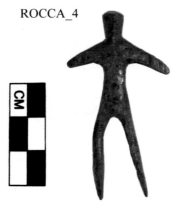

FIGURE A131
Highly schematic male figure (inv. N. 109558; by permission of the Polo Museale dell'Umbria).

ROCCA_5

FIGURE A132
Highly schematic male figure (inv. N. CS1729; by permission of the Polo Museale dell'Umbria).

ROCCA_6

FIGURE A133
Highly schematic male figure (inv. N. CS1728; by permission of the Polo Museale dell'Umbria).

CATALOG OF UMBRIAN FIGURATIVE VOTIVE OFFERINGS 259

7.2 Foligno Group

ROCCA_2

FIGURE A134
Highly schematic warrior figure (inv. N. 109578; by permission of the Polo Museale dell'Umbria).

ROCCA_1

FIGURE A135
Highly schematic warrior figure (inv. N. 109559; by permission of the Polo Museale dell'Umbria).

7.3   *Nocera Umbra Group*

ROCCA_8

FIGURE A136
Highly schematic warrior figure (inv. N. 337381; by permission of the Polo Museale dell'Umbria).

ROCCA_9

FIGURE A137
Schematic figure of a striding male (inv. N. 305069; by permission of the Polo Museale dell'Umbria).

7.4 Amelia Group

ROCCA_10

FIGURE A138
Schematic figure of a striding male (inv. N. CS172; by permission of the Polo Museale dell'Umbria).

7.5 Archaic Anatomicals

ROCCA_11

FIGURE A139
Bronze arm (inv. N. 305671; by permission of the Polo Museale dell'Umbria).

7.6 *Anatomical Terracottas*

FIGURE A140   Fragments of feet, toes and fingers (inv. NN. 305628, 305631—feet; 305626, 305627—toes; 305629, 305630—fingers; after Pani 2011, fig. 23).

FIGURE A141
Fragments of two uteri (inv. NN. 305645 and 305645).

CATALOG OF UMBRIAN FIGURATIVE VOTIVE OFFERINGS 263

FIGURE A142
Fragment of male genitalia (inv. N. 275102).

FIGURE A143   Fragment of a head (left) and veiled head (right) (inv. NN. 305632 and 305652).

7.7 Animals

FIGURE A144
Fragment of a terracotta bovine (inv. N. 305623).

8 Monte Subasio

8.1 Esquiline Group

FIGURE A145
Highly schematic male figure (inv. N. 10; after Monacchi 1986, tav. 38b).

CATALOG OF UMBRIAN FIGURATIVE VOTIVE OFFERINGS 265

8.2   *Amelia Group*

CSRufino_9

FIGURE A146
Schematic figure of a striding male (inv. N. NA; after Monacchi 1986, tav. 38b).

8.3   *Other*

CSRufino_1

FIGURE A147
Schematic figure of a warrior with situla (inv. N. 1; after Monacchi 1986, tav. 38a).

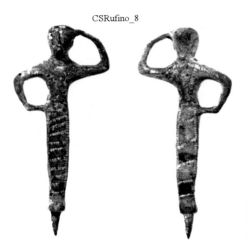

FIGURE A148
Dancing figure (inv. N. 18; after Monacchi 1986, tav. 39c).

FIGURE A149
Pendant in the shape of a quadruped (inv. N. 12; after Monacchi 1986, tav. 38d).

8.4   *Hellenistic Worshiper*

FIGURE A150   Schematic figures of female and male worshiper (left and center); arm of worshiper with patera (right) (inv. NN. 10, 13, and 18; Monacchi 1986, tav. 39a–c).

CATALOG OF UMBRIAN FIGURATIVE VOTIVE OFFERINGS 267

9 Monte Ansciano

9.1 *Esquiline Group*

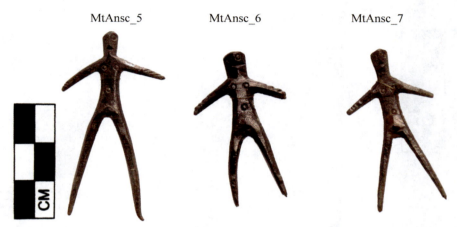

FIGURE A151   Highly schematic male figures (from left to right: inv. NN. 625958, 625959, 625960; by permission of the Soprintendenza ABAP dell'Umbria).

FIGURE A152
Highly schematic male figure (inv. N. 41; by permission of the Soprintendenza ABAP dell'Umbria).

268 APPENDIX 3

MtAnsc_20

FIGURE A153
Highly schematic male figure (inv. N. 93; by permission of the Soprintendenza ABAP dell'Umbria).

MtAnsc_21

FIGURE A154
Highly schematic male figure (inv. N. 146; by permission of the Soprintendenza ABAP dell'Umbria).

MtAnsc_42

FIGURE A155
Extremely schematic warrior figure (inv. N. 80; by permission of the Soprintendenza ABAP dell'Umbria).

CATALOG OF UMBRIAN FIGURATIVE VOTIVE OFFERINGS 269

MtAnsc_3

FIGURE A156
Highly schematic female figure (inv. N. 625955; by permission of the Soprintendenza ABAP dell'Umbria).

MtAnsc_2

FIGURE A157
Highly schematic female figure (inv. N. 625954; by permission of the Soprintendenza ABAP dell'Umbria).

MtAnsc_18

FIGURE A158
Highly schematic female figure (inv. N. 65; by permission of the Soprintendenza ABAP dell'Umbria).

9.2 Nocera Umbra Group

MtAnsc_15

FIGURE A159
Highly schematic warrior figure (inv. N. 44; by permission of the Soprintendenza ABAP dell'Umbria).

MtAnsc_16

FIGURE A160
Extremely schematic warrior figure (inv. N. 46; by permission of the Soprintendenza ABAP dell'Umbria).

9.3 Archaic Heads

MtAnsc_10

FIGURE A161
Fragment of terracotta head (inv. N. 625969; by permission of the Soprintendenza ABAP dell'Umbria).

CATALOG OF UMBRIAN FIGURATIVE VOTIVE OFFERINGS 271

9.4 Hellenistic Worshiper

MtAnsc_19

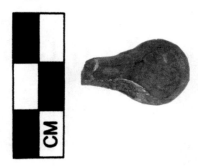

FIGURE A162
Hand holding a patera (inv. N. 73; by permission of the Soprintendenza ABAP dell'Umbria).

10 Monte Acuto

10.1 Esquiline Group

MTS_27

FIGURE A163
Highly schematic male figure (inv. N. 122218; by permission of the Soprintendenza ABAP dell'Umbria).

MTS_16

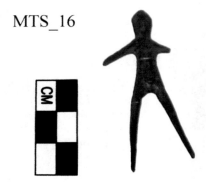

FIGURE A164
Highly schematic male figure (inv. N. 122218; by permission of the Soprintendenza ABAP dell'Umbria).

MTA_39

FIGURE A165
Highly schematic female figure (inv. N. 114347; by permission of the Soprintendenza ABAP dell'Umbria).

MTA_42

FIGURE A166
Highly schematic female figure (inv. N. 11686; by permission of the Soprintendenza ABAP dell'Umbria).

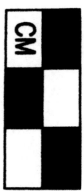

MTA_5

MTA_12

FIGURE A167
Highly schematic warrior figures (inv. NN. 116864 and 116847; by permission of the Soprintendenza ABAP dell'Umbria).

10.2 Animals

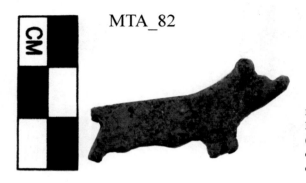

FIGURE A168
Highly schematic figure of a pig (inv. N. 1222412; by permission of the Soprintendenza ABAP dell'Umbria).

FIGURE A169
Highly schematic figure of a sheep (inv. N. 114341; by permission of the Soprintendenza ABAP dell'Umbria).

FIGURE A170
Highly schematic figure of an ox (inv. N. 116848; by permission of the Polo Museale dell'Umbria).

MTA_61

FIGURE A171
Highly schematic figure of a goat (inv. N. 116845; by permission of the Polo Museale dell'Umbria).

MTA_78

FIGURE A172
Highly schematic figure of a quadruped (inv. N. 116845; by permission of the Soprintendenza ABAP dell'Umbria).

10.3 Bronze Sheets

MTA_105

FIGURE A173
Schematic male figure (inv. N. 113498; by permission of the Polo Museale dell'Umbria).

CATALOG OF UMBRIAN FIGURATIVE VOTIVE OFFERINGS 275

MTA_94

FIGURE A174
Schematic male figure (inv. N. 113498; by permission of the Soprintendenza ABAP dell'Umbria).

10.4 *Nocera Umbra Group*

MTA_1

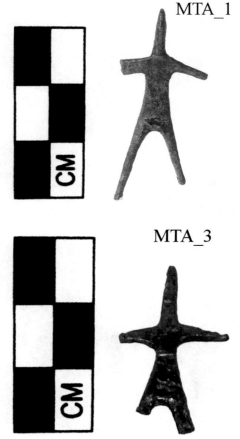

FIGURE A175
Highly schematic warrior figure (inv. N. 113499; by permission of the Soprintendenza ABAP dell'Umbria).

MTA_3

FIGURE A176
Highly schematic warrior figure (inv. N. 116871; by permission of the Soprintendenza ABAP dell'Umbria).

10.5 Amelia Group

MTA_34

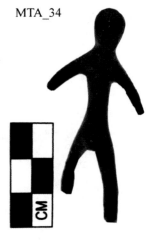

FIGURE A177
Highly schematic figure of a male striding forward (inv. N. 114344; by permission of the Soprintendenza ABAP dell'Umbria).

MTA_33

FIGURE A178
Highly schematic figure of a male striding forward (inv. N. 116846; by permission of the Polo Museale dell'Umbria).

10.6 Archaic Heads

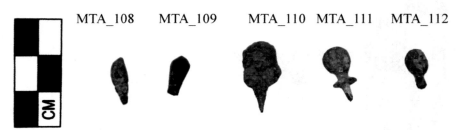

FIGURE A179 Bronze heads (inv. NN. NA; by permission of the Soprintendenza ABAP dell'Umbria).

CATALOG OF UMBRIAN FIGURATIVE VOTIVE OFFERINGS 277

10.7 *Archaic Anatomicals*

MTA_114

FIGURE A180
Bronze leg (inv. N. NA; by permission of the Soprintendenza ABAP dell'Umbria).

MTA_106

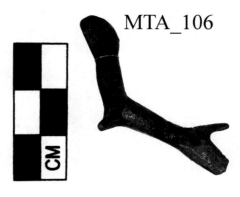

FIGURE A181
Bronze arm (inv. N. 116872; by permission of the Soprintendenza ABAP dell'Umbria).

MTA_107

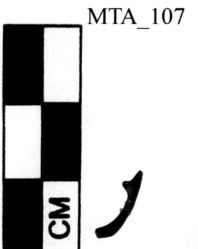

FIGURE A182
Bronze hand (inv. N. 116844; by permission of the Soprintendenza ABAP dell'Umbria).

11 Colle Mori

CM_5

FIGURE A183
Highly schematic male figure (inv. N. 361784; by permission of the Soprintendenza ABAP dell'Umbria).

CM_7

FIGURE A184
Highly schematic male figure (inv. N. 361875; by permission of the Soprintendenza ABAP dell'Umbria).

CM_9

FIGURE A185
Highly schematic male figure (inv. N. 88988; by permission of the Soprintendenza ABAP dell'Umbria).

11.1 Foligno Group

CM_10

FIGURE A186
Highly schematic warrior figure (inv. N. 174766; by permission of the Soprintendenza ABAP dell'Umbria).

11.2 Archaic Heads

CM_1

FIGURE A187
Lower half of terracotta head (inv. N. 361878; by permission of the Soprintendenza ABAP dell'Umbria).

11.3 Hellenistic Worshipers

FIGURE A188
Female worshiper holding a patera (inv. N. 211373; by permission of the Soprintendenza ABAP dell'Umbria).

11.4 Terracotta Heads

FIGURE A189
Terracotta head (inv. N. 361899; by permission of the Soprintendenza ABAP dell'Umbria).

CM_3

FIGURE A190   Terracotta head (inv. N. 364985; by permission of the Soprintendenza ABAP dell'Umbria).

12   Cancelli

12.1   *Foligno Group*

Cancelli_1

FIGURE A191
Highly schematic warrior figure (inv. N. 637473; modified after Manca et al. 2014, 56 n. 31).

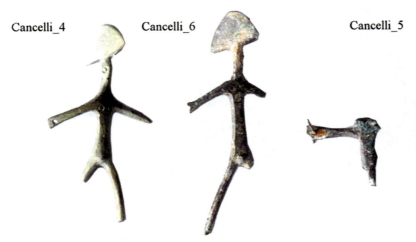

FIGURE A192 Highly schematic warrior figures (inv. NN. NA; modified after Manca et al. 2014, 56 n. 31).

12.2 *Esquiline Group*

Cancelli_8

FIGURE A193
Highly schematic male figure (inv. N. 646185; after Manca et al. 2014, 56 n. 36).

Cancelli_7

FIGURE A194
Highly schematic female figure (inv. N. 637518; after Manca et al. 2014, 56 n. 35).

Cancelli_3

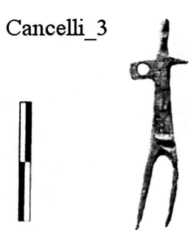

FIGURE A195
Highly schematic warrior figure (inv. N. 643123; after Manca et al. 2014, 56 n. 34).

12.3 *Animals*

Cancelli_13

FIGURE A196
Schematic figure of a bull (inv. N. 679455; after Manca et al. 2014, 56 n. 34).

12.4 *Nocera Umbra Group*

Cancelli_2

FIGURE A197
Highly schematic warrior figure (inv. N. 637436, after Manca et al. 2014, 56 n. 32).

12.5 *Bronze Sheets*

Cancelli_9

FIGURE A198
Highly schematic male figure (inv. N. 737440; after Manca et al. 2014, 56 n. 37).

12.6 *Eyed Crests*

Cancelli_10

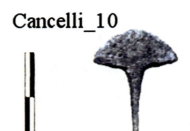

FIGURE A199
Schematic crest with eyes (inv. N. 637443; after Manca et al. 2014, 56 n. 38).

CATALOG OF UMBRIAN FIGURATIVE VOTIVE OFFERINGS 285

12.7   *Archaic Heads*

Cancelli_11

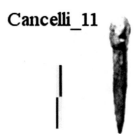

FIGURE A200
Schematic head (inv. N. 637459; after Manca et al. 2014, 56 n. 39).

12.8   *Archaic Anatomicals*

Cancelli_12

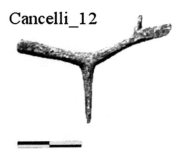

FIGURE A201
Schematic representation of an arm (inv. N. 637466; after Manca et al. 2014, 56 n. 39).

12.9   *Hellenistic Worshipers*

Cancelli_17

FIGURE A202
Drawing of Hellenistic worshiper figure (Picuti 2009, 9).

12.10 Anatomical Terracottas

Cancelli_16

FIGURE A203
Fragment of a foot (inv. N. 695199; after Manca et al. 2014, 51 n. 5).

12.11 Terracotta Heads

Cancelli_15

FIGURE A204
Fragment of the upper half portion of a male head (inv. N. 643009; after Manca et al. 2014, 51 n. 4).

13 Campo la Piana

13.1 Esquiline Group

CPL_1

FIGURE A205
Highly schematic male figure (inv. N. NA; by permission of the Soprintendenza ABAP dell'Umbria).

CPL_4

FIGURE A206
Highly schematic figure of male striding forward (inv. N. NA; by permission of the Soprintendenza ABAP dell'Umbria).

13.2   *Other*

CPL_5

FIGURE A207
Terracotta head of a male wearing a tall hat (inv. N. NA; by permission of the Soprintendenza ABAP dell'Umbria).

14 Monte Pennino

FIGURE A208   Highly schematic human figures (inv. NN. NA; by permission of the Soprintendenza ABAP dell'Umbria).

15 Sanctuary of Cupra at Colfiorito

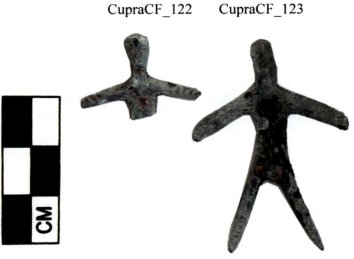

FIGURE A209   Highly schematic male figures (inv. N. 764031; by permission of the Soprintendenza ABAP dell'Umbria).

CATALOG OF UMBRIAN FIGURATIVE VOTIVE OFFERINGS 289

CupraCF_118

FIGURE A210
Highly schematic male figure (inv. N. 721905; by permission of the Polo Museale dell'Umbria).

CupraCF_81

FIGURE A211
Highly schematic female figure (inv. N. 721900; by permission of the Polo Museale dell'Umbria).

CupraCF_191

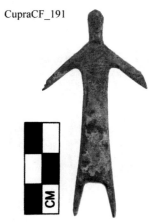

FIGURE A212
Highly schematic female figure (inv. N. 763932; by permission of the Polo Museale dell'Umbria).

15.1 Bronze Sheets

FIGURE A213
Extremely schematic male figures (inv. N. 764033; by permission of the Soprintendenza ABAP dell'Umbria).

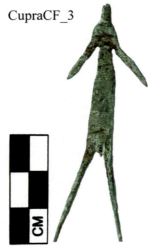

FIGURE A214
Extremely schematic male figure (inv. N. 721902; by permission of the Polo Museale dell'Umbria).

15.2   Nocera Umbra Group

CupraCF_208

FIGURE A215
Highly schematic female figure (inv. N. 601919; by permission of the Soprintendenza ABAP dell'Umbria).

Cupra_CF_207

FIGURE A216
Highly schematic female figure (inv. N. 341593; by permission of the Soprintendenza ABAP dell'Umbria).

CupraCF_240

FIGURE A217
Highly schematic warrior figure (inv. N. A1748; by permission of the Polo Museale dell'Umbria).

CupraCF_226

FIGURE A218
Highly schematic warrior figure (inv. N. 76318; by permission of the Soprintendenza ABAP dell'Umbria).

15.3 *Amelia Group*

CupraCF_246

FIGURE A219
Schematic figure of a striding male (inv. N. 601918; by permission of the Soprintendenza ABAP dell'Umbria).

CATALOG OF UMBRIAN FIGURATIVE VOTIVE OFFERINGS

CupraCF_241

FIGURE A220
Schematic figure of a striding male (inv. N. 721906; by permission of the Polo Museale dell'Umbria).

15.4 *Animals*

CupraCF_251

FIGURE A221
Highly schematic figure of a horse (inv. N. 764006; by permission of the Soprintendenza ABAP dell'Umbria).

CupraCF_250

FIGURE A222 Highly schematic figure of an ox (inv. N. 721896; by permission of the Polo Museale dell'Umbria).

15.5 Foligno Group

CupraCF_210

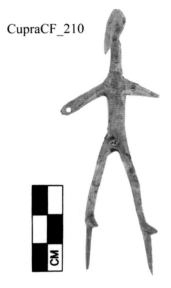

FIGURE A223
Highly schematic warrior figure (inv. N. 341637; by permission of the Soprintendenza ABAP dell'Umbria).

15.6 Fabriano Group

CupraCF_248

FIGURE A224
Schematic warrior figure (inv. N. 354776; by permission of the by permission of the Soprintendenza ABAP dell'Umbria).

15.7 Fossato di Vico Group

FIGURE A225
Schematic warrior figure (inv. N. 351595; by permission of the Soprintendenza ABAP dell'Umbria).

15.8 Archaic Anatomicals

FIGURE A226
Schematic representation of a foot (inv. N. 601896; by permission of the Soprintendenza ABAP dell'Umbria).

15.9 Others

CupraCF_259

FIGURE A227
Schematic figure with bird-like features (inv. N. A1732; by permission of the Soprintendenza ABAP dell'Umbria).

CupraCF_257

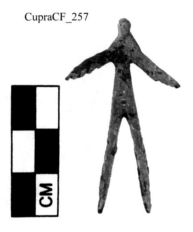

FIGURE A228
Schematic figure with bird-like features (inv. N. 76350; by permission of the Soprintendenza ABAP dell'Umbria).

CupraCF_255

FIGURE A229
Schematic figure with bird-like features (inv. N. 764035; by permission of the Polo Museale dell'Umbria).

CATALOG OF UMBRIAN FIGURATIVE VOTIVE OFFERINGS 297

CupraCF_260

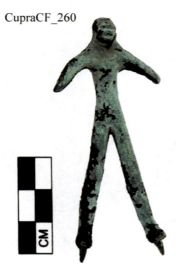

FIGURE A230
Schematic figure with monkey-like features (inv. N. 601926; by permission of the Soprintendenza ABAP dell'Umbria).

15.10 *Anatomical Terracottas*

CuprCF_267

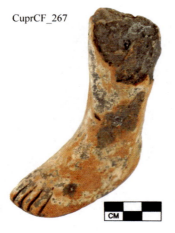

FIGURE A231
Terracotta foot (inv. N. 601922; by permission of the Soprintendenza ABAP dell'Umbria).

15.11 Tanagra Figurines

CupraCF_265   CupraCF_264

FIGURE A232 Tanagra figurines (inv. NN. 602018 and 602016; by permission of the Soprintendenza ABAP dell'Umbria).

15.12 Other

CupraCF_268

FIGURE A233
Schematic figure of Heracles (inv. N. 341601; by permission of the Soprintendenza ABAP dell'Umbria).

Bibliography

Agostiniani, L., A. Calderini, and R. Massarelli (eds.) 2011. *Screhto est: lingua e scrittura degli antichi Umbri: catalogo della mostra.* Perugia: Università degli studi.

Almagro-Gorbea, M. 1982. *El Santuario de Juno en Gabii: Excavaciones 1956–1969.* Roma: Escuela española de historia y arqueología.

Aigner Foresti, L. 1991. "Etruria orientale, Umbria occidentale: un'area di confine," in G. Bonamente and F. Coarelli (eds.), *Assisi e gli Umbri nell'antichità, Atti del convegno internazionale, Assisi 1991:* 11–27. Assisi: Minerva.

Albanesi, M. and M.R. Picuti (eds.) 2013. *Guida del Museo Archeologico.* Nocera Umbra: Comune

Amann, P. 2011. *Die antiken Umbrer zwischen Tiber und Apennin: Unter besonderer Berücksichtigung der Einflüsse aus Etrurien.* Wien: Holzhausen.

Ammerman, R. (2002) *The Sanctuary of Santa Venera at Paestum II: the Votive Terracottas.* Ann Arbor: University of Michigan Press.

Andrén, A. 1940. *Architectural Terracottas from Etrusco-Italic Temples.* Lund: Gleerup.

Angelelli, C. and L. Ponzi (eds.) 2006. *Terni—Interamna Nahars: Nascita e sviluppo di una città alla luce delle più recenti ricerche archeologiche.* Roma: École française de Rome.

Asdrubali-Pentiti, G. 1981–1982. "Etruschi e Umbri nella guerra sociale." *Annali della Facoltà di Lettere e Filosofia dell'Università degli studi di Perugia* 19: 261–268.

Arena, M.S. 1981–1982. "Montecastrilli." *Fasti Archeologici* 30–31: 50–65.

Badian, E. 1958. *Foreign clientelae (264–270 B.C.).* Oxford: Clarendon Press.

Bagnasco Gianni, G. 2005. "Sui contienitori arcaici di ex-voto nei santuari etruschi," in A. Comella and S. Mele (eds.), *Depositi votivi e culti dell'Italia antica dall'età arcaica a quella tardo repubblicana:* 351–358. Bari: Edipuglia.

Baggieri, G. and M.L. Veloccia, 1996. *"Speranza e sofferenza" nei votivi anatomici dell'antichità: Complesso monumentale del S. Michele di Roma, Sala degli aranci, ottobre-novembre 1996.* Roma: Bretschneider.

Barrett, J.C. 1994. *Fragments from Antiquity: An Archaeology of Social Life in Britain, 2900–1200 BC.* Oxford: Blackwell.

Barrett, J.C. 1997. "Stone Age Ideologies." *Analecta Praehistorica Liedensia* 29: 121–129.

Barth, F. 1969. *Ethnic Groups and Boundaries: The Social Organization of Culture Difference.* Bergen: Universitetsforlaget.

Battiloro, I. 2018. *The Archaeology of Lucanian Cult Places, Fourth Century BC to the Early Imperial Age.* Basingstoke: Taylor & Francis.

Barrowclough, D. and Malone, C. (eds.) 2007. *Cult in Context: Reconsidering Ritual in Archaeology.* Oxford: Oxbow Books.

Becker, H. 2002. "The Etruscan Castellum: Fortified Settlements and Regional Autonomy in Etruria." *Etruscan Studies* 9, 1: 85–96.

Bell, C.M. 1992. *Ritual Theory, Ritual Practice*. New York: Oxford University Press.

Bell C.M. 1997. *Ritual: Perspectives and Dimensions*. New York: Oxford University Press.

Benelli, E. 2017. "Problems in Identifying Central Italic Ethnic Groups," in G.D. Farney and G.J. Bradley (eds.), *The Peoples of Ancient Italy*: 89–104. Boston: De Gruyter.

Betts, E. 2013. "Cubrar matrer: Goddess of the Picenes." *Accordia Research Papers* 12: 119–147.

Bianchi Bandinelli, R. 1970. *Rome: The Centre of Power: Roman Art to AD200*. London: Thames and Hudson.

Bispham, E.H. 2000. "Mimic? A Case Study in Early Roman Colonization," in E. Herring and K. Lomas (eds.), *The Emergence of State Identities in Italy*: 157–186. London: Accordia Research Institute.

Bispham, E.H. 2006. "*Coloniam deducere*: How Roman was Roman Colonization during the Middle Republic?" in G.J. Bradley and J.P. Wilson (eds.), *Greek and Roman Colonization: Origins, Ideologies and Interactions*: 73–160. Swansea: Classical Press of Wales.

Bittarelli, A.A. 1987. "Stipi votive e strade sui valichi dell'Appennino sud occidentale," in *Atti e Memorie della R. Deputazione di Storia Patria per le Provincie Delle Marche, Atti del Convegno Fano, Fabriano, Pesaro, Ancona (11–14 ottobre 1984)*: 583–595.

Blake, E. 2014. *Social Networks and Regional Identity in Bronze Age Italy*. Cambridge: Cambridge University Press.

Bloch, M. 1989. *Ritual, History and Power: Selected Papers in Anthropology*. London: Athlone.

Bonfante, L., H. Nagy and J. Collins-Clinton, 2015. *The Collection of Antiquities of the American Academy in Rome*. Ann Arbor: Published for the American Academy in Rome by University of Michigan Press.

Bonghi Jovino, M. 2005. "Mini muluvanice-mini turace. Depositi votivi e sacralità. Dall'analisi del rituale alla lettura interpretativa delle forme di religiosità", in A. Comella and S. Mele (eds.), *Depositi votivi e culti dell'Italia antica dall'età arcaica a quella tardo repubblicana*: 31–46. Bari: Edipuglia.

Boni, M. 1999. *Fulginates e plestini popolazioni antiche nel teritorio di Foligno: Mostra archeologica, Foligno, Palazzo Trinci, 10 aprile–31 dicembre 1999*. Foligno: Comune di Foligno.

Bonomi Ponzi, L. 1982. "Alcune considerazioni sulla situazione della dorsale appenninica umbro-marchigiana tra il 9. e il 5. secolo a.C." *Dialoghi di archeologia* 2: 138–142.

Bonomi Ponzi, L. 1985. "Topographic Survey of the Colfiorito di Foligno Plateau: A Contribution Towards the Study of the Population in the Territory of the Plestini," in C. Malone and S. Stoddart (eds.), *Papers in Italian Archaeology*, 4, 1: 201–238. Oxford: British Archaeological Reports.

Bonomi Ponzi, L. 1985. *Il territorio Nocerino tra preistoria ed alto medioevo*. Firenze.

BIBLIOGRAPHY

301

Bonomi Ponzi, L. and M.C. De Angelis. 1988. "La necropoli delle Acciaierie di Terni", in C. Pietrangeli (ed.), *Gens Antiquissima Italiae: Antichità dall'Umbria in Vaticano*: 44–54. Perugia: Electa.

Bonomi Ponzi, L. 1989. *Cesi: Cultura e ambiente di una terra antica*. Todi, PG: Ediart.

Bonomi Ponzi, L. 1990. "Aspetti dell'Orientalizzante nell'Umbria appennica", in F. Roncalli and B. Adembri (eds.), 1990. *Gens antiquissima Italiae. Antichità dall'Umbria a Leningrado*: 118–152. Perugia: Electa.

Bonomi Ponzi, L. 1991. "Gli Umbri: territorio, cultura, società," in F, Roncalli (ed.) *Gens antiquissima Italiae. Antichità dall'Umbria a New York*: 53–66. Perugia: Electa.

Bonomi Ponzi, L. 1992. "Occupazione del territorio e modelli insediativi nel territorio plestino e camerte di età protostorica", in *La civiltà picena nelle Marche: studi in onore di Giovanni Annibaldi*: 204–242. Ripatransone: G. Maroni.

Bonomi Ponzi, L. 1997. *La necropoli plestina di Colfiorito di Foligno*. Perugia: Quattroemme.

Bonomi Ponzi, L. (ed.) 1999. *Fulginates e plestini popolazioni antiche nel teritorio di Foligno: Mostra archeologica, Foligno, Palazzo Trinci, 10 aprile–31 dicembre 1999*. Foligno: Comune di Foligno.

Bonomi Ponzi, L. 2010. "Terni, Colfiorito, Gualdo Tadino. Tre casi emblematici dell'Umbria antica", in P. Fontaine (ed.), *L'Étrurie et l'Ombrie avant Rome. Cité et Territoire. Actes du colloque International Louvain-la-Neuve Halles Universitaires, Sénat Académique 13–14 février 2004*: 165–193. Bruxelles; Rome: Institut Historique Belge de Rome.

Bonomi Ponzi, L. 2014. "L'evoluzione del sistema insediativo umbro dalle origini alla conquista romana," in O. Paoletti (ed.), *Gli Umbri in età preromana*: 189–213. Pisa: Fabrizio Serra.

Bonomi Ponzi L., L. Ermini Pani, and C. Giontella (eds.) 1995. *L'Umbria meridionale dalla protostoria all'alto Medioevo*. Terni: Provincia di Terni.

Bourdin, S. 2012. *Les peuples de l'Italie préromaine: identités, territoires et relations interethniques en Italie centrale et septentrionale*. Rome: École francaise de Rome.

Boss, M. 2000. *Lakonische Votivgaben aus Blei*. Würzburg: Königshausen und Neumann.

Bourdieu, P. 1977. *Outline of a Theory of Practice*. Cambridge: Cambridge University Press.

Bradley, R. 2000. *An Archaeology of Natural Places*. London: Routledge.

Bradley, G. 1997. "Archaic Danctuaries in Umbria." *Cahiers du centre Gustave Glotz* 8: 111–129.

Bradley, G. 2000. *Ancient Umbria: State, Culture, and Identity in Central Italy from the Iron Age to the Augustan Era*. Oxford; New York: Oxford University Press.

Bradley, G. 2000b. "States, Cities, and Tribes in Central Italy," in E. Herring and K. Lomas (eds.), *The Emergence of State Identities in Italy in the First Millennium BC*: 109–129. London: Accordia Research Institute.

Bradley, G. 2005. "Aspects of the Cult of Hercules in Central Italy," in H. Bowden and L. Rawlings (eds.), *Herakles and Hercules: Exploring a Graeco-Roman Divinity*: 129–151. Swansea: Classical Press of Wales.

Bradley, G. 2006. "Colonization and Identity in Republican Italy," in G. Bradley and J.P. Wilson (eds.), *Greek and Roman Colonization: Origins, Ideologies, and Interactions*: 161–187. Swansea: Classical Press of Wales.

Bradley, G. 2014. "The Nature of Roman Strategy in Mid-Republican Colonization and Road Building," in T. Stek and J. Pelgrom (eds.), *Roman Republican Colonization: New Perspectives from Archaeology and Ancient History. Papers of the Royal Netherlands Institute in Rome*: 60–72. Rome: Palombi.

Bradley, G. 2015. "Investigating Aristocracy in Archaic Rome and Central Italy: Social Mobility, Ideology and Cultural Influences," in N. Fisher and H. Van Wees (eds.), *'Aristocracy' in Antiquity: Redefining Greek and Roman Elites*: 85–124. Swansea: Classical Press of Wales.

Bradley, G. and F. Glinister, 2013. "Italic Religion," in L. Bredholt Christensen, O. Hammer, and D.A. Warburton (eds.), *The Handbook of Religions in Ancient Europe*: 173–192. Durham: Acumen.

Bravi, A. and D. Monacchi 2017. *Amelia preromana e romana*. Amelia: Fondazione per il cammino della luce: Centro studi Via Amerina e Corridoio Bizantino.

Brizio, E. 1891. "Resti di un antico santuario riconosciuti in contrada Campo La Piana", in *Notizie degli scavi di antichità*: 308–313.

Brosius, C., A. Michaels, and P. Schrode (eds.) 2013. *Ritual und Ritualdynamik*. Stuttgart: UTB GmbH.

Brown, F.E. 1980. *Cosa: The Making of a Roman Town*. Ann Arbor: University of Michigan Press.

Brumfiel E. 2001. "Aztec Hearts and Minds: Religion and the State in the Aztec Empire," in S. Alcock, T.N. D'Altroy, K.D. Morrison, and C.M. Sinopoli (eds.), *Empires: Perspectives from Archaeology and History*: 283–310. Cambridge: Cambridge University Press.

Bruni, B. 1983. *La rocca di Spoleto: Studi per la storia e la rinascita*. Cinisello Balsamo: Silvana Editoriale.

Bruschetti, pP. 1987–1988. *Il Museo dell'Accademia Etrusca di Cortona: Catalogo delle collezioni*. Cortona: Calosci.

Bruschetti, P. 1989. "Il santuario di Pasticcetto di Magione e i votivi in bronzo," in R. Roncalli (ed.), *Gens Antiquissima Italiae. Antichità dall'Umbria a Budapest e Cracovia*: 113–123. Perugia: Electa Editori Umbri.

Bruschetti, P. 2001 "Cultura etrusca e mondo italico: l'esempio di Todi." *Annali della Fondazione per il Museo Claudio Faina*, 7: 141–161.

Bruschetti, P. and A. Trombetta, 2002. *Antiquitates: Testimonianze di età classica dal territorio di Corciano*. Corciano: EFFE.

BIBLIOGRAPHY

Burkert, W. 1987. *Ancient Mystery Cults*. Cambridge, MA: Harvard University Press.

Braidotti, R. 2013. *The Posthuman*. Cambridge: Polity Press.

Briault, C. 2007. "High Fidelity or Chinese Whispers? Cult Symbols and Ritual Transmission in the Bronze Age Aegean." *Journal of Mediterranean Archaeology* 20: 239–265.

Buck, C.D. 1928. *A Grammar of Oscan and Umbrian: With a Collection of Inscriptions and a Glossary*. Boston: Ginn.

Calvani, M., R. Curina, and E. Lippolis (eds.) 2000. *Aemilia: la cultura romana in Emilia Romagna dal III secolo a.C. all'età constantiniana*. Venezia: Marsilio.

Calzoni U. 1947. "La stipe votiva di Colle Arsiccio nei pressi di Magione." *Bollettino della Deputazione di Storia Patria perl'Umbria* 44: 44–45.

Capriotti, T. 2020. *L'Adriatico medio-occidentale: Coste, approdi e luoghi di culto nell'antichità*. Roma: Arbor Sapientiae editore.

Carafa, P. 2008. *Culti e santuari della Campania antica*. Roma: Istituto Poligrafico.

Carlà-Uhink, F. 2017. *The "Birth" of Italy: The Institutionalization of Italy as a Region, 3rd–1st Century BCE*. Berlin: De Gruyter.

Catalli, F. 1989. "Monetazione preromana in Umbria: le zecche di Tuder ed Iguvium." In *Antichità umbre nei Musei di Budapest e Cracovia*: 140–152. Città di Castello: Electa Editori Umbri Associati.

Catalli, F. 2005. "Materiali numismatici del santuario di Casalvieri (Sora)," in A. Comella and S. Mele (eds.), *Depositi votivi e culti dell'Italia antica dall'età arcaica a quella tardo-repubblicana*: 145–151. Bari: Edipuglia.

Cavanagh, W. and R. Laxton, 1984. "Lead Figures from the Menelaion and Seriation." *Annual of the British School at Athens* 79: 23–36.

Cederna, A. 1951. "Carsoli. Scoperta di un deposito votivo del III secolo a.C." *Notizie Scavi, 5*: 169–224.

Cenciaioli, L. 1991. "Monte Acuto di Umbertide," in F: Roncalli (ed.), *Gens Antiquissima Italiae. Antichità dell'Umbria a New York*: 211–216. Perugia: Electa.

Cenciaioli, L. 1996: "Un santuario di altura nella valle tiberina. Monte Acuto di Umbertide," in G. Bonamente and F. Coarelli (eds.), *Assisi e gli Umbri nell'antichità: atti del Convegno internazionale*, Assisi 18–21 dicembre 1991: 193–234.

Cenciaioli, L. (ed.) 1998. *Umbri ed Etruschi. Genti di confine a Monte Acuto e nel territorio di Umbertide*. Ministero per bene culturali e ambientali: Soprintendenza archeologica per l'Umbria: Comune di Umbertide.

Chaniotis, A. 2011. *Ritual Dynamics in the Ancient Mediterranean: Agency, Emotion, Gender, Representation*. Stuttgart: F. Steiner.

Chieco Bianchi, A.M. 2002. *Le statuette di bronzo dal santuario di Reitia a Este: (scavi 1880–1916 e 1987–1991) = Die Bronzestatuetten aus dem Reitia-Heilgtum von Este: (Ausgrabungen 1880–1916 und 1987–1991)*. Mainz: Verlag Philipp von Zabern.

Cifani, G. and S. Stoddart (eds.) 2012. *Landscape, Ethnicity and Identity in the Archaic Mediterranean Area*. Oxford: Oxbow Books.

Ciotti U. 1964. "Nuove conoscenze sui culti dell'Umbria antica," in F. Ugolini (ed.), *Problemi di storia e archeologia dell'Umbria. Atti del I Convegno di Studi Umbri* (Gubbio, 26–31 maggio 1963): 99–112. Gubbio: Centro di studi umbri.

Coarelli, F. 1986. *Fregellae: 2*. Roma: Edizioni Quasar.

Coarelli, F. 2000. "Il lucus Pisaurensis e la romanizzazione dell'ager Gallicus," in C. Bruun (ed.), *The Roman Middle Republic: Politics, Religion and Historiography c. 400–133 B.C.: Papers from a Conference at the Institum Romanum Finlandiae, September 11–12, 1998*: 195–205. Rome: Institutum Romanum Finlandiae.

Coarelli, F. and H. Patterson (eds.) 2008. *Mercator placidissimus: The Tiber Valley in Antiquity: New Research in the Upper and Middle River Valley: Rome, 27–28 February 2004*. Roma: Quasar.

Cohen, A.P. 1985. *The Symbolic Construction of Community*. Chichester: E. Horwood.

Coles, A.J. 2009. *Not effigies parvae populi Romani: Gods, Agency, and Landscape in Mid-Republican Colonization*, PhD dissertation, University of Pennsylvania.

Coli, U. 1964. "L'organizzazione politica dell'Umbria preromana," in *Problemi di storia e archeologia dell'Umbria. Atti del primo convegno di Studi Umbri, 26–31 maggio, 1963*: 133–159. Gubbio: Centro di Studi Umbri presso la Casa di Sant'Ubaldo in Gubbio.

Colivicchi, F. and C. Zaccagnino, 2008. *Umbria*. Roma: Libreria dello Stato.

Colivcchi, F. 2015. "After the Fall: Caere after 273 BCE." *Etruscan Studies* 18: 178–199.

Colonna, G. 1970. *Bronzi votivi Umbro-Sabellici a figura umana*. Firenze: Sansoni.

Colonna G. 1974. "Ricerche sugli Etruschi e sugli Umbri a nord degli Appennini." *Studi Etruschi* 42: 3–24.

Colonna, G. 1985. *Santuari d'Etruria*. Milano: Electa.

Colonna, G. 2006. "Sacred Architecture and the Religion of the Etruscans," in N.T. de Grummond and E. Simons (eds.), *The Religion of the Etruscans*: 132–168. Austin: University of Texas Press.

Comella, A. 1981. "Tipologia e diffusione dei complessi votivi in Italia in epoca medio- e tardo-repubblicana", in *Mélanges de l'École française de Rome* 93, 2: 717–803.

Comella, A. 1982. *Il deposito votivo di Ara della Regina*. Roma: Bretschneider.

Comella, A. 1986. *I materiali votivi di Falerii*. Roma: Bretschneider.

Comella, A. 1993. *Le terrecotte architettoniche del santuario dello Scasato a Falerii: scavi 1886–1887*. Napoli: Edizioni scientifiche italiane.

Comella, A. 1997. "Circolazione di matrici in area etrusco-laziale e campana," in A : Muller, *Le Moulage en terrecuite dans l'antiquité: création et production dérivée, fabrication et diffusion, Actes du XVIIIe Colloque de Recherches Archéologiques, (Lille III, 7–8, décembre 1995)*: 333–351. Villeneuve: Presses Universitaires du Septentrion.

Comella, A. and Stefani, G. 1990. *Materiali votivi del santuario di Campetti a Veio. Scavi 1947 e 1969*. Rome: Bretschneider.

Comaroff, J. 1985. *Body of Power, Spirit of Resistance: The Culture and History of a South African People*. Chicago: University of Chicago Press.

BIBLIOGRAPHY

Connerton, P. 1989. *How Societies Remember*. Cambridge: Cambridge University Press.

Cooley, A.E. 2016. *A Companion to Roman Italy*. Oxford ; Malden, MA ; Chichester: Wiley Blackwell.

Cornell, T. 2004. "Deconstructing the Samnite Wars: An Essay in Historiography," in H. Jones (ed.), *Samnium: Settlement and Cultural Change: The Proceedings of the Third E. Togo Salmon Conference on Roman* Studies: 115–131. Providence, R.I.: Center for Old World Archaeology and Art.

Costamagna, L. 1998. *Monte Moro. Nuovi dati archeologici dalla Valle del Nera*. Roma: Comune di Montefranco.

Costamagna, L. 2002 "Monteleone di Spoleto. Il santuario di forma Cavaliera; Monteleone di Spoleto. Il santuario di Monte Aspra; Montefranco. Il santuario di Monte Moro," in C.P. Cardinali e D. Manconi (eds.), *Spoleto e la Valnerina: Documenti archeologici dal territorio*: 15–23. Perugia: Ministero per i beni e le attività culturali, Soprintendenza per i beni archeologici dell'Umbria.

Cristofani, M. 1985. "Una dedica ad Asclepio da Felsina e i culti salutari in Etruria settentrionale." *Annali della Scuola Normale Superiore di Pisa, Cl. di Lettere e Filosofia* 15: 1–5.

Crawford, M.H. 1975. *Roman Republican Coinage*. Cambridge: Cambridge University Press.

Crawford, M.H. 2006. "From Poseidonia to Paestum via the Lucanians," in G. Bradley and J.P. Wilson (eds.), *Greek and Roman Colonization: Origins, Ideologies, and Interactions*: 59–72. Swansea: Classical Press of Wales.

Crawford, M.H. 2011. *Imagines Italicae: A Corpus of Italic Inscriptions* (3 vols.). Bulletin of the Institute of Classical Studies supplement 110. London: Institute of Classical Studies University of London.

Crawford, M.H. 2012 "Review of Sisani 2007." *Athenaeum* 100: 737–742.

Cunningham, G. 1999. *Religion and Magic: Approaches and Theories*. New York: New York University Press.

Dart, C.J. 2015. *The Social War, 91 to 88 BCE: A History of the Italian Insurgency against the Roman Republic*. Farnham: Ashgate.

Dämmer H. 1986. *San Pietro Montagnon (Montegrotto): Ein vorgeschichtliches Seeheiligtum in Venetien = un santuario protostorico lacustre nel Veneto*. Mainz: P. von Zabern.

D'Alessio, A. 2008. "Santuari terrazzati e sostruiti italici di età tardo-repubblicana: spazi, funzioni, paesaggi." *Bollettino di Archeologia online*: 17–31.

D'Ercole, V. 2000. "I paesaggi di potere dell'Abruzzo protostorico." *Paesaggi di potere. Problemi e prospettive. Atti del seminario, Udine 16–17 maggio 1996*: 121–152.

De Angelis, M.C. 1994. *Spoleto: Il colle della Rocca: primi risultati di scavo*. Perugia: Quattroemme.

de Cazanove, O. 2000. "Some Thoughts on the 'Religious Romanization' of Italy before the Social War," in E. Bispham and C. Smith (eds.), *Religion in Archaic Rome and Italy: Evidence and Experience*: 71–76. Edinburgh: Edinburgh University Press.

de Cazanove, O. 2015. "Per la datazione degli ex voto anatomici d'Italia," in T.D. Stek and G.-J. Burgers. (eds.), *The Impact of Rome on Cult Places and Religious Practices in Ancient Italy*: 26–99. London: Institute of Classical Studies.

de Grummond, N.T. 2006. *Etruscan Myth, Sacred History, and Legend*. Philadelphia: University of Pennsylvania Museum of Archaeology and Anthropology.

de Grummond N.T. and E. Simon (eds.) 2006. *The Religion of the Etruscans*. Austin: University of Texas Press.

de Grummond, N. and I. Edlund-Berry 2011. *The Archaeology of Sanctuaries and Ritual in Etruria*. Portsmouth, R.I.: Journal of Roman Archaeology.

De Lucia Brolli, M.A. 2018. *Riti e cerimonie per le dee nel santuario di Monte Li Santi-Le Rote a Narce*. Pisa: Edizioni ETS.

Demarest, A.A. and G.W. Conrad (eds.) 1992 *Ideology and Pre-Columbian Civilizations*. Santa Fe: School of American Research Press.

DeMarrais, E., L.J. Castillo, and T.K. Earle. 1996. "Ideology, Materialization, and Power Strategies." *Current Anthropology* 37: 15–31.

Demetriou, D. 2012. *Negotiating Identity in the Ancient Mediterranean: The Archaic and Classical Greek Multiethnic Emporia*. Cambridge: Cambridge University Press.

Dench, E. 1995. *From Barbarians to New Men: Greek, Roman, and Modern Perceptions of Peoples from the Central Apennines*. Oxford: Clarendon Press.

de Polignac, F. 1991. *Cults, Territory, and the Origins of the Greek City-State*. Chicago: University of Chicago Press.

De Vecchi, P. 2002. *Museo civico di Gualdo Tadino: Rocca Flea 2: materiali archeologici e ceramiche dal XVI al XX secolo*. Milano: Electa: Editori Umbri Associati.

Devoto, G. 1947. *Le tavole di Gubbio*. Perugia: Deputazione di storia patria per l'Umbria.

Dicus, K. 2012. *Actors and Agents in Ritual Behavior: The Sanctuary at Grasceta dei Cavallari as a Case-Study of the E-L-C Votive Tradition in Republican Italy*. PhD dissertation, University of Michigan.

Dommelen, P. and A. Knapp, 2010. *Material Connections in the Ancient Mediterranean: Mobility, Materiality, and Mediterranean Identities*. Abingdon: Routledge.

Donald, M. 2001. *A Mind So Rare: The Evolution of Human Consciousness*. New York: W.W. Norton.

Draycott, J.L. and E.J. Graham (eds.) 2017. *Bodies of Evidence: Ancient Anatomical Votives Past, Present and Future*. London: Routledge.

Droogan, J. 2013. *Religion, Material Culture and Archaeology*. London: Continuum International Publishing Group.

Dupraz, E. 2012. *Sabellian Demonstratives: Forms and Functions*. Leiden: Brill.

Edlund, I.E.M. 1987. *The Gods and the Place: The Location and Function of Sanctuaries in the Countryside of Etruria and Magna Graecia* (700–400 B.C.). Stockholm: Svenska Institutet i Rom.

Erdkamp, P. 2007. *A Companion to the Roman Army*. Malden, MA: Blackwell.

BIBLIOGRAPHY

Eriksen, T.H. 1993. *Ethnicity and Nationalism: Anthropological Perspectives*. London: Pluto.

Ermini Pani, L. 2011. *Il colle Sant'Elia e il futuro della rocca a Spoleto: Atti delle giornate di studio, Spoleto, 12–13 marzo 2010*. Spoleto: Fondazione Centro italiano di studi sull'alto Medioevo.

Eroli, G. 1860. "Scavi di Amelia." *Bulletino dell'Istituto di Corrispondenza Archeologica*: 118–122.

Eroli, G. 1864. "Scavi di Amelia." *Bulletino dell'Istituto di Corrispondenza Archeologica*: 56–59.

Eroli, G. 1867. "Scavi di Amelia." *Bulletino dell'Istituto di Corrispondenza Archeologica*: 169–172.

Fabbricotti, E. 1969. *Ritrovamenti archeologici sotto la Chiesa della Visitazione di Santa Maria "in Camuccia"*. Todi: Tipografia Porziuncola.

Falconi Amorelli, M.T. 1977. *Todi preromana: Catalogo dei materiali conservati nel Museo comunale di Todi*. Perugia: Tip. Giostrelli.

Faloci Pulignani, M. 1980. "Scoperte di antichità in Foligno e nel suo territorio. X. Cancelli." *Notizie degli scavi di antichità 5, 10*: 312–315.

Farney, G.D. 2007. *Ethnic Identity and Aristocratic Competition in Republican Rome*. Cambridge: Cambridge University Press.

Farney, G.D. and G.J. Bradley (eds.) 2017. *The Peoples of Ancient Italy*. Boston: De Gruyter.

Faro, E. 2008. *Ritual Activity and Regional Dynamics: Towards a Reinterpretation of Minoan Extra-Urban Ritual Space*. PhD dissertation, University of Michigan.

Faustoferri, A. and S. Lapenna 2014. *Iuvanum tra Sangro e Aventino: Ricerca, tutela, valorizzazione: Atti del Convegno Internazionale in ricordo di Walter Pellegrini tenuto a Montenerodomo (CH) il 30 e 31 maggio 2008*. Firenze: All'Insegna del Giglio.

Fenelli, M. 1975a. "Contributo per lo studio del votivo anatomico: i votivi anatomici di Lavinio." *Archeologia Classica* 27: 206–225.

Fenelli, M. 1975b. "Votivi anatomici (D)," in F. Castagnoli, L. Cozza, and M. Fenelli (eds.), *Lavinium II: Le Tredici Are*: 253–303. Roma: De Luca.

Fentress, E. 2000. "Frank Brown, Cosa and the Idea of a Roman City", in E. Fentress (ed.), *Romanization and the City: Creation, Transformation, and Failures*: 11–24. Portsmouth, RI: Journal of Roman Archaeology.

Feruglio, A.E. 1966. "Rassegna degli scavi." *Studi Etruschi* 34, 306.

Feruglio, A.E. 2001: "La fortuna di Arna: materiali archeologici dalle collezioni Eugeni e Bellucci." *Bollettino della Deputazione di Storia Patria per l'Umbria*: 225–243.

Feruglio, A.E., D. Manconi, and L. Bonomi Ponzi, 1991. *Mevania: Da centro umbro a municipio romano*. Perugia: Electa Editori Umbri.

Fincham, G. 2002. "A Consumer Theory and Roman North Africa: A Post-Colonial Approach to the Ancient Economy." *Theoretical Roman Archaeology Journal* 2001: 34–44.

Fogelin L. 2006. *Archaeology of Early Buddhism*. Lanham, MD: AltaMira Press.

Fogelin, L. 2007. "The Archaeology of Religious Ritual." *Annual Reviews in Anthropology* 36: 55–71.

Fogelin, L. 2008a. "Delegitimizing Religion: The Archaeology of Religion as ... Archaeology," in D. Whitley and K. Hays-Gilpin (eds.), *Belief in the Past: Theoretical Approaches to the Archaeology of Religion*: 121–141. Walnut Creek, Calif: Left Coast Press.

Fox, J. 2012. *An Introduction to Religion and Politics*. London: Routledge.

Fracchia, H. 2013: "Survey, Settlement and Land Use in Republican Italy," in J. DeRose Evans (ed.), *A Companion to the Archaeology of the Roman Republic*: 181–197. Oxford; Malden: Wiley-Blackwell.

Frederiksen, M.W. and J.B. Ward-Perkins 1957. "The Ancient Road Systems of the Central and Northern Ager Faliscus." *Papers of the British School at Rome* 25: 67–208.

Freeman P.W.M. 1993 "'Romanization' and Roman Material Culture." *Journal of Roman Archaeology*, 6: 438–435.

Freeman, P.W.M. 2007. *The Best Training-Ground for Archaeologists: Francis Haverfield and the Invention of Romano-British Archaeology*. Oxford: Oxbow Books.

Fulminante, F. 2012. "Ethnicity, Identity and State Formation in the Latin Landscape: Problems and Approaches," in G. Cifani and S. Stoddart (eds.), *Landscape, Ethnicity and Identity in the Archaic Mediterranean Area*: 89–107. Oxford: Oxbow Books.

Gabba, E. 1972. "Urbanizzazione e rinnovamenti urbanistici nell'Italia centro-meridionale del I sec. a.C." *Studi classici e orientali* 21: 73–112.

Gabba, E. 1994. *Italia romana*. Como: Ed. New Press.

Galestin, M.C. 1987. *Etruscan and Italic Bronze Statuettes*. Leiden: Warfhuizen.

Gambacurta, G. and G. Fogolari, 2001. *Materiali veneti preromani e romani del santuario di Lagole di Calalzo al Museo di Pieve Cadore*. Roma: Bretschneider.

Gardner, A., E. Herring, and K. Lomas. (2013). *Creating Ethnicities and Identities in the Roman World*. London: Institute of Classical Studies.

Gargola, D.J. 2009. *Lands, Laws, and Gods: Magistrates and Ceremony in the Regulation of Public Lands in Republican Rome*. Chapel Hill: University of North Carolina Press.

Gatti Lo Guzzo, L. 1978. *Il deposito votivo dall'Esquilino detto di "Minerva Medica"*. Firenze: Sansoni.

Gell, A. 1998. *Art and Agency: An Anthropological Theory*. Oxford: Clarendon Press.

Gentili, M. 2005. "Riflessioni sul fenomeno storico dei depositi votivi di tipo etrusco-laziale-campano", in A. Comella and S. Mele (eds.), *Depositi votivi e culti dell'Italia antica dall'età arcaica a quella tardo-repubblicana*: 367–378. Bari: Edipuglia.

Geertz, C. 1973. *The Interpretation of Cultures: Selected Essays*. New York: Basic Books.

Gherardi, L. 2014. *Santuari E Luoghi Di Culto Nell'umbria Preromana*. Edizioni Accademiche Italiane.

Giontella, C. 1995. "Gli Umbri", in L. Bonomi Ponzi, L. Ermini Pani, and C. Giontella (eds.), *L'Umbria meridionale dalla protostoria all'alto Medioevo*: 18–61. Terni: Provincia di Terni.

Giontella, C. 2006. *I luoghi dell'acqua divina: Complessi santuariali e forme devozionali in Etruria e Umbria fra epoca arcaica ed età romana*. Roma: Aracne.

Giorgi, E. 2020. *Il santuario di Monte Rinaldo: La ripresa delle ricerche (2016–2019)* (Prima edizione.). Bologna: Bononia University Press.

Given, M. 2004. *The Archaeology of the Colonized*. London: Routledge.

Gleba, M. and H. Becker (eds.) 2009. *Votives, Places and Rituals in Etruscan religion: studies in honor of Jean MacIntosh Turfa*. Leiden: Brill.

Glinister, F. 1987. "What is a Sanctuary?" *Cahiers du Centre Gustave Glotz* 8: 61–80.

Glinister, F. 2000. "Sacred Rubbish", in E.H. Bispham and C. Smith (eds.), *Religion in Archaic and Republican Rome and Italy: Evidence and Experience*: 54–70. Edinburgh: Edinburgh University Press.

Glinister, F. 2006a. "Reconsidering 'Religious Romanization'," in C.E. Schultz and P.B. Harvey (eds.), *Religion in Republican Italy*: 10–33. Cambridge: Cambridge University Press.

Glinister, F. 2006b. "Women, Colonisation and Cult in Hellenistic Central Italy." *Archiv für Religionsgeschichte* 8: 89–104.

Glinister, F. 2015. "Colonies and Religious Dynamism in Mid-Republican Italy," in T.D. Stek and G.J. Burgers (eds.), *The Impact of Rome on Cult Places and Religious Practices in Ancient Italy*. Bulletin of the Institute of Classical Studies Supplement 132: 145–156. London: Institute of Classical Studies.

Gnade, M. 2007. *Satricum: Trenta anni di scavi olandesi*. Amsterdam: Amsterdams Archeologisch Centrum.

Gonlin, N. and J.C. Lohse 2007. *Commoner Ritual and Ideology in Ancient Mesoamerica*. Boulder: University Press of Colorado.

Gosden, C. 2004. *Archaeology and Colonialism: Cultural Contact from 5000 B.C. to the Present*. Cambridge: Cambridge University Press.

Gosden, C. 2005. "What Do Objects Want," in *Journal of Archaeological Method and Theory*, 12, 3: 193–211.

Graham, E.-J., 2020: *Reassembling Religion in Roman Italy*. Abingdon: Routledge.

Graepler, D. 1994 "Corredi funerary con terrecotte figurate," in E. Lippolis and D. Boschung (eds.), *Catalogo del Museo nazionale archeologico di Taranto: Aspetti e problemi della documentazione archeologica tra VII e I sec. a.C.*: 282–298. Taranto: La Colomba.

Groppo, V. 2011: "I bronzetti preromani dalle ricerche di superficie", in V. Girotto (ed.), *Alle foci del Medoacus Minor. La carta archeologica*, 89–102. Padova: Esedra.

Griffith, A. 2013. "Reconstructing Religious Ritual in Italy," in J. DeRose Evans (ed.), *A Companion to the Archaeology of the Roman Republic*: 392–405. Chichester: Wiley-Blackwell.

Grifoni Cremonesi, R. 1987. "Il Neolitico della Toscana e dell'Umbria," in *Atti della XXVI riunione scientifica dell'Istituto Italiano di Preistoria e Protostoria, Il Neolitico in Italia*: 229–237. Florence: Istituto Italiano di Preistoria e Protostoria.

Gualandi, G. 1973. Un santuario felsineo nell'ex villa Cassarini (Facoltà di ingegneria), in *Atti e Memorie della Deputazione di Storia Patria per le Province di Romagna* n.s. 24, 315–345.

Gualandi, G.1974. "Santuari e stipi votive dell'Etruria padana." *Studi Etruschi* 42: 27–68.

Gualtieri, M. "Fortifications and Settlement Organization: An Example from Pre-Roman Italy." *World Archaeology* 19, 1: 30–46.

Guzzo, P.G. 1987: "Schema per la categoria interpretativa del 'santuario di frontiera' ", in *Scienze dell'Antichità*, 1: 373–379.

Haack M-L. 2002. "Haruspices publics et privés: tentative d'une distinction." *Revue des Études Anciennes* 104, 1–2: 111–133.

Hall, J.M. 1997. *Ethnic Identity in Greek Antiquity*. Cambridge: Cambridge University Press.

Harding, D.W. 2012. *Iron Age Hillforts in Britain and Beyond*. Oxford: Oxford University Press.

Harris, W.V. 1971. *Rome in Etruria and Umbria*. Oxford: Clarendon Press.

Harris, O.J.T. and C.N. Cipolla. 2017. *Archaeological Theory in the New Millennium: Introducing Current Perspectives*. London: Routledge.

Haumesser, L. 2017. "Hellenism in Central Italy," in A. Naso (ed.), *Etruscology*: 645–665. Berlin: De Gruyter.

Haverfield, F. 1912. *The Romanization of Roman Britain*. Oxford: Clarendon Press.

Hawkes, C. 1954. "Archaeological Theory and Method: Some Suggestions from the Old World." *American Anthropologist* 56: 155–168.

Hayden B. 2003. *Shamans, Sorcerers, and Saints*. Washington, DC: Smithson Books.

Haynes, S. 1960. "The Bronze Priests and Priestesses from Nemi." *Mitteilungen des deutschen archaologischen Instituts, Römische Abteilung* 67: 34–102.

Heilmeyer, W-D. 1979. *Frühe Olympische Bronzfiguren. Die* Tiervotive (Olympische Forschung 12). Berlin: De Gruyter.

Helbig, W. 1880. "Scoperta di una di una stipe votiva al Monte Subasio." *Bullettino dell'Instituto di corrispondenza archeologica*: 249–250.

Heldring, B. 2007. "Il deposito votivo III. Una cisterna prima, un deposito votivo dopo," in M. Gnade (ed.), *Satricum Trenta anni di scavi olandesi*: 78–81. Amsterdam: Amsterdams Archeologisch Centrum.

Herring, E. 1996. "Using your Religion: Native Ritual and Belief in South Italy in the 5th and 4th Centuries BC," in J. Wilkins (ed.), *Approaches to the Study of Ritual: Italy and the Ancient Mediterranean*: 143–182. London: Accordia Research Centre.

Hicks, D. 2010. *The Oxford Handbook of Material Culture Studies*. Oxford: Oxford University Press.

BIBLIOGRAPHY

Hingley, R. 2000. *Roman Officers and English Gentlemen: The Imperial Origins of Roman Archaeology*. London: Routledge.

Hobsbawm, E.J. and T.O. Rogers 1992. *The Invention of Tradition*. Cambridge: Cambridge University Press.

Hodder, I. 1982. *Symbols in Action: Ethnoarchaeological Studies of Material Culture*. Cambridge: Cambridge University Press.

Hodder, I. 2012. *Entangled: An Archaeology of the Relationships between Humans and Things*. Malden, MA: Wiley-Blackwell.

Hoer, A. (2024). *Die Höhenbefestigungen Samniums: Eine landschafts- und siedlungsarchäologische Analyse*. Basel; Frankfurt a.M.: LIBRUM Publishers & Editors.

Hughes, J. 2008. "Fragmentation as Metaphor in the Classical Healing Sanctuary." *Social History of Medicine* 21: 217–236.

Humphrey, C. and J. Laidlaw. 2004. *The Archetypal Actions of Ritual: A Theory of Ritual Illustrated by the Jain Rite of Worship*. Oxford: Clarendon Press.

Insoll, T. 2004. *Archaeology, Ritual, Religion*. London: Routledge.

Insoll, T. 2011. *The Oxford Handbook of the Archaeology of Ritual and Religion*. Oxford: Oxford University Press.

James, S.L. and S. Dillon (eds.) 2012. *A Companion to Women in the Ancient World*. Malden, MA: Wiley-Blackwell.

Jeammet, V. and Aravantinos, V.L. (eds.) 2010. *Tanagras: Figurines for Life and Eternity: The Musée du Louvre's Collection of Greek Figurines*. Valencia: Fundación Bancaja.

Jannot, J.R. 2005. *Religion in Ancient Etruria*. Madison: University of Wisconsin Press.

Jehne, M. et al. (2013). *Religiöse Vielfalt und soziale Integratio: Die Bedeutung der Religion für die kulturelle Identität und die politische Stabilität im republikanischen Italien*. Mainz: Verlag Antike.

Jones, S. 1997. *The Archaeology of Ethnicity: Constructing Identities in the Past and Present*. London: Routledge.

Karageorghis, V. 2012. *Ancient Art from Cyprus: The Cesnola Collection in the Metropolitan Museum of Art*. New York: Metropolitan Museum of Art.

Käner, R.F. 2001 *Bilderzyklen aus Terrakotta, Untersuchungen zur etrusckisch-italischen Baudekoration des 3. und 2. Jahrhunderts v.Chr.* München: Universität.

Kelly, J. and M. Kaplan, 1990. "History, Structure, and Ritual," in *Annual Reviews of Anthropology* 19: 119–150.

Kertzer, D.I. 1988. *Ritual, Politics and Power*. New Haven: Yale University Press.

Kilmer, M.F. 1977. *The Shoulder Bust in Sicily and South and Central Italy: A Catalogue and Materials for Dating*. Göteborg: Studies in Mediterranean Archaeology.

Knappett, C. 2005. *Thinking through Material Culture: An Interdisciplinary Perspective*. Philadelphia: University of Pennsylvania Press.

Knappett, C. 2014. "Mediterranean Archaeology and Ethnicity," in J. McInerney (ed.),

A Companion to Ethnicity in the Ancient Mediterranean: 34–50. Chichester: Wiley-Blackwell.

Koutrafouri, V.G. and J. Sanders, 2017. *Ritual Failure: Archaeological Perspectives*. Leiden: Sidestone Press.

Koch C. 1954. "s.v.Praetor Etruriae" in *Realencyclopädie der classischen Altertumswissenschaft*, 22, 2, col. 1606 s.

Kraus, C.S. and A.J. Woodman. 1997. *Latin Historians*. Oxford: Oxford University Press.

Kyriakidis, E. (ed.) 2007. *The Archaeology of Ritual*. Los Angeles: Cotsen Institute of Archaeology Press.

La Regina, A 1970. "Note sulla formazione dei centri urbani in area sabellica," in *Studi sulla città italica preromana: Atti del convegno di studi sulla città etrusca e italica preromana*: 197–207. Bologna: Istituto per la storia di Bologna.

La Regina, A 1975. "Centri fortificati preromani nei territori sabellici dell'Italia centrale adriatica." *Posebna Izdania* 24: 271–284.

La Regina, A. 1976. "Il Sannio", in P. Zanker (ed.), *Hellenismus in Mittelitalien: Kolloquium in Göttingen vom 5. bis 9. Juni 1974*: 216–248. Göttingen: Vandenhoeck & Ruprecht.

La Regina, A. 1999. "Le istituzioni agrarie italiche", in E. Petrocelli (ed.), *La civiltà della transumanza: storia, cultura e valorizzazione dei tratturi e del mondo pastorale in Abruzzo, Molise, Puglia, Campania e Basilicata*: 3–18. Isernia: C. Iannone.

La Rocca, E 1996. "Graeci artifices nella Roma repubblicana: lineamenti di storia della scultura," in C. Pugliese Carratelli (ed.), *I Greci in Occidente*: 607–626. Milano: Bompiani.

Larson, J. 2007. *Ancient Greek Cults: A Guide*. New York: Routledge.

Laurence, R. 1999. *The Roads of Roman Italy: Mobility and Cultural Change*. London: Routledge.

Lawson, E.T. and R.N. McCauley. 1990. *Rethinking Religion: Connecting Cognition and Culture*. Cambridge: Cambridge University Press.

Leach. E. 1976. *Culture and Communication: The Logic by which Symbols are Connected*. Cambridge: Cambridge University Press.

Leonelli, V. 2003. *La necropoli della prima età del ferro delle acciaierie di Terni: Contributi per un'edizione critica*. Firenze: All'insegna del giglio.

Letta, C. 1992. "I santuari rurali nell'Italia centro-appenninica: valori religiosi e funzione aggregativa." *Mélanges de l'École française de Rome* 104, 1: 109–124.

Lévi-Strauss, C. 1966. *The Savage Mind*. London: Weidenfeld & Nicolson.

Lévi-Strauss, C. 1996. *The Raw and the Cooked*. Chicago: University of Chicago Press.

Liebmann, M. and U. Rizvi 2008. *Archaeology and the Postcolonial Critique*. Lanham, MD: AltaMira Press.

Lloyd, J. 1991. "Farming the Highlands: Samnium and Arcadia in the Hellenistic and Early Roman Imperial Periods," in G. Barker/J. Llyod (eds.), *Roman Landscapes:*

BIBLIOGRAPHY   313

Archaeological Survey in the Mediterranean Region: 180–193. London: British School at Rome.

Lomas, K., 2017. "The Veneti," in G.D. Farney and G.J. Bradley (eds.), *The Peoples of Ancient Italy*: 701–718. Boston: De Gruyter.

Lotti, B. 1902. "Sulla costituzione geologica del gruppo montuoso di Amelia (Umbria)." *Bollettino del Reggio Comitato Geologico d'Italia* 33, 89–103.

Lyons, C.L. and J.K. Papadopoulos. 2002. *The Archaeology of Colonialism*. Los Angeles: Getty Research Institute.

Lucero, L.J. 2003. "The Politics of Ritual: The Emergence of Classic Maya Rulers." *Current Anthropology* 44: 523–558.

Maddoli, G. 2014. "Gli umbri nella storiografia greca," in *Gli umbri in età preromana: atti del XXVII Convegno di studi etruschi ed italici: Perugia-Gubbio-Urbino, 27–31 ottobre 2009*: 17–27.

Maetzke G. 1957. "Per un corpus dei bronzetti etruschi. La Collezione del Museo Archeologico Nazionale di Chiusi." *Studi Etruschi* 25: 489–523.

Mackil, E.M. 2016. *Creating a Common Polity: Religion, Economy, and Politics in the Making of the Greek koinon*. Berkeley: University of California Press.

Maggiani A. 2002. "I culti di Perugia e del suo territorio." *Annali della Fondazione Claudio Faina* 9: 267–299.

Maioli, M. and A. Mastrocinque, 1992. *La stipe di Villa di Villa e i culti degli antichi Veneti*. Rome: Bretschneider.

Malone, C. and S. Stoddart 1994. *Territory, Time, and State: The Archaeological Development of the Gubbio Basin*. Cambridge: Cambridge University Press.

Manca, M.L. and A. Menichelli (eds.) 2014. *MAC Museo archeologico di Colfiorito: Guida*. Foligno (PG): Comune di Foligno.

Manca, M.L., M.R. Picuti, and M. Albanesi (eds.) 2014. *Il santuario umbro-romano a Cancelli di Foligno: archeologia a scuola*. Sisto Perugia: Fabrizio Fabbri.

Manconi, D., M.A. Tornei, and M. Vezar 1981. "La situazione in Umbria," in A. Giardina and A. Schiavone (eds.), *Società romana e produzione schiavistica*: 371–406. Roma: Laterza.

Manconi, D. and F. Marcattili, 2008. *Gubbio: Scavi e nuove ricerche*. Città di Castello: edimond.

Manconi, D. 2017. "The Umbri", in G.D. Farney and G.J. Bradley (eds.), *The Peoples of Ancient Italy*: 603–637. Boston: De Gruyter.

Mansuelli, G.A. 1983. *Guida alla città etrusca e al museo di Marzabotto*. Bologna: Alfa.

Marcotte, D. 1986. "Le périple dit de Scylax: Esquisse d'un commentaire épigraphique et archéologique." *Bollettino dei Classici* 7: 166–182.

Marini, C.M., Curina, R., and E. Lippolis, 2000. *Aemilia: La cultura romana in Emilia Romagna dal III secolo a.C. all'età costantiniana*. Venezia: Marsilio.

Mariotti, E., and J. Tabolli, 2021. *Il santuario ritrovato: Nuovi scavi e ricerche al Bagno Grande di San Casciano dei Bagni*. Livorno.

Marroni, E. 2012. *Sacra Nominis Latini: I santuari del Lazio arcaico e repubblicano: atti del Convegno Internazionale, Palazzo Massimo, 19–21 febbraio 2009*. Napoli: Loffredo editore.

Matteini Chiari, M. and S. Stopponi (eds.) 1996. *Museo comunale di Amelia: Raccolta archeologica: cultura materiale*. Perugia: Electa, Editori umbri associati.

Mattingly, D.J. 1997. *Tripolitania*. Ann Arbor: The University of Michigan Press.

Mattingly, D.J. 2011. *Imperialism, Power, and Identity: Experiencing the Roman Empire*. Princeton: Princeton University Press.

McAnany, P.A. and E.C. Wells, 2008. "Toward a Theory of Ritual Economy." *Research in economic anthropology* 27: 1–16.

McInerney, J. 2014. *A Companion to Ethnicity in the Ancient Mediterranean*. Chichester: Wiley-Blackwell.

Meiser, G. 1986. *Lautgeschichte der umbrischen Sprache*. Innsbruck: Institut für Sprachwissenschaft der Universität Innsbruck.

Meskell, L. 2004. *Object Worlds in Ancient Egypt: Material Biographies Past and Present*. New York: Berg.

Miari, M. 2000: *Stipi votive dell'Etruria Padana*. Roma: Bretschneider.

Micozzi, M. 2014. "I corredi di Gualdo Tadino nel Museo di Villa Giulia", in O. Paoletti (ed.), *Gli umbri in età preromana: Atti del XXVII Convegno di studi etruschi ed italici: Perugia-Gubbio-Urbino, 27–31 ottobre 2009*: 327–356. Pisa: Serra.

Mills, B.J. and W.H. Walker, 2008. *Memory Work: Archaeologies of Material Practices*. Santa Fe: School for Advanced Research Press.

Mingazzini, P. 1932: "Edicola e Stipe Votiva nella Villa Già di Proprietà Marchi." *Notizie Scavi di Antichità*: 442–481.

Monacchi, D. 1984. "Resti della stipe votiva del Monte Subasio di Assisi (Colle S. Rufino)." *Studi Etruschi* 52: 77–89.

Monacchi, D. 1988. "Note sulla Stipe Votiva di Grotta Bella (Terni)." *Studi Etruschi* 54: 75–89.

Monacchi, D. 1997. "Terracotte architettoniche del santuario di Pantanelli di Amelia." *Studi Etruschi* 97, 63: 167–194.

Moore, J.D. 1996. "The Archaeology of Plazas and the Proxemics of Ritual: Three Andean Traditions." *American Anthropologist* 98, 4: 789–802.

Morley, N. 2013. "Religion, Urbanisation and Social Change," in M. Jehne et al. (eds.), *Religiose Vielfalt und soziale Integration: Die Bedeutung der Religion für die kulturelle Identitat und die politische Stabilitat im republikanischen Italien*: 61–68. Heidelberg: Verlag Antike.

Morris, B. 2006. *Religion and Anthropology: A Critical Introduction*. Cambridge: Cambridge University Press.

Mouritsen, H. 2007. *Plebs and Politics in the Late Roman Republic*. Cambridge: Cambridge University Press.

BIBLIOGRAPHY

Muskett, G. 2014. "Votive Offerings from the Sanctuary of Artemis Orthia, Sparta, in Liverpool collections." *The Annual of the British School at Athens* 109: 159–173.

Nagy, H. 2016. "Votives in their Larger Religious Context," in S. Bell and A.A. Carpino (eds.), *A Companion to the Etruscans*: 261–275. Chichester, West Sussex: John Wiley & Sons Inc.

Nijboer A.J. 2001. *Interpreting Deposits: Linking Ritual with Economy: Papers on Mediterranean Archaeology*. Groningen: Groningen Institute for Archaeology.

Nocentini, A., S. Sarti, and P.G. Warden (eds.) 2018. *Albagino: Per una lettura del paesaggio sacro etrusco = Albagino: Toward an Understanding of the Etruscan Sacred Landscape*. Firenze: Consiglio regionale della Toscana.

Oakley, S.P. 2005. *A Commentary on Livy, books VI–X: 4*. Oxford: Clarendon Press.

Ohnefalsch-Richter, M. 1893. *Kypros: The Bible and Homer: Oriental Civilization, Art and Religion in Ancient Times*. London: Asher & Co.

Orlandini, S. and A. Passigli 1990. *Fiesole archeologica = Archaeology in Fiesole*. Milano: Idea Books.

Ortner, S.B. 1989. *High Religion: A Cultural and Political History of Sherpa Buddhism*. Princeton, NJ: Princeton University Press.

Osborne, R. 2004. "Hoards, Votives, Offerings: The Archaeology of the Dedicated Object." *World Archaeology* 36, 1: 1–10.

Östenberg, C.E., 1967. "Luni sul Mignone e problemi della preistoria d'Italia." *Acta Instituti Romani Regni Sueciae* 4, 25: 1–306.

Oswald, A., S. Ainsworth, T. Pearson, and P. Frodsham, 2013. *Hillforts: Prehistoric Strongholds of Northumberland National Park*. New York: English Heritage Publishing.

Pakkanen, P. and S. Bocher. 2016. *Cult Material: From Archaeological Deposits to Interpretation of Early Greek Religion*. Helsinki: Foundation of the Finnish Institute at Athens.

Pallottino, M. 1940. "Tradizione etnica e realtà culturale dell'Etruria, Umbria e Romagna prima dell'unificazione augustea," in *Atti della Società italiana per il progresso delle scienze*: 81–102. Roma: Società italiana per il progresso delle scienze.

Paribeni, R. 1937. *Scritti in onore di Bartolomeo Nogara: Raccolti in occasione del suo 70 anno*. Città del Vaticano.

Patterson, J.R. 2006. "Colonization and Historiography: The Roman Republic," in G. Bradley and J.P. Wilson (eds.), *Greek and Roman Colonization: Origins, Ideologies, and Interactions*: 189–218. Swansea: Classical Press of Wales.

Pauketat, T.R. 2013. *An Archaeology of the Cosmos: Rethinking Agency and Religion in Ancient America*. Abingdon: Routledge.

Pensabene, P. 1980. *Terracotte votive dal Tevere*. Roma: L'Erma di Bretschneider.

Perego, E. and R. Scopacasa (eds.) 2016. *Burial and Social Change in First-millennium BC Italy. Approaching Social Agents: Gender, Personhood and Marginality*. Oxford: Oxbow Books.

Perna, R., R. Rossi and V. Tubaldi, 2011. "Scavi e ricerche nell'antica Plestia" in *Picus*, 31: 213–278.

Peroni, R. 1959. "Per una definizione dell'aspetto culturale 'subappenninico' come fase cronologica a sé stante." *Memorie della Accademia Nazionale dei Lincei*, 8, 9: 1–253.

Picuti, M.R. 1999. "Il territorio fulginate in età arcaica," in L. Bonomi Ponzi (ed.), *Fulginates e Plestini. Popolazioni antiche nel territorio di Foligno: Mostra archeologica: Foligno, Palazzo Trinci, 10 aprile–31 dicembre 1999*: 28–29. Foligno: Comune di Foligno.

Picuti, M.R. 2006. "Un santuario lungo la via Plestina: le terrecotte architettoniche da Pale di Foligno (Perugia)", in I. Edlund-Berry, G. Greco, and J. Kenfield (eds.), *Deliciae fictiles III: Architectural terracottas in Ancient Italy: New Discoveries and Interpretations: Proceedings of the International Conference Held at the American Academy in Rome*: 194–209. Oxford: Oxbow Books.

Picuti, M.R. 2009. "Ricerche vecchie e nuove sul territorio di Cancelli di Foligno (PG) in epoca Romana", in M. Cancelli (ed.), *Cancelli, l'arte del gregge*: 8–19. Milano: Politi.

Plunket, P. (ed.) 2002. *Domestic Ritual in Ancient Mesoamerica*. Los Angeles: Cotsen Institute of Archaeology Press.

Potter, T.W. 1979. *The Changing Landscape of South Etruria*. London: P. Elek.

Potter, T. 1989. *Una stipe votiva da Ponte di Nona*. Roma: De Luca.

Potts, C.R. 2018. *Religious Architecture in Latium and Etruria, c. 900–500 BC*. Oxford: Oxford University Press.

Poultney, J.W. 1959. *The Bronze Tables of Iguvium*. Oxford: Blackwell.

Prosdocimi, A.L. 1989. "Le religioni degli Italici," in G. Pugliese Carratelli (ed.), *Italia omnium terrarum parens*: 475–545. Milano: Schewiller.

Puglisi, S.M. 1954. "Civiltà appenninica e sepolcri di tipo dolmenico a Pian Sultano." *Rivista di Antropologia*, 41: 3–32.

Quinn J.C. and A. Wilson 2013. "Capitolia." *Journal of Roman Studies* 103: 117–173.

Raja, R. 2015. *A Companion to the Archaeology of Religion in the Ancient World*. Chichester: Wiley-Blackwell.

Rainini, I. (1976) "Valle d'Ansanto, Rocca S. Felice. II deposito votivo del santuario di Mefite." *Notizie degli Scavi*: 23–47.

Rappaport, R. 1979. "Ritual Regulation of Environmental Relations among a New Guinea People," in R. Rappaport (ed.), *Ecology, Meaning, and Religion*. Berkeley: North Atlantic Books.

Recke, M. 2013. "Science as Art: Etruscan Anatomical Votives", in J.M. Turfa (ed.), *The Etruscan World*: 1068–1085. London: Routledge.

Reggiani Massarini, A.M. 1988. *Santuario degli Equicoli a Corvaro: oggetti votivi del Museo Nazionale Romano*. Roma: De Luca.

Rendini, P. 2001 "Stipi votive e culti nella valle dell'Albenga in età ellenistica," in A. Comella and S. Mele (eds.), *Depositi votivi e culti dell'Italia antica dall'età arcaica a quella tardo repubblicana*: 285–293. Bari: Edipuglia.

BIBLIOGRAPHY

Renfrew, C. 1985. *The Archaeology of Cult: The Sanctuary at Phylakopi*. London: British School of Archaeology at Athens.

Renfrew, C. and I. Morley (eds.) 2009. *Becoming Human: Innovations in Prehistoric Material and Spiritual Culture*. Cambridge: Cambridge University Press.

Renfrew, C., I. Morley, M.J. Boyd, and P.P.G. Bateson (eds.) 2018. *Ritual, Play and Belief in Early Human Societies*. Cambridge: Cambridge University Press.

Richardson, E. 1983. *Etruscan Votive Bronzes: Geometric, Orientalizing, Archaic*. Mainz am Rhein: Verlag P. von Zabern.

Riva, C. and S.K.F. Stoddart, 1996. "Ritual Landscapes in Archaic Etruria," in J.B. Wilkins (ed.), *Approaches to the Study of Ritual: Italy and the Mediterranean*: 91–109. Accordia Research Centre, University of London: London.

Rizzello, M. 1980. *I santuari della media valle del Liri, 4.–1. sec. a. C: Depositi votivi e rinvenimenti di: Arce, Arpino, Atina, Boville, Canneto, Casalvieri, Ceprano, Colli, Sora, Veroli*. Sora: Centro studi sorani Patriarca.

Rix, H. 2002. *Sabellische Texte: Die Texte des Oskischen, Umbrischen und Südpikenischen*. Heidelberg: Universitätsverlag C. Winter.

Roncalli, F. 1973. *Il Marte di Todi: Bronzistica etrusca ed ispirazione classica*. Roma: Tipografia poliglotta vaticana.

Roncalli, F. (ed.) 1989. *Gens antiquissima Italiae: Antichità dall'Umbria a Budapest e Cracovia*. Perugia: Electa Editori Umbri.

Roncalli, F. and B. Adembri (eds.) 1990. *Gens antiquissima Italiae. Antichità dall'Umbria a Leningrado*. Perugia: Electa.

Roncalli, F. and L. Bonfante (eds.) 1991. *Antichità dall'Umbria a New York*. Perugia: Electa.

Rudhart, J. 1992. *Notions fondamentales de la pensée religieuse et actes constitutifs du culte dans la Grèce classique*. Paris: Picard.

Salmon, E.T. 1969. *Roman Colonization under the Republic*. London: Thames and Hudson.

Salvatore, M. 2008. *Museo archeologico di Spoleto: La formazione della città, dalle origini al municipio (90 a.C.): le sculture del Teatro romano*. Perugia: Soprintendenza per i beni archeologici dell'Umbria.

Sassatelli, G. and R. Macellari 2002. "Perugia, gli Umbri e la val Padana." *Annali della Fondazione per il Museo Claudio Faina* 9: 407–434.

Scarpignato, M. 1989. "La stipe votive di Bettona," in R. Roncalli (ed.), *Gens antiquissima Italiae. Antichità dall'Umbria a Budapest e Cracovia*: 124–133. Perugia: Electa Editori Umbria.

Schultz, C.E. 2006. *Women's Religious Activity in the Roman Republic*. Chapel Hill: University of North Carolina Press.

Schippa F. 1979. "Il deposito votivo di Ancarano di Norcia." *Studi in onore di Filippo Magi*: 203–211. Perugia: E.U. Coop.

Schippa F. 1983. "Scavi e scoperte: Gubbio (Perugia)", in *Studi Etruschi*, 51: 456–457.

Scopacasa, R. 2015a. *Ancient Samnium: Settlement, Culture, and Identity between History and Archaeology*. Oxford: Oxford University Press.

Scopacasa, R. 2015b. "Moulding Cultural Change: A Contextual Approach to Anatomical Votive Terracottas in Central Italy, Fourth–Second Centuries BC." *Papers of the British School at Rome* 83: 1–27.

Scopacasa, R. 2016. "Rome's Encroachment on Italy," in A.E. Cooley (ed.), *A Companion to Roman Italy*: 35–56. Chichester: Wiley-Blackwell.

Scopacasa, R. 2017. "Ethnicity," in G.D. Farney and G.J. Bradley (eds.), *The Peoples of Ancient Italy*: 105–127. Boston: De Gruyter.

Selsvold, I. and L. Webb (eds.) 2020. *Beyond the Romans: Posthuman Perspectives in Roman Archaeology*. Oxford: Oxbow Books.

Sewell, J. 2014. "Gellius, Philip II and a Proposed End to the 'Model-Replica' Debate", in T.D. Stek and J. Pelgrom (eds.), *Roman Republican Colonization: New Perspectives from Archaeology and Ancient History*: 125–139. Roma: Palombi & Partner.

Sillar, B. 2009. "The Social Agency of Things? Animism and Materiality in the Andes." *Cambridge Archaeological Journal* 19, 3: 366–377.

Sigismondi, G. 2009. *Nuceria in Umbria*. Foligno (PG): Il salvalibro.

Sisani, S. 2001. *Tuta Ikuvina: Sviluppo e ideologia della forma urbana a Gubbio*. Roma: Quasar.

Sisani, S. 2002. "British Umbria (quasi una recensione ad uno studio recente)." *Eutopia* 2, 1: 123–139.

Sisani, S. 2006. *Umbria e Marche*. Bari: Laterza.

Sisani, S., 2007. *Fenomenologia della conquista. La romanizzazione dell'Umbria tra il IV sec. a.C. e la guerra sociale*. Roma: Quasar.

Sisani, S. 2008. "Dirimens Tiberis? I confini tra Etruria e Umbria," in F. Coarelli and H. Patterson (eds.), *Mercator placidissimus: The Tiber Valley in Antiquity*, 45–85. Roma: Quasar.

Sisani, S. 2009. *Umbrorum gens antiquissima Italiae. Studi sulla società e le istituzioni dell'Umbria preromana*. Perugia: Deputazione di storia patria per l'Umbria.

Sisani, S. 2012. "I rapporti tra Mevania ed Hispellum" in G.M. Della Fina (ed.) *Il fanum voltumnae e i santuari comunitari dell'italia antica: Atti del XIX convegno internazionale di studi sulla storia e l'archeologia dell'Etruria*: 409–463. Roma: Quasar.

Sisani, S. 2013. *Nursia e l'ager Nursinus: un distretto sabino dalla praefectura al municipium*. Roma: Quasar.

Sobel E. and Bettles G. 2000. "Winter Hunger, Winter Myths: Subsistence Risk and Mythology among the Klamath and Modoc." *Journal of Anthropological Archaeology* 19: 276–313.

Sommella, pP. 1971–1972. "Heroon di Enea a Lavinium: Recenti scavi a Pratica di Mare." *Rendiconti della Pontificia Accademia Romana di Archeologia* 44, 47–74.

BIBLIOGRAPHY

Söderlind, M. 2002. *Late Etruscan Votive Heads from Tessennano: Production, Distribution, Sociohistorical Context*. Roma: L'Erma di Bretschneider.

Staffa, R. 2001. "Nuove acquisizioni dal territorio di Lanciano", in A. Comella and S. Mele (eds.), *Depositi votivi e culti dell'Italia antica dall'età arcaica a quella tardo repubblicana*: 411–436. Bari: Edipuglia.

Stefani, E. 1935. "Gualdo Tadino: Scoperte varie." *Notizie degli scavi di antichità*: 155–173.

Stek, T. 2009. *Cult Places and Cultural Change in Republican Italy: A Contextual Approach to Religious Aspects of Rural Society after the Roman Conquest*. Amsterdam: Amsterdam University Press.

Stek T. 2013. "Material Culture, Italic Identities and the Romanization of Italy," in J. DeRose Evans (ed.), *Companion to the Archaeology of the Roman Republican Period*: 337–353. Chichester: Wiley-Blackwell.

Stek 2017. "The Impact of Roman Expansion and Colonization on Ancient Italy: From Diffusionism to Networks of Opportunity," in G.D. Farney and G.J. Bradley (eds.), *The Peoples of Ancient Italy*: 269–294. Boston: De Gruyter.

Stek, T. and J. Pelgrom (eds.) 2014. *Roman Republican Colonization: New Perspectives from Archaeology and Ancient History*. Rome: Palombi.

Stek, T.D. and G.J. Burgers (eds.) 2015. *The Impact of Rome on Cult Places and Religious Practices in Ancient Italy*, BICS Supplement 132. London: Institute of Classical Studies.

Stoddart, S. 1994. "Text and Regional Setting," in C.A.T. Malone and S.K.F. Stoddart (eds.), *Territory, Time and State: The Archaeological Development of the Gubbio Basin*: 172–177. Cambridge: Cambridge University Press.

Stoddart, S. 2010. "Changing Views of the Gubbio Landscape," in Fontaine, P. (ed.) *L'Étrurie et l'Ombrie avant Rome. Cité et Territoire. Actes du colloque International Louvain-la-Neuve Halles Universitaires, Sénat Académique 13–14 février 2004*: 211–218. Rome: Belgisch Historisch Instituut te Rome.

Stoddart, S. 2013. "Physical Geography and Environment," in N.S. Rosenstein and R. Morstein-Marx (eds.), *A Companion to the Roman Republic*: 102–123. Malden, MA: Blackwell.

Stoddart, S. and W. Whitley. 1988. "Gubbio, loc. Monte Ansciano (Perugia)." *Studi Etruschi* 54: 379–382.

Stoddart, S., P. Barone, J. Bennett, L. Ceccarelli, G. Cifani, J. Clackson, and N. Whitehead (2012a). "Opening the Frontier: The Gubbio-Perugia Frontier in the Course of History." *Papers of the British School at Rome* 80: 257–294.

Stoddart, S., L. Ceccarelli, and D. Redhouse 2012b. "Before the Frontier: Gubbio and Its Landscape before the State," in N. Negroni Catacchio (ed.), *L'Etruria dal Paleolitico al Primo Ferro lo stato delle ricerche: atti del decimo incontro di studi, Valentano (VT)—Pitigliano (GR) 10–12 settembre 2010*: 677–687. Milano: Centro studi di preistoria e archeologia.

Stoddart, S. and D. Redhouse, 2014. "The Umbrians: Archaeological Perspective: Simon Stoddart, David Redhouse," in M. Aberson, M. Di Fazio, M. Wullschleger, and M C. Biella, *Entre Archéologie et Histoire: Dialogues Sur Divers Peuples de L'Italie Préromaine*: 107–124. Genève: Université de Genève—Faculté des Lettres—Département des Sciences de l'Antiquité.

Stopponi, S. 2011. "Campo della Fiera at Orvieto–New Discoveries," in N. de Grummond and I. Edlund-Berry (eds.), *The Archaeology of Sanctuaries and Ritual in Etruria*: 16–43. Portsmouth, RI: Journal of Roman Archaeology.

Strazzulla, M.J. 1981. "Le terrecotte architettoniche. Le produzioni dal IV al I sec. a.C.", in A. Giardina and A. Schiavone (eds.), *Società romana e produzione schiavistica*, 2: 187–207. Roma: Laterza.

Strazzulla, M.J. 2012. "I santuari italici: le prime fasi dell'emergere del sacro" in *Quaderni di Archeologia d'Abbruzzo*, 2: 255–273.

Suano, M. and R. Scopacasa, 2013. "Central Apennine Italy: The Case of Samnium," in J. DeRose Evans (ed.), *A Companion to the Archaeology of the Roman Republic*: 387–405. Chichester: Wiley-Blackwell.

Swenson, E. 2015. "The Archaeology of Ritual." *Annual Review of Anthropology* 44: 329–345.

Tabone, G.pP. 1995–1996. *I bronzetti a figura umana etruschi ed italici a nord del Po. Diffusione dei modelli ed alaborazioni locali in età arcaica*. PhD dissertation, University of Roma "La Sapienza".

Tagliamonte, G. 2005. *I Sanniti: Caudini, Irpini, Pentri, Carricini, Frentani*. Milano: Longanesi.

Tarpin, M. 2014. "Strangers in Paradise: Latins (and Some Other Non-Romans) in Colonial Context: A Short Story of Territorial Complexity," in T. Stek and J. Pelgrom (ed.), *Roman Republican Colonization New Perspectives from Archaeology and Ancient History*: 160–191. Roma: Palombi editori.

Tascio, M. 1989. *Todi: Forma e urbanistica*. Roma: L'Erma di Bretschneider.

Termeer, M.K. 2016. "Votives in Latin Colonies: A Perspective beyond Religious Romanization," in D. Bolder-Boos and D. Maschek (eds.), *Orte der Forschung, Orte des Glaubens: neue Perspektiven für Heiligtümer in Italien von der Archaik bis zur Späten Republik*: 117–127. Bonn: Dr. Rudolf Habelt Verlag.

Terrenato, N. 1998. "The Romanization of Italy: Global Acculturation or Cultural *bricolage*?" in *Theoretical Roman Archaeology Journal* 97: 21–27.

Terrenato, N. 2007: "The Essential Countryside: Farms, Villages, Sanctuaries, Tombs," in S. Alcock and R. Osborne (eds.), *Classical Archaeology*: 139–161. London: Blackwell.

Terrenato, N. 2008. "The Cultural Implications of the Roman Conquest" in E.H. Bispham (ed.), *Roman Europe (The Short Oxford History of Europe)*: 234–264. Oxford: Oxford University Press.

BIBLIOGRAPHY

Terrenato N., 2014, "Private Vis, Public Virtus: Family Agendas during the Early Roman Expansion", in T. Stek and J. Pelgrom (eds.), *Roman Republican Colonization: New Perspectives from Archaeology and Ancient History*: 45–59. Rome: Palombi.

Terrenato, N. 2019. *The Early Roman Expansion into Italy: Elite Negotiation and Family Agendas*. Cambridge: Cambridge University Press.

Terrenato, N. 2021. "The Romanization of Rome," in O. Belvedere and J. Bergemann (eds.), *Imperium Romanum: Romanization between Colonization and Globalization*: 77–88. Palermo: Palermo University Press.

Torelli, M. 1973. "Le stipi votive," in *Roma medio repubblicana: Aspetti culturali di Roma e del Lazio nei secoli IV e III a. C.*: 138–139. Roma: Assessorato antichità, belle arti e problemi della cultura.

Torelli, M. 1982. *Etruria*. Etruria. Bari: Laterza.

Torelli, M. 1983. "Edilizia pubblica in Italia centrale tra guerra sociale ed età augustea. Ideologia e classi sociali": in M. Cébeillac-Gervasoni, *Les "Bourgeoisies" municipales italiennes aux IIe et Ier siècles av. J.-C: Centre Jean Bérard. Institut Français de Naples 7–10 décembre 1981*: 241–250. Paris: Centre Jean Bérard.

Torelli, M. 1993. "Fictiles fabulae: Rappresentazione e romanizzazione nei cicli figurati fittili repubblicani." *Ostraka. Rivista di antichità* 2: 269–299.

Torelli, M. 1995. *Studies in the Romanization of Italy*. Edmonton: University of Alberta Press.

Torelli, M. 1999. *Tota Italia: Essays in the Cultural Formation of Roman Italy*. Oxford: Clarendon Press.

Torelli, M. 2010. "Etruschi e Umbri: interferenza, conflitti, imprestiti," in P. Fontaine (ed.), *L'Étrurie et l'Ombrie avant Rome: Cité et territoire. Actes du colloque International, Louvain-la-Neuve 13–14 février 2004*: 219–230. Bruxelles: Brepols.

Torelli, M. 2016. "The Roman Period," in N.T. de Grummond and L. Pieraccini (eds.), *Caere*: 263–279. Austin: University of Texas Press.

F. Trenti (ed.) 2013. *Museo archeologico del Casentino Piero Albertoni. Catalogo dell'esposizione*. Arezzo: Fruska.

Turfa, J.M. 1994. "Anatomical Votives and Italian Medical Traditions," in R.D. De Puma and J.P. Small (eds.), *Murlo and the Etruscans: Art and Society in Ancient Etruria*: 224–224. Madison, WI: University of Wisconsin Press.

Turfa, J.M. 2004. "Anatomical Votives," in *Thesaurus Cultus et Rituum Antiquorum* (ThesCRA), 1: 359–368. Los Angeles: Getty Publications.

Turfa, J.M. (ed.) 2013. *The Etruscan World*. London: Routledge.

Turner, V. 1987. *The Anthropology of Performance*. New York: PAJ Publications.

Vagnetti, L. 1971. *Il deposito votivo di Campetti a Veio: (Materiale degli scavi 1937–1938)*. Firenze: Sansoni.

Van Dyke, R.M. and S. Alcock. 2003. *Archaeologies of Memory*. Malden, MA: Blackwell.

Vetter, E. 1953. *Handbuch der italischen Dialekte*. Heidelberg: C. Winter.

Verhoeven, R. 2002. "Ritual and Its Investigation in Prehistory," in H.G. Gebel, B.D. Hermansen, and C. Hoffmann Jensen, *Magic Practices and Ritual in the Near Eastern Neolithic: Proceedings of a Workshop Held at the 2nd International Congress on the Archaeology of the Ancient Near East*: 5–42. Berlin: Ex Oriente.

Vilucchi, S., P. Zamarchi Grassi and S. Baldassarri, 2001. *Etruschi nel tempo: i ritrovamenti di Arezzo dal '500 ad oggi*: luglio-dicembre 2001. Arezzo: Provincia di Arezzo.

Wallace-Hadrill, A. 2008. *Rome's Cultural Revolution*. Cambridge: Cambridge University Press.

Warden, P.G. 2012. "Monumental Embodiment: Somatic Symbolism and the Tuscan Temple," in M.L. Thomas and G.E. Meyers (eds.), *Monumentality in Etruscan and Early Roman Architecture: Ideology and Innovation*: 82–110. Austin: University of Texas Press.

Warren, P. 1988. *Minoan Religion as Ritual Action*. Göteborg: Lindgren.

Webster, J. 2001. "Creolizing the Roman Provinces." *American Journal of Archaeology* 105, 2: 209–225.

Wesler, K. 2012. *An Archaeology of Religion*. Lanham, MD: University Press of America.

Weiss, M.L. 2010. *Language and Ritual in Sabellic Italy: The Ritual Complex of the Third and Fourth Tabulae Iguvinae*. Leiden: Brill.

White, R. 1991. *The Middle Ground: Indians, Empires, and Republics in the Great Lakes Region*; 1650–1815. Cambridge: Cambridge University Press.

Whitley D.S. and K. Hays-Gilpin (eds.) 2008. *Belief in the Past: Theoretical Approaches to the Archaeology of Religion*. Walnut Creek, CA: Left Coast Press.

Winter, F.E. and J. Fedak 2016. *Studies in Hellenistic Architecture*. Toronto: University of Toronto Press.

Woolf, G.D. 1992. "The Unity and Diversity of Romanisation." *Journal of Roman Archaeology* 5: 349–352.

Woolf, G.D. 1998. *Becoming Roman: The Origins of Provincial Civilization in Gaul*. Cambridge: Cambridge University Press.

Zaccagni, P. 1980. "Palestrina. Materiali votivi di Piazza Ungheria." *Archeologia laziale*, 3: 188–191.

Zapelloni Pavia, A. 2024. "When Bodies Fall Apart: Anatomical Votives in Pre-Roman Italy," in D. Bartus and M. Szabó (eds.), *Proceedings of the 21st International Congress on Ancient Bronzes*. Dissertationes Archaeologicae Supplementum 4. Budapest: 113–139.

Zapelloni Pavia, A. and F. Larocca, 2023. "Grotta Bella: The Evolution of a Meeting Place." *Studia Hercynia* 16, 1: 39–54.

Zapelloni Pavia, A. 2020. "Decentralizing Human Agency: A Study of the Ritual Function of the Votive Figurines from Grotta Bella, Umbria," in I. Selsvold and L. Webb (eds.), *Beyond the Romans: Posthuman Perspectives in Roman Archaeology*. TRAC Themes in Roman Archaeology 3: 41–54. Oxford Philadelphia: OXBOW books.

Zecchini, G. 2009. *Le guerre galliche di Roma*. Roma: Carocci.

Index

Actor-Network Theory   34, 34*n*19, 35

Anatomical votives   41, 42, 46, 85, 85*n*2, 156,157, 176–180, 190–191, 200, 200*n*78, 202*n*91

Archaeology of Religion   31,38

Archaeology of Ritual   33, 37–38, 178

Arezzo   53, 141, 188*n*80, 199, 199*n*75, 200

Asclepius   22, 22*n*60, 169

Asia Minor   53,201

Assisi   66, 79, 122–123, 129, 143, 165, 182*n*64, 194, 201, 204

Battiloro, Ilaria   186

Bettona   78, 197, 199, 200

Blake, Emma   58

Bispham, Edward   22

Bonomi-Ponzi, Laura   44

Bourdin, Stephan   58, 58*n*47, 59

Bradley, Guy   3, 15, 25–29, 43–45, 61–62, 73*n*117, 82, 159–167, 172, 175, 182, 185

Bricolage   11, 13

Bronze figurines   1, 6, 40*n*49, 43–44, 46, 69, 95, 100, 104, 108, 114

Caere   73*n*117, 188, 202

Calvi dell'Umbria   129, 194–196, 198–200

Camerinum   57, 71, 74, 75*n*132

Campo La Piana   87, 143–146, 162*n*8, 164, 181, 205*n*1, 286–287

Cancelli   86, 138–142, 157, 161–163, 177, 181, 182, 185–186, 195–201, 281–285

Capitolium, Capitolia   20*n*51, 21, 23

Carafa, Paolo   18

Cenciaioli, Luana   44, 49, 130, 198

Cerveteri   43, 170

Chaniotis, Angelos   36

Cicero   50, 71, 74–75

Citizenship   2–3, 16, 20, 49, 72*n*117, 74, 76, 78, 117

Code-switching   11–13, 190

Cognitive approach   32, 40

Colfiorito   65–67, 69, 87, 143, 147, 149–150, 161, 163–164, 166, 177, 181–182, 186, 193–194, 198, 200, 203–204, 288–298

Colle Mori   66–68, 86, 133–134, 136–137, 156–157, 161–164, 182, 195, 197, 199, 201, 278–281

Colonization   9, 16, 23, 49, 50, 53, 71, 78*n*144, 157, 184

Colonna, Giovanni   25, 43–44, 45*n*74, 70, 70*n*140, 116, 124, 132, 168, 193–195, 198, 206

Comella, A.M.   122, 122*n*79, 177, 202

Cosa   23

Crawford, Micheal   95*n*26

Creolization   11–12

de Cazanove, Olivier   20, 22, 42

de Grummond, Nancy   42

de Polignac, Francois   17, 27

Demetriou, Denise   58

Dionysius of Halicarnassus   50–51, 74*n*121

Discrepant identities   11, 13

Edlund-Berry, Ingrid   39, 42

Elite   10, 13, 26–27, 37, 41, 44–45, 67, 81–82, 160, 164, 175, 187–190

Etruria   1, 14, 21, 24, 42, 54, 56–58, 60, 67, 72, 77–78, 94, 97, 99, 113, 141, 145, 150, 156, 163–164, 173, 186, 188, 190, 198, 201–203, 206

Etruscan sanctuaries   18, 39, 161, 200

Etruscans   14, 42, 51–53, 55–56, 69–72, 76

Etrusco-Latial-Campanian group   202–203

Fabriano   66, 67*n*91, 152, 165, 193

Falerii   71, 74, 99, 156, 202

Fenelli, Maria   156

Fentress, Elizabeth   22

Fiesole   70*n*104, 195, 199–200

Fogelin, Lars   33, 37–38

Fowler, Chris   171

Foligno   43, 67, 101, 122, 138, 143, 149, 165, 195–204

Fossato di Vico   133, 165–166, 193

Fregellae   23, 41, 169, 179*n*52

Fulginiae   72, 73*n*117, 80*n*153, 185

Gell, Alfred   34–35

Gentili, Anna-Maria   23–24, 46, 180*n*60

INDEX

325

Glinister, Fay   3, 23–24, 29, 45n73, 46, 157, 159, 169–171,177, 180, 184

Gosden, Chris   9, 11, 35, 171, 187

Graham, Emma-Jayne   41–41, 171

Gravisca   58, 170

Greek votive practice   40

Greek influence   23

Grotta Bella   27, 86–87, 91, 93–94, 96, 98, 161–166, 177, 181, 183, 196, 198–201, 203, 205, 208–221

Gualdo Tadino   63, 65–67, 78, 122, 126, 133–134, 144, 195, 197, 199, 201, 207

Gubbio   46, 49, 55, 63–65, 125–126, 129, 134, 196, 201, 207

Guzzo, Pier Giovanni   17

Hall, Jonathan   57

Harris, William   14

Haverfield, Francis   8–9

Heracles   17, 116n69, 155, 159, 168, 171

Herodotus   51

Hillforts   27, 66–67, 77, 149–150, 162

Hodder, Ian   33–35

Iguvine Tablets   55, 59, 61, 80n153, 80n154, 134, 172

Iguvium   55, 59, 61–63, 67–68, 74–76, 77, 125, 160, 172, 182, 185

La Regina, Adriano   16, 19, 25

La Rocca   86, 115, 117, 118n72, 119, 121, 157, 162–163, 176–177, 181–184, 186, 194–196, 200, 204, 258–264

Latium   1, 14, 20–22, 24, 26, 29, 41, 58–60, 62, 64, 74, 77, 79, 162–164, 169, 186, 188, 190–191, 201, 203, 206

Language   10, 12, 55–56, 61, 79, 80–81, 163, 186, 189

Latour, Bruno   34–35

Lavinium   162, 170

lex Sempronia agraria   75

Livy   50, 70–72, 82, 188n81, 189

Maevania   80n154, 145n116

Maggione   197

Manconi, Dorica   26, 60–61

Manganello   169

Mars   114, 124, 132, 165

Mattingly, David   9–10, 13

Middle Ground Theory   7, 11, 14, 161

Millet, Martin   9–10

Minoan votive practice   40

Monacchi, Daniela   26, 44, 93, 97, 98n31, 123, 125

Monte Acuto   86, 129, 130–133, 149, 160, 162–163, 174, 181–183, 194, 196, 198-, 200, 271–277

Monte Ansciano   27, 46, 86, 125–126, 128–129, 156, 160–163, 172–173, 181–182, 196, 201, 267–271

Montefranco   171, 195, 199

Monte Moro   86, 109, 157, 161–164, 174, 176–177, 182–183, 185–186, 195, 198–199, 239–244

Monte Pennino   86, 143, 147, 149, 161, 164, 181, 288

Monte San Pancrazio   86, 100, 103, 129, 157, 161–162, 166, 173, 177, 181, 185–186, 194, 197–200, 223–229

Monte Santo   78, 86, 113–115, 117, 166, 181, 194–199, 247–257

Monte Subasio   63, 86, 122–123, 129, 132, 157, 160–162, 167, 181, 201, 264–266

Monte Torre Maggiore   65–66, 86, 100, 102–103, 129, 149, 157, 161–163, 165, 174, 177, 181, 183, 185–186, 195–196, 198–201, 229–239

Nagy, Helen   43

Nocera Umbra   122, 143, 147, 196, 207

Object agency   34

Ocriculum   56, 72n110, 74, 78, 82, 100

pagus-vicus system   19, 26

Pantanelli   78, 86, 93, 96–98, 157, 162, 165–166, 174, 177, 181, 186, 196, 203, 221–222

Picenum   7, 67, 72, 77, 124–125, 143, 184, 191, 198

Polybius   22n61, 70, 72n116, 74

Ponte di Nona   170

Pozzarello   169

Practice theory   36–37

Pseudo-Skymnos   53–54

Pseudo-Skylax   53

Pliny the Elder   49, 49–50, 52, 57, 61, 71n107

Rafael Scopacasa 18–19, 24–25, 59, 85, 157, 180, 186

Religious Romanization 7, 20, 22, 47

Renfrew, Colin 34, 178

Roads 24, 67, 69, 74, 78–79, 95, 96, 134, 143, 147, 149, 160, 180, 183

Romanization 7–11, 14–15, 20, 22, 24–25, 42–43, 46–47, 59, 83, 85, 176, 202

Samnium 1, 14, 17–19, 59, 77, 186, 190–191, 203

Samnites 72

Scopacasa, Rafael 18–19, 24–25, 54, 59, 85, 157, 180, 186

Sisani, Simone 14–15, 26, 49, 60, 71, 73n118, 79

Social War 3, 5, 14–15, 20, 74, 76–77, 157

Stek, Tesse 17, 19, 42, 59–60, 85, 178, 184

Stoddart, Simon 15, 18, 46, 62, 69n99, 162

Strabo 52

Tarquinia 109, 122, 170, 188

Terni 63–68, 77, 88, 96, 102, 129, 195–196, 199–201, 207

Terrenato, Nicola 9, 11, 13, 81–82, 160, 187, 188n80

Tessennano 102, 109, 122

Todi 64–65, 67–68, 78, 89, 101, 113–117, 165–166, 194–199, 207

Torelli, Mario 10, 21, 42, 55, 60, 73n117, 202

Tratturi 17

Tuder 56, 62–63, 68, 74, 87, 95, 114–115, 166

Umbertide 129, 194, 196, 198–200, 207

Veii 43, 128, 136, 156, 169–170, 202

Venetic sanctuaries 173n36, 200

Veneto 156n135, 173, 195–196, 200

Via Amerina 50, 74, 78, 87, 96

Via Flaminia 74, 78, 118, 122, 126, 134, 143, 183

Via Plestina 138

Via Salaria 183

Votive deposit 1, 5, 7, 28–29, 39, 4142, 46–47, 70, 79, 86–87, 148, 160, 189, 191

Votive religion 29, 38–39, 42, 47

Vulci 102, 122

Wallace-Hadrill, Andrew 9, 12

Woolf, Greg 9–10